BATTLE OF BRITAIN
Volume 2
The Breaking Storm

*Dedicated to the aircrew of Fighter Command,
Bomber Command and Coastal Command killed,
posted missing or wounded in Britain's defence,
10 July 1940 to 12 August 1940*

BATTLE OF BRITAIN
Volume 2
The Breaking Storm
10 July 1940 – 12 August 1940

Dilip Sarkar MBE FRHistS

BATTLE OF BRITAIN: VOLUME 2
THE BREAKING STORM
10 July 1940 – 12 August 1940

First published in Great Britain in 2023 by
Air World
An imprint of
Pen & Sword Books Ltd
Yorkshire – Philadelphia

Copyright © Dilip Sarkar, 2023

ISBN: 978 1 39905 641 0

The right of Dilip Sarkar to be identified as Author of this work has been asserted by him in accordance with the Copyright, Designs and Patents Act 1988. A CIP catalogue record for this book is available from the British Library All rights reserved.

No part of this book may be reproduced or transmitted in any form or by any means, electronic or mechanical including photocopying, recording or by any information storage and retrieval system, without permission from the Publisher in writing.

Typeset by SJmagic DESIGN SERVICES, India.

Printed and bound in the UK by CPI Group (UK) Ltd.

Pen & Sword Books Ltd incorporates the imprints of Pen & Sword After the Battle, Archaeology, Air World Books, Atlas, Aviation, Battleground, Discovery, Family History, History, Maritime, Military, Naval, Politics, Social History, Transport, True Crime, Claymore Press, Frontline Books, Praetorian Press, Seaforth Publishing and White Owl

For a complete list of Pen & Sword titles please contact:

PEN & SWORD BOOKS LTD
George House, Units 12 & 13, Beevor Street, Off Pontefract Road,
Barnsley, South Yorkshire, S71 1HN, England
E-mail: enquiries@pen-and-sword.co.uk
Website: www.pen-and-sword.co.uk

or

PEN AND SWORD BOOKS,
1950 Lawrence Road, Havertown, PA 19083, USA
E-mail: uspen-and-sword@casematepublishers.com
Website: www.penandswordbooks.com

Contents

Foreword by Air Chief Marshal Sir Stephen Dalton vii
   GCB, ADC, FRAeS

Author's Note and Glossary viii

Acknowledgements xii

Introduction xiii

Part I   KANALKAMPF DIARY, 10 JULY – 31 JULY 1940 1

Part II   KANALKAMPF DIARY, 1 AUGUST – 12 AUGUST 1940 197

Reflections 294

Bibliography 298

Other Books by Dilip Sarkar MBE FRHistS 307

Index 309

Foreword

The Battle of Britain Memorial Trust, in addition to maintaining the National Memorial to the Few, also exists to advance education in and understanding of the contributions made by aircrew from the UK and Commonwealth and Allied countries who flew operationally in the Battle thus ensuring that future generations are aware of the importance of this event and its place in history.

In this second volume of the series, Dilip Sarkar MBE, FRHistS explores the early phase of the Battle using his unique archive of personal testimonies and other rare sources, often challenging accepted narratives whilst weaving an eminently readable account which references both British and German aspects of the conflict.

This volume complements the earlier volume in the series which will build into a unique and invaluable work which will contribute greatly to the understanding of the Battle and will help to sustain the work of the Trust.

ACM Sir Stephen Dalton GCB, ADC, FRAeS
President, The Battle of Britain Memorial Trust CIO

Author's Note and Glossary

The aviation-minded reader will notice that I have referred to German *Messerschmitt* fighters by the abbreviation 'Me' (not 'Bf', which is more technically correct), or simply by their numeric designation, such as '109' or '110'. This not only reads better but is authentic: during the Battle of Britain, Keith Lawrence, a New Zealander, flew Spitfires and once said to me 'To us they were just 'Mes', '109s' or '110s', simple, never 'Bf'.'

In another attempt to preserve accuracy, I have also used the original German, wherever possible, regarding terms associated with the *Luftwaffe*. These include the following:

Adlerangriff	'Attack of the Eagles'.
Adlertag	'Eagle Day'.
Bordfunker	Radio operator.
Eichenlaub	The Oak Leaves, essentially being a bar to the Ritterkreuz.
Erprobungsgruppe	Experimental group, in the case of Erprobungsgruppe 210 a skilled precision bombing unit.
Experte	A fighter 'ace'. Ace status, on both sides, was achieved by destroying five enemy aircraft.
Freie Hunt	A fighter sweep.
Führer	The German leader (Hitler).
Gefechstand	Operations headquarters.
General der Jagdflieger	General of fighter pilots.
Geschwader	The whole group, usually of three gruppen.
Geschwaderkommodore	The group leader.
Gruppe	A wing, usually of three squadrons.
Gruppenkeil	A wedge formation of bombers, usually made up of vics of three.
Gruppenkommandeur	The wing commander.
Heer	The German army.
Jagdbomber ('Jabo')	Fighter-bomber.
Jagdflieger	Fighter pilot.
Jagdgeschwader	Fighter group, abbreviated JG.
Jagdwaffe	The fighter force.
Jäger	Hunter, in this context a fighter pilot or aircraft.
Kampffleiger	Bomber aircrew.

AUTHOR'S NOTE AND GLOSSARY

Kampfgeschwader	Bomber group, abbreviated KG.
Kanal	English Channel.
Kanalkampf	Channel Battle.
Katchmarek	Wingman.
Kriegsmarine	The German navy.
KanalkampfFührer	Channel Battle Leader.
Lehrgeschwader	Literally a training group, but actually a precision bombing unit, abbreviated LG.
Luftflotte	Air Fleet.
Oberkannone	Literally the 'Top Gun', or leading fighter ace.
Oberkommando des Heeres (OKH)	The upper command of the German army.
Oberkommando der Luftwaffe (OKL)	The upper command of the German air force.
Oberkommando der Wehrmacht (OKW)	The German armed forces high command.
Reichstag	The national parliament of Nazi Germany.
Reichskuftfahrministerium (RLM)	The German Air Ministry.
Ritterkreuz	The Knight's Cross of the Iron Cross.
Rotte	A pair of fighters, comprising leader and wingman, into which the Schwarm broke once battle was joined.
Rottenführer	Leader of a fighting pair.
Schwarm	A section of four fighters.
Schwarmführer	Section leader.
Schwimmweste	Life-jacket.
Seelöwe	*Sealion*, the codenamed provided Hitler's proposed seaborne invasion of the UK.
Seenotflugkommando	Luftwaffe air sea rescue organisation
Stab	Staff.
Stabschwarm	Staff flight.
Staffel	A squadron.
Staffelkapitän	The squadron leader.
Störflug	Harassing attacks, usually by lone Ju 88s.
Stuka	The Ju 87 dive-bomber.
Sturkampfgeschwader	Dive-bomber group, abbreviated StG.
Vermisst	Missing.
Wehrmacht	Armed forces.
Zerstörer	Literally 'destroyer', the term used for the Me 110.
Zerstörergeschwader	Destroyer group, abbreviated ZG.

Each *geschwader* generally comprised three *gruppen*, each of three *staffeln*. Each *gruppe* is designated by Roman numerals, i.e. III/JG26 refers to the third *gruppe* of

Fighter Group (abbreviated 'JG') 26. *Staffeln* are identified by numbers, so 7/JG26 is the 7th *Staffel* and belongs to III/JG26.

Rank comparisons may also be useful:

Gefreiter	Private 1st Class.
Unteroffizier	Corporal, no aircrew equivalent in Fighter Command.
Feldwebel	Sergeant.
Oberfeldwebel	Flight Sergeant.
Leutnant	Pilot Officer.
Oberleutnant	Flight Lieutenant.
Hauptmann	Squadron Leader.
Major	Wing Commander.
Oberst	Group Captain.
General-Admiral	Admiral.
Grand-Admiral	Admiral of the Fleet.

RAF and British Abbreviations:

AA	Anti-aircraft.
AAF	Auxiliary Air Force.
AASF	Advance Air Striking Force.
A&AEE	Aeroplane and Armament Experimental Establishment.
AC1	Aircraftsman 1st Class.
AFC	Air Force Cross.
AFDU	Air Fighting Development Unit.
AI	Airborne Interception Radar.
AOC	Air Officer Commanding.
AOC-in-C	Air Officer Commanding-in-Chief.
ATA	Air Transport Auxiliary.
ATS	Armament Training School.
BEF	British Expeditionary Force.
CAS	Chief of the Air Staff.
CFS	Central Flying School.
CGS	Central Gunnery School.
CO	Commanding Officer.
DAF	Desert Air Force.
DCAS	Deputy CAS.
DES	Direct Entry Scheme.
DFC	Distinguished Flying Cross.
DFM	Distinguished Flying Medal.
DSO	Distinguished Service Order.
E/A	Enemy Aircraft.

AUTHOR'S NOTE AND GLOSSARY

FAA	Fleet Air Arm.
FIU	Fighter Interception Unit.
FTS	Flying Training School.
GPC	Guinea Pig Club.
ITW	Initial Training.
LAC	Leading Aircraftman.
MAP	Ministry of Air Production.
MC	Military Cross.
MRAF	Marshal of the Royal Air Force.
MSFU	Merchant Ship Fighter Unit.
MTB	Motor Torpedo Boat.
NCO	Non-Commissioned Officer.
OR	Other Ranks.
ORB	Operations Record Book.
OTC	Officer Training Corps.
OTU	Operational Training Unit.
PAF	Polish Air Force.
PDC	Personnel Distribution Centre.
RAF	Royal Air Force
RAFVR	Royal Air Force Volunteer Reserve.
RDF	Range and Direction Finding (Radar Detection System).
RFS	Reserve Flying School.
RN	Royal Navy.
R/T	Radio Telephone.
SASO	Senior Air Staff Officer.
SEAC	South East Asia Command.
SHAEF	Supreme Headquarters Allied Expeditionary Force.
SOO	Senior Operations Officer.
SSC	Short Service Commission.
TAF	Tactical Air Force.
UAS	University Air Squadron.
U/S	Unserviceable.
WAAF	Women's Auxiliary Air Force.
WDAF	Western Desert Air Force.
W/T	Wireless Telephone.

Note: 'Angels' refers to height measured in thousands of feet, hence 'Angles One-Five' means 15,000ft. A 'vector' is a compass course, measured in degrees, a 'Bandit' is a confirmed enemy aircraft while a 'Bogey' and an 'X-Raid' are as yet unidentified but potentially hostile radar plots. 'Tally Ho!' was shouted when the enemy were sighted and the leader was ordering an attack.

Acknowledgements

This series of books has arisen from over forty years of research and study of the subject, throughout which time I led a privileged relationship with survivors, and the relatives of casualties – too many to thank individually, but all have my appreciation.

As always, my old friend Andy Long was ever-helpful, and, in relation to this particularly special project, I must thank Charles Hewitt, Martin Mace and Matthew Potts of Pen & Sword, Amy Jordan and the production and marketing teams, who are always a pleasure to work with and collectively do a first-class job.

I must thank Hannah and Peter Tutton for taking me to visit Auckland's War Memorial Museum, where I saw Air Chief Marshal Sir Keith Park's medals. The following all played a part in my subsequent research journey leading to Sir Keith being accepted by the RAF AHB as one of The Few: Gail Romano, the Museum's Associate Curator, War History; Simon Moody, Research Curator at the RNZAF Museum in Christchurch, New Zealand; Stephen Park, Sir Keith's great-nephew; Squadron Leader Jon Rooke.

Finally, it has been an absolute privilege to produce this work for the Battle of Britain Memorial Trust and National Memorial to The Few, and I must thank our Chairman, Richard Hunting CBE, Honorary Secretary, Group Captain Patrick Tootal OBE DL RAF, Trustee Wing Commander Andrew Simpson RAFVR(T), Major (Ret'd) Jules Gomez, Site Manager, National Memorial to The Few, and both Malcolm Triggs and Becca Collier-Cook for their help in promoting 'Battle of Britain: The People's Project'.

Introduction

On 18 June 1940, the British Prime Minister, Winston Churchill, addressed the House of Commons, predicting that, 'What General Weygand called the Battle of France is over. I expect that the Battle of Britain is about to begin.'

That night, the lull following the Dunkirk evacuation broke when the *Luftwaffe*, now operating from bases in north-west France, launched the greatest air attack so far on mainland Britain, when over seventy intruders bombed a wide range of targets. That attack was so comparatively heavy, in fact, as to inspire Pilot Officer David Scott-Malden, a young RAF fighter pilot converting to Spitfires at Aston Down in Gloucestershire, to consider in his diary that 'The "Battle of Britain" starts with an air raid on the East Coast.' Nothing else of significance, however, occurred until the beginning of July 1940.

At lunchtime on 1 July 1940, a coal convoy, codenamed *Jumbo*, was steaming towards Plymouth when dive-bombed by *Stukas*. Fortunately no ships were sunk, and sections of 213 Squadron's Hurricanes, although arriving after the Germans' departure, successively kept guard overhead thereafter. This daylight attack on shipping, however, represented a change in German tactics, which continued over the next few days.

On 4 July 1940, 79 Squadron's Sergeant H. Cartwright DFM was shot down and killed in combat with Me 109s over St Margaret's Bay, becoming the first fatal Fighter Command casualty in this contest over the Channel. Between then and 9 July 1940 inclusive, seven further RAF fighter pilots were killed or missing, seven others wounded and two more later died of wounds.

On 11 September 1946, Air Chief Marshal Dowding's despatch on the Battle of Britain was published in *The London Gazette*. In this important document, Lord Dowding, Fighter Command's chief during that epic summer of 1940, clearly felt the Battle of Britain's start-date was unclear:

> The Battle may be said to have started when the Germans had disposed of the French resistance in the summer of 1940, and turned their attention to this country. The essence of their strategy was to so weaken our fighter defences that their air arm should be able to give adequate support to an attempted invasion of the British Isles.

It is difficult to fix the exact date on which the 'Battle of Britain' can be said to have begun. Operations of various kinds merged into each other almost insensibly, and there are grounds for choosing 8 August, on which was made the first attack in force against land objectives in this country, as the beginning of the Battle.

On the other hand, the heavy attacks made against our Channel convoys probably constituted, in fact, the beginning of the German offensive; because the weight and scale of the attack indicates that the primary object was rather to bring our fighters to battle than destroy the hulls and cargoes of the small ships engaged in coastal trade. While we were fighting in Belgium and France, we suffered the disadvantage that even the temporary stoppage of an engine involved the loss of pilot and aircraft, whereas, in similar circumstances, the German pilot might be fighting again the same day, and his aircraft be airborne again in a matter of hours.

In fighting over England these considerations were reversed, and the moral and material disadvantages of fighting over enemy country may well have determined the Germans to open a phase of fighting in which the advantages were more evenly balanced. I have therefore, somewhat arbitrarily chosen the events of 10 July 1940 as the opening of the Battle. Although many attacks had previously been made on convoys, and even land objectives such as Portland, 10 July saw the employment by the Germans of the first really big formation (seventy aircraft) intended primarily to bring our fighter defence to battle on a large scale.

Significantly, Dowding acknowledged that the enemy's ultimate objective was invasion. That being so, surely the enemy's invasion plans appended to *Luftwaffe* air operations dictated when the Battle of Britain began?

It has often been argued that had Hitler not delayed after the Fall of France and instead pressed on with a seaborne invasion of England, this ambitious combined operation could have succeeded, given the British disarray immediately after Dunkirk. In *Hitler's Naval War*, however, Cajus Bekker makes a pertinent point – after the evacuation, which significantly damaged the potential invasion embarkation points of Dunkirk and Calais,

> the Germans found virtually no seaworthy craft they could use. The British had taken the lot ... or if not had destroyed them. This fact alone makes nonsense of the idea ... that the German should have pursued the beaten foe and landed straightaway on his island sanctuary. There were just no vessels then at hand for such a purpose. Now they had to be brought painstakingly from Germany.

INTRODUCTION

While this undertaking went ahead, on 2 July 1940, the German high command (OKW) informed the *Wehrmacht* that the invasion of Britain may possibly proceed, providing certain conditions were obtained – essentially control of the air. 'Seldom,' Bekker commented, 'can the text of an order been more equivocal: "It must be borne in mind that no landing in England has yet to be decided upon, and that all preparations will be made on a hypothetical basis."'

In truth, Hitler was reluctant to destroy Britain and its empire, and was still hopeful that terms could still be agreed, while preferring a policy of blockade to invasion. Nonetheless, if we are to accept that the Battle of Britain was fought to prevent a German seaborne invasion of southern England, then surely 2 July 1940 is actually the date on which the Battle began – because from this point on and until the proposed landings were postponed indefinitely, enemy air operations were appended to an invasion plan – 'hypothetical' or otherwise. Some previous commentators have argued that the Dunkirk air fighting was the start of what became the Battle of Britain – but that was clearly not the case given that those air battles were unconnected with an invasion of Britain.

Dowding mentions 8 August 1940 as a potential start-date, when the Germans began stepping up attacks on land targets, but clearly, as far as the enemy was concerned, military preparations, in the air, on land and at sea, had begun the previous month; so, again, we return to the OKW directive of 2 July 1940. Certainly Air Commodore Al Deere, the celebrated fighter ace from New Zealand, writing in 1959, was convinced that the start-date was 2 July 1940. Indeed, a line in his 54 Squadron's Operations Record Book [ORB], dated 10 July 1940, is telling: As a result of the first phase of the Battle of Britain, the squadron could only muster eight aircraft and thirteen pilots.

That 'first phase' then, as far as 54 Squadron was concerned, was the period 2–9 July 1940. And yet, officially, the Battle of Britain did not actually commence until the following day. This is important, because after Germany's eventual total defeat on 24 May 1945, the Air Ministry announced that there would be a special clasp to the 1939–45 Star, indicating that the recipient had been fighter aircrew during Britain's darkest days. On 23 July 1945, the Air Ministry further announced the issue of the clasp and appended rosette, to be worn on the medal ribbon, to 'aircrew personnel who flew in fighter aircraft engaged in the Battle of Britain between 10 July 1940 and 31 October 1940'.

Over time, further qualification criteria emerged, which will be discussed in this and future volumes, but what is significant is the start-date of 10 July 1940. This means that those aircrew lost or maimed between 2–9 July 1940 inclusive did not receive the coveted Battle of Britain Clasp, and nor, consequently, are they remembered among The Few. Their battles and sacrifice were covered in Volume 1, which concluded with the events of 9 July 1940.

This successive work begins on Wednesday, 10 July 1940, covering the first phase of the Battle of Britain, as far as the official dates are concerned, which lasted until Monday, 12 August 1940. This narrative is presented in diary format, placing the air fighting within a much broader context of human experience – and carefully considers the evolving German invasion plans.

Britain's salvation in 1940 arguably relied upon one of two things: American intervention and aid, or her own defences. This was touched upon by US Senator Key Pittman, Chairman of the Senate Foreign Relations Committee. 'It is no secret,' he wrote in his statement advising the British Government to surrender to Nazi Germany, 'that Great Britain is totally unprepared for defence and that nothing the United States has to give can more than delay the result.'

As Pilot Officer Scott-Malden also wrote in his diary, 'Cannot yet conceive the enormity of it all. I suppose it will not be long before we start defending England in earnest.'

And, although a surprise to Senator Pittman, among others, it would be an 'earnest' and ultimately successful defence – as our unique narrative continues to explore.

Dilip Sarkar MBE FRHistS, 2023

Part I

KANALKAMPF DIARY
10 July – 31 July 1940

WEDNESDAY, 10 JULY 1940

Perhaps ironically, considering that in popular myth and memory the summer of 1940 is remembered as one of idyllic weather, dawn on the first official day of the Battle of Britain heralded a day of rain, wind, storm clouds and thunder. As daylight broke, eight convoys were steaming through British coastal waters, and despite the poor weather conditions, Fighter Command mounted standing convoy protection patrols from Exeter, on the South Coast, and Wick, near John O'Groats.

Inevitably, sunrise of this historically significant day once more saw enemy reconnaissance aircraft active over Britain – and one such was about to become the first casualty of the Battle of Britain proper. Perhaps surprisingly, this first action was not fought over the South Coast or English Channel, but off the East Coast.

For 66 Squadron's Spitfire pilots, based at Coltishall in Norfolk, dawn patrols seeking reconnaissance bombers and patrolling over North Sea convoys was becoming routine. That morning, Red Section, comprising Pilot Officers Charles Cooke (Red 1) and John Mather (Red 2), and Sergeant Fred Robertson (Red 3), was at readiness when scrambled at 00.40 hrs to investigate an 'X-Raid'.

Pilot Officer Mather:

> At 0515 'Jaybo' [Coltishall Control] informed Red 1 we were in vicinity of one bandit. Red 1 ordered me to patrol above 8/10 cloud at 10,000ft. As soon as I penetrated cloud I saw one Do 17 about 4,000ft above and one mile to my starboard. I informed Red 1 and followed the bandit. When half a mile behind him I saw Red 1 and 3 and re-joined the Section. Before starting No 1 Attack, enemy aircraft (E/A) jettisoned his bombs.
>
> After Red 1 had attacked, I opened fire at 400 yards from astern and slightly below. Enemy fire was not very accurate. I fired all my ammunition in three bursts and broke away and watched Red 3 attack. E/A started a shallow dive and when at about 8,000ft flames appeared from his port engine. He continued his dive down to sea level and Red 3 then attacked again. E/A continued to fly immediately above the sea, leaving a trail of oil.
>
> After another six to eight miles he suddenly shot into the sea and three survivors started swimming. One of them had some bright green liquid which he trailed in the sea for conspicuousness. I continued to circle round while Red 3 climbed to height sufficient to contact 'Jaybo'. I circled for about half an hour, hoping to attract attention.

Of this combat, which occurred at 05.20 hrs off Winterton, at 17,000ft, Sergeant Robertson reported:

> When E/A was sighted it was about 5,000ft above us. Red 1 and 2 did their attacks, then I went in and opened fire at 300 yards range, closing to about fifty yards, and broke away. At the start of my attack the rear gunner was firing at me, but as I closed up the fire ceased and as I broke away the port engine of the Do 17 burst into flames. The aircraft began to lose height and I followed it down on an easterly course. When it reached 500ft it appeared to level out and, thinking it was getting away, I did another stern attack, opening fire at 150 yards, closing right up to within fifty yards before breaking away. The starboard engine was then on fire and about three minutes later it struck the sea and disintegrated, about fifteen minutes after the first attack was delivered. I experienced no return fire from the enemy during my second attack. Three persons were floating in the water after the crash. The return fire from the E/A appeared to be tracer and seemed to come from the top turret.

Pilot Officer Cooke's combat report has not survived, but we do know that the windscreen of his Spitfire, N3042, was damaged by return fire from the Do 17.

The first German aircraft to fall in the Battle of Britain, this Do 17Z of II/KG3, came down in the sea between Great Yarmouth and Harwich. Although three of the enemy crew were seen swimming in the water, one even having activated the fluorescein dye he was equipped with, and in spite of the gallant Pilot Officer Mather orbiting the crash-site in the hope of attracting the assistance of a passing ship, there were no survivors. Of the four-man crew, the bodies of *Oberleutnant* Hilmar Bott and *Leutnant* Friedrich-Karl Schroder washed up on the British coast the following day, while *Oberfeldwebel* Franz Puk and *Gefreiter* Edi Frenz remain missing. These enemy airmen were, therefore, the very first *Luftwaffe* casualties in what would be a bloody sixteen-week conflict.

At exactly the same time as 66 Squadron's Red Section scored first blood, 05.20 hrs (ten minutes earlier according to the 145 Squadron ORB, but that is incorrect) the Hurricanes of 145 Squadron's Red Section, comprising Flight Lieutenant Roy Dutton (Red 1), Flying Officer Michael Newling (Red 2) and Pilot Officer Robert Yule (Red 3, a New Zealander) were also up, from Tangmere, and in action over the 'Southampton area'; Flight Lieutenant Dutton:

> I was Red Section Leader and ordered to patrol Beachy Head at 10,000ft, taking-off at about 0500 hrs. I arrived on patrol above clouds and received information of the presence of one bandit at an unknown height. At about 0510 hrs I sighted a white smoke trail about five or six miles South of me, going north-west at a height of 20,000ft. I immediately sighted bandit ahead of smoke trail and gave chase. After a chase lasting about ten minutes I came within range of E/A, which turned out to be a Do 17 at 21,000ft.

The E/A dived steeply for a cloud layer at 15,000ft. I followed, giving a series of short bursts until I had to break away owing to lack of ammunition, and the fact that I was overtaking in cloud. The E/A appeared to be hit many times and was seen to emit brown-black smoke from the starboard engine. Bits and pieces were also seen to fall off as the result of fire.

After breaking away, I turned back and sighted the E/A flying south-east, among cloud. My No 2 attacked but owing to the slow speed of the target overshot very quickly. I continued to keep sight of E/A until lost it in thick cloud at 12,000ft. I was unable, however, to direct my No 3 to the target as he was unable to see it.

During the engagement I was hit in the starboard wing root, the bullet entering the petrol tank. My No 3 was hit at extreme range – one bullet entering starboard wing-tip and three others only dinting leading edge. The Do 17 has since been reported down in sea.

According to Red 3, Pilot Officer Yule, the 'E/A appeared to be very badly hit and flying very slowly'.

There is no record, however, of an enemy aircraft down in the sea. This aircraft might have been the Do 215 of *Aufklarangsgruppe Ob.d.L*, which crashed and burned out near Le Havre that morning, killing two crew-men and wounding another, or a Do 17P of 4(F)/121 which crash-landed after combat near Boulogne with one crewman killed, two missing and another wounded.

That morning, based on the South Coast, 145 Squadron was kept busy by the enemy reconnaissance incursions, sections being scrambled nine times between 05.00 and 11.30 hrs. According to the squadron's ORB, 'Green Section chased a second Dornier across the Channel and gave it bursts at long range, without apparently doing it serious damage; this Dorner maintained great speed throughout'. Already, it was becoming clear that shooting at long-range was largely ineffective – close-in was best, although with the German bombers being increasingly armoured they were clearly difficult to bring down with rifle-calibre machine-guns.

At this time, 253 Squadron was based at Kirton-in-Lindsey, seven miles South-east of Scunthorpe on the North Lincolnshire coast. Like 66 Squadron, the unit's Hurricanes patrolled the coast and North Sea shipping; that morning Sergeant Ian Charles Cooper Clenshaw was up on the dawn patrol.

The 22-year-old pilot from Southend, Essex, had joined the RAFVR in February 1939, learning to fly on Tiger Moths before mobilisation in September 1939. After advanced service flying training, he joined 253 Squadron at Kirton in early June 1940, surviving a crash on 7 July 1940, in which he suffered minor burns. Three days later, the young and comparatively inexperienced pilot lost control of his fighter in bad weather, his Hurricane, P3359, crashing near the Church of St Andrew's, at Irby-upon-Humber, near Grimsby. Sadly, Sergeant Clenshaw was killed, becoming

KANALKAMPF DIARY, 10 JULY – 31 JULY 1940

Fighter Command's first aircrew casualty of the Battle of Britain. Within less than two hours, therefore, the reaper had consumed souls from both sides.

The next action also occurred over East Anglia and involved another Coltishall-based squadron, namely 242 – and therein lies a tale.

Wing Commander A.B. 'Woody' Woodhall, Station Commander RAF Duxford:

> Soon after the Fall of France, Air Vice-Marshal Leigh-Mallory, our 12 Group AOC, rang me to say that 242 (Canadian) Squadron was reporting to Coltishall and would be under the operational control of my Duxford Sector. He told me that the squadron had had a tough time in France, and that the groundcrews had only just been evacuated via Cherbourg thanks to the resourcefulness of their adjutant, Flight Lieutenant Peter MacDonald MP. Their own CO had left them to their own devices after the pilots had landed in England, and the squadron, led by Flying Officer Stan Turner, had landed at Coltishall with nothing but the uniforms they were wearing. Tools, spare kit, baggage, the lot, had been abandoned.
>
> LM said 'I've got to find them a new squadron commander but he's got to be good, because these chaps are Canadians and they've had a rough time. They are browned off with authority and need a good leader – any suggestions?'
>
> At once I said 'What about Douglas Bader?'
>
> LM replied 'I thought you'd say that. I think you are right'.

Bader was already a legend in the service. A gifted sportsman and aerobatic pilot, in 1931 the headstrong young Cranwellian suffered the amputation of both legs as the result of a blameworthy low-flying accident. A lesser man would have died, but Bader overcame his disability, mastering mobility on artificial limbs, and was determined to continue flying. Although he passed a flying test, King's Regulations did not provide for disabled pilots, so having refused a ground commission, Bader left the service in disgust. Friends in high places, however, arranged that in the event of war, if Bader passed another flying test he would be reinstated.

This duly came to pass and in February 1940, Flying Officer Bader found himself flying Spitfires on 19 Squadron at Duxford, commanded by his old friend and fellow Cranwellian, Squadron Leader Geoffrey Stephenson. Although well-known and older than the other pilots, being subservient to his former equal, and junior to younger pilots, far from suited Bader – who was only a team player if leader of it. Another Cranwell chum, Squadron Leader H.W. 'Tubby' Mermagen, however, agreed to have Bader as a flight commander on his 222 Squadron, with which the legless pilot saw action over Dunkirk, scoring his first aerial victories.

Squadron Leader Mermagen:

> By the time Bader was promoted to command 242 Squadron, a Canadian unit suffering from poor morale, he was known personally to the AOC, Air Vice-Marshal Leigh-Mallory, who knew of his record and had particular respect for the way in which he had dealt with both the crash and amputations. I had spoken to Leigh-Mallory on several occasions, confirming that Bader was an 'above average' Spitfire pilot, a most mature character and quite an outstanding personality in Fighter Command. I feel certain that my high opinion of Douglas Bader helped him achieve such rapid promotion which he rightly deserved and as proven by his later service record.

Squadron Leader Bader:

> The AOC told me that the Two-Hundred-and-Forty-Second (Canadian) Squadron was a pretty brassed-off bunch; they lacked discipline and he thought that I might be some use in getting the thing straight. So I rushed off, thinking that this would be absolutely splendid!

Driving through the night, confounded by the lack of sign posts and uncooperative locals, who viewed his inquiries as to Coltishall airfield's location with suspicion, Bader arrived at the main gate tired and frustrated. It was not a good mixture, leading to an inauspicious start, which was far from 'splendid': 'When I got to the station where this squadron was I had some difficulty getting in, because the chap on the gate said "What's the password?" I replied, "You stupid prick, I don't know!"'

According to Bader's first post-war biographer, Paul Brickhill, 242's new CO 'exploded'. He was, nonetheless, forced to simmer by the barrier for twenty minutes until the Duty Officer 'ruled that he was admissible'.

The following morning, Bader was delighted to find that Coltishall's resident Spitfire squadron, 66, was commanded by an old friend: Squadron Leader Rupert 'Lucky' Leigh. Breakfast was followed by an interview with the Station Commander, Wing Commander Walter 'Bike' Besiegel, who briefed Squadron Leader Bader on his new command.

No.242 Squadron had been formed at Church Fenton on 30 October 1939, as the first Canadian squadron. It had arrived at Coltishall only a short time before Squadron Leader Bader, having been severely mauled during the Battle of France. When the *Blitzkrieg* began, the squadron had been operating with 1 Squadron at Châteaudun, from which it rapidly withdrew to Le Mans.

By the campaign's conclusion what was left of 242 Squadron was at Nantes, without effective leadership, cohesion – or even its ground personnel, which were somewhere between Le Mans and the coast with the adjutant, Flight Lieutenant Peter 'Boozy Mac' MacDonald. There had certainly been a crisis of leadership in France, as far as this particular fighter squadron was concerned, which was perhaps unsurprising given that the former CO, a French Canadian, had a background in Training Command – not as a fighter leader. In the face of Hitler's onslaught, however, inspirational leadership was required – but not the CO or his flight commanders had the ability to provide it. The outcome was inevitable: only nine pilots survived the crucible of France. Bader clearly had work to do, to both restore morale and gain 242 Squadron's confidence – and, for all his faults, it was exactly this kind of challenge that brought out the best in Douglas Bader.

Squadron Leader Douglas Bader:

> I found myself ... in conjunction with my Adjutant, an elderly gentleman of the finest class who had been Member for the Isle of Wight for the past plus 500 years, and had fought in World War One, he took me into a dispersal hut where these chaps were lying about on beds, wearing Mae Wests and flying clothes, and all reading comic strips. He said 'Gentlemen, this is your new Squadron Commander, Squadron Leader Bader' – and for some extraordinary reason, because I had been trained at the RAF College Cranwell, I thought they might stand up.
>
> In fact some of them lowered their comics, looked over the top, obviously didn't care for what they saw, put the comics back up and went on reading! There was one chap lying with his back to me. He actually turned over, had a look, then turned back again and went on reading! I then told the adjutant that I wanted to see all of the pilots in my office.

During the interval, of an hour and ten minutes, 242 Squadron's new CO took off in Hurricane P2967 on what he described in his logbook as 'Practice on type'. More accurately, this was a breath-taking display of low-level aerobatics – intended to impress upon the disgruntled pilots that, even without legs, their new CO was no passenger and that things had changed.

Squadron Leader Douglas Bader:

> They arrived and I gave them what I thought was a reasonable three-minute talk. When finished I said 'Has anybody got anything to say?' There was a long silence, then, from the back of the room a voice said 'Horseshit!' Again, they hadn't taught me at Cranwell what to do in such a situation. As I was getting rather red around the neck and face, and was about to make a bloody fool of myself, the same voice added 'Sir!'.

A lively discussion then ensued, in which the new CO was enlightened as to why morale was so poor: even the pilots' clothes, left behind in France, had yet to be replaced, and neither had they been paid for some time. Immediately recognising the urgent need for strong leadership in all aspects, Bader firstly sent his pilots clothes-shopping in Norwich, personally guaranteeing payment, then established a new command team. Flight Lieutenant Eric Ball was brought in from 19 Squadron to command 'A' Flight, and Flight Lieutenant George Powell-Sheddon, an ex-Cranwellian, came from the Fighter Command Pool to command 'B' Flight.

There was already another young British officer flying with 242 Squadron, Pilot Officer Denis Crowley-Milling, an Old Malvernian and former Rolls-Royce apprentice who had joined the RAFVR pre-war:

> When he received command of 242 Squadron, Douglas Bader was approaching thirty whist the rest of us were around twenty or twenty-one. After France we were in a bad state, but less than a month after Douglas took command the squadron was fully operational – and our morale was high. Fear was always there, of course, but Bader was afraid of nothing. Through personal example and constant encouragement he helped us all conquer our anxieties. You always felt perfectly safe when flying with Douglas Bader. For me, his arrival at Coltishall was the start of eighteen exciting months of operational flying together, an unforgettable experience which helped shape my subsequent career.

Suddenly, with the swashbuckling Bader's arrival, 242 Squadron was rapidly becoming supercharged.

In addition to 242 Squadron's pilots' problems, though, its Hurricanes had suffered too; although eighteen new aircraft were on charge, no spare parts or tools were on the inventory. Bader's next port of call was the squadron's Engineering Officer, Warrant Officer Bernard 'Knocker' West.

For the next few days, Bader berated Coltishall's Stores Officer, but his forthright demands for equipment fell upon deaf ears. After a week of this, West informed his CO that stores had cited an obscure regulation confirming a three month wait before fresh equipment could be ordered. Justifiably on this occasion, Bader was absolutely furious.

In response, on 4 July 1940, he sent an unprecedented signal to 12 Group HQ: '242 Squadron now operational as regards pilots but non-operational repeat non-operational as regards equipment.' He then lurched into the Station Commander's office and showed the signal flimsy to him. A heated scene ensued, and West could not believe his eyes when he read the signal shortly afterwards. What Bader failed to tell his boss, but not Mr West, was that a copy had also been sent to Fighter Command HQ.

The response came that evening from the latter. An unhelpful squadron leader concluded by pointing out that Dowding himself was 'furious' – before having the phone virtually rammed down his ear by 242's angry CO. Two days later Squadron Leader Bader was carpeted before the AOC himself, Air Chief Marshal Sir Hugh Dowding. Suffice it to say that Bader got his way: the obstructive stores officer found himself removed from his cushy HQ post and 242 Squadron's much-needed equipment was soon arriving.

Wing Commander 'Woody' Woodhall:

> Douglas was very apt to cut corners and ignore regulations or interpret them his own way in order to get on with the war. On one occasion when he had offended against some rule, I was given orders from a higher authority to reprove him. He was ordered to report to my office, and when he stumped in and saluted with his usual cheerful grin he noticed that I was wearing my cap and did not tell him to sit down, indicating an official interview.
>
> Douglas stood to attention and with an impish grin said 'Woody, you're not going to be rotten to me, are you?' What could I do but laugh, then tell him to sit down? Needless to say the reproof was passed to him as a joke – but the fact that it was passed on proved quite effective. The administrative and operational tasks and problems increased daily, and hampered as we were by a set of peacetime rules and regulations, designed as they were in the main to prevent petty pilfering, it is not surprising that everyone trying to do his job had to cut the red tape in order to get on with the war.
>
> In this Douglas Bader and I saw eye-to-eye, and I can state that we backed each other up loyally in this matter of tape-cutting. LM, our AOC, was always on our side too, which was very comforting!

LAC David Evans was a member of 242 Squadron's groundcrew:

> When Douglas Bader arrived at Coltishall, there was a little resentment and the feeling generally was 'Who the hell is this newly promoted squadron leader without legs, who has seen little action, coming to tell us how to do it after we had been in the Battle of France?' By example, however, Squadron Leader Bader gained our respect – but he was undoubtedly an autocrat. I always felt that Squadron Leader Bader bullied our Engineering Officer, Warrant Officer West, a bit to keep the aircraft serviceable.
>
> At the time Coltishall was a grass airfield, and the squadron was soon flying endless convoy protection patrols. I was a flight mechanic and in view of this constant flying keeping our Hurricanes serviceable was an exhausting undertaking. We used to work a

pattern of shifts, 0800 hrs until noon on the first day, 1630 – 0800 the following, and finally 1430 – 1630. We had the use of a Nissen hut at dispersal but it was such a lovely summer that more often than not we would just kip down beneath the mainplanes.

Many of the ground personnel were Canadians who had enlisted in the RAF with a view to flying – an ambition some later achieved through Squadron Leader Bader's encouragement, help and recommendation. Certainly our CO couldn't tolerate inefficiency or incompetence and made this very plain to all and sundry.

I wonder whether this is why he fast gained a reputation of being rather bloody-minded and arrogant. I would prefer to think it more a case of single-mindedness as his priority was to beat the Germans – which was after all the object of the exercise. I will always recall Squadron Leader Bader working his way backwards on his backside along the port mainplane until reaching the cockpit, when he then went into a practised routine of swinging his right leg up into it. He was a very brave man – make no mistake.

Hard taskmaster though Squadron Leader Bader was, he was in his element – and would defend any member of 242 Squadron to the hilt, if necessary:

I felt they were *mine*, all the pilots and troops. I used to get furious if anyone said anything about them or did anything to them, and I arranged with Norwich police that they never put my chaps on a charge but sent the matter to me to deal with. I was tough with them myself, but always closed ranks if anyone else tried to interfere. I suppose I was unreasonable in my attitude to the squadron, but it was an obsession with me and I would not brook interference.

Incredibly, this stance even extended to the Station Commander. When several of 242 Squadron's groundcrew contravened blackout restrictions, Besiegel's punishment was making them sleep in a hangar. This, however, was done without reference to 242 Squadron's CO, who, furious, stormed into the wing commander's office and called him a 'bastard'. Such insubordination was, and is, unthinkable. In the face of such a determined verbal assault the Station Commander backed down – no one, it seemed, could resist the sheer force of Douglas Bader's incredible personality.

On 29 June 1940, Squadron Leader Bader began an intensive programme of flying training for his new command. Naturally, the emphasis was on aerobatics – but not to thrill crowds at the Hendon Air Pageant: there was now a deadly purpose to those loops and rolls, as Bader himself wrote:

If you have been used to controlling an aeroplane upside down, sideways or in a vertical dive or upward zoom you have become used to being in those odd positions with the ground instead of the sky above your head and your mind remains clear. You find yourself in all these positions in combat and you don't get flustered. As a result you can shoot in whatever position you may find yourself.

Over a period of eight days, 242 Squadron practised aerobatics for ten hours and twenty minutes, a punishing schedule requiring utmost concentration. On 6 July 1940, 242 Squadron spent the day practice firing at Sutton Bridge – achieving a record score and evidencing the fact that 242 Squadron had been restored to a disciplined, motivated fighting unit. As Bader later said, 'It did not take long for me to get this Squadron back into first class shape'.

While based at Coltishall, 242 Squadron made good its personnel losses suffered in France, receiving replacement pilots. On 1 July 1940, for example, three volunteers from the Fleet Air Arm arrived, namely Sub-Lieutenant Dicky Cork, Sub-Lieutenant Richard Gardner and Midshipman Peter Patterson.

On 9 July 1940, the day before the Battle of Britain's official start-date, Squadron Leader Bader declared 242 Squadron to be 'fully operational'. The newly re-formed Squadron's first aerial victory would fall to Sub-Lieutenant Gardner, now a member of 'B' Flight, who was at readiness with Green Section the following morning.

Sub-Lieutenant Richard Gardner:

> Take-off at 0755 hrs, headed out to relieve Red Section on convoy patrol. AA fire from RN ships drew our attention to E/A at about 15,000ft. Our Section climbed to the attack. The E/A disappeared into clouds at about 17,000ft.
>
> I set gyro on his course and climbed to 24,000ft when I was ordered to return by convoy by R/T. On returning to convoy I noticed aircraft about four miles south-east of convoy. After catching aircraft I determined that it was an enemy and dived to the attack in direct line astern. The second attack I came in at about angle of 25° port side. Port engine and undercarriage was put out of action. After the third attack the E/A either crashed or pancaked at a medium speed. E/A sank in about two minutes and one person climbed onto the wing.
>
> During attacks I found that the sights were obscured by the reflection of the sun of the water. I tried the smoked glass screen but found that too dark.

Gardner's combat had taken place twenty-five miles off Lowestoft at 08.20 hrs. The enemy bomber involved was a He 111 of III/KG53; there were no survivors.

So far, the day's events had focused upon 12 Group and concerned lone raiders. This pattern, however, was about to change.

At 10.00 hrs, a substantial convoy, codenamed *Bread*, rounded the North Foreland, travelling West, and was spotted by a heavily escorted German reconnaissance machine. In response, Spitfires of 74 Squadron were scrambled from Manston at 10.37 hrs.

Pilot Officer John Freeborn:

> I was flying as Red Leader, leading 'A' Flight ... I was ordered to patrol base and then sent to investigate the bombing of a convoy two miles East of Deal.
>
> Four bombs were dropped near to the convoy but no direct hits. I was then ordered to patrol the convoy. I was flying at 12,000ft and saw two aircraft. I then climbed for height and saw a Do 17 or Do 215 escorted by thirty Me 109s. I had advantage of height and ordered 'line astern' and attacked the Me 109s as they climbed to attack.
>
> I engaged one enemy aircraft and opened fire at approximately fifty yards. My bullets entered the E/A and seemed to knock it sideways. This aircraft then just 'dropped out of the sky' and was seen to go down out of control by observers at Manston.
>
> I then turned to attack another Me 109, and I myself was then attacked by another Me 109. This latter E/A was taken off my tail by Red 2. Several other enemy aircraft then got onto my tail. These were very easy to shake off, but due to superior numbers I could not shake them all off. I was finally shot down by E/A and made a successful forced-landing at Manston aerodrome.

Pilot Officer Peter Stevenson (Yellow 3):

> We climbed for position and attacked the Me 109s from behind. The first two Me 109s I was about to engage already had Spitfires on their tails, so I climbed up and engaged an Me 109 doing a steep left-hand turn. I gave him a three-second deflection burst and saw ammunition enter the left-hand wing of the E/A. I saw liquid stream out from underneath the wing.
>
> As the E/A had an Me 109 guarding his tail I kept on climbing up. I met another Me 109 which immediately dived when I got on his tail. I only got a 2-second burst into his fuselage before he did a half-roll and dived out.
>
> After this, another Me 109 dived past me. I opened up and went vertically down towards the sea, following him. I gave him a 6-second burst and saw really thick black smoke pouring out from the sides and underneath his engine. I was fired on from behind by an Me 109, so I broke away, leaving the attacked E/A still going vertically downwards at about 4,000ft.

KANALKAMPF DIARY, 10 JULY – 31 JULY 1940

> I climbed again and looked for more E/A. The sky was clear of E/A so I returned to Manston, having used 160 rounds per gun.

Stevenson was credited with one Me 109 probably destroyed, another damaged, in what was a typical cut and thrust fighter combat. Pilot Officers St John, Draper and Cobden were also engaged, claiming damaged Me 109s. In addition to Pilot Officer Freeborn being shot-up, Sergeant Tony Mould's Spitfire was also damaged by enemy fire and he too forced-landed back at Manston.

Although no claims were made regarding the lone Do 17, a machine of 4(F)/121 reportedly crashed at Boulogne at 10.50 hrs, having apparently been damaged in this action. The Me 109 pilots involved were from II and III/JG51, who claimed six Spitfires destroyed for the loss of *Feldwebel* Wolfgang Stocker of 5/JG51.

Flight Lieutenant Edward Smith had led Red, Yellow and Blue Sections of 610 Squadron up on patrol from Biggin Hill at 10.00 hrs that morning, the Spitfires encountering marauding Me 109s over Dover at 11.10 hrs. Smith's Spitfire, L1000, was hit by cannon fire and damaged, probably by *Feldwebel* Bernard Lausch of 8/JG51, sending Red 1 diving away from the action to crash-land at Hawkinge; fortunately Smith, an experienced pilot and pre-war auxiliary, was unhurt. In this sharp and violent combat, Flying Officer William Warner fired three bursts at and hit an Me 109, which was claimed as destroyed, but unconfirmed. The 109s withdrew, having actually suffered no loss.

The action now shifted to South Wales. The Spitfires of 92 Squadron had arrived at Pembrey, West of Swansea and overlooking Carmarthen Bay, on 18 June 1940, to afford some protection to South Wales and the West Country. Lone Ju 88s were active over the area on the morning of 10 July 1940, as 92 Squadron's Flight Lieutenant Brian Kingcome reported:

> I was Red 1 and at 1110 hrs was ordered to patrol Llanelli at 10,000ft. When about ten miles north-east of Pembrey aerodrome at 6,000ft I saw a Ju 88 drop a stick of bombs. The E/A came out of cloud, dropped the bombs and went back into the cloud. I circled the cloud and every time it came out I just managed to get in a 1 second deflection snap shot. I had several sort bursts at it, but eventually lost it in the cloud. I was recalled and returned to base for rearming.

The other two members of Red Section, namely Pilot Officer Tony Bartley and Sergeant Stanley Barraclough, also got deflection shots in, the Ju 88 subsequently and somewhat optimistically being shared as 'damaged'.

Given that orders had still not been issued by OKW, across the Channel the battle was being directed at *Luftflotten* level. On 4 July 1940, *Oberst* Johannes 'Papa' Fink, *Kommodore* of the Do 17 equipped KG2 *Holzhammer*, based at Cambrai-Épinoy, was appointed *KanalkampfFührer* (Channel Battle Leader). It was not so much the shipping and ports involved that were the *Luftwaffe's* primary objective, though – these targets were more a means to an end, to draw Fighter Command to battle for destruction over the sea. The Germans would dictate the time and place of battle, and therefore have the tactical advantage.

It was impossible for Fighter Command to mount standing patrols from dawn to dusk, there simply being insufficient resources to do so, and, even with radar, given speed and the distances involved, warning of such attacks was short. The enemy's intention, therefore, was to overwhelm small formations of RAF fighters patrolling over convoys, then annihilate reinforcing RAF squadrons which would be met by German fighters sweeping in strength. And now, Fink, having grown in confidence, unleashed the heaviest attack so far.

At 13.15 hrs, six Hurricanes of 32 Squadron's 'B' Flight, Green and Blue Sections, led by Flying Officer John Humpherson were scrambled from Biggin Hill to patrol Convoy CW3, codenamed *Bread*, now steaming South-west, two miles off Dungeness. Five minutes later, RDF stations in Kent detected the assembly of a large enemy formation over the Pas-de-Calais, which soon struck out towards the convoy, the presence of which had not gone unnoticed by the enemy. After a short briefing the German bomber crews had taken off, and just a few minutes later were bearing down on the convoy, the ships of which scattered, taking evasive action by steering a zig-zag course.

Flying Officer John Humpherson:

> As we approached our patrol line at about 10,000ft I noticed that the escorting destroyers were firing their AA guns. Immediately afterwards I saw a formation of about fifty Do 215s approaching convoy from the south-east. Blue Section had become separated from my Section as we had just passed through a heavy rain cloud.

Humpherson, now leading just two other Hurricanes now that Blue Section was detached, was actually looking at twenty-six Do 17s of I/KG 2 escorted by all three *Staffeln* of I/ZG26 (Me 110s), and two *Staffeln* of I/JG3 (Me 109s), incoming at 7,000ft.

Humpherson continues:

> I put Green Section into line astern and carried out a No 1 Attack on a single E/A that had become separated from the rest of the formation. I opened fire at about 250 yards and then closed to about fifty yards, firing two bursts of about ten seconds' duration. I encountered heavy fire from the rear gunner of the Dornier, but this ceased about three-quarters way through my attack.
>
> Just before the firing ceased I noticed a minor explosion in the bottom gun turret. As I broke away, I noticed that the Dornier carried three guns in the bottom turret, one firing astern and one on each side.

KANALKAMPF DIARY, 10 JULY – 31 JULY 1940

The other two pilots of Green Section, Sub-Lieutenant Geoffrey Bulmer and Sergeant Leonard Pearce, also attacked the same Do 17, the latter following the bomber to mid-Channel, by which time the enemy aircraft had dropped to 3,000ft, emptying his remaining ammunition into the bomber before returning to base.

Reinforcements were rapidly sent to help the outnumbered 32 Squadron pilots. At 12.45 hrs, Flight Lieutenant Edward 'Jumbo' Gracie of North Weald's 56 Squadron had led 'B' Flight to operate from Manston, so these seven Hurricanes were well-placed when scrambled at 13.30 hrs. Vectored to Dover, having patrolled for five minutes, Gracie espied the enemy formation attacking *Bread*, making off to the south-east after dropping their bombs:

> I put the Flight into line astern and climbed in an endeavour to get above the fighters and dive through them onto the bombers. This proved impossible owing to the large numbers of fighters at all heights, and Blue Section attacked fifteen or twenty Me 110s which were maintaining a left-hand circle in line astern.
>
> I fired a long burst of about ten seconds at an Me 110 and parts of its tail were seen to fall off. My range was then about 200/300 yards. Little or no evasive action was taken. One of the crew was seen to bale out and E/A went into a low spin. Pilot Officer Wicks and Flight Lieutenant Coghlan saw E/A's tail come adrift, and Flight Sergeant Higginson saw it spinning towards the sea, out of control.
>
> I was hit from behind and oil, petrol and glycol were leaking from my aircraft. My engine seized at 500ft over Manston and I had no time or height to let down my undercarriage and I was enveloped in smoke. I crashed on landing and my aircraft was written-off, but I was uninjured.

The Me 110 was confirmed as destroyed, as was one claimed by Sergeant Clifford Whitehead, while Flight Lieutenant John Coghlan claimed one Me 110 destroyed and another damaged.

At 13.00 hrs, Squadron Leader John Thompson had led eight Hurricanes of his 111 Squadron up from Croydon with orders to proceed to and operate from Hawkinge. En route, Thompson was vectored to the action over Convoy *Bread* and hastened to the scene.

Approaching the enemy head-on, the Hurricanes continued until wheeling around to attack the two rearmost sections of bombers. Several of Thompson's pilots attacked and destroyed a Do 17, the crew of which bailed out. *Oberleutnant* Walter Oseau of III/JG51, however, picked out and attacked the Hurricane of Flying Officer Thomas Higgs, who immediately flung his machine into a violent evasive manoeuvre – colliding with a Do 17 in the process. A wing was torn from the British fighter in the collision, and Higgs baled out. The Do 17 involved, of 3/KG3, crashed near the Dungeness Buoy; two of the crew were captured while the other pair remain missing. Of Higgs, no trace was found until his body washed ashore on a Dutch beach the following month.

Meanwhile, Flying Officer Henry Ferriss DFC,

> drove an Me 109 into the sea and was in turn attacked by three Me 109s who shot away one aileron control. He was persistently attacked for about twenty miles but avoided further damage by gentle turns, which he steepened as he followed the course of tracer bullets. He did this about a dozen times and finally the Me 109s abandoned their attacks [111 ORB].

Flying Officer John Mungo-Park was leading the Spitfires of 74 Squadron's 'B' Flight, up from Manston, patrolling over the Dover Strait when at 13.35 hrs he too sighted the enemy over Convoy *Bread*. Ordering line-astern, Mungo-Park opened fire at 400 yards, closing to 100 yards, emptying all his ammunition into a Do 17, setting its starboard engine alight before breaking away. Flight Lieutenant William 'Tink' Measures damaged an Me 110, Pilot Officer Peter Stevenson damaging two more; Measures, Pilot Officers Bryan Draper and Don Cobden, a New Zealander, also claimed Do 17s damaged. The latter, however, was shot-up, crash-landing his battered Spitfire at Lympne, the pilot fortunately unhurt.

While in line astern during 74 Squadron's initial charge, Flying Officer Peter St John, Yellow 3, sighted a formation of Me 109s 'to the left and slightly above'. Mungo-Park, Yellow leader, also saw the trouble and the pair of Spitfire pilots climbed to engage the German fighters, which split up. St John 'picked one and gave him a short deflection burst. I did not have time to see the effect of my burst as another 109 was on my tail. I outclimbed the 109 without any difficulty. When I got on his tail I gave him all the ammunition I had and saw tracers going in.'

The 109, which 'flew off very unsteadily towards the French coast', was credited as damaged.

As the enemy withdrew, 'B' Flight of Kenley's 64 Squadron was urgently vectored to the Dover – upon the order 'Buster!' the Spitfire pilots rammed their throttles forward and made all haste. Upon arrival, 64 Squadron found the Me 110s, which had been milling around in a defensive circle, heading back to France. The Spitfires harried the enemy across the Channel to Calais.

Sub-Lieutenant Francis Dawson-Paul:

> As Blue 3 I was ordered to patrol Tenterden with Yellow Section. Blue Section was airborne at 1345 hrs. We were vectored 120° and crossed the coast just West of Folkestone. I saw ahead a large number of aircraft obviously engaged in a dogfight. I selected an Me 110 as my first target and positioned myself on his tail at a distance of 150 yards.
>
> After two bursts his port motor caught fire and he dived down and crashed into the sea. I then selected another Me 110 as a target

and approached from the port quarter. I gave one long burst and his tail unit broke right off and the E/A went into a spin and crashed into the sea. The rear gunner baled out and was picked up by a destroyer.

Three Me 110s were lost by 8/ZG26 in the engagement and it is likely that Dawson-Paul's second victim was one of either two of these casualties, both of which suffered a crewman missing and the other captured. Me 110s were also claimed by 64 Squadron's Flying Officers Donald Taylor and Hubert Patten.

So ended the air battle, prompting Air Chief Marshal Dowding to consider 10 July 1940 as the Battle of Britain's start-date. Certainly, the defending RAF fighter pilots had done well; for the loss of one pilot, seven enemy aircraft had been destroyed, while Convoy *Bread* lost just one ship of 400 tons. As the official Air Historical Branch (AHB) narrative concludes: 'A ludicrously small return for so great an effort on the part of the Germans' – although KG2 claimed a heavy cruiser and four merchantmen sunk, and another damaged, in addition to eleven RAF fighters destroyed or damaged. Overclaiming, in the confusion of a fast-moving air battle, was on occasion something both sides suffered from. The problem with this, as we will see in subsequent volumes, is that inaccurate figures could wrongly influence strategy and tactics, providing a false impression of the enemy's strength and deployment.

For Air Vice-Marshal Park, the fighting over the sea was ever a vexing issue. On this day, the AOC 11 Group took-off from Northolt in his personal Hurricane, 'OK1', to see for himself what was happening. In his flying logbook, Park recorded that he had first flown to Lympne, on the southern Kentish coast, then proceeded out to sea, over a 'Convoy', before returning inland and landing at West Malling. It was an historic flight, because although not officially awarded the Battle of Britain Clasp to the 1939-45 Star, Air Chief Marshal Sir Keith Park, as he became, included the clasp in his medal group, which can be seen today at the Auckland War Memorial Museum in Auckland, New Zealand. It would not be until 2023, when this author personally viewed the medals and queried inclusion of the Clasp that evidence from Sir Keith's logbook, preserved by the RNZAF Museum, was submitted to the RAF's AHB - which accepted that Sir Keith was, indeed, 'a legitimate recipient' of the Clasp. So it was that this otherwise insignificant flight would lead, 83 years later, to Air Chief Marshal Sir Keith Park formally joining the ranks of The Few.

Although the attack on *Bread* represented the day's major effort, raiders were active elsewhere. While Fighter Command was preoccupied with defending *Bread*, a lone bomber from Cherbourg sallied forth and successfully bombed Falmouth harbour – sinking one ship of over 6,000 tons and setting two larger vessels ablaze.

Given that the Red warning only sounded two minutes before the first bomb exploded, the official narrative admits that the 'intelligence organisation in the south-west was not yet working with proper efficiency'. Another issue was that there were insufficient fighters in that area – and yet the region accommodated a number of aircraft factories, at Filton, Yeovil and Yate. The hard-pressed 92 Squadron, based at Pembrey, failed to contact an intruder that afternoon, which dropped three bombs on the Royal Ordnance Factory, near the airfield, killing twelve workers and injuring fourteen more.

Another bomber on the prowl over South Wales, however, infuriated Wing Commander Ira Jones, a decorated First World War fighter pilot and now commanding No.7 Bombing and Gunnery School at Stormy Down, to the East of Swansea, near Porthcawl:

> The Observer Corps kept on ringing up to tell me there was a Nazi over Swansea. I could see the blighter through my binoculars and a maddening situation he was putting me in. I could not tell the Observer boys over the telephone that since all my aircraft were used for drogue-towing, I had no suitable machine for air fighting.
>
> At last I got fed up with that ringing telephone. Jumping into a Henley (a two-seater of the Hurricane type), I fairly leapt into the air and climbed for a position in which I could approach the Nazi out of the sun, so that it would be difficult for his gunner to spot me. The enemy was a Ju 88, obviously on photographic duties over the dock area.
>
> The sun was South of Swansea, so I flew out to sea and made for Mumbles Head before turning around to approach the bomber, which was flying at 12,000ft. I climbed to 15,000ft and made a steady dive at 300 mph, with my throttle full on. When I got near enough to see the black crosses on the Hun's wing and rudder, I felt the old joy of action coursing through my body, though my only armament was a Very pistol which fired a cartridge of varicoloured lights.
>
> A bare 100 yards in front of the bomber I pressed the trigger of the pistol. Then I turned gently to the left. The lights went floating prettily down in front of the Junkers, and the pilot made a sharp flick turn towards the open sea. He put his diving flaps into action and nosed vertically into billowy clouds at about 8,000ft. I screamed along the top of the cloud, just to have the fun of seeing him run away.
>
> After passing Mumbles Head the aircraft came out of the cloud about 300 yards ahead of me. The gunner was obviously looking out for me. I could see the flashes from his guns as he fired. When a bullet hole suddenly appeared in my port wing, I decided it was time to turn back. Flying back to base at Stormy Down, the Henley developed a tail flutter which frightened me more than the Nazi bullets. In fact, I got back safely and quite enjoyed my lunch!

The Blenheims of 2 Group, Bomber Command, however, were somewhat less fortunate than the raider chased off by the exasperated Wing Commander Jones. Forty Blenheims were ordered to attack the airfields at Amiens and St Omer, although most were unable to find their targets owing to bad weather.

At 11.40 hrs, six Blenheims of 107 Squadron left Wattisham to attack aerodromes in the Amiens-Glissy area. On the approach to the target area, however, intense flak was experienced, breaking up the formation. The Blenheims were then set upon by Me 109s of 9/JG3 – five Blenheims were claimed destroyed twenty kilometres West of Arras, and two more over Le Touquet. Five of the six Blenheims, in fact, were destroyed, only one aircraft returning safely, the formation leader, Flight Lieutenant Harold Pleasance, a Canadian, who had dropped to 0ft and shaken off his pursuers by taking violent evasive action. Skimming over the sea, the Blenheim pilot saw the two 109 pilots break off the chase – waving as they did so. A sixth Blenheim was claimed by 3/Flak Regiment 141 fourteen kilometres North-east of Poix on what was a costly day indeed for 2 Group – and further evidence of how ill-advised was sending unescorted bombers over enemy territory in daylight.

As ever, Coastal Command was also active on reconnaissance and convoy protection patrols. At 03.35 hrs, Pilot Officer A.J. Pearson of 22 Squadron took off from Leuchars in Hudson P5122, to patrol a convoy; at 07.05 hrs, a Do 215 was sighted, which turned away as Pearson gave chase. Having fired one burst, Pearson was forced to break off the engagement when his aircraft was raked with bullets from the enemy bomber – badly wounding his wireless operator, Sergeant R.C. Christie.

Immediately, Pearson headed back to the Scottish coast, landing at RAF Lossiemouth. Sadly, it was too late to save Sergeant Christie, who died en route – another unsung hero of summer 1940.

On the Home Front, donations had begun pouring into the Air Ministry during the previous month for what became the 'Spitfire Fund' (see Volume 1), and on this first day of battle the *Daily Express* published an appeal by Lord Beaverbrook, the Minister for Aircraft Production, 'To the Women of Britain':

> Give us your aluminium ... We will turn pots and pans into Spitfires and Hurricanes, Blenheims and Wellingtons.
>
> I ask therefore that everyone who has pots and pans, kettles, vacuum cleaners, hat pegs, coat hangers, shoe trees, bathroom fittings ... made wholly or in part of aluminium ... should hand them over at once to the local headquarters of the Women's Voluntary Services.

Edward Bishop, journalist:

> Lord Beaverbrook's competitors in Fleet Street took up the cry. 'From the Frying Pan into the Spitfire' – somewhat inevitably.
>
> It needs now be no military secret that the mountains of pots, pans and all the other articles collected so assiduously by the housewives for Lord Beaverbrook were never of much practical assistance in building fighters for the Battle of Britain. But his appeal was worth its weight in all the bathroom fittings alone for the uplift it brought to civilian morale.

People said 'Here is action. Here is something *we* can do. Here is something being done.' A nation that had been so horrified by pre-war pictures of Italian widows parting with their wedding rings to be melted down for Mussolini, surrendered its aluminium pots with a will.

While British housewives created huge mountains of pots and pans, some German *hausfrau* were reflecting on the current situation.
Frau Else Wendel:

> I loved that spring and summer, and so did everybody in Berlin. Victory flags, victory music, victory gaiety. Everything was alright in Germany ... England had asked for it and she has got Dunkirk. Feverishly we waited for the invasion of England. Some of us were astonished that it didn't come at once ... We didn't hate the English so much now but just felt rather sorry for what was coming to them ... England would no doubt turn out to be quite a valuable ally when she had swallowed her pride and acknowledged defeat.

The German mood was entirely confident. General Erwin Rommel wrote to his wife from France: 'Would you cut out all the newspaper articles about me, please. I have no time to read at the moment, but it will be fun to look at them later ... by my estimate the war will be won in a fortnight. Lovely weather – if anything, too much sun.'

Across the Channel, however, according to the Daily Home Intelligence Report (HIR), 'There is little change in morale: people are generally cheerful, although in those areas which have been constantly raided there is anxiety and lassitude. There is no diminution in determination.' Although the report went on to document that '[t]he morale of women in working-class raided areas is being lowered by lack of sleep and by the family responsibilities with which they are burdened.'

Interestingly, in direct contravention of the mythical narrative telling of a united nation pulling together, the HIR also states that 'reports on the state of feeling among young people show that many have failed to identify themselves with the war, and many are consciously as well as unconsciously non-cooperative'. Nonetheless, reports regarding residents in 'areas considered likely of invasion show that the population is confident (if not over-confident)'.

While still hopeful that Britain would come to terms, on 10 July 1940 Hitler ordered that all heavy naval artillery should be used to provide frontal and flanking fire to support the projected landing operations. To this end, gun emplacements were hastily constructed along the Channel coast between Calais and Boulogne, a firm indication of the enemy's resolve and intended focus of operations.

THURSDAY, 11 JULY 1940

Once more, the day's action began with German reconnaissance aircraft snooping around, the first shots again occurring off the East Coast. Throughout the morning, these intruders constantly monitored British coastal waters, with over eighty such sorties plotted by RDF stations from the north of Scotland to Land's End.

On one such flight a Do 17 of *WetterkingsdungsStaffel* 261 was off Yarmouth, reporting on weather conditions when it was intercepted at 06.00 hrs by Squadron Leader Rupert Leigh and Sergeant Reg Hyde of 66 Squadron. Return fire from the bomber's alert gunner, however, holed Leigh's oil tank, forcing the CO of 'Clickety-Click' to abandon the engagement and return to Coltishall. Doubtless, thankfully, the enemy aircraft slid into low cloud and made off.

The weather early that morning was bad, so when the Coltishall Controller enquired of Squadron Leader Bader whether a section of 242 Squadron could search for a 'bandit' off Cromer, the legless CO declined – but agreed to go himself. Given the weather, with thick cloud between 1,000–2,500ft, his take off, at 06.00 hrs, was virtually on instruments. Discovering cloud base to be at 700ft, Bader continued to the coast, where it lifted to 1,000ft.

Squadron Leader Douglas Bader:

> Then I saw him 400 yards in front of me. As I closed on him I recognised the narrow fuselage and twin fins of a Do 17, the aeroplane nicknamed the 'flying pencil'. The enemy had not seen me. I imagine the crew did not expect to be intercepted at that height and in that weather, so were taking it a bit easy.
>
> We continued flying along with my Hurricane gaining on the Dornier. At 250 yards I had just re-set my reflector sight to 200 yards range when the enemy rear-gunner opened fire. The flashes from his machine-gun were vivid. That crew had woken up!
>
> I remember thinking to myself as the Dornier gunner opened up on me: 'I've got a twelve-cylinder engine shielding me, a bullet-proof windscreen, *and* eight machine-guns'. I was totally relaxed. I fired at the Dornier, observing no effect other than a steeply banked turn to the left, but he was still below the cloud. I followed him round and he straightened up after a complete 180°. Then he started a shallow climb into cloud, with me in position behind him. I fired a second burst as he disappeared and continued into cloud behind him, still shooting. With blistering curses I gave him up and reported my failure to the Operations Room.
>
> About fifteen minutes later the Controller telephoned to say that a Home Guard observation post had reported a Dornier crashing into the sea near Cromer at the exact time of my action. This proved a lucky start for the new CO of 242 Squadron.

> After the incident, I remember thinking how easy it had been shooting from the Hurricane. Apart from the smell of cordite in the cockpit and noise of the guns I might have been keeping line-astern formation on the Dornier at some peace-time air display.

Air Ministry policy at the time was not to identify individuals in the press, so the media made much of this victory attributed to an anonymous – legless – squadron commander. Already, though, the Bader story was becoming mythicised.

An example of this appeared in Worcestershire's *Malvern Gazette* in July 1940, aimed at encouraging donations to the town's Spitfire Fund:

> Remember the story of the young pilot who lost his legs in a crash? Fitted with artificial legs he argued his way back into the RAF; argued his way through the medical boards; argued his way into a squadron, and one day, quite recently, he went up alone and shot a *Dornier* down into the sea. Did he say 'I've given the country my legs; why should I now be expected to give them my neck?' Not a bit! Like all those gallant lads he was ready to give the extra. God bless them for it.

As mentioned earlier, in reality Bader had lost his legs in a blameworthy pre-war flying accident. A legless fighter pilot, though, was inspirational at a time when Britain needed heroes – so Douglas Bader's usefulness and contribution to the war effort actually far exceeded fighting the hot war from a Hurricane cockpit. He was, in short, a propagandist's dream and would increasingly find himself used in that direction.

Another RAF squadron commander was leading a section of Hurricanes off the East Coast that morning, at 06.15 hrs. That was Squadron Leader Peter Townsend of 85 Squadron, based at Debden, in Essex:

> The weather was filthy, heavy rain and cloud. I encountered a *Dornier* in cloud, managed to get up close and fire, causing a lot of damage, but the rear-gunner, Werner Borner, shot it out with me. His MG15 was actually knocked out of his hands in the exchange, but beforehand Werner hit my Hurricane. There was an explosion in the cockpit and I broke away, trailing smoke. My engine packed up. So, I was 200 miles from land in one direction, and twenty from the British East Coast. No option but to bale out.
>
> Baling out was a pretty dicey business, really, as Air Sea Rescue was not very well organised, and as I went down I looked for a ship but couldn't see one anywhere. Then, at the last moment, there was this little trawler, which picked me up. A sailor brought me half a glass of rum, bit early for me, but I drank it, then had breakfast with them, rum for breakfast, then more rum, and I almost washed my teeth in rum, and by the time we got to Harwich and I tottered ashore,

I could hardly stand up. I had to present myself to a naval officer and tell him that I was Commanding Officer of 85 Squadron – which he had some difficulty in believing!

The Do 17 involved, of II/KG2, got home, crash-landing at St Leger Arras with three wounded men aboard.

By this time, Squadron Leader Harry Hogan's 501 'County of Gloucester' Squadron had regrouped after the fighting in France and was now based in the Middle Wallop Sector in Hampshire, inland of Southampton. Hogan's Hurricanes also operated from the forward base of Warmwell, near Weymouth in Dorset, and at 07.30 hrs 501's Green Section was scrambled from the latter airfield to patrol base.

Then, two formations of enemy aircraft were detected by RDF, heading North from Cherbourg towards an eastbound convoy traversing Lyme Bay, so Green Section, Pilot Officers Edmund Sylvester (Green 1) and Ralph Don, and Sergeant Frederick Dixon, were vectored to intercept.

Shortly before 08.00 hrs, the three Hurricanes were fifteen miles South of Portland when ten or more *Stukas* were sighted at 7,000ft, escorted by twenty Me 109s of III/JG27 positioned half a mile behind and 5,000ft higher. In the ensuing combat, Sergeant Dixon was shot down by *Oberleutnant* Ludwig Franziket; the 21-year-old pilot baled out but was not rescued – his body was later washed ashore in France. The other two Hurricanes managed to escape unscathed.

At dawn, the Spitfires of 609 Squadron had flown from Middle Wallop down to the forward base at Warmwell, from which, at 08.00 hrs, 'B' Flight was scrambled to reinforce 501 Squadron. Five minutes later, the fast-moving Spitfires arrived on the scene.

Pilot Officer Adolf Blayney:

> Blue (three aircraft) and Green (two aircraft) Sections ordered on patrol South of Portland Bill. After covering twelve miles observed dive-bombing attacks on one ship. Blue 1 (Flight Lieutenant Barran) ordered line astern with Green Section to form above guard ... Blue Section went into attack a Ju 87. Before Blue 1 opened fire, Blue 3 [Pilot Officer Blayney, writing in and out of the third person in this report] noticed bullets passing his windscreen from the rear. Made a sharp turn left at the same time broadcasting 'Evasive Action'!

Flying Officer Bernard Little:

> Blue Section moved into attack in line astern and I (Green 1) ordered No 2 in line astern and climbed up behind Blue Section, to act as rear-guard and began to weave about, looking behind.
>
> Almost instantly the bombers broke up and the dogfight developed, including Me 109s which must have come down from

the sun. During this dogfight I found myself among three or four Ju 87s which were diving to sea-level, and fired a quick burst – five or six seconds – into the under surface of one of them.

I saw the bullets strike home and the last I saw of the machine it was dropping away on its back with small pieces of it falling away. Being attacked by 109s I was unable to watch the E/A any further.

The Ju 87 hit by Little was credited as a 'probable'.

Pilot Officer Adolf Blayney continues:

> Blue 3 saw no E/A on his tail after the turn. Proceeded to attack a Ju 87. Gave him 2–3-second burst at 200 yards and closing to 50 yards. Height 1,500ft. At first the Ju 87 zig-zagged down to sea. After the first burst I noticed black smoke from the fuselage. As Blue 3 finished last burst I observed more bullets coming from the rear, so broke off engagement and endeavoured to turn in order to engage E/A on tail, which was not to be seen.
>
> After that all E/A had disappeared. Blue 3 continued to patrol the bombed vessel, and noticed a Sorbo [609 Squadron's callsign] aircraft making for the English coast on fire, so followed him until his engine stopped and pilot baled out by parachute. This occurred five or six miles South of Portland Bill. Blue 3 continued to circle over the pilot in the water and instructed Green 1 (Flying Officer Bernard Little) to inform Control to send out rescue launches. Blue 3 continued to circle position of pilot.

'Sorba Squadron' had in fact lost two Spitfires to the pouncing Me 109s: Pilot Officer Gordon Mitchell and Flight Lieutenant Phillip 'Pip' Barran. Both pilots baled out and splashed-down in the sea, it being likely that the pilot seen by Blayney and Little was Barran, who abandoned Spitfire L1069 five miles off the Dorset coast and baled out badly burned.

Although rescued from the water, he died before making landfall. Mitchell was sadly not found, and his body later washed up on the Isle of Wight. Only one Spitfire, unusually, was claimed by the German pilots, namely *Oberleutnant* Max Dobislav of 9/JG27, who recorded his second victory South of Portland.

No.609 'West Riding' Squadron was an Auxiliary Air Force (AAF) squadron, locally raised on the territorial principle, and within such units it was common for personnel to be friends or even related. Over time, replacement pilots arrived from the RAFVR and regular service, including men from the Empire and Commonwealth and occupied lands, changing the identity of these close-knit squadrons.

These early casualties, however, among the original auxiliaries, hit such squadrons hard. Only two days previously, 609 had suffered its first casualty operating from the Middle Wallop Sector, namely the popular Flying Officer Peter

KANALKAMPF DIARY, 10 JULY – 31 JULY 1940

Drummond-Hay, shot down by an Me 109 over Portland and reported missing (again see Volume 1). Pilot Officer David Crook was an auxiliary member of 609, and, suffering from the death of his room-mate. Drummond-Hay, was on leave the following day, catching the afternoon train to London for an evening out with his wife, Dorothy (known to all as 'D'). Of his return to Middle Wallop at lunchtime on 11 July 1940, in his diary Crook wrote:

> I got back ... and heard that 'Pip' Barran and Gordon [had] been killed that morning. The whole squadron was down at Warmwell and apparently a lot of fighting was going on all along the South Coast.
>
> I could get no details of what had happened, and I sat alone in the Mess all afternoon, feeling more miserable and more stunned than I had never felt before.
>
> Everybody arrived back after dark, dog tired and utterly depressed. I shall never forget seeing them all come into the mess – people who normally appeared not to have a care in the world, just flopped into chairs and sat there and said not a word.
>
> I rang up D and told her the news and I think that she was as shocked as I was. She had only met 'Pip' on a few occasions, but of course knew Gordon very well indeed ...
>
> It is difficult to describe my feelings during the next few days. We had lost three pilots in thirty-six hours, all of them in fights in which we had been hopelessly outnumbered, and I felt that there was really nothing left to care about, because obviously from the law of probability one could not expect to survive many more encounters of a similar nature.
>
> When one thinks of the losses sustained in war – particularly by the Army – to lose three people in two days seems very trifling. But in a squadron, there are so few pilots and it really seems more like a rather large family than anything else, and therefore three deaths at once and seems very heavy indeed.
>
> Again, compared with the experiences of squadrons during the fighting in France such losses were small, because some squadrons in France were wiped out almost to a man in a few days.
>
> But they were taking part in heavy and continuous fighting where one expects losses, and also they were destroying very much greater numbers of Germans than they themselves were losing, so they could feel, to put it bluntly, that they were getting value for money, which is a very big factor in maintaining spirits and morale.
>
> But our losses had been sustained in two small encounters and we had hardly anything to count against it, in the way of enemy shot down.
>
> So quite apart from the death of one's friends we all felt very depressed and miserable, because obviously things weren't going well.

Gordon's death in particular made a very deep impression on me, because I knew him very much better than I knew Pip, and he, Michael and I had spent the whole war together, and were so accustomed to being together that I could not then (and still cannot now) get used to the idea that we should not see Gordon again, or spend any more of our gay evenings together, or rag him about the moustache of which he was so proud. He was a very delightful person – possibly rather inclined to be moody at times, but generally a very gay and charming companion, and always exceedingly generous, both as regards material matters and – more important still – in his outlook and views. He was also a brilliant athlete, a Cambridge Hockey Blue and Scotch International.

It always used to delight me to watch Gordon playing any game, whether hockey, tennis or squash because he played with such a natural ease and grace – the unmistakable signs of a first-class athlete. He was the second Old Leysian to be killed in the air during this war.

But if Gordon's death was a greater shock to me personally, Pip's death was a terrible blow to the squadron.

He was more than a mere member of the squadron – you might almost say that he was the foundation stone upon which it was formed and built. He was one of the first people to join the squadron when it was started, and he was, I think, easily the outstanding personality of us all. I don't think anybody could mention 609 without immediately thinking of Pip, and his death in the face of such overwhelming odds was characteristic of a very brave and resolute man.

Squadron Leader Horace 'Uncle George' Darley, 609 Squadron's CO, was not an auxiliary but a Short Service Commissioned (SSC) officer, who asked Flight Lieutenant Barran if he needed a rest after the Dunkirk fighting:

He answered that he wished to stay with the squadron. I was certainly glad to keep him, for he was by far the most competent pilot and leader among the auxiliaries, and his posting would have been a severe blow to already shaken morale [609 Squadron lost four pilots killed during the Dunkirk evacuation]. But when he was shot down I did ask myself whether it could have been due to tiredness.

The mood was certainly dark that afternoon, as far as 609 Squadron was concerned, the squadron diarist being untypically critical of tactics:

The utter futility of sending up very small sections of fighters to cope with the intense enemy activity in the Portland area is bitterly resented by the pilots. The fact that they have so often been sent off to make an interception – as a Section, or possibly a flight – only to find themselves hopelessly outnumbered by enemy fighters acting as guard to the bombers, is discouraging because the British fighter then finds himself unable to do his job of destroying the bombers, and is compelled to fight a defensive action.

The situation is keenly felt by this Squadron, whose 'score' of enemy aircraft is in too close a ratio to its own losses. It is felt that we happen to have been particularly unlucky at Dunkirk and at Portland. Our contacts with the enemy have taken place when the numerical odds were rather too unreasonable.

The problem was that there was so little experience of modern fighter combat, and the German advance to the Channel coast, putting even London within range of the lethal Me 109 had changed the whole tactical and strategic scenario (see Volume 1). Indeed, before the war it was even doubted by the Air Ministry that owing to the high speeds and g-force achieved by the new monoplanes, fighter versus fighter combat would be impossible, because such physical exertions would be beyond the human body's capacity.

Understandably, it was also perceived that any attack on England would be made solely by unescorted bombers, approaching Britain's East Coast from bases in Germany. Consequently, pre-war Fighter Command tactics had focused upon set-piece formation attacks against bombers, not fighters, which were found to be inappropriate (again, see Volume 1). With the Air Fighting Manual firmly thrown in the bin after the Fall of France and Dunkirk, squadrons were literally learning on the job, with little or no helpful precedent.

Forward-thinking squadron commanders, like the legendary South African Squadron Leader 'Sailor' Malan, began experimenting with their own tactical formations, rejecting the stipulated Fighter Command 'vic' of three tightly bunched fighters. Some began flying a more stretched out line astern or abreast formation, although why it took so long to emulate the German *Schwarm* is difficult to understand.

Another issue (again covered in Volume 1) was that Fighter Command tactics revolved around the section of three aircraft, or flight of two sections, rather than the whole squadron operating together as a cohesive unit. Again, this was largely because it was anticipated only bombers would be encountered, which were slow and ponderous, and doubtless the mass formations now being seen were unimagined before the war. Moreover, the TR9D radio set had great limitations, enabling an airborne squadron to communicate with each other and ground control – but not other airborne squadrons.

Furthermore, Air Chief Marshal Dowding was naturally unwilling to lose pilots over the sea, and had no intention of being drawn to battle over the Channel *en masse*, so this was another reason for using what Squadron Leader Darley described as 'penny packet formations'. However, sections of three, or flights of six, fighters intercepting infinitely larger formations of German bombers and fighters was the start of the perception that Britain was saved by a handful of RAF aircrew prevailing against overwhelming odds.

In truth, the two air forces were well-matched on paper, and Dowding wisely spread his resources around the country, every inch of which was within the range of German bombers and had to be defended. Consequently, there was no question of the bulk, or all, of Fighter Command's resources being deployed to the South Coast. It was a question of preserving limited resources while executing maximum damage to the enemy – and learning on the job.

Squadron Leader 'Uncle George' Darley:

> Each combat produced its own lessons, the fault in the past having been the inability to draw the correct conclusions. Formations had to be flexible, with a protective section weaving up-sun and higher than the main body. [Team-work, Darley, impressed, was key.] If eight of our aircraft were engaged by sixteen of the enemy, the odds would be 2:1 (in actual practice an unusually low ratio). If, however, four of our aircraft, willingly or unwillingly, left the formation, the odds would be 4:1 – a ratio that might spell *finito* for the remaining four ... I made it abundantly clear that I would not welcome personal 'aces'. As far as I was concerned, the only figures that counted were Squadron ones, and an immediate and lasting improvement in the kill/loss ratio.

For 609 Squadron, things would improve – in time.

On this day, 11 July 1940, another AAF squadron was poised to enter the fray – namely the fabled 601 'County of London' Squadron, based at Tangmere, that most famous of fighter stations near Chichester.

If the AAF was considered socially elite, then 601 was undoubtedly the elite of the elite, known as 'The Millionaire's Mob'. The Squadron's origins were in London's most exclusive gentleman's club: White's, at 37 St James's Street, Mayfair, members of which were drawn from royalty, the aristocracy and high society. No.601's founder, Lord Edward Arthur 'Ned' Grosvenor (son of the first Duke of Westminster, an Old Etonian, adventurer and passionate aviator), was naturally a member. Indeed, Grosvenor had bought two of the first commercially produced aeroplanes made by the pioneering Frenchman Louis Blériot, learning to fly at Brooklands before putting himself and his machines at the country's disposal for the First World War.

During the conflict, 'Ned' learned about military aviation, afterwards promoting civilian aviation. Grosvenor believed that in addition to the regular air force, the country also required a part-time, essentially civilian, reserve, seizing the chance, when news filtered through of Trenchard's intention to create the AAF, to host a dinner at White's and propose the foundation of 601 Squadron.

Grosvenor then recruited his like-minded and high-born friends to form a unit of trained pilots, under his command, presenting this to the Air Staff on a plate.

Initially, five squadrons were formally raised, 601 'County of London' Squadron's formation as a bomber unit being announced on 14 October 1925. Based at Northolt, equipped with Avro 504s, summer camps were held at Lympne. There, on Romney Marsh, the two landowners adjacent to the airport, namely the actor Noel Coward and none other than the Undersecretary of State for Air, Sir Philip Sassoon, opened their homes to Grosvenor's officers. Sassoon's generous hospitality at his Porte Lympne mansion was such that 601's annual training camp became known as the 'Summer Outing of White's Club'!

While this sets the scene, there is more: the eccentric and autocratic Grosvenor was, bizarrely considering his background, a former member of the French Foreign Legion – for which reason 601 became known as the 'Legion', its members 'Legionnaires'. A silver figure of a legionnaire brandishing a rifle in one hand and a sword held high in the other gave rise to the squadron's famous badge: the winged sword. Grosvenor, however, died prematurely in 1929, and was succeeded in command of 601 Squadron by that great friend of the 'Millionaire's Mob', Sir Phillip Sassoon.

Before the war, 601 shared Hendon with its sister-squadron, 600 'City of London', where, according to Group Captain Sir Hugh Dundas, an auxiliary with 616 'South Yorkshire' Squadron, could be found 'a group of enthusiasts, well laced with young men of great wealth, giving every moment of their spare time to the squadrons, many of them affecting an approach to their training as to appear almost frivolous, yet achieving a standard of efficiency in the air which surpassed many regular squadrons'.

Initially, 601 flew the Hawker Demon biplane light-bomber, then the Gloster Gauntlet biplane fighter, before converting to the twin-engine Blenheim Mk IF monoplane fighter in January 1939. Mobilised on 25 August 1939, 601 Squadron moved to Biggin Hill the day before Britain and France declared war on Germany.

Among the squadron's exulted members was none other than Flight Lieutenant Max Aitkin, son of Lord Beaverbrook, who, on 27 November 1939, commanded the section of 601 Squadron contributing to the audacious and highly publicised raid on Borkum, a German seaplane base in the Frisian Islands. A month later, 601 moved to Tangmere, exchanging its Blenheims for Hawker Hurricanes in March 1940.

After participation in the Fall of France, the 'Legionnaires' regrouped at Middle Wallop under Aitkin's command, now promoted to squadron leader, before returning to Tangmere on 17 June 1940. Eleven days later Squadron Leader Aitkin destroyed a He 111 at night, following which 601 Squadron, being well-placed, had seen action over the Channel from 2 July 1940 onwards.

At 10.15 hrs, 601 Squadron's Flight Lieutenant Willie Rhodes-Moorhouse – son of the first ever air VC – was patrolling with 'B' Flight and encountered a reconnaissance bomber, variously reported as either a Do 215 or 17; the former reported that:

> When just South of the Isle of Wight E/A was sighted in the South, flying westerly about 10–15 miles away. On catching up I had

difficulty in identifying E/A as it had circles on upper side of wing with black crosses in the middle, which were difficult to see until very close. I attacked from the stern and saw my fire going into E/A's fuselage. E/A then dived almost vertically onto the sea, flattening out at 500ft. I made another beam attack when E/A had gone down to 100ft. Shortly after it was seen to be flying one wing low and I saw E/A crash into the sea. It sank immediately.

The kill was shared with Flying Officer Michael Doulton and was either a Do 17 of *Wetterkundungs Staffel* 26 or 2(F)/11, both of which units lost an aircraft that morning.

It would, in fact, be a busy day for 601 Squadron.

Shortly after 11.00 hrs it was the turn of 601 Squadron's 'A' Flight, led by Flight Lieutenant Sir Archibald Hope, to scramble from Tangmere with orders to intercept yet another reconnaissance bomber. Minutes later RDF revealed increased enemy air activity in the Channel, it being obvious that the Lyme Bay convoy was again under threat.

The six Hurricanes were diverted to intercept and sighted the incoming raid. Immediately, the enemy's position was reported, 10 and 11 groups, in a direct contrast to the earlier action involving 501 and 609 Squadrons, scrambled more fighters: six Hurricanes of 238 from Warmwell (11.42 hrs), three of 501 from Middle Wallop (11.50 hrs), and three of 87 Squadron (newly arrived at Exeter on 5 July 1940, exact take-off time unknown, as ORB conflicts with combat reports), and nine more of 213 from the same station (11.55 hrs). Also at 11.55 hrs, 'B' Flight of 601 Squadron was scrambled from Tangmere.

Flight Lieutenant Sir Archibald Hope, 601 Squadron:

> Over Portland Bill at 16,000ft at 1133 hrs ... we sighted a large formation of E/A to the West (about one mile), flying North. I counted twenty-one Ju 87s and then observed about five formations in vic behind, stretching right out of sight. Each formation of seven aircraft, at least. The leading E/A were about 14,000ft, the rear ones at 16,000ft, the same as us. The E/A were getting into line astern and then turning right and diving. I turned right and my Flight got into line astern, also.
>
> There were no 110s above us so I turned left and we all attacked the mass of Ju 87s below us. I opened fire on one at about 300 yards. Its rear gunner ceased to fire and it turned and slipped over to the left, disappearing in a most peculiar manner. I then pulled up on two more Ju 87s about 200ft above and 200 yards away and fired a 4-second burst at one which appeared to fall away to the right, out of control. I carried on and at once saw an Me 110 ahead of me which I finished by bullets. There were three other 110s just above on the right so I dived to sea level and came home.

> All the 87s had long-range tanks on the wings, rather larger but the same shape as those on a long-range Hurricane. They were coloured pale green or green/blue below with black crosses. The 110s were standard camouflaged.
>
> The Me 110 escort appeared very inefficient to me. They were only about 1,000 – 1,500ft above the 87s and were half to five miles behind. As the bombers turned East and formed line-astern, the 110s also turned East and were completely out of position when we attacked from the north-west.

The Me 110s involved, of III/ZG76, were, in fact, new to the battle, having only flown their first sortie over the *Kanal* that morning. That afternoon, operating from forward airfields at Dinard and Lannion in Normandy to increase range, the same *gruppe* escorted the *Stukas* to Portland, which sank *Warrior* of 530-tons.

In response, 601 Squadron's pilots claimed three Ju 87s destroyed, two probables and one damaged, although only one dive-bomber, of 9/StG2, was actually lost. The Me 110s, however, were about to suffer grievous losses.

Flight Lieutenant Stuart Walch (Australian), 238 Squadron:

> 'B' Flight detailed to patrol Warmwell, 1140 hrs. Diverted to Portland at 1155 hrs. E/A reported over Portland at 4,000ft. Saw AA fire about 5,000ft. At this time my Flight was at 10,000ft. I ordered aircraft line astern. Climbed towards combat taking place ahead (South), above, about three miles distant.
>
> One Me 110 observed diving towards ship off Portland Bill at 10,000ft. I ordered Green Section to stay above in case of escort fighters. Blue 1, 2 and 3 attacked in order. E/A turned towards me and I fired two 3-second bursts from range 300-200 yards. Again attacked after Blue 3 from beam, closing to line-astern.
>
> I closed to fifty yards, E/A straightening out, white and black smoke coming from port engine, which caught fire in dive. I followed E/A down and saw it crash into the sea. E/A had black 'X' on fuselage.

The victory was confirmed by Pilot Officers Jack Urwin-Mann and Brian Considine. This was, in fact, 238 Squadron's first 'scalp' [ORB], the squadron only having reformed in May 1940. According to the ORB, Pilot Officer Urwin-Mann, Flying Officer MacCaw and Sergeant Parkinson all attacked a 'Ju 88', although this would have been another Me 110, as no 88s were involved.

Squadron Leader Johnny Dewar, 87 Squadron:

> Leading a flight of three Hurricanes at 5,000ft west of Weymouth; sighted nine enemy aircraft approaching Portland from south at

15,000ft. Commenced climbing south, to get in between E/A and sun. Saw nine more E/A and one group of twelve Me 110s as we were going up. Got level and up-sun of enemy at 12,000ft.

As we approached, some aircraft dived to attack shipping. Enemy did not appear aware of our presence. Saw two other Hurricanes attacking and swung into Me 110s, which seemed to be flying to form, a circle. Saw a Hurricane diving and turning slowly with 110 on his tail, so put four bursts into 110. On last burst the port engine appeared to blow up.

Aircraft flicked onto its back and dived almost vertically. Owing to presence of numerous E/A, I did not watch this aircraft hit the sea, but feel certain it must have gone in, four miles east of Shambles. Method of approach was line astern, then 'free for all'.

The Me 110 concerned is believed to be the aircraft of 9/ZG76, which crashed onto the Verne's chalk heights with such violence that no trace of the crew has ever been found.

The pilot was actually *Reichsmarschall* Göring's nephew, *Oberleutnant* Hans-Joachim Göring – whose *zerstörer* was the first enemy aircraft to crash in England during the Battle of Britain; it was also the new RAF Exeter's first 'kill'. Later, a survivor of the combat, *Leutnant* Richard Marchfelder, the *Gruppe* Technical Officer, recalled that Göring had 'stupidly tried to take on the whole RAF', and that 'The old uncle stirred up quite a fuss'.

The action, however, was not yet over for 87 Squadron's CO:

I went into a full turn to review progress of battle and remove two other E/A trying to get on my tail. Saw a bomb exploding by shipping in the harbour and two E/A diving for ground. One E/A still pursued me.

My Hurricane turned easily onto his tail – he was vertically banked. He then dived for ground, going east – I followed but withheld fire as I was getting short of rounds. E/A pulled out about 1,000ft and continued in 'S' turns. I gave him a burst from about 100 yards and vapour came out of both engines. I had to slam throttle back to avoid over-shooting. Vapour then ceased to come from one engine and he gathered way again.

I was very close and there was no rear gun fire, so I held my position and took careful non-deflection shot, using all ammunition. E/A at once turned inland, going very slowly. Seeing me draw away, he turned seawards again. I went to head him off and he, apparently thinking I had more rounds, turned for land again, sinking slowly.

At about 200ft, another Hurricane came up and fired a short burst at him. He immediately turned and landed on Grange Heath (or near). Both crew got out, wearing yellow jackets. Army was close by. Number of other Hurricane was UW-F (I think).

This was another machine of 9/ZG76, which had previously been attacked by 238 Squadron's Green Section; the Hurricane that Dewar reported as having also attacked the enemy aircraft was Flying Officer Hugh Riddle of 601 Squadron (and whose Hurricane was more likely UF-W). The enemy unit's *Staffelkapitän*, *Oberleutnant* Gerhard Kadow, and his gunner, *Gefreiter* Helmut Scholz, were both captured unhurt having forced-landed at Grange Heath, near Lulworth.

Oberleutnant Gerhard Kadow, 9/ZG76:

> As I approached the English coast, I was confronted with the enemy. I counted about twenty dark dots in the distance, somewhat higher than myself. As they came nearer, I was certain they were British fighters, though I could not see if they were Spitfires or Hurricanes.
> I knew that the twin-engine Me 110 was not as manoeuvrable as these fighters and there was little chance of winning a battle with them, especially as there were only seven Me 110s in my *Staffel* and we were outnumbered three to one. Our orders, however, were to defend the *Stukas* and so we must engage the enemy.
> Our offensive armament consisted of two 20mm cannon and 7.92mm machine-guns in the nose, so I made a head-on attack. I pressed the gun buttons and a stream of bullets flew out like water from a hosepipe. Our closing speed was very high and we both broke away to avoid collision.
> In the next moment, two fighters were behind me and firing. My engines stopped and I knew that returning to France was impossible. The fighters followed me down and stopped firing, they could see what trouble I was in. I jettisoned my cockpit hood in the hope that it might hit one of the fighters, but rather obviously this failed! I ordered Helmet Scholz to do the same, but he reported that his hood was damaged and jammed, so now we could neither bale out or ditch in the sea, as Helmut may not have escaped before the machine sank.
> I therefore decided to make a forced-landing, which I did, rather well, at Povington Heath, near Wareham, at about 1245 hrs I then discovered that I could not leave the aircraft immediately because a bullet had blown a hole in my seat and the sharp edges had been forced into my parachute pack. I pulled forward and got out to help Helmut, who had been injured by splinters.
> Now, I must destroy my aircraft. At this time we had no demolition device fitted, so I tried to set light to the fuel tanks by firing my pistol into them. I used all eight rounds but failed, probably just as well because it would probably have exploded and killed us both!

As I was trying to destroy the aircraft I could hear gunfire and bullets hitting it. I went around the aircraft to see where the bullets were coming from and was hit in the heel of my boot, the bullet causing a flesh wound.

Both of us left the aircraft well alone and looked around to see about twenty soldiers approaching. An officer ordered 'Hands up!' and took us prisoner. I later told him that it was unfair to shoot aircrew who had been shot down, but he said that he was trying to prevent us destroying our aircraft and I should be glad not to have been shot dead.

The action had been fast, violent and furious. No.87 Squadron's Flying Officer Dickie Glyde, Blue 2, an Australian, shot down *Leutnant* Jochen Schröder, who ditched his aircraft in the sea, just off the Ney breakwater – fortunately close to the Weymouth lifeboat, which picked up the downed pilot. Schröder's gunner, *Gefreiter* Franz Sorokoput, however, was picked up dead.

In turn, Glyde was attacked from astern by another 110, resulting the Hurricane pilot having, notes the ORB, 'a close call from a bullet which pierced the central panel of his hood and struck the armour plating close to his head'.

Pilot Officer Dudley Jay, was Blue 3 in Squadron Leader Dewar's Section:

One Me 110 went straight across the front of me in a steep turn and I fired a burst, the E/A then went into a dive and I turned to follow, on his tail, firing fairly long bursts; the enemy continued his dive and hit the sea at over 300 mph.

This was the 9/ZG76 Me 110 of *Leutnant* Fredrich-Wolfgang Graf von und zu Castell and his gunner, *Gefreiter* Heinz Reder, which crashed near the Shambles lightship – neither airman was ever found.

In total, the enemy had lost four Me 110s – an early indication that the type was generally no match for Hurricanes and Spitfires – and two *Stukas*. Fighter Command suffered no loss, in what was an entirely successful action. Although he took no part in the action, among Squadron Leader Dewar's 87 Squadron pilots at Exeter was another exceptional fighter pilot and leader, namely Flight Lieutenant Ian 'Widge' Gleed – who commented after this battle that, 'We were all as pleased as Punch, and had a grand party at our pub that night'.

By 12.20 hrs, the sky was clear of enemy aircraft and remained so for the next three hours, excepting nuisance attacks on shipping in the Thames Estuary. So far, the main attacks on Channel shipping had been launched in the morning, the action not resuming until night raiders began intruding at dusk.

Unusually, at 17.46 hrs, an enemy formation was detected flying North, fifteen miles off Cherbourg. This new threat comprised twelve He 111s of *Oberst* Stoeckl's Villacoublay-based KG55 (specifically 2/KG55) escorted by a *Staffel* of Me 110s – all bound for the great naval base at Portsmouth.

At 17.15 hrs, Flight Lieutenant Rhodes-Moorhouse (Blue 1) had led his 'B' Flight Hurricanes of 601 Squadron up from Tangmere to patrol base, so were already airborne and well-positioned when vectored to intercept this latest threat. With the Hurricanes arriving on the scene, a running battle developed over the Solent, Portsmouth and East of the Isle of Wight. Among the 601 Squadron pilots was Bristol's Sergeant Redvers 'Reg' Hawkings, a 22-year-old VR pilot and already a veteran; he reported the following on the combat, which took place between 17.55 and 18.15 hrs, at heights of 17,000–12,000ft:

> As Blue 2 I followed Blue 1 in a quarter attack upon E/A, but lost formation in breakaway, in order to avoid collision with another Hurricane. One burst of five seconds (no apparent result). Attacked from astern another He 111. One burst of five seconds delivered (no apparent result). Upon turning, sighted E/A heading South about fifteen miles South of Bognor.
>
> Gave chase and delivered quarter attack on port engine, which caught fire, emitting black smoke. E/A lost height rapidly and turned to left. My ammunition ran out, so I broke away to right but upon turning could see no sign of E/A. I returned to base to rearm and refuel.

Perhaps surprisingly, considering the inconclusive nature of the combat, Hawkings was credited with a 'probable', as were Flying Officer Cleaver and Pilot Officer Dickie, and Flight Sergeant Pond, while an 'unconfirmed' destroyed Me 110 was accredited to Flying Officer Davis, and similarly a He 111 to Flight Sergeant Pond, the latter reporting that:

> I was Yellow 3 in the right-hand Section. The bombers were flying from West to East over Portsmouth. I followed Yellow 1 in line astern and pursued the bombers. I first attacked the middle E/A of those flying in a wide vic. I approached from slightly below and to the right, and opened fire from 250 yards, closing to 100 yards, the burst took about eight seconds.
>
> I observed flashes from the starboard blister guns but saw no tracer or other missiles coming in my direction. I finished the attack in the line astern position, the E/A began to break up and emit black smoke. When last seen it was in a shallow dive towards the ESE. I then attacked the port E/A of two, closing to about 100 yards.
>
> This aircraft also began to break up and emit smoke, and the aircraft fell down. This expended all my ammunition so I was unable to carry on the attack. I dived steeply and returned to base.

On this occasion, 601 Squadron suffered a casualty when Sergeant Arthur Woolley was hit, either by return fire while attacking a He 111 or possibly by 'friendly' anti-aircraft fire, igniting his gravity tank. The pilot, although wounded and suffering from burns, managed to bale out safely, his Hurricane crashing at Cranmore on the Isle of Wight.

Also in action over Selsey Bill was 145 Squadron, the whole squadron, led by Squadron Leader John Peel, having been scrambled from Tangmere at 18.00 hrs – just as bombs began exploding in Portsmouth. The squadron subsequently shared the destruction of a 2/KG55 He 111 which crashed just off Selsey Beach. Two of the enemy crew, *Unteroffizier* Mueller and *Oberfeldwebel* Shlueter, were killed, while *Oberleutnant* Schweinhagen, *Oberfeldwebel* Slotosch and *Feldwebel* Steiner were all wounded and captured. Flight Lieutenant Boyd claimed an Me 110 destroyed, and Flight Lieutenant Dutton and Pilot Officer Storrar both claimed He 111s destroyed. Again, this was not without loss:

> [No.145 Squadron] lost the CO, Squadron Leader J.R.A. Peel, whose aircraft was hit and made a forced descent into the sea. Squadron Leader Peel narrowly escaped drowning, but was picked up after an hour in a semi-conscious condition by a Selsey lifeboat. He eventually recovered and returned to the squadron in a bruised condition. [ORB]

In this engagement, another 2/KG55 He 111 was lost, crashing into the sea, the crew of which remain missing, while another crash-landed back at base, damaged with two wounded crewmen aboard. As is so often the case, excepting the He 111 on Selsey Beach, it is impossible to say which of the 145 and 601 squadrons' pilots were responsible. No Me 110s were lost however, notwithstanding the RAF pilots claiming two of the type destroyed.

Over twenty HE bombs had fallen on Portsmouth, starting various fires, including one at the Airspeed aircraft factory, although this was soon extinguished and damage was slight. Although only three barges were sunk, sadly the Drayton Road School was hit, which doubled as a first aid centre. A total of nineteen civilians were killed and twenty-six injured as a result of the raid.

The Portsmouth raid was the last daylight attack on this day – which had seen the heaviest fighting thus far. The nature of these attacks on Channel-bound convoys placed great strain on the fighter squadrons based on the South Coast. Only a small number of aircraft could be deployed at any one time to patrol over a convoy, usually just a section of three, and so few fighters were clearly vulnerable to being overwhelmed by superior numbers in the event of an attack incoming before reinforcements could arrive.

Experience to date indicated that while RDF could identify approaching threats, the notice was often insufficient for 10 and 11 groups' sector controllers to scramble and have fighters in position to prevent targets being bombed. Clearly both Portland and Portsmouth were to continue being prime targets, and in order to increase resources available in the area, on this evening Air Chief Marshal

Dowding ordered the Spitfires of Squadron Leader Peter Devitt's 152 'Hyderabad' Squadron from Acklington to Warmwell.

On the morning of 11 July 1940, there had also been action for Coastal Command's 217 Squadron based at St Eval:

> One Anson was ordered to take off (0911 hrs) and search for an E/A twenty miles SE of Start Point. Sighted the enemy seaplane and opened fire with front gun at 600 yards, at 1011 hrs. E/A slowed up, upon being hit and turned to starboard to land on the sea. Seeing this manoeuvre, Anson turned to port, allowing navigator and rear gunner to open fire.
>
> At 1012 hrs the E/A was shot down into the sea. The crew were as follows: Captain of aircraft, Flight Sergeant NH Webb; Navigator, Pilot Officer HT Smith; Wireless Operator, AC2 Holiday; air gunner, Sergeant PH Botha. [ORB]

The seaplane was another He 59 of *Seenotflugkommando* 1, the crew of which took to their dinghy and captured near the Channel Islands when RN destroyers D78 and D76 appeared.

The He 59's distress calls had drawn a Ju 88 of I/KG51 to the scene; three Blenheims of 236 Squadron, also based at St Eval, which were escorting the two destroyers en route to the downed seaplane, were despatched to investigate:

> At noon, a signal was received from the destroyers to attack a Ju 88, which was chased by our aircraft. Pilot Officer Riley used up his ammunition and got hits on fuselage and tail. The Ju 88 got away, being faster. At 1230 hrs an E/A was seen and our machines turned and attacked.
>
> Pilot Officer BM McDonough got in a good burst and chased it down to the sea. It was last seen obviously in trouble, close to the water, heading for France and pilot thought it would come down in sea. Our aircraft was hit in one cylinder and one wing and had to be left at St Eval for repairs. [ORB]

Pilot Officer McDonough, an Australian, was right: the Ju 88 failed to return, its crew all still missing.

That evening, a 217 Squadron Anson was despatched at 19.15 hrs on an 'Anti-invasion patrol. Sighted for E-Boats [a motor torpedo boat]. Dropped one bomb which fell ten yards astern of E-Boat, steering gear believed damaged. There was pom-pom and concentrated machine-gun fire from the E-boats.'

At 21.50 hrs, two further Ansons were scrambled to attack the E-boats, but the enemy had disappeared into the gathering dusk.

By day, Bomber Command sent forty Blenheims to attack various targets, but owing to cloud-cover none of the targets in Germany were bombed, and only ten aircraft managed to bomb airfields in France and the Netherlands. One Blenheim was lost, although Me 109 pilots of 7/JG51 claimed two destroyed, one North-west of Watten at 14.25 hrs, the other fifteen kilometres northeast of Deal at 19.45 hrs.

That night, the weather continued to hamper operations, only forty-five of sixty-four Bomber Command aircraft managing to locate and attack their targets. One Hampden, a Wellington and a Whitley were lost on these raids.

It was clear to all by now that the enemy's air effort was intensifying. Nonetheless, the HIR on this day recorded:

> The public is cheerful and there is little change in morale ... Hitler's failure to arrive is promoting an apprehensive feeling that 'he must have something very unpleasant in store for us'. Determination to challenge and meet this surprise is widespread, and confidence in the Navy is at a high level. 'The Navy will win the war for us in the end.'
>
> Air raids continue to be taken calmly. In heavily raided areas there is a demand for further reprisals and aggressive RAF action is strongly applauded. Official policy about the publication of air-raid casualties and damage is not understood and widely resented. Local information about casualties, which are not reflected in official bulletins, has brought suspicion on other official communiques, and on the honesty of official news as a whole.

At the Berghof, his mountain retreat near Berchtesgaden in Bavaria, the *Führer* remained indecisive as far as Britain was concerned, and hence his ongoing 'failure to arrive'. The German leader still believed that Britain could be persuaded to come to terms, rendering ongoing prosecution of the war in the West and Operation *Seelöwe* unnecessary. But how to make the stubborn British see sense? Hitler's exasperation at the British stance remains almost palpable, all these years later.

The answer, he was mulling over, was offering Britain one last chance of accepting Germany's peace terms via a high-profile *Reichstag* speech. On this day, 11 July 1940, Hitler was visited by *Grand-Admiral* Raeder, the *Kriegsmarine* chief, who opined that 'the British people should be given a sharp taste of war at first-hand: first by strangling their ocean supply lines, second by heavy air-raids on the main centres'. Raeder, however, who was now proposing the bombing of civilian centres, remained opposed to a sea-crossing – unless as an absolute last resort to subdue Britain.

Poor intelligence, misinforming the actual situation regarding Britain's well-organised aerial defences and the RAF's actual strength, persuaded Hitler and his vain henchman, the *Luftwaffe* chief, Göring, that their air force was capable of delivering such intensive bombing attacks that Britain would have no option but to sue for peace. In truth, the advantage lay with the British, given that the 'System' was the most advanced air defence in the world, designed for exactly the kind of battle now being fought – and yet the Germans understood little of the crucial importance of radar and how the 'System' worked. Inaccurate intelligence estimated British aircraft production to be 180 machines in July 1940, which would substantially reduce once air attacks began; in fact, it was 496, and would drop by less than thirty aircraft per month as the battle wore on – and German monthly fighter production figures were on average less than half of Britain's.

Furthermore, the *Luftwaffe* had been established primarily to provide a bombardment ahead of advancing ground troops, and provide close tactical support to the army. Consequently, its bombers were of medium range and with comparatively small bomb loads, there being no heavy strategic bomber available. The Me 110 enjoyed longer range than the Me 109 fighter, but was already showing itself to be unsuitable for the role into which it was now pressed, and the Me 109, a short-range defensive fighter, lacked the range for offensive operations over England.

Moreover, Germany's lightning advance to the Channel coast had surprised everyone involved, including the OKW, and so the opportunity to invade southern England by sea was unanticipated and lacked appropriate planning and preparation. Germany was un-resourced for such an immense undertaking, and, notwithstanding Norway, lacked the necessary experience of combined operations – and the *Kriegsmarine* was well-aware of the RN's superiority at sea. No wonder, then, that Raeder supported aerial attacks in preference to a seaborne operation.

Göring, however, remained entirely confident that the *Luftwaffe* would prevail, and on the *Kanalfront* the *KanalkampfFührer*, *Oberst* Fink, was already emboldened and increasing the size of his attacking formations. For now, then, while Hitler pondered how successful or otherwise his proposed 'final appeal to common-sense and reason' speech might be, he was content to allow the air war against Britain continue, in the hope that these shows of aerial strength would be pivotal in persuading the British to abandon the fight – and in the process see Dowding's pilots perish in dangerous battles over the sea. And so what Edward Bishop rightly described as 'Air Fleet Diplomacy' continued, while the *Führer* went on considering his options.

FRIDAY, 12 JULY 1940

After a night of bombing which left twenty-nine dead and 103 injured, the day dawned fair, turning to rain later. The fighting that morning would revolve around the Convoy *Booty*, steaming South from the Thames Estuary.

At 08.40 hrs, a 500 Squadron Anson, based at Detling and flown by Pilot Officer D. Pain, with Pilot Officer G. Bliss his air gunner, was patrolling in the vicinity of *Booty* when the convoy was attacked by nine He 111s. The under-armed Coastal Command aircraft engaged, claiming one of the raiders destroyed.

At 06.30 hrs, 'A' Flight of 17 Squadron had taken-off from Debden Sector Station to operate from their forward base at Martlesham Heath, on the East Coast, near Ipswich in Suffolk. At 08.48 hrs, the Hurricanes were patrolling *Booty* when:

> Pilot Officer Manger and Sergeant Griffiths of Yellow Section sighted twelve He 111s at 8,000ft, bombing the convoy. The Section delivered a line-astern attack on an He 111 which had broken away from the formation, and Pilot Officer Manger, firing continuously from 350 to 50 yards range, sent the E/A gliding down through clouds with both engines on fire. Sergeant Griffiths closed in and fired a burst of about nine seconds, and left the E/A 'generally falling to pieces'.
>
> Sergeant Griffiths then sighted four He 111s flying East, and attacked one which was 500 yards behind the others. He sent it down in a spiral dive with both engines on fire, and saw it crash into the sea and sink.
>
> At 0850 hrs, Pilot Officer Pittman and Sergeant Fopp of Red Section sighted nine He 111s approaching the convoy, and delivered a series of quarter attacks on one of them which had straggled. The E/A dropped its undercarriage and went down with port engine silent and petrol streaming from it, finally crashing into the sea, near a trawler which picked up three survivors.
>
> At 0926 hrs, Flying Officer Czernin and Pilot Officer Hanson of Red Section saw three Do 17s bombing the convoy, and Pilot Officer Hanson made two head-on attacks on one of the Dorniers, which dived to sea level. He then delivered a stern attack, and last saw the enemy aircraft wallowing badly with one engine out of action, at a speed of only about 120 mph. He did not consider that it could have reached its base.
>
> Flying Officer Czernin attacked another Do 17, which had already been attacked and shot down by Hurricanes of 151 Squadron. [ORB]

In this action, 17 Squadron claimed the destruction of three He 111s confirmed and two Do 17s (unconfirmed). This generated a signal from the 12 Group AOC, Air Vice-Marshal Sir Trafford Leigh-Mallory: 'Congratulations on this morning's very excellent show.'

No.85 Squadron, operating from Martlesham, also engaged the *Booty* raiders, at 09.10 hrs:

> Pilot Officer Bickerdyke, Sergeant-Pilot Rust and Sergeant-Pilot Jowitt went into action. Pilot Officer Bickerdyke delivered two attacks on a He 111 from quarter starboard, which accounted for the rear-gunner, and the second from quarter port, which put paid to the E/A, which crashed into the sea: a conclusive victory.

KANALKAMPF DIARY, 10 JULY – 31 JULY 1940

> Sergeant-Pilot Rust attacked another E/A which made for home – he put in one attack from three-quarters astern which silenced the rear-gunner; the E/A escaped in a dive through clouds.

However, 85 Squadron suffered a casualty: Sergeant Leonard Jowitt was shot down into the sea, never to be seen again. From Failsworth, Lancashire, Jowitt had joined the RAF as an Aircraft Apprentice at RAF Halton, the service's technical training school, instantly becoming a so-called 'Trenchard Brat'. Passing out as an airframe fitter, Jowitt served in India with 20 Squadron before, back home, applying for pilot training in 1937.

As explained in Volume 1, the expansion process had made it possible for existing non-commissioned airmen to apply for pilot training, the concept being that they would fly for four years before reverting to their original roles, thereby increasing the number of operational pilots and providing a trained reserve. Having successfully won his 'wings', Sergeant Jowitt joined 85 Squadron at Debden on 20 August 1938.

On 19 May 1940, he destroyed a He 111 in France, being one of the squadron's survivors of the Fall of France – when withdrawn to Northolt just ten days after the *Blitzkrieg* began, 85 Squadron mustered only three serviceable Hurricanes. Sergeant Jowitt was, therefore, a professional and experienced airman and pilot – the very backbone of the service – and the loss of such men Fighter Command could ill-afford.

On this occasion, the 12 Group Controller had acted swiftly and decisively, also scrambling three Hurricanes of 242, six Defiants of 264, and eleven Hurricanes of 151 Squadrons. At 08.30 hrs, Squadron Leader Teddy Donaldson, commanding the latter, had led a section of Hurricanes up from Martlesham Heath to patrol *Booty*, the North Weald Station Commander, that indomitable Irishman Wing Commander Victor Beamish, following five minutes later with two more sections of 151 Squadron.

At 09.30 hrs, twenty miles East of Orfordness, 151 Squadron ran into II/KG2, as Beamish reported:

> Squadron Leader Donaldson attacked the three Do 17s with his Section but owing to a steep turn only he himself got in an attack and his aircraft was quickly severely damaged.'

The 151 Squadron ORB adds that:

> Squadron Leader Donaldson came under very heavy cross-fire during his attack and among other things his rudder controls were shot away. By use of his engine he guided his aircraft back to Martlesham and the engine failed just before he landed. The extensive damage done by enemy fire included a punctured tyre, but a successful landing was made.

Indeed, Wing Commander Beamish considered Donaldson's effort 'magnificent', and continued:

> I immediately followed and was met by heavy cross-fire with red tracer. After long bursts at the left-hand Dornier, his port engine blew up and stopped, his undercarriage dropped down and he broke away from the formation. I know he was badly crippled and could not get away. I immediately attacked the leader but had little ammunition left. I then broke away. Flying Officer Hamar saw the port engine stop and the Dornier severely damaged. Other pilots came up and gave him further bursts – and he crashed into the sea.

Beamish's Hurricane was also badly damaged, and he too forced-landed back at base. No.151 Squadron, however, lost a pilot in this action – Flying Officer James Allen, a New Zealander and former sailor:

> Flying Officer Allen was last seen following an attack, gliding down into the sea with a dead engine and no trace of him or his aircraft were seen again, although Sergeant Hewett circled the spot for five minutes. [ORB]

In total, the RAF pilots engaged claimed the destruction of six He 111s and Do 17s, two Do 17s and three He 111s actually being lost, offset against two pilots killed, two aircraft destroyed and two more damaged. Convoy *Booty* suffered the loss of the 2,162-ton coaster SS *Hornchurch*, the 1,926-ton SS *Josewyn* being damaged.

The attack on *Booty*, dealt with by 12 Group, was the only major threat this day, although small formations of enemy bombers were intercepted hither and thither; one such, a He 111, being intercepted three miles East of Portland at 10.04 hrs by Red Section of 609 Squadron, led by Flight Lieutenant Frank Howell:

> Red 3 (Pilot Officer John Curchin) reported E/A on starboard beam ... I ordered 'Line astern' and immediately delivered an attack from below and in front. The *Heinkel* immediately went into a steep right-hand turn. I peeled off, allowing Red 2 (Flying Officer AR Edge) and Red 3 to come into the attack.
>
> I saw Red 2 and 3 delivering attack in thick haze. I climbed above and behind and delivered a quarter attack from fifty – 100 yards range. There was return fire in the first attack but none in the second. The E/A did excessive evasive action. No known result.

The enemy bomber was chalked up as a 'possible', and may have been a machine of *Stab*/StG3 which forced-landed, damaged, near Cherbourg.

At 12.45 hrs, a Norway-based He 111 of 9/KG26 attacked the Hall Russell shipyard in Footdee, Aberdeen, although no air raid warning sounded. Sixteen bombs cascaded down onto the Boiler Works and the London Boat at Waterloo Quay, causing twenty-five civilian deaths. In what was the first daylight attack on Aberdeen, damage was also caused to the Domestic Science School and the *Neptune Bar* in King Street.

The raid was recalled by Aberdeen resident Ada Stewart:

> I was eleven when war broke out in 1939. My most vivid memory was in 1940 when Hall Russell Shipyard was bombed. My brother had just got a job there and I was worried about his safety.
>
> I was in our house (4 Link Street) when the bombing started. I remember the front door crashing shut and pushing me right over! I heard a terrible noise so I went out to see what all the commotion was about. I saw civilians taking injured people up the road on a horse and cart and any other available vehicle.
>
> My dad was away working and came home to check my brother was okay. Many workers who were having a lunchtime drink in the Neptune Bar were killed in this incident. A number of the bar's windows were blown in, causing havoc for those customers inside.

The raider would not escape, however; Pilot Officer George 'Sheep' Gilroy, a Spitfire pilot of Dyce's 603 Squadron:

> As Yellow 1, at 1243 hrs I was ordered off to intercept E/A flying south-west from Collieston at 12,000ft. I sighted E/A flying south-east about five miles West of Aberdeen, climbing into cloud.
>
> Yellow Section being in wide line-astern, I approached E/A from starboard quarter and just before coming into range observed E/A jettison bombs. I opened fire on E/A from starboard quarter, coming into line astern – undercarriage was observed to drop and considerable oil covered my windscreen before breaking away. Yellow 2, Sergeant Caistor, was in position to fire and covered my break-away. E/A then assumed gliding attitude with engines throttled back or unserviceable.
>
> After several deflection attacks by Yellow Section I gave a 'cease fire' order as E/A appeared to coming down on town. There was, however, much low cloud and Control ordered 'resume fire and make sure of E/A'. I therefore carried out one attack from the port-quarter and one from above, both being short bursts. E/A finally crashed in flames onto Aberdeen's new ice rink.

The ice rink in Anderson Drive was under construction, but would never be completed and was demolished post-war. Tragically, the He 111's tail fell on the

Hall Russell canteen, causing more casualties. The German crew involved were all killed. Twenty-nine civilians were killed in total, and two ARP wardens, Alfred Carson and Frazer Allen, were both awarded the George Medal for their courage and efforts to rescue the injured on what became known locally as 'Black Friday'.

Off Portland, reconnaissance bombers remained active, seeking convoys. To counter this ongoing nuisance, 501 Squadron's Hurricanes flew South from Middle Wallop to Warmwell, operating from that forward base alongside the Spitfires of 609.

At 15.15 hrs, Flight Lieutenant Gus Holden led 'B' Flight of 501 to patrol the Channel off Portland, the Hurricanes intercepting a Do 17 at 15.50 hrs:

> E/A was sighted diving to sea level off Lyme Regis. In dive he jettisoned four bombs into the sea. Blue 1 attacked at 1,000ft from 400 yards, range, closing to 200 yards. Rear gunner thought to be silenced after about five seconds firing as he appeared to cease fire at that time. E/A continued on course at sea level without apparent damage but Blue 3 thinks he saw white smoke from the Dornier's port engine. Blue 2 struck the sea before firing. Blue 3 did not fire, stating he could not catch the enemy.

The Do 17 was claimed as a 'possible', but Blue 2, the experienced Canadian Pilot Officer Duncan Hewitt, was missing, having apparently been buffeted by the bomber's slipstream and crashing into the sea. Although the pilot's body was seen floating on the surface, he was not recovered and remains missing.

Further East along the South Coast, at Tangmere, when Squadron Leader George Lott was wounded and lost an eye on 9 July 1940, he was succeeded in command of 43 Squadron by Squadron Leader John 'Tubby' Badger. At 15.40 hrs on 11 July 1940, Squadron Leader Badger led 'B' Flight's Hurricanes up from Tangmere. Five minutes later, Flight Lieutenant Tom Dalton-Morgan took off after them, engaging a He 111 at 16.05 hrs, 8,000ft over Portsmouth:

> I saw E/A on port side below me at 8,000ft. I turned onto his tail and came into the attack. I opened fire at 200 yards and closed to 100 yards. During this burst the starboard wing broke up and the starboard engine blew up. I was enveloped in smoke and fragments for about three seconds. I broke away and followed him through cloud. I made a second attack and opened fire at 200 yards, closing to 100 yards.
>
> This time, fragments and black smoke came from the port engine. The E/A then commenced a glide towards the ground. I followed him down. He selected a field four miles North of Fort Nelson and landed in a northerly direction, ending up in a hedge near a farmhouse. No one was observed to leave the aircraft. I was fired on by air-gunner and he scored one round in my tailplane.

On the ground was a young schoolboy, Alexander McKee (later a well-known and accomplished historian and author):

> With one engine spluttering and banging, it came towards a field near the village of Southwick; wheels up, it passed over a hedge and went skidding and bumping wildly across a ploughed field, coming to a stop fifty yards from a public house. The observer, shot through the head, lay dead across the bombsight. A subaltern from one of the forts on Portsdown Hill took surrender of the crew.

The 'subaltern' was in fact Sam Brown, the landlord of the *Horse and Jockey*, at Hipley, just inland of Portsmouth. Brown captured *Oberfeldwebels* Fritz Knecht and Philipp Muller, and *Feldwebel* Heinz Kalina, all of whom were wounded. Inside the He 111 of *Stab*/KG55, the aircraft captain, *Oberleutnant* Walter Kleinhaus, lay dead.

After soldiers had arrived and removed the prisoners and their dead comrade's remains, the young McKee, eager for souvenirs, seized an opportunity to enter the bomber while temporarily left unguarded. Entering via a small hatch on the port side, the curious schoolboy walked inside the fuselage to the glazed nose, whereupon he,

> settled into the pilot's seat and tried out the controls and then had a look at the instrument panel ... I got into the front gunner's position – the nose was entirely Perspex, now rather blood-spattered. There was a trap door where he lay when firing the gun. I slid back the trap door revealing a blood-drenched bombsight and compass. The blood must have pumped out because every cranny was thickly saturated with it.

Then, further to the south-west, just before 16.30 hrs, a lone Ju 88 dropped bombs on the 10 Group aerodrome at St Eval, in Cornwall. Blue Section of 234 Squadron was scrambled, as the New Zealander Pilot Officer Keith Lawrence later reported:

> I took off as Blue 2 some seconds after Blue 1 (Pilot Officer WHG Gordon). As soon as I was airborne I turned and looked back, seeing the E/A behind me on a course almost parallel to my own.
>
> I immediately turned towards the E/A and climbed steeply, closing to about 275 yards before opening fire with a burst of one second, before E/A disappeared in cloud; tracer appeared to enter lower gun position.

In that one-second burst, the Spitfire pilot's eight Browning machine-guns had spat 160 rounds at the Ju 88, which was credited as 'unconfirmed'.

According to the 74 Squadron ORB (Form 540, monthly summary of events, day-by-day) for 12 July 1940:

> At 1630 hrs, Red Section left (Hornchurch) to investigate a raid fifteen miles off Margate. AA fire was sighted from a ship which was being bombed by a He 111. Flight Lieutenant Malan DFC, leading Red Section, gave order to attack in line astern and opened attack, closing to 300 yards range.
>
> Heavy fire from the aircraft's rear gunner was silenced by Red Leader. Sergeant Mould and Pilot Officer Stevenson also attacked in turn and enemy aircraft seen to crash into the sea.

Strangely, however, the 74 Squadron Form 541, the daily record of events, makes no mention of such a patrol, and nor does a combat report appear to have survived. Moreover, there is no German loss correlating to this apparent combat casualty.

The previous day, Squadron Leader John Peel, commanding 145 Squadron, had been shot down and rescued from the sea 'semi-conscious', returning to the squadron 'in a bruised condition'. This traumatic experience, however, did not prevent the gallant Peel leading 'B' Flight up from Tangmere on a patrol at 17.00 hrs on 12 July 1940. Having landed from that patrol at 18.05 hrs, Peel was scrambled with 'B' Flight twenty-five minutes later:

> Red Section (Squadron Leader Peel, Pilot Officers Yule and Newling) encountered a large enemy formation three miles off St Catherine's Point at 1830 hrs. Squadron Leader Peel and Pilot Officer Newling each damaged an Me 110. Pilot Officer Yule also damaged an Me 110, and shot a Ju 88 down into the sea. This combat took place just under, and in and out of, dense clouds which came as low as 700ft. [ORB]

There are no Me 110 losses recorded on this day, nor a Ju 88 lost at sea, although Yule's victim may have been the Ju 88A of I/KG51 (listed in some secondary sources) which apparently crashed at Villaroche while engaged on an operational sortie, although no mention of this is made in the unit history (see Bibliography).

Earlier on the day in question, Squadron Leader Peter Devitt had led his 152 Squadron Spitfires up from Acklington in fine weather – later landing at Warmwell, the squadron's new home,

> in a very low rain cloud. Remainder of personnel came by special train. The aerodrome was covered in Harrow and Wellington aircraft of 10 Bombing & Gunnery School. These went the next day, which left the aerodrome a bit clearer. Central Gunnery School remained, which kept the aerodrome still fairly blocked. [ORB]

No.152 Squadron now joined the Spitfires of 609 Squadron to bolster the defence of Portland.

Squadron Leader Peter Devitt:

> We were sent forward to fly from Warmwell, very close to the coast, which didn't give us much time to get up there. Middle Wallop was a bit further inland, so really it made more sense to leave us there so that we had more time to climb to an appropriate combat altitude. The lack of air sea rescue provision also concerned me very greatly, and I told Group, in simply understood terms, that this needed rectifying quickly.

Devitt was 27 during the Battle of Britain, and married with two children. A stockbroker who had made his money with Lloyd's before the war, one of his pilots, Pilot Officer Roger Hall, described him as 'a debonair sort of chap, an excellent pilot and a very capable leader'.

Among 152 Squadron's groundcrew was Ray Johnson, an armourer:

> And then it happened. What is now known as the Battle of Britain started. On 12 July 1940, 152 Squadron moved south from Acklington to Warmwell in Dorset. An advance party, including myself, was flown down in a Handley Page Harrow, which was a high-wing monoplane, to Warmwell, which was a grass airfield inland of Weymouth and not far from the army camp at Bovington.
>
> In fact, it was adjacent to the spot where Lawrence of Arabia was killed on his motorcycle. Warmwell was, in fact, a pre-war practice camp, using the nearby Lulworth Cove bombing and gunnery ranges.
>
> About a week or so after our arrival the Station Commander, a Group Captain, had the whole station parade; until then we had all operated from the concrete apron in front of the hangars, but the Groupie's address was to change all that. It went something like this: 'One of these days in the not too distant future, the Hun is going to appear over those Purbeck Hills and knock three kinds of shit out of us. Therefore No 152 Squadron will disperse to the far side of the airfield in an effort to ensure that minimum damage will be occasioned. The hangar will only be used for major inspections and repairs.' He was right about being hit. We were, several times, but luckily nowhere near as badly as some of the airfields in the London area.
>
> The squadron's duties were in defence of the Portland naval base, Southampton docks, Yeovil aircraft factory etc, and throughout 152 Squadron managed to give a good account of itself, accounting for fifty or sixty confirmed victories. They were certainly hectic

days, from dawn to dusk we were at dispersal. It seemed as though we were always at readiness, rearming, re-fuelling, daily inspections of aircraft all seemed to follow each other without pause. It was certainly thrilling to see your aircraft return with its gun ports in the wing leading edges open and black streaks down the underside of the wings, indicating that it had been in action.

Very often there was a victory roll before the undercarriage was lowered and the pilot brought it in to land. Sometimes, though, your aircraft did not return, and you were left wondering what had happened to it. Sometimes a Spit[fire] would land badly shot-up.

From the beginning, the squadron's mascot was a white bull terrier known as 'Pooch'. Now Pooch was not an easy animal to get on with, and if he only suspected that you were afraid of him that was sufficient to make your life a misery and a continual hazard.

A very good mate of mine, the squadron Parachute Packer, was one of these, and among his duties was a daily visit to the pilots' dispersal tent to carry out his inspection. I am sure that Pooch heard or sensed this coming from afar, and it was the duty of whoever was there to grab Pooch and picket him down. To do so was indeed difficult, for he had been known to move the NAAFI wagon, given a strong rope and enough encouragement! Pooch even until then had a somewhat colourful career having previously belonged to a Canadian officer pilot stationed at Digby. The pilot was with the RAF on some kind of scheme. When he returned to Canada, Pooch was given to Tommy Thomas who gave the dog to his wife as a present. For some time, understandably, she was scared stiff of the dog but eventually they became very attached.

When 152 Squadron re-formed in 1939, Tommy became Commander of 'B' Flight and remained so until he was promoted to squadron leader and posted as a controller to Middle Wallop, Warmwell's Sector Station. His good lady had by this time relinquished ownership of Pooch, who was taken over by 152 and Flying Officer Cox in particular. Now Cocky Cox was equivalent in weight and strength to Pooch, but luckily his disposition was more docile! He and the dog became great friends.

Wherever the squadron went until sometime in 1942, Pooch was there and in every place the pilots sought female companionship for him, so much so that I am sure he had more than the rest of the squadron put together!

During the summer and early autumn of 1940, the invasion of this country was more than a distinct possibility. Suffice it to say that the danger eventually receded and as the days shortened so did air activity and we were given a little time off. Bus trips into neighbouring

Bournemouth and Weymouth were arranged, and evenings we would visit hostelries in the more immediate vicinity, such as at Woodsford, Puddletown, Broadmaine and Dorchester. Pilots had their own haunts, although occasionally our paths would cross, such as at the Gloucester Hotel in Weymouth, which was popular with all ranks.

Returning to the events of 12 July 1940, Coastal Command was ever-active, it being another busy day for the Blenheim-equipped 59 Squadron, based at Thorney Island, near Tangmere:

> The squadron carried out six anti-invasion Channel sweeps. On one of these Pilot Officer A.E.R. Fry dropped two 250lb bombs on hangars at Boulogne, damage done not known. Otherwise nothing reported. Two port recces were sent out but one returned owing to bad weather.
> The other, Pilot Officer R.W. Ayers, penetrated Cherbourg and dive-bombed the aerodrome, damage not known. Aircraft damaged by AA fire and on return intercepted by twelve Me 109s which pressed attack in pairs until within five miles of Isle of Wight. Aircraft considerably damaged and Air Gunner, Sergeant Webb slightly wounded, but managed to reach base. [ORB]

Pilot Officer Ayers and his crew, it seemed, had a miraculous escape.

The bad weather, however, saw no 2 Group Blenheims despatched to attack their usual daylight targets of invasion ports and airfields, and for the same reason Bomber Command nocturnal operations were reduced to twenty-three Whitleys sent to attack Kiel and Emden, only fourteen of which found and bombed their targets.

On 12 July 1940, Air Vice-Marshal Park made a further operational flight from Northolt in his personal Hurricane: 'To Kenley, to meet PM and escort back to Northolt'. Indeed, throughout the Battle of Britain, Park flew himself around his fighter stations (and after the Battle officially concluded on 31 October 1940, even flew from Northolt on a 'Biggin-Kent Patrol'). All of these many flights he recorded in his logbook, confirming beyond doubt that Air Vice-Marshal Park was a true fighter pilot and leader - and ready for action.

And so ended the third day of battle.

On this day, *Generaloberst* Alfred Jodl, the OKW's head of Operations Staff, recorded his initial thoughts on a 'Landing in England', which was approved and supported by General Keitel, the OKW chief. In this document, three difficulties were outlined. First, the RN's command of the sea could be negated by a landing on the South Coast: 'in the Channel we can substitute command of the air for naval supremacy which we do not possess, and the sea crossing is short there'. Second, being aware of this, Britain had concentrated its land forces so that they could move rapidly to the likely landing grounds. Third, Jodl recognised the impossibility of achieving strategic surprise, given that the necessary shipping concentrations in the Channel ports could not be concealed and were in any case under British surveillance.

Therefore, Jodl wrote, the landing:

> Must ... take place in the form of a river crossing in force on a broad front. In this operation the role of artillery will fall to the *Luftwaffe*; the first wave of fighting troops must be very strong (seven divisions landing between Dover and Bournemouth); and in place of bridging operations, a sea lane completely secure from naval attacks must be established in the Dover Straits.

Finally, Jodl urged that the OKW should draft a directive on 'preparation and general execution'.

Significantly, the OKW's invasion plan was codenamed 'Operation *Löwe*' (*Lion*) – soon to be revised and go down in history as 'Operation *Seelöwe*' (*Sea Lion*).

SATURDAY, 13 JULY 1940

That day, Generals Walther von Brauchitsch, the head of the German army, and his chief of staff, Franz Halder, were received at the Berghof by Hitler to outline their proposed plan for operations against Britain. Both men were enthusiastic; Halder, in fact, had begun detailed planning on 1 July 1940.

Now, Hitler approved the plan, ordering that preparations should begin immediately, and even wrote to Mussolini confirming that a landing in Britain had been definitely decided. That may have been so, but in reality, the *Führer* remained indecisive.

General Franz Halder:

> The *Führer* is very much preoccupied with the problem of why England does not wish to come to terms. Like us, he sees the answer in the fact that England will place some hope in Russia. He therefore expects that he will have to compel her by force to make peace. But he does not do this willingly.
>
> Reason: if we crush England by force of arms, the British Empire will fall to pieces. But this would be of no advantage to Germany. We should spill German blood only in order that Japan, America, and others, might benefit.

General Gerhard Engel, Hitler's Army Adjutant: 'It's my impression that the *Führer* is still unsure and doesn't know what to do.'

In his diary, Count Ciano, The Italian Foreign Minister, wrote that, 'We are awaiting a speech from Hitler. We shall learn the decisions from him'.

Although overcast once more, enemy aircraft continued to seek convoys in the Channel. At 09.45 hrs, Flight Lieutenant John Gibson, a New Zealander, was leading Yellow Section of 501 Squadron, up from Warmwell, on patrol over Swanage when a lone Do 17 was sighted:

> [It was] immediately attacked from quarter. Air gunner ceased to fire, then got into position astern and fired off rest of ammunition into E/A. Port engine emitted black smoke. After attack, E/A dived into cloud and disappeared. It was subsequently reported as having come down in the sea.

At 11.20 hrs, Blue Section of Tangmere's 43 Squadron (Flight Lieutenant Dalton-Morgan, Pilot Officers Gorrie and de Mancha) were patrolling at 12,000ft over the Solent and Isle of Wight, when a He 111 was sighted.

Flight Lieutenant Dalton-Morgan:

> I led Section in No 1 Attack ... I got in an effective burst on port wing. The wing was damaged and port undercarriage fell down. In second attack I received no return fire from E/A. I closed and fired two bursts and further fragments fell from fuselage. In third attack I concentrated on port engine, and gave it two effective bursts ...
>
> Smoke and flames began to issue from port engine and E/A commenced final dive towards sea. I watched E/A crash into the sea and explode. I made one circuit of wreckage and told Section to re-form. We then returned to base.

The He 111 was jointly shared by the pilots of Blue Section, but was more likely a Ju 88 of II/KG51 which failed to return from an operational flight, the crew of which remain missing.

A new German unit would enter the fray this particular morning, one which would be heavily engaged throughout the Battle of Britain: *Erprobungsgruppe* 210. Formed at Köln-Ostheim on 1 July 1940, equipped with both the Me 110 and 109, this would be a *gruppe*-strength low-level precision fighter-bomber unit. Designated an experimental formation, *Erprobungsgruppe* 210 was commanded by the Swiss born *Hauptmann* Walter Rubensdörffer, a highly respected former test-pilot and Spanish Civil War veteran.

On the Battle of Britain's official start-date, 10 July 1940, *Erprobungsgruppe* 210 moved to Denain in *Luftflotte* 2's area of north-west France, where it undertook a short period of training prior to commencing active operations against England. Shortly after 06.00 hrs on 13 July 1940, *Erprobungsgruppe* 210 left Denain to operate, for the next three weeks, from St Omer, closer to the Channel coast.

At 11.45 hrs, eight *Erprobungsgruppe* 210 Me 109s, ten Me 110 '*Jabos*' (abbreviation for *Jagdbomber*: fighter-bomber), and four Me 110 fighters took-off, the formation further supported by Me 109s of I/JG52, with orders to attack a convoy in the Thames Estuary. Two, in fact, comprising some sixty-five ships, were subsequently attacked, *Erprobungsgruppe* 210 claiming four direct hits, although no ships were sunk, however, or reported damaged that day. The raid went in low and fast, which may be why Fighter Command failed to react. The Germans suffered no combat casualties, but a faulty supercharger caused one Me 110 to make a forced-landing at Ghent.

Next, the action shifted to a westbound convoy approaching Lyme Bay. At midday, Flight Lieutenant Carr Withall, an Australian, was leading 'A' Flight of 152 Squadron up from Warmwell, comprising Red and Yellow Sections, on patrol at 8,000ft over Portland. A Ju 88 appeared from the South-east, which Red Section attacked, down-sun, twenty miles North of Portland. Hits were scored on the raider but it was lost, according to Withall, 'when cloud cover became solid'.

By early afternoon, the ships were entering Lyme Bay, and just before 15.00 hrs, three Spitfires of 609 Squadron at Warmwell and the twelve Middle Wallop-based Hurricanes of 238 Squadron were scrambled to provide protection. However, because the convoy had (sensibly) adopted a zig-zag course it was behind schedule, so the Hurricanes found no ships – only about fifty enemy aircraft, a single Do 17 escorted by Me 110s of IV/LG1 and Me 109s of II/JG51, equally surprised by the convoy's non-appearance.

Pilot Officer Charles Davis (Red 2), a Cranwellian, of 238 Squadron:

> Over Portland Harbour at 12,000ft ... saw one Do 17 proceeding out to sea in a shallow dive. Twenty Me 110s about 3,000ft above. Went into line astern and followed Do 17 out to sea. Red 1 (Flight Lieutenant John Kennedy, commanding 'A' Flight) went in, probably killed rear-gunner and damaged aircraft. E/A turned back towards the shore and Red 2 (himself) went in and fired several 2-second bursts, and then Red 3 (Sergeant Cecil Parkinson) went in and did likewise. E/A then turned across Portland Bill very low and Red 3 again went in and fired several bursts. The Dornier crashed into the sea, close to Chesil Bank.

Two of the bomber's crew, of 2(F)/123, were killed, and the aircraft captain, *Oberleutnant* Graf von Kesselstadt, was captured. Flight Lieutenant Kennedy, however, was hit by return fire during the action; he was killed when his Hurricane stalled while avoiding high-tension cables during the subsequent forced-landing at Southdown Farm, Lodmore, in Weymouth. It was a sad loss, as the 238 Squadron ORB recorded: 'The squadron lost an officer of high calibre.' Kennedy was also the first of ten Australians to die in the Battle of Britain.

In the same action, Sergeant Eric Bann of 238 Squadron's Yellow Section claimed an Me 110 destroyed:

Line astern formation when ordered to tackle individually. Got inside Me 110 and detached it from formation and made a quarter attack. One 2-second burst and he immediately dived into the sea ... he went straight in.

This Me 110 was a machine of 14/LG1, the crew of which were lost.

Two miles South-east of Portland, Pilot Officer Brian Considine, 238 Squadron's Blue 2, also attacked a 110, which he 'gave a full deflection shot turning inside turn. Burst was about eight seconds. His port engine caught fire and he dived vertically down. Did not see him hit, being engaged with 110 on my tail.'

The 609 Squadron Spitfires were also now in action; Pilot Officer Rogers Miller, Yellow 3, reported that:

> I was on patrol with Yellow Section (led by Flying Officer John Dundas, Yellow 2 was Pilot Officer Overton) at 4,000ft looking for Convoy *CRUMB* which was not in position stated. Suddenly I noticed a large number of aircraft circling at a great height on our starboard beam.
>
> I informed Yellow Leader and he told me to lead. I climbed right to one side of E/A, into the sun until I was 1,000ft above. I waited for an E/A to break from the very wide circle in which they were milling. It was straight below and towards me. I fired a short burst ahead of him and he flew straight into it and disappeared underneath me. I regained height and waited again.
>
> Then a Do 17 came out of the circle across me. I gave three 1-second bursts from quarter beam ahead and then followed him round and opened again from 200 yards, following him closely and firing continuously up to fifty yards, throttling right back.
>
> This attack started from quarter ahead and developed through a quarter attack to more or less astern. I was overshooting and broke away as my ammunition was expended and there were so many Me 110s about. This aircraft was later seen diving with the starboard motor on fire, going south.

Although in what was his first action against the enemy Pilot Officer Miller's attack on the Me 110 was inconclusive, pilots of 238 Squadron confirmed seeing the Do 17 heading out to sea, 'with his port engine on fire and losing height rapidly'. It was credited as a 'probable'.

Flying Officer Dundas destroyed an Me 110 with 800 rounds, but Pilot Officer 'Teeny' Overton was unable to gain sufficient height quickly enough and was unable to engage. Nonetheless, considering 609's run of bad luck to date, this result was certainly a 'good show'.

At 17.20 hrs, eleven Spitfires of Kenley's 64 Squadron were scrambled from Kenley to patrol Dover. Five minutes later, Blue Section of 54 Squadron, namely

Flight Lieutenant Basil 'Wonky' Way, Pilot Officer Colin Gray and Sergeant John Norwell, scrambled from Manston; while patrolling base a few minutes later, Blue Section sighted some Me 109s approaching; Gray, a New Zealander, reported that:

> While attempting to intercept twelve bandits, Blue Section encountered two Me 109s at 12,000ft, five miles off Deal. Both E/A dived to sea-level and pulled up sharply. Blue Leader took the right-hand E/A and I took the left, which then separated and dived to sea-level. I fired two or three bursts of my ammunition at fairly close range and bullets appeared to be striking E/A.
>
> Another Me 109 then appeared on my tail. After firing a final burst I pulled away and went home. Sergeant Smythe, 56 Squadron, who was piloting a Hurricane in the vicinity at the time confirms that this enemy aircraft crashed into the sea, immediately after I broke away.

Only one Me 109 was lost in what would be a developing combat: *Leutnant* Joachim Lange of 9/JG51, who was killed. This was also the 109 attacked and claimed destroyed by Sub-Lieutenant Dawson-Paul of 64 Squadron:

> As Blue 3 I was ordered with my Section and three other sections to patrol Dover at a height of 20,000ft ... we orbited Dover and saw twenty Me 109s approaching from our rear and slightly above. I broke off and approached two Me 109s, which were in formation. I gave one a short burst at 200 yards, which had no effect.
>
> They then dived at high speed. On looking round I saw that they were being chased by a Spitfire. One Me 109 manoeuvred himself onto the tail of the Spitfire, who was firing at the other 109.
>
> I dived ... and attacked the rear-most Me 109 from very nearly head-on. I fired one long burst into his belly and smoke poured out. He rolled over on his back and I stall-turned and gave him another burst, which hit him. The pilot then baled out and the E/A crashed into the sea.
>
> This action was seen by the pilot of the other Spitfire, Flying Officer Woodward. I landed at an advanced base, as there were no signs of other E/A.

Also down at Hawkinge, on the coast, was 64 Squadron's Sergeant Arthur Binham, whose Spitfire was damaged by AA fire over Dover at 17.45 hrs.

The Spitfires had encountered the Me 109s of III/JG51, being led by their exulted *Kommodore*, *Oberst* Theo Osterkamp. At 42 years old, Osterkamp was a remarkable man by any standards: a thirty-two victory First World War ace, in this action he claimed a Spitfire destroyed, his fifth Second World War kill and thereby qualifying him as an ace in both world wars. No Spitfires, however, were actually lost in this combat.

The next raid saw the Me 109s of II/JG51 escorting the *Stukas* of II/StG1, which was intercepted by eleven 56 Squadron Hurricanes on a 'special patrol'. Squadron Leader Graham 'Minnie' Manton:

> I left Rochford at 1745 hrs to patrol Canterbury, then vectored to Dover, subsequently to carry out sweep to within ten miles of French coast. Flew westwards, then turned East near French coast, intercepting E/A, of which Ju 87s were in sections of three (vic formation) and climbing at the time.
>
> I was leading second (Yellow) section and followed Red Section into attack. Red had dived onto the formation, which then broke up and I turned towards the French coast. Dogfight ensued. I attacked three 87s, one after the other, the first two without visible effect.
>
> I sat behind the third, firing continuously, expending all my ammunition, and I last saw it dicing steeply towards the sea with petrol coming from port tanks, then at a height of 2,000ft ... I was then attacked by a He 113 from above and the rear. I then broke off the engagement and returned to North Weald at 2005 hrs, via Manston. The rear gunner of the third Ju 87 fired only one burst, so I presume he was knocked out.

Manton was credited with a Ju 87 destroyed (unconfirmed). His reference to the 'He 113', however, is completely erroneous. This prototype fighter was much-vaunted by the German propagandists but never actually existed. So successful was the ruse, however, that RAF pilots' combat reports throughout the Battle of Britain frequently mention 113s, when in fact they were fighting Me 109s.

Also in action some three miles off Calais at 18.30 hrs was Pilot Officer Geoffrey Page, who attacked two *Stukas* without apparent effect, chasing one down to sea-level:

> I then saw a Hurricane being attacked by a He 113, which I attacked. This was about 500ft. I attacked from practically dead astern and gave E/A three short bursts at about 300 yards, using slight deflection. I could see my tracers flying all around him. E/A turned over on its side an dived rapidly towards the sea.
>
> I was then attacked from above and in front on my port side by another E/A and I turned towards this E/A and climbed to meet him, but he then broke off the attack. I was thus unable to see the He 113 crash, but from its angle of dive I have no doubt at all that it fell into the sea. Flight Lieutenant Coghlan saw me attack and saw E/A fall into the sea.

Clearly, the 109 attacked by Page was destroyed, and witnessed – but, again, no possible candidate appears in German records.

In addition to these victories, Flight Lieutenant John Coghlan claimed a Ju 87 and a 'He 113' destroyed; Sergeants James Cowsill, George Smythe, Peter Hillwood and Ron Baker each claimed Ju 87 destroyed. This result, however, was not without loss. Unfortunately for 56 Squadron, when positioning to attack the Ju 87s, the Hurricanes were sandwiched between the dive-bombers and close escort fighters. The Me 109s of 4/JG51 were led by *Oberleutnant* Josef Fözö:

> We opened fire immediately and three Hurricanes separated from the formation, two dropping and one gliding down to the water, smoking heavily. At that moment I saw a *Stuka* diving for the water to head back to France. It was being chased by a single Hurricane. I saw the deadly dangerous situation and dived to assist.
>
> There were now five aircraft nosing down to the water. The *Stuka* received heavy damage and crashed on the beach near Wissant, with the crew badly wounded. *Feldwebel* Hans John hit the Hurricane, which disappeared into the Channel, the right wing cutting the water like a shark's fin, and 'my' Hurricane dropped like a stone, close to the one John had shot down.

John, of 4/JG51, had shot down Sergeant Cowsill, while Sergeant Joseph Whitfield fell to Fözö; both British pilots were killed. Flight Lieutenant Coghlan's Hurricane was also damaged, the slightly injured pilot safely returning to base. Sergeant Ron Baker's Hurricane was also damaged in the action, forcing him to crash-land at Rodmersham, near Sittingbourne.

Fözö claimed a second Hurricane destroyed, and *Unteroffizier* Ernst Buder, *Hauptmann* Horst Tietzen (5/JG51) and *Feldwebel* Heinrich Tornow also, somewhat optimistically, claimed Hurricanes destroyed.

So ended the daylight fighter battles on 13 July 1940.

That day, Bomber Command sent twenty-two Blenheims to attack various locations in France, Belgium and Germany, but owing to the poor weather only eight found and bombed their targets. Two Blenheims were lost, both of Watton's 82 Squadron, one being shot down over the North Sea off Borkum by 6/JG52, the other by *Stab*/JG1.

By night, ninety-seven Bomber Command aircraft sowed mines and attacked targets far and wide. Among them was Pilot Officer Charles Price and his Waddington-based 44 Squadron crew, who took off in their Hampden at 21.50 hrs, subsequently dropping six 250lb General Purpose bombs and sixty 4lb incendiaries from 500ft on the aircraft factory at Lemwerder, Bremen, home of Weser Flugzeugbau who manufactured the high-flying Ju 86 reconnaissance aircraft. This attack was pressed home despite heavy flak. Poor visibility caused by low cloud prevented results being recorded, but on the return flight, while passing over the North Sea island of Borkum, two Me 110s were seen in the circuit of the airfield there, preparing to land.

Price immediately attacked, positioning the bomber so that his rear-gunner got in a shot at – and hit – one of the enemy machines, before engaging the second, which was shot down into the sea. Having 'displayed great courage, initiative and determination throughout the operation', as his citation read, Price was awarded the DFC for this night's work. The following year saw Price become a flight lieutenant on 97 Squadron, flying Avro Manchesters at Coningsby.

On 8 November 1941, he took off at 13.20 hrs on a search of the cold North Sea for ditched aircrew but failed to return. Flight Lieutenant Price and his crew remain missing – he was 20 years old.

Coastal Command was also active on the night of 13/14 July 1940, Blenheims of Detling's 53 Squadron and 59 Squadron based at Thorney Island struck at barges congregating in canals around Bruges. An aircraft of the latter inexplicably crashed into the Channel off Shoreham, killing the crew.

SUNDAY, 14 JULY 1940

Even though bad weather served to protect the nine convoys steaming through Channel waters, Fighter Command still flew a total of 597 sorties on this day. That afternoon, Convoy *Booty*, off Dover, attracted the enemy's attention in the shape of forty IV/LG 1's *Stukas*, escorted by thirty Me 109s of III/JG3 and II/JG51.

Battle was joined when the raiders were intercepted by the Hurricanes of 615 and 151 squadrons, and the Spitfires of 610. Among the 151 Squadron pilots engaged was Pilot Officer Jack Hamar, who later reported vividly on the action:

> At 1500 hrs the squadron was ordered off from Rochford to intercept E/As south of Dover. At approximately 1520 hrs, when the squadron was almost over Dover, a bunch of Me 109s were sighted about 5,000ft above our formation, in which I was flying Red Two. As it looked as though the E/A were about to attack us, the leader ordered our defensive line astern tactics.
>
> As we turned sharply to port, two Me 109s were seen diving to attack the last aircraft in our formation. 'Milna Leader' attacked the leading Me 109 and I the second. I turned inside the E/A, which had pulled up into a steep left-hand climbing turn. I closed rapidly and opened fire at about 250 yards with a 45° deflection shot.
>
> The E/A seemed to falter and straightened out into a dive. I placed myself dead astern at about 50 yards. I opened fire, closing to almost no distance. I saw a large explosion just in front of the pilot and a large amount of white smoke poured from the E/A, which by this time was climbing steeply. I was then forced to break away quickly due to fire from the rear, lost sight of the E/A and therefore did not see it crash. This action was also witnessed by Flying Officer Forster

Squadron Leader Teddy Donaldson:

> Jack Hamar was my Number Two. A leader has to navigate as we as coordinate and lead attacks. He can only do this if he has a good Number Two, whom he can completely rely on. A CO then knows that no one can creep up behind him as long as his Number Two is in place.
>
> I always knew that Jack would be there. If he were shot down, I knew that the last thing he would do would be to tell me on the radio that he had 'had it'. Looking after me was an extremely hazardous task. Jack did it loyally and even managed to shoot down six and a half enemy aircraft. The half was for a German bomber which we shared; I had damaged it but it may have returned to its base, so Jack blew it out of the sky in flames.
>
> I made nine forced-landings in total but was never shot down with Jack Hamar my Number Two.

In this combat, Squadron Leader Donaldson also destroyed a 109 in this action, as did Flight Lieutenant Rod Smith, commanding 'B' Flight, who was flying an experimental Hurricane armed with 20mm cannon:

> About two minutes after the squadron had whipped around onto two Me 109s, I had climbed with my Section above the other sections and saw a Hurricane chasing another aircraft across my bows. I turned in to the left and cut off the corner, and when about 300 yards away identified the leading (chased) aircraft as a 109, as I had suspected.
>
> I opened fire as he straightened up out of his turn on seeing me, and closed from beam to quarter and pulled up when very close to avoid the fire of the pursing Hurricane, which aircraft missed me by a few feet only. I looked down to my left and saw the 109 going almost vertically down with smoke coming out of it in puffs. I had fired a 2-second burst from my two cannons and had used eighteen rounds from one and twenty from the other, on inspection.
>
> I could not say, of course, whether it was my fire or the other Hurricane which brought the 109 down – I did not watch it for more than 2,000ft, as I was looking for other E/A, so cannot say if or where it hit the ground, but from the amount of various coloured smoke I should say it was well on fire.

At 13.00 hrs that day, Squadron Leader Joe Kayll had led thirteen Hurricanes of his 615 'County of Surrey' Squadron from Kenley to operate from Hawkinge. Two hours later, Kayll was leading Red Section (Pilot Officers Cecil Montgomery and Michael Mudie) on patrol over *Booty* when the enemy attack came in. Me 109s of

II/JG51 set upon the Hurricanes, shooting down Red 3, Pilot Officer Mudie, who baled out, badly wounded, suffering from severe burns and a gunshot wound to the face. Although rescued from the sea in St Margaret's Bay by the RN, the 24-year-old pilot died in Dover hospital the following day.

In response, Kayll and Montgomery managed to fire several bursts at the *Stukas* but had to break away owing to further attacks from the escorting fighters. While the combat was ongoing, the remaining aircraft of 615 Squadron scrambled to assist, the three pilots of Yellow Section, namely Flying Officers John Gayner and Peter Collard, and Pilot Officer Petrus 'Dutch' Hugo) all claiming Ju 87s destroyed. Blue Section chased the 109s but made no claim, but 'Green Section missed the fun' (ORB).

That evening 615 Squadron would receive congratulations from none other than the Prime Minister, who was Honorary Commodore of this AAF squadron, which proudly called itself 'Churchill's Own'.

At 14.50 hrs, the twelve Spitfires of Biggin Hill's 610 Squadron, led by Squadron Leader Andrew Smith, were scrambled to patrol Hawkinge at 10,000ft. Approaching Dover, however, the air battle over the Channel was all too evident and the Spitfires joined in. Green Leader, Pilot Officer Peter Litchfield, followed three Me 109s down to 3,000ft, firing three bursts at the leading enemy fighter, which dived away, enveloped in smoke.

Up at 20,000ft, Blue Section, providing top cover, saw the dive-bombers attacking *Booty* but lost sight of the enemy formation before it could be attacked.

This great combat over the Channel, within sight of the white cliffs of Dover, was actually being witnessed from that vantage point by veteran BBC reporter Charles Gardner, who was sitting in a recording van and whose radio broadcast that evening marked an important milestone in the history of war reporting:

> The Germans are dive-bombing a convoy out at sea: there are one, two, three, four, five, six, seven German dive-bombers, *Junkers* 87s. There's one going down on its target now – bomb! No! He missed the ships, it hasn't hit a single ship – there are about ten ships in the convoy but he hasn't hit a single one and – There, you can hear our anti-aircraft going at them now. There are one, two, three, four, five, six – there are about ten German machines dive-bombing the convoy, which is just out to sea in the Channel.
>
> I can't see anything! No! We thought he had got a German one at the top then, but now the British fighters are coming up. Here they come. The Germans are coming in an absolutely steep dive, and you can see their bombs actually leave the machines and come into the water. You can hear our guns going like anything now. I can hear machine-gun fire but I can't see our Spitfires. They must be somewhere there. Oh! Here's one coming down.
>
> There's one going down in flames. Somebody's hit a German and he's coming down with a long streak – coming down completely out

of control – a long streak of smoke – and now a man's baled out by parachute. The pilot's baled out by parachute. He's a *Junkers* 87 and he's going slap into the sea – and there he goes: SMASH! A terrific column of water and there was a *Junkers* 87. Only one man got out by parachute, so presumably there was only a crew of one in it.

Now then, oh, there's a terrific mix-up over the Channel! It's impossible to tell which are our machines and which are the Germans. There was one definitely down in this battle and there's a fight going on. There's a fight going on and you can hear the little rattles of machine-gun bullets. Crump! That was a bomb, as you may imagine. Here comes one Spitfire. There's a little burst. There's another bomb dropping. Yes, it has dropped. It has missed the convoy. You know, they haven't hit the convoy in all this.

The sky is absolutely patterned with bursts of anti-aircraft fire, and the sea is covered with smoke where bombs have burst, but as far as I can see there is not one single ship hit, and there is definitely one German machine down. And I am looking across the sea now. I can see the little white dot of a parachute as the German pilot is floating down towards the spot where his machine crashed with such a big fountain of water two minutes ago.

Well, now everything is peaceful again, for the moment. The Germans, who came over in about twenty or twenty-five dive-bombers, delivered their attack on the convoy, and I think they made off as quickly as they came. Oh yes, I can see one, two, three, four, five, six, seven, eight, nine, ten Germans haring back towards France now for all they can go – and here are our Spitfires coming after them. There's going to be a big fight, I think, out there, but it will be too far away for us to see. Of course, there are a lot more German machines up there, 'Can you see, Cyril?', yes, there are one, two, three, four, five, six, seven on the top layer, one, two, three – there's two layers of German machines. They are all, I think, I could not swear to it, but they were all *Junkers* 87s.

Well, that was a really hot little engagement while it lasted. No damage done, except to the Germans who lost one machine and the German pilot who is still on the end of his parachute, although appreciably nearer the sea than he was. I can see no boat going out to pick him up, so he'll probably have a long swim ashore.

Well, that was a very unsuccessful attack on the convoy, I must say.

Oh, there's another fight going on, away up, now – I think about 20, 25 or even 30,000ft above our heads, and I can't see a thing of it. The anti-aircraft guns have put up one, two, three, four, five, six bursts, but I can't see the aeroplanes. There we go again – oh, we

KANALKAMPF DIARY, 10 JULY – 31 JULY 1940

have just hit a *Messerschmitt*! Oh, that was beautiful! He's coming right down, I think it was definitely that burst got him. Yes, he's come down. You hear those crowds? He's finished! Oh, he's coming down like a rocket now. An absolute steep dive.

Let us move round so we can watch him a bit more. Here he comes, down in a steep dive – the *Messerschmitt*. No, no, the pilot's not getting out of that one. He's being followed down. What, there are two more *Messerschmitts* up there? I think they are all right No – that man's finished. He's going down from about 10,000, oh, 20,000 to about 2,000ft, and he's going straight down – he's not stopping. I think that's another German machine that's definitely put paid to. I don't think we shall actually see him crash because he's going into a bank of cloud. He's smoking now.

I can see smoke, although we cannot count that as a definite victory because I did not see him crash. He's going behind a hill. He looked certainly out of control.

Now, we are looking up to the anti-aircraft guns. There's another! There's another *Messerschmitt*. I don't know whether he's down or whether he's trying to get out of the anti-aircraft fire, which is giving him a very hot time. There's a Spitfire! Oh! There's about four fighters up there, and I don't know what they are doing. One, two, three, four, five fighters fighting right above our heads. Now there's one coming right down on the tail of what I think is a *Messerschmitt*, and I think it's a Spitfire behind him. Oh darn! They've turned away and I can't see. Where's one crashing? No, I think he's pulled out. You can't watch these fights very coherently for long. You just see about four twirling machines, you just hear little bursts of machine-gunning, and by the time you've picked up the machines they've gone.

Hello, there are one, two, three, and look, there's a dogfight going on up there! There are four, five, six machines wheeling and turning around. Now – hark at all the machine-guns going! Hark! One, two, three, four, five, six. Now there's something coming right down on the tail of another. Here they come. Yes, they are being chased home! There are three Spitfires chasing three *Messerschmitts* now. Oh boy! Look at them going!

Oh, look how the *Messerschmitts* – oh boy – look at them going! Oh, look how the *Messerschmitts* – oh boy – that was really grand! There's a Spitfire behind the first two. He will get them. Oh yes! Oh boy! I've never seen anything so good as this! The RAF fighters have really got these boys taped. Our machine is catching up the *Messerschmitt* now. He's catching it up! He's got the legs of it, you know. Now, right in the sights, go on, George! You've got him!

Bomb – bomb. No, no, the distance is a bit deceptive from here. You can't tell but I think something is definitely going to happen to that first *Messerschmitt*. Oh yes – just a moment – I think I wouldn't like to be in that first *Messerschmitt*. I think he's got him. Yes? Machine-guns are going like anything.

No, there's another fight going on. No, they've chased him right out to sea. I can't see, but I think the odds would certainly be on that first *Messerschmitt* catching it. Yes, they've got him down too, yes, he's pulled away from him. Yes, I think that first *Messerschmitt* has crashed on the coast of France all right!

To many, Gardner's now famous broadcast was inspirational and morale boosting; others wrote to the *Times*, complaining that he had reduced the whole matter of men fighting for their lives to the level of a cup final. They had a point: the first aircraft Gardner saw crash was not, in fact, a *Stuka*, but the 615 Squadron Hurricane of Pilot Officer Michael Mudie, who was the only RAF casualty in this engagement, which cost the Germans two Ju 87s destroyed and their crews killed.

Of the convoy, the coaster *Mons* was damaged, and *Dlader* was set ablaze, its stern blown off. Gardner's recording was broadcast on the wireless at 21.00 hrs to a mixed reaction. Home Intelligence subsequently canvassed 300 people for their view on the piece, concluding that 'a considerable majority spoke enthusiastically of the broadcast', but women especially objected to what some perceived as war being treated as a sporting contest, and felt that 'his callous Oxford accent made it worse'.

Edward Bishop, journalist:

> War reporting was to become so much more cold, precise and expert with practice ... In the emergency of the hour, however, the rumpus aroused by Gardner's broadcast was worth any number of BBC headaches to Britain. Its unique quality helped alert those who were still mentally or geographically adrift from the reality that no such dangerous enemy had been so near to London since Harold and his bowmen awaited defeat at the hands of the Conqueror from Normandy.
>
> The broadcast also provided a disc which sold well in neutral America. The profits, suitably enough, were devoted to purchase of mufflers, balaclavas, woolly mitts, cricket bats, footballs and other 'comforts' for the RAF.

Perhaps that the RAF benefited from the 'comforts' arising from Gardner's broadcast was especially appropriate, given that Gardner possessed a private pilot's licence and, in due course, joined up, flying Coastal Command Catalina long-range flying-boats over the Atlantic and Far East.

While Gardener inadvertently caused a 'rumpus' on 14 July 1940, however, it was a quieter day for Coastal Command – although a 53 Squadron Blenheim was lost attacking oil and petrol tanks on the Ghent-Selzaette Canal, and a 59 Squadron Blenheim, engaged on an 'anti invasion patrol', was shot-up by four Me 109s off Selsey Bill; the pilot, Pilot Officer M.D. Sanders, managed to crash-land back at Thorney Island.

Bomber Command continued the dangerous practice of sending unescorted Blenheims over enemy territory by day, although a lack of cloud cover dictated that a proposed attack on Kiel by six aircraft had to be abandoned. That night, eighty RAF bombers again sowed mined and attacked various targets in Germany; only one Wellington was lost.

By now, it was clear to the Air Staff that the failure to provide an appropriate air sea rescue service was somewhat of an omission, considering how the majority of fighting was now over the sea and nose-heavy fighters like the single-engine Spitfires and Hurricanes tended to dive vertically underwater within a few seconds of being ditched. Pilots without immersion protection suits or even dinghies could not survive long in the cold sea, especially when wounded, and were reliant upon their position having been noted and either being picked up by a passing vessel or one specifically launched from shore.

Conversely, information gleaned from enemy aircrew prisoners confirmed that the Germans had set up an efficient rescue service before Norway, which now comprised at least twelve aircraft, mostly He 59 seaplanes. As we have seen, such red-cross emblazoned and unarmed enemy ambulance aircraft were deliberately attacked and destroyed by RAF pilots on 1 and 9 July 1940. All German aircrew serving with the *Seenotdienst* were members of the *Luftwaffe*, but nonetheless this was a *bona fide* rescue service, the personnel of which being appropriately equipped and trained for this humanitarian and essential purpose, and one crew was even officially registered with the International Red Cross at Geneva; the only evidence of impropriety, in fact, was one ambulance aircraft being used as a taxi for German staff officers.

On 14 July 1940, however, Fighter Command ordered that if found close to the British coast or convoys, the red-crossed aircraft must be destroyed. The problem, in simple terms, was that some 400 German airmen captured since the war began had been returned to Germany by the French after the Armistice, so many of the aircrew involved were now flying operationally again. The German Red Cross seaplanes exacerbated this scenario further still, as Air Chief Marshal Dowding wrote in his Despatch:

> They were engaged in rescuing combatants and taking them back to fight again, and they were also in a position if granted immunity, to make valuable reconnaissance reports. In spite of this, surviving crews of these aircraft appeared to be surprised and aggrieved at being shot down.

This was supported by the British Government, however, which, a fortnight later, would formally protest regarding such a use of the Red Cross. Nonetheless, this remained controversial.

After the war, former *Luftwaffe* officers serving in the post-war German air force opined that all the aerial intelligence required was obtained through normal means, and no misuse of, or subterfuge by, ambulance aircraft was necessary. The German veterans' perception, which was partially true, was that what the British were really trying to prevent was the capture of downed RAF aircrew by the *Seenotdienst* seaplanes, and similarly prevent German airmen being rescued to fight another day. The evidence from the examination of captured He-59s, however, confirmed that they were equipped to make immediate reports regarding the position of convoys.

A German newspaper reported on the matter as one of a lack of chivalry and fair play:

> It has been observed on several occasions when German Red Cross planes were rescuing shipwrecked Englishmen, the English fighter planes circled round to see their comrades had been rescued by Germans, and then flew away. But when Germans were being rescued the English attacked at once.

There was still no expressed intention by Hitler to invade Britain. The prospect of invasion, however, had been very much in British minds since mid-May 1940, and certainly after Dunkirk. On this day, Churchill wrote:

> We may ... be sure that there is a plan – perhaps built up over years – for destroying Great Britain, which has the honour to be his main and foremost enemy.

Churchill was wrong. As we have seen, there was no plan.

MONDAY, 15 JULY 1940

Persistent low cloud and rain severely hampered offensive air operations for both sides. Nonetheless, the enemy continued prowling over the Channel, and at 10.15 hrs 151 Squadron, operating from Manston, was scrambled 'to intercept E/A bombing shipping in the Dover area. An attack was made but owing to cloud the result was not ascertainable. 'The E/A was a Do 215, apparently unescorted, and it escaped into cloud,' noted the ORB.

First blood of the day, however, would go to 603 Squadron in the Turnhouse Sector of 13 Group; Pilot Officer Dudley Stewart-Clark:

At 1155 hrs, two aircraft of Yellow Section were ordered to intercept a bandit off Peterhead. The weather was cloudy and the clouds came almost down to sea-level. I sighted the E/A flying south-east at 500ft, five miles south-east of Peterhead and one-mile East of me. E/A turned north-east and turned into cloud, but shortly afterwards came out again about 500 yards from my machine and a bit below.

I delivered a burst of three seconds from slightly astern and on the quarter of about three seconds which silenced the rear gunner, and then delivered another from slightly below, closing from 300 yards to 100 yards, using all my ammunition.

My windscreen, propeller and wings were covered in oil from the E/A.

Yellow 1 (Pilot Officer James Morton) then delivered two attacks and the E/A disappeared into thick cloud, and was not seen again by me. We subsequently ascertained from four prisoners recovered from the aircraft that it forced-landed on the sea twenty miles East of Peterhead at 1230 hrs.

The two Spitfire pilots shared the victory equally, this being a He 111 of 2/KG26 based in Norway. The pilot, *Oberleutnant* Ottmar Hollman, ditched his crippled bomber some fifty miles off Peterhead. The rear-gunner, *Feldwebel* Reinhard, was killed, but the five surviving Germans, having taken to their dinghy, were fortunate to be picked up by a passing trawler two days later.

At 14.15 hrs, Blue Section of North Weald's 56 Squadron was patrolling a convoy off Harwich when a dozen twin-engine German aircraft appeared. Flight Sergeant Frederick 'Taffy' Higginson:

I was flying No 3 and I suddenly saw the E/A dive out of the clouds to comb the convoy. I broke formation and fired a preliminary burst from the beam, to try to distract the E/A's attention from the bombing. Most of the E/A broke away except two or three, the leader of which dropped a bomb directly on a big ship, which burst into flames. Two E/A then broke away to the right in line astern and I got on the tail of the last one.

I opened fire at first at about 300 yards with a quarter attack, which must have put his gunner out of action, and E/A then adopted echelon right formation to give the other E/As' gunners a chance to get at me. I closed into range again and opened fire at about 300 yards from astern. Both E/A then dived to sea-level and closed in to about 75/100 yards, firing continuously. E/A then turned and dived straight into the sea. I was fired at by rear gunners of both aircraft but not hit.

Visibility was very bad, with rain and clouds. The rest of the E/A jettisoned their bombs and turned eastwards. I saw no fighter escort.

Flight Sergeant Higginson's claim for a Do 17 was confirmed, and his Flight Commander, Flight Lieutenant 'Jumbo' Gracie, was credited with a 'probable'.

The ship Higginson saw 'burst into flames' was the 2,855-ton SS *Heworth* of Convoy *Pilot*, which was en route from London to Sunderland, in ballast. The cargo ship sank near the Aldeburgh Light Vessel, four of her crew being killed while the survivors were picked up by HMS *Valorous*; a Polish freighter was also damaged. It was not 'Do 17s', however, that the Hurricanes engaged that afternoon, but Me 110s of *Erprobungsgruppe* 210.

That morning *Hauptmann* Rubensdörffer's men had flown from Denain to St Omer at dawn, but owing to the bad weather, the first and third *Staffeln* were recalled. Eventually, a mission was decided upon and this was flown by two Me 110s of the *Stabschwarm* and eight of 2/*Erprobungsgruppe* 210. That this raid was made by 110s explains the lack of a fighter escort and no losses are recorded, although the German crews' aircraft identification was as suspect as 56 Squadron's, it seems, given that they reported seeing a flight of Spitfires, and over-estimated the tonnage of the ship they sank at 4,000 tons.

On this day, despite the bad weather, 213 Squadron's Hurricane pilots flew nine convoy patrols from Exeter off Portland. According to the ORB, at 13.00 hrs, 'One aircraft of Yellow Section patrolled base and Dartmouth. Shot down but believed to have got two enemy aircraft.' This was Sub-Lieutenant Henry Bramah, an FAA pilot seconded to Fighter Command, who was shot down by return fire from a Do 17 over Old Mill Creek, near Dartmouth, and baled out, landing in the sea. Picked up by HMS *Scimitar*, the pilot was badly wounded but refused to have a mangled arm amputated (eventually recovering and serving in the RN until 1955). No enemy loss can be attributed to Bramah on 15 July 1940, however.

In the afternoon, a small formation of Ju 88s from LG1 appeared from the clouds over Yeovil in Somerset, dropping twelve bombs on the Westland Aircraft Company's factory and airfield. A flight shed was hit and the runway cratered, but fortunately the new cannon-armed and twin-engine Westland Whirlwind fighters escaped damage.

According to various secondary sources, at 17.15 hrs, Pilot Officer Bob Holland of 92 Squadron, based at Pembrey to afford protection to South Wales and the West Country aircraft factories, destroyed a Ju 88 over the Bristol Channel, near Cardiff. Certainly a Ju 88 of II/LG1 failed to return from operations that day, the crew of which remain missing, but if Holland did indeed destroy it, it is surprising that no mention is made of this success in the 92 Squadron ORB, and nor does the pilot's personal combat report exist.

The 145 Squadron ORB notes the following:

> Very heavy continuous rain – visibility almost nil ... At about 1900 hrs, Green Section (Flying Officers Guy Branch and Pilot Officers Peter Parrott and Jas Storrar) were ordered to patrol between cloud layers in the Portsmouth – Chichester area. They sighted and

attacked a Do 17 which escaped into cloud. Pilot Officer Storrar was lucky enough to emerge from cloud on the tail of this Dornier and a long chase ensued across the Channel, this pilot giving the E/A short bursts on every possible occasion.

Eventually he ran out of ammunition some thirty miles South of Selsey Bill, and left the Dornier on fire, in starboard engine and wing, and losing speed, but with the rear gunner still firing. Flying Officer Branch and Pilot Officer Parrott sighted another Do 17 near Selsey and gave it short bursts before it was lost in the clouds. No damage to this plane can be claimed.

During the day, Coastal Command undertook various reconnaissance flights but given the weather, results were unremarkable. Bomber Command sent a combined force of seventeen Blenheims from Nos. 107 and 110 squadrons to airfields in France and the industrial Ruhr, but thirteen aborted due to the weather; the remaining four aircraft pressed home attacks on Evreux and Lisieux.

Most night raids were cancelled, although 5 Group Hampdens successfully sowed mines off Copenhagen and attacked various targets in Germany.

On 15 July 1940, Fighter Command was doubtless heartened to hear that the Air Ministry was working with the Admiralty for inshore patrols to be conducted by motor launches while air battles were ongoing, and the 300 small craft under Admiralty orders surrounding the British coastline were given a watching brief when air battles were in progress.

The RAF also possessed high speed launches, moving five of these to the southeastern ports of Ramsgate, Newhaven and Calshot. What limited these vessels operationally, however, was the inability to see beyond the horizon, so it was clear that like the Germans, dedicated aircraft were required for this purpose; surprisingly, this would not happen until September 1940.

On the Home Front, people remained upbeat and were beginning to question whether Hitler would launch an invasion after all.

TUESDAY, 16 JULY 1940

Despite the weather severely curtailing air operations, 16 July 1940, was nonetheless enormously significant.

On this day, Hitler, as '*Führer* and Supreme Commander of the *Wehrmacht*', issued his infamous '*Führer* Directive No.16' – outlining, at last, his intention to *possibly* invade Britain. Arguably, 16 July 1940 is, therefore (if we are to understand that the Battle of Britain revolved around a proposed German invasion) another contender to be considered the aerial conflict's start-date.

The text of Hitler's order is rarely reproduced in full, as it is here:

ON PREPARATIONS FOR A LANDING OPERATION AGAINST ENGLAND

Since England, in spite of her hopeless military situation, shows no signs of being ready to come to an understanding, I have decided to prepare a landing operation against England, and if necessary, to carry it out.

The aim of this operation will be to eliminate the English homeland as a base for the prosecution of the war against Germany, and if necessary occupy it completely.

I therefore order as follows:

1. The landing will be in the form of a surprise crossing on a wide front from about Ramsgate to the area west of the Isle of Wight. Units of the Air Force will act as artillery, and units of the Navy as engineers.

   The possible advantages of limited operations before the general crossing (e.g. the occupation of the Isle of Wight or of the county of Cornwall) are to be considered from the point of view of each branch of the Armed Forces and the results reported to me. I reserve the decision to myself. Preparations for the entire operation must be completed by the middle of August.

2. These preparations must also create such conditions as will make a landing in England possible, viz:
   a) The English Air Force must be so reduced morally and physically that it is unable to deliver any significant attack against the German crossing.
   b) Mine-free channels must be cleared.
   c) The Straits of Dover must be closely sealed off with minefields on both flanks; also the Western entrance to the Channel approximately on the line Alderney–Portland.
   d) Strong forces of coastal artillery must command and protect the forward coastal area.
   e) It is desirable that the English Navy be tied down shortly before the crossing, both in the North Sea and in the Mediterranean (by the Italians). For this purpose we must attempt even now to damage English home-based naval forces by air and torpedo attack as far as possible.

3. Command organisation and preparations. Under my overriding command and according to my general instructions, the

Commanders-in-Chief will command the branches of the Armed Forces for which they are responsible. From 1st August the operations staffs of Commander-in-Chief Army, Commander-in-Chief Navy, and Commander-in-Chief Air Force are to be located at a distance of not more than 50 kilometres from my Headquarters (Ziegenberg).

It seems to me useful that the inner operations staffs of Commander-in-Chief Army and Commander-in-Chief Navy should be placed together at Giessen.

Commander-in-Chief Army will detail one Army Group to carry out the invasion.

The invasion will bear the cover name '*Seelöwe*'.

In the preparation and execution of this operation the following tasks are allotted to each Service:

a) Army: The Army will draw up the operational and crossing plans for all formations of the first wave of the invasion. The anti-aircraft artillery which is to cross with the first wave will remain subordinate to the Army (to individual crossing units) until it is possible to allocate its responsibilities between the support and protection of troops on the ground, the protection of disembarkation points, and the protection of the airfields which are to be occupied. The Army will, moreover, lay down the methods by which the invasion is to be carried out and the individual forces to be employed, and will determine points of embarkation and disembarkation in conjunction with the Navy.

b) Navy: The Navy will procure the means for invasion and will take them, in accordance with the wishes of the Army, but with due regard to navigational considerations, to the various embarkation points. Use will be made, as far as possible, of the shipping of defeated enemy countries.

The Navy will furnish each embarkation point with the staff necessary to give nautical advice, with escort vessels and guards. In conjunction with air forces assigned for protection, it will defend the crossing of the Channel on both flanks. Further orders will lay down the chain of command during the crossing. It is also the task of the Navy to coordinate the setting up of coastal artillery-i.e. all artillery, both naval and military, intended to engage targets at sea-and generally to direct its fire. The largest possible number of extra-heavy guns will be brought into position as soon as possible in order to cover the crossing and to shield the flanks against enemy action at sea. For this purpose railway guns will also be used (reinforced by all available captured weapons) and will be sited on railway turntables. Those batteries intended only to deal with targets on the English mainland (K5 and K12) will not be included. Apart from this the existing extra-heavy platform-gun batteries are to be enclosed in concrete opposite the Straits of Dover in such a manner that they can withstand the heaviest air attacks and will permanently, in all conditions, command the Straits of Dover within the limits of their range. The technical work will be the responsibility of the Organisation Todt.

c) The task of the Air Force will be: To prevent interference by the enemy Air Force. To destroy coastal fortresses which might operate against our disembarkation points, to break the first resistance of enemy land forces, and to disperse reserves on their way to the front. In carrying out this task the closest liaison is necessary between individual Air Force units and the Army invasion forces. Also, to destroy important transport highways by which enemy reserves might be brought up, and to attack approaching enemy naval forces as far as possible from our disembarkation points. I request that suggestions be made to me regarding the employment of parachute and airborne troops. In this connection it should be considered, in conjunction with the Army, whether it would be useful at the beginning to hold parachute and airborne troops in readiness as a reserve, to be thrown in quickly in case of need.

4. Preparations to ensure the necessary communications between France and the English mainland will be handled by the Chief, Armed Forces Signals. The use of the remaining eighty kilometres of the East Prussia cable is to be examined in cooperation with the Navy.

5. I request Commanders-in-Chief to submit to me as soon as possible:
    a) The plans of the Navy and Air Force to establish the necessary conditions for crossing the Channel (see paragraph 2).
    b) Details of the building of coastal batteries (Navy).
    c) A general survey of the shipping required and the methods by which it is proposed to prepare and procure it. Should civil authorities be involved? (Navy).

d) The organisation of Air Defence in the assembly areas for invasion troops and ships (Air Force).
e) The crossing and operation plan of the Army, the composition and equipment of the first wave of invasion.
f) The organisation and plans of the Navy and Air Force for the execution of the actual crossing, for its protection, and for the support of the landing.
g) Proposals for the use of parachute and airborne troops and also for the organisation and command of antiaircraft artillery as soon as sufficient English territory has been captured.
h) Proposal for the location of Naval and Air Headquarters.
i) Views of the Navy and Air Force whether limited operations are regarded as useful before a general landing and, if so, of what kind.
j) Proposal from Army and Navy regarding command during the crossing.

[signed] Adolf Hitler

Some have considered this a definite commitment to invade southern England 'if necessary', meaning that in the absence of the British accepting terms, with Hitler's forthcoming Reichstag speech very much in mind, there would be no other means of eliminating 'the English homeland as a base for the prosecution of the war against Germany, and if necessary occupy it completely'. That masterful Hitler biographer and scholar Ian Kershaw, however, interprets the use of such language as reflecting Hitler's 'half-heartedness' towards the proposed invasion.

Ciano's diary, though, references the fact that on the same day, Hitler 'sent a long letter to the Duce. It announces the attack against England as something decided upon.' Moreover, Göring had total confidence in his *Luftwaffe*'s ability to defeat the RAF. Raeder, however, was under no illusion that given its strength, the *Kriegsmarine* was not adequately resourced to fulfil Hitler's requirements to maintain the sea-crossing lane mine-free, or sow sufficient minefields itself to keep the RN away; there was also no chance, he knew, if the survival of Britain was at stake, of pinning down RN ships away from the invasion area.

Hitler was aware of these things, leading the German historian Cajus Bekker to suggest that the dictator 'may well have deliberately made his conditions difficult as to bar any landing at all, or at least to provide an excuse for cancelling *Seelöwe*, should one of them not be fulfilled'.

Nonetheless, as Ronald Wheatley argues, 'With the signing of this Directive the invasion plan became a serious and important element in Hitler's strategy. No longer a tentative scheme, the landing was to be prepared as a major operation, ready for launching, if necessary, at the appointed time.'

That is true. However, Hitler was a master of 'brinkmanship', and this directive, along with the ongoing 'Air Fleet Diplomacy' in advance of his proposed speech, which he knew would represent a last appeal for the British to see reason, may well have been bluff in the hope of frightening Britain into submission. Whatever the truth of it, the whole enterprise clearly hung on the *Luftwaffe* achieving aerial supremacy, which – in spite of Göring's confidence – remained to be seen. So, if Britain still refused terms, now that Directive No.16 existed, there would come a time when either *Seelöwe* would go ahead – or be abandoned. Only time would tell, so these days in mid-July 1940 were pivotal to subsequent events.

From an air fighting perspective that day, perhaps ironically it was a quiet one. Fog enveloped northern France and south-east England, providing an opportunity for the day fighter squadrons to enjoy some rare off duty time. Instead of Spitfires, Hurricanes and Defiants droning over convoys, Blenheim night-fighters fulfilled the convoy protection role until midday, when the weather improved sufficiently for 242 Squadron to get up from Coltishall and cover a convoy off Great Yarmouth. In the south-west, although 238 Squadron sighted some Me 110s off Portland, these were quickly lost in the haze.

Again, first blood fell to Pilot Officer Dudley Stewart-Clark of 13 Group's 603 Squadron:

> At 1524 hrs Red Section was ordered to patrol Kinnaird's Head at Angels 20 when we were told that an E/A was bombing Peterhead and then Fraserburgh. Red 1 sighted the E/A and we went into line astern. E/A was making evasive turns and as he turned in front of me, across my sights and in range, I attacked first, opening with a short burst at about 250 yards on the quarter.
>
> I then got into an astern position and gave a long burst, closing from 300 yards to fifty yards. I saw my bullets entering the E/A, the end of the burst being at point blank range, and broke away. I experienced return fire from the E/A. Red 1 and 2 then attacked in turn and the E/A subsequently forced-landed in the sea. Two survivors in a rubber boat were picked up. I landed at 1646 hrs.

The victory was jointly shared by Red Section, Red 1 and 2 being Flying Officer Ian Ritchie and Pilot Officer James Morton respectively. The He 111 was another Norway-based bomber of 9/KG26, two of the crew being killed while the pilot, *Oberleutnant* Gerhard Lorenz, and *Unteroffizier* Heinz Beer were the survivors who Stewart-Clark had seen captured.

The next action for Fighter Command came South-west of Southampton at 17.00 hrs, as reported by Flight Lieutenant Willie Rhodes-Moorhouse of Tangmere's 601 Squadron:

> I was leading 'B' Flight and we took off at 1644 and 1658 hrs. I sighted one Ju 88 flying north-east just above 9/10 cloud over the West end of the Solent. I ordered an attack and followed E/A into

cloud where I lost it. I pulled up out of cloud to find Blue 2 and 3 making an attack, after E/A itself had pulled up.

I then made another attack and E/A went into vertical right-hand dive into cloud; I followed it and it continued vertically into the sea, hitting the water mid-way between The Needles and the mainland, slightly West of North of The Needles. Being the only aircraft below cloud I then reported E/A hitting the sea and ordered Blue Section to reform below cloud.

I then saw yet another Ju 88, about 900ft above, flying South, just coming out of cloud – so I climbed and made a beam attack after which I was just above E/A and made a steep-right-hand turn down on top of E/A, making another attack at point blank range until my ammunition ran out. I then saw that the starboard engine of E/A was stopped and the 'prop' was stationary with airscrew fully feathered. It then went into a shallow dive South until about 50–100ft above the sea.

I followed E/A, asking the Ground Station to send an aircraft with ammunition to finish it off. I eventually got into R/T communication with Green Section, whom I saw about 3,000ft above me and on my right. As Green Section saw me, the Ju 88 crashed into the sea and a yellow rubber boat appeared with one man in it and one swimming towards it. Green Section then circled the rubber boat and after about an hour the Germans were picked up. I then returned to base, landing at 1804 hrs. This E/A crashed about 10–15 miles South of The Needles.

Flight Lieutenant Rhodes-Moorhouse was credited with one Ju 88 destroyed, shared with members of Blue Section, and another personally destroyed. Again, the records appear deficient, because clearly there was no mistaking the fate of these two enemy bombers, but only one such loss appears recorded, a Ju 88 of 6/KG54, the two captured survivors from which being the pilot, *Feldwebel* Rudolf Forteman, and *Gefreiter* Herbert Augustin.

As far as Bomber Command was concerned, the bad weather in the morning of 16 July 1940 forced eleven Bomber Command Blenheims to abort raids on enemy airfields and invasion preparations. Of the four aircraft which continued their sorties, one attacked St Ingelvert airfield; another attacked some 300 barges, all lashed together, in the canal between Merville and Armentières, scoring a direct hit on one which sank, blocking the canal.

One of the Blenheims was intercepted by 6/JG54's Me 109s, the crew all killed. No nocturnal raids were made, again because of the weather, and Coastal Command's sorties this day were routine.

As we have seen, the surviving written documentation from the period can be contradictory, inconsistent and even incomplete, none of which is helpful to the provision of an entirely accurate interpretation of events. With great foresight, however, the Air Ministry issued a bulletin regarding the recording of reports:

It is natural that pilots should look upon the writing of combat reports as almost superfluous after they land. They may not realise the value of the flimsy green foolscap sheets of paper ... But history must be written as it is made and the reports ... are carefully filed away after they have been read by those officers who frame the policy of the Service. Combat Reports teach the lessons of experience, and any one sentence, written by a tired pilot who is impatient of the official appetite for foolscap paper, may be of great value to those in command.

Doubtless the Air Ministry was not thinking of such reports being such a crucial source to historians nearly a century after the Battle of Britain. Indeed, as Supermarine Test-Pilot and one of The Few Jeffrey Quill once said to me: 'Our minds were not focused on posterity in 1940'!

WEDNESDAY, 17 JULY 1940

After the Fall of France, many *Luftwaffe* units had withdrawn to bases in Germany to rest and re-fit, not least the fighters, which had ruled the skies, and *Stuka* dive-bombers, which had wrought such terrifying destruction. This meant that the bombers available to *Luftflotten* 2 and 3 for the ongoing war against Britain was a comparatively small force – until this day, when full readiness was ordered.

By now, the *Luftwaffe* was largely deployed to bases between Hamburg and Brest, facing West and within range of British targets – and the striking force now available for the war's ongoing prosecution had been increased to its intended strength.

To re-cap, the *Luftwaffe* in northern France comprised *Luftflotten* 2 and 3, their common boundary being the mouth of the Seine, and invisible northern line extending through the centre of England, thereby defining the formation's geographic area of responsibility. The brunt of fighting ahead would fall to these *Luftflotten*, the combined strength of which, by mid-July 1940, was:

Long-range bombers	1,200 (69 per cent of which actually serviceable by 20 July 1940)
Dive-bombers	280
Single-engine fighters	760 (*Luftflotte* 2: 460, 3: 300)
Twin-engine fighters	220 (*Luftflotte* 2: 90, 3: 130)
Long-range reconnaissance	50
Short-range army cooperation	90
Total	*2,600*

To the North lay the smaller *Luftflotten* 5, based in Norway, with 190 long-range bombers and reconnaissance aircraft, and twin-engine fighters. This would play little significant part until one particular day in August 1940, as we will in due course see, but the presence of this threat meant that Fighter Command had to also resource defence of north-east England – and figures available for 15 July 1940 indicate its strength at 603 fighters.

The fighter forces of *Luftflotten* 2 and 3 were reorganised under the tactical command of a *JagdfliegerFührer*, who enjoyed a degree of independence when planning fighter operations. Unlike Fighter Command's radar informed System of Fighter Control, however, the Germans had no such technology and so were unable to plot the disposition of enemy aircraft or track and control their own formations once airborne – which would prove a colossal disadvantage in the battle ahead.

As always, on this day of 17 July 1940, German reconnaissance bombers were active in the morning, regardless of the weather. At 12.10 hrs, Spitfires of Kenley's 64 Squadron intercepted a Do 17 prowling around South-west of base, but the enemy aircraft escaped in cloud. Then, at about 13.00 hrs, Red Section of 615 Squadron was scrambled from Hawkinge to intercept a Do 17, but although Red 2, Pilot Officer 'Dutch' Hugo, sighted and attacked a Do 17, the outcome was inconclusive as this intruder also made off into cloud.

At 13.30 hrs, twelve Spitfires of 64 Squadron were scrambled to patrol Beachy Head but were bounced by a single Me 109 South of the Isle of Wight – *Oberleutnant* Helmut Wick, an ace and *Staffelkapitän* of 3/JG2, based at Beaumont-le-Roger in *Luftflotte* 3's area.

At 14.07 hrs Wick claimed his fourteenth kill – a Spitfire destroyed. Wick, a protégé of *Major* Werner Mölders, wrote:

> In my first air battle I was terribly strung up ... the first air battles are tricky affairs ... your nerves are whipped up into fever pitch and your brain is all confused. After all, we are only human. After my first 'kill' I was much calmer.

On this occasion, Wick shot-up 64 Squadron's Flying Officer Don Taylor, who crashlanded at Hempstead Lane, Hailsham, wounded, and was admitted to Eastbourne Hospital with shrapnel in his head, torso, right arm and leg. Fortunately, Taylor survived his encounter with the deadly Wick in what was the perfect ambush by a lone hunter; none of 64 Squadron's pilots even saw the aircraft which attacked Taylor in what was inevitably a high-speed, fleeting, diving pass from high above.

To the West, three sections of Exeter's 213 Squadron were among those fighter squadrons patrolling without contact this day. Among the Hurricane pilots of 213 Squadron concerned was 25-year-old volunteer reservist Pilot Officer Alexander Osmand, a Londoner who had joined the squadron at Wittering on 17 June 1940, having converted to Hurricanes at 6 OTU, Sutton Bridge.

Between 14.55 and 15.40 hrs, Yellow Section, comprising Pilot Officer Osmand, Sub-Lieutenant William Moss of the FAA, and Flying Officer Raymond Kellow, patrolled Exeter without incident. It was, nonetheless, a significant sortie for Osmand, being his first operational patrol of the Battle of Britain.

Pilot Officer Osmand exchanged hundreds of letters with his intended, Miss Marjorie Hodges who lived in Peckham. Her letter to him on this particular day in part read:

> I did hear the commentary by Charles Gardner – it truly was amazing darling! You men of the RAF certainly know how to do things – we heard it at Pound Hill, and we were all positively jumping with excitement. As for our Winston and his 1942 – well I guess if the war goes on until then – I will marry an Air Force Officer ... Darling – I shall make an amazing wife. I shall be so terribly happy and thrilled all the time you are there that I wouldn't do anything else – instead of doing anything at all really useful. I should want to be in your arms every precious moment you were with me.
>
> I suppose dearest that in time I should settle down to become a model wife etc. but I can't see that happening – all my life I shall want you not as the ordinary run of husbands just become a mere man about the house – but always my sweetheart and my lover. Our love will never grow old or less full – with time it will grow and our life will be full of joy and peace with each other wherever we may go, whatever we may do, and whatever may go on in the world around.

Whether Marjorie's hopes for a utopian existence with her beloved were but a forlorn hope remained to be seen.

Returning to the action on 17 July 1940, 145 Squadron would be the next engaged, up from Tangmere at 14.55 hrs.

Flight Lieutenant Roy Dutton reported that:

> I was leading Red Section of 'A' Flight on interception patrol. While patrolling near St Catherine's Point, Yellow Leader (Squadron Leader John Peel) decided to investigate a smoke trail over the Cherbourg peninsula. When 15–20 miles North of the peninsula two aircraft was sighted heading North, approaching from the direction of Le Havre.
>
> Yellow Leader went down to investigate while I stayed above with my Section, to act as a guard in the event of enemy fighters appearing. It was my impression at first that these aircraft were Blenheims. I became suspicious, however, when they turned SW and then towards Cherbourg. They appeared to have Blenheim-type camouflage and yellow rings on the wings.

I attacked the starboard E/A following attacks made by Yellow Section. I received considerable fire from the rear gunner but was not hit by any bullets. As I closed range to 250 yards the E/A released two large bombs, also a considerable quantity of bits and pieces, some of which appeared to be bands of wire, then came past me and one burst damaged the leading edge of my starboard wing root.

Shortly after my opening burst the starboard engine began to smoke heavily and the E/A broke formation and slow down. After firing all my rounds I broke off to the right. During this break-away I noticed that I was being fired at by the top rear-gunner. I circled for a while but did not see the E/A crash.

I then turned for home and was joined by the remainder of the Flight.

Squadron Leader Peel's Hurricane was badly damaged in the engagement, but he escaped injury and all 145 Squadron's aircraft had landed safely back at base by 16.00 hrs. Flight Lieutenant Dutton was accredited with two Ju 88s damaged, although it seems one of these, an aircraft of I/KG51, was lost in combat over the Channel, the crew were all killed.

The final fighter action of the day occurred at 19.15 hrs when, as the ORB notes, Pilot Officer Cecil Saunders of 92 Squadron 'contacted a Ju 88 over Bristol. It got away after Pilot Officer Saunders had used up all his ammunition and had received several bullet holes in his wings.'

That day, Coastal Command lost a 59 Squadron Blenheim, shot down by *Leutnant* Hans-Folkert Rosenboom of 3/JG27, ten kilometres North of Cherbourg.

By day, Bomber Command sent thirteen Blenheims to attack airfields and barges, only two of which found their targets, owing to the poor weather, and likewise by night only a handful of RAF bombers hit their marks.

The Battle of Britain was now officially a week old – and there was no sign of Fighter Command being weakened by the enemy's efforts to date.

AC1 Bill Ellams was an Airframe Rigger on 611 Squadron's 'B' Flight at Digby, in 12 Group, and remembered life on a Spitfire squadron during the Battle of Britain:

> God I was thrilled when they gave me a Spitfire to look after! We slept in dug-outs on dispersal near the aircraft, and were up every morning at dawn to run up and check everything. Despite it being summer, as the flight mechanic revved up the Merlin, we riggers were straddled over the tailplane, to hold the aircraft down, frozen in the slipstream! Once a Spitfire overrode the chocks and moved forward despite the brakes being applied! I was so cold and numb that I didn't give a damn.

Incidentally, the Dunlop air brakes were the weak part of the Spitfire. I must have spent hours of my time upside down in the cockpit adjusting the air valves to synchronise the pressure with the rudder bar.

While on standby we would clean the Spitfires with a wax dissolved in a petrol mixture, let it dry then polish it like hell to get a shine. The crew undertaking this often included the pilot who also mucked in. By doing this we could get an extra 5 mph in flight. At Digby we very much regarded ourselves as a team, including the pilot who was more or less considered a friend. We would discuss with him things like the 'hands off' technique. I would place a bit of string doped on the control surfaces or trimming tabs to get perfection – amazing what a little knowledge of aerodynamics could do!

Getting the Spitfire back in the air as quickly as possible was very important to the rigger, mechanic and armourer. Our team would rehearse the routine over and over again. We could all check control surfaces, refuel and rearm in just four minutes. We made short-handled screwdrivers to undo and fasten the *Dzus* buttons which secured the panels. Believe me, these were exciting times! During a panic turnaround, I was passing along the leading edge of the mainplane, the armourer was rearming and reloading the Browning guns when as he was pulling back the striking pin with his toggle he slipped – there was a round up the spout, the bullet passed by my face but I didn't even pause; afterwards, when the kite had taken off, I said a prayer and broke out into a sweat!

Another nasty piece of work was on take-off. The rigger stood by the starter trolley while the pilot primed the engine. When the engine fired I had to pass along the leading edge of the mainplane and take out the plug just behind the airscrew, fasten up the little panel with the *Dzus* fastener, run back and pull the chocks away. That airscrew so near one's arm and shoulder was not at all nice, especially as the pilot was anxious to get moving forward to take-off in formation! Many a time I had to duck to let the mainplane pass above my head.

I remember our Sergeant Levenson taking off early one morning in his pyjamas, with flying helmet, jacket, one boot and no trousers – panic stations! He was a shade of blue upon return, but it was no funk. A particular officer pilot even used to spray the inside of his cockpit with lavender water but he was no pansy. Other pilots had lucky charms but I never once saw a frightened face. The comradeship between pilots and groundcrews was wonderful.

While on duty we were never allowed away from the Spitfires, meals were brought out to dispersal. While stood down we had hobbies: I made model aircraft, Gilly Potter grew vegetables, Len Carver made paper knives out of old salvaged flying wire and put Perspex handles on them. Some made a poker and pontoon gang and played with matches, others tried to filter the green dye out of the 100-octane petrol, to sell to the pilots who often had cars but no fuel. I bought an old bicycle and did it up like new, and while off duty used to cycle to Lincoln and enjoy egg and chips at the Salvation Army Canteen, price one shilling!

THURSDAY, 18 JULY 1940

On the Axis political stage, the tension was building regarding what Hitler would do next, and the outcome of his forthcoming and all-important speech.

In his diary, Count Ciano wrote that 'The Germans inform us at the last moment that Hitler's speech will be made tomorrow at 7 pm.' The Italian foreign minister left for Berlin immediately, meeting with his Nazi counterpart, the Reichsminister for Foreign Affairs, Joachim von Ribbentrop, who confirmed that Hitler's long-awaited speech really would be 'a last appeal to Great Britain'.

Candidly, Ciano added in his diary: 'I understand that, without their saying so, however, they are hoping and praying that this appeal will not be rejected.'

The British, though, had already made the unwavering and momentous decision to fight it out behind Churchill – although Hitler's hopes for a negotiated peace were understandable, given previous diplomatic events.

During the 1930s, Britain had to deal with a changing European order, dominated by fascist Germany and Italy, both states hell-bent on aggressive territorial expansion. Unprepared for war, Britain's National Government under Neville Chamberlain preserved peace through conceding to Hitler's demands. On 20 February 1938, British Foreign Secretary Anthony Eden, resigned in protest after Chamberlain, in the wake of the Italian-Ethiopian War, entered into friendly relations with Mussolini's Italy. However, at no time during Eden's term of office (1935–38) did he oppose the policy of appeasing Hitler, or condemn the Nazi dictator's contravention of Versailles when the Rhineland was reoccupied. Eden's successor was Lord Halifax, a supporter of Chamberlain.

Going forward, Halifax's diplomacy focused upon an alliance with the Soviets – ultimately thwarted on 29 August 1939, when the Soviet foreign minister, Molotov, and von Ribbentrop signed the Treaty of Non-Aggression between Germany and the Union of Soviet Socialist Republics – an unholy alliance indeed. After Germany invaded Poland on 1 September 1939, although 'Lord Holy Fox' refused to negotiate with Hitler while German troops remained on Polish soil, he supported Chamberlain's view that Britain should not declare war against Nazi Germany until France committed to such a conflict.

A Cabinet revolt, however, insisted that Britain honour the guarantee previously made to Poland and so, reluctantly, Britain and France declared war on Germany two days later. In fairness to Halifax, from that point on he refused to negotiate with Germany or compromise throughout the 'Phoney War'.

When Chamberlain resigned in May 1940, over Norway, the Conservative Halifax was the preferred successor of the King, Chamberlain, and even the Labour Party. Halifax himself disagreed – believing that the energetic and indomitable Churchill was the best and rightful war leader. When the BEF became isolated around Dunkirk, however, Halifax argued for a peace with Germany, negotiated through Mussolini. Churchill countered that 'nations which went down fighting rose again, but those which surrendered tamely were finished'. Moreover, Churchill argued that Hitler was hardly likely to honour any agreement, and rightly believed that his determination to fight back rather than compromise or negotiate was supported by the British people.

Given the years of Appeasement and lack of decisive action by Britain, it is easy to understand why Hitler still felt that Britain could be persuaded to back down – and in Germany, with Europe at his feet, Hitler was the man of the hour. Berlin newspapers were cock-a-hoop, predicting with joyful optimism Britain's impending downfall, the *Nachtausgabe* evening paper reporting that: 'The whole of England is trembling on the brink of a decision. There is only the slight possibility of England offering any military resistance ... The British people are in downright fear of forthcoming military and political events.'

Continuation of the war, the German newspapers proclaimed, was 'Churchill's crime against the British people'. German radio announced that:

> In England, men and women feel the urge to raise their courage by resorting to drink ... Alcoholic poisoning is increasing by leaps and bounds ... Press gangs under Sergeants are visiting cinemas, cabarets and tea rooms to enrol young civilians as trench diggers ... Fear in England is indeed terrific. Evidence of this is that the Jews are having their hair bleached and noses straightened.

For three days, between 25 and 28 May 1940, Halifax and Churchill made out their cases to the War Cabinet. The latter, however, called his Outer Cabinet together, delivering an impassioned appeal, convincing all present that Britain must fight on with these grim words:

> If this long island story of ours is to end at last, let it end only when each of us lies choking in his own blood upon the ground.

With Churchill at the helm, there was no ambiguity as to Britain's direction of travel – and that was far away from any suggestion of a negotiated peace with a deluded and over-confident Nazi Germany. Halifax lost the argument, and Britain had emerged

KANALKAMPF DIARY, 10 JULY – 31 JULY 1940

from the Fall of France and entered the Battle of Britain resolved to fight on. On the eve of Hitler's 'last appeal to reason', that resolve remained unwavering.

Although the weather was poor, cloudy, unsettled and punctuated by thunderstorms, German bombers were active over Britain by night and into the early hours of 18 July 1940. At 00.11 hrs 928 (Balloon Barrage) Squadron, based at Harwich on the East Coast, reported a 'balloon cable struck by plane'. Later that morning raiders were active over Scotland, four people being killed and others injured when the Rolls-Royce factory in Glasgow was targeted by four Do 17s, and a lone He 111 attacked Montrose airfield, damaging aircraft on the ground and killing two airmen.

A Spitfire pilot, Pilot Officer 'Raz' Berry, also of 603 Squadron, however, engaged the bomber without making a claim subsequently, but at 16.40 hrs, Pilot Officer 'Sheep' Gilroy of the same unit was hit in the coolant system (Spitfire R6755) by return fire from another He 111, and forced-landed at Old Meldrum, while Pilot Officer James Morton's Spitfire (L1049) was damaged while engaging another intruder. Sergeant James Caistor was also in action, attacking a Ju 88 ten miles off Aberdeen, which was considered to have very probably crashed – the bomber, of I/KG30, crash-landed at Aalborg in Norway with a wounded crewman aboard. Inevitably, however, these engagements were a sideshow, the main action taking place over southern England.

At 09.37 hrs, Flight Lieutenant E.B.B. Smith scrambled from Biggin Hill, leading eleven other 610 Squadron Spitfires, 'ordered to investigate E/A reported to be approaching Ramsgate from between Calais and Dunkirk'. As ever, convoys chugged along the Channel, and it is likely that the 11 Group Controller assumed that the German formation represented yet another threat to the merchantmen. While radar provided the defenders with the immeasurable advantage of an early warning of enemy formations assembling over France and striking out towards the English coast, what it could not do was identify the aircraft types involved.

On this occasion, at 6,000ft over the Channel and some ten miles off Calais, the Spitfires were met not by a formation of bombers as expected, but ambushed by the high-flying Me 109s of 5/JG51. With the advantage of height and surprise, the German *Staffelkapitän*, *Hauptmann* Horst Tietzen, a veteran of the Spanish Civil War, led his fighters into a fleeting, high-speed, diving pass through the Spitfires, picking off a British fighter as he flashed by. Owing to cloud cover, and speed of the enemy attack, only two Spitfire pilots managed ineffective snapshots at their assailants. 'One aircraft was seen to go straight down into the sea', this being Tietzen's eighth victim, 25-year-old Pilot Officer Peter Litchfield, who remains missing (Spitfire DW-T, P9452).

Next, the action shifted to the south-west. At 10.10 hrs, the three Spitfires of Yellow Section, 152 Squadron, which had only recently arrived at Warmwell, was scrambled to patrol a convoy passing Portland. The ships had already attracted the enemy's attention, however, and almost immediately after take-off and reaching the nearby coast, the 'Hyderabad' pilots sighted forty enemy aircraft flying at just 2,000ft.

Yellow Leader, Pilot Officer Ian Bayles, put the Section in line astern and headed for the trouble. The Spitfires were outnumbered by over 13:1 – and here we have the myth of 'The Few'. The popular narrative, propagandised in wartime, is that the Battle of Britain was fought and won by a handful of plucky Hurricane and Spitfire pilots facing overwhelming odds. In truth, on paper, the opposing forces were reasonably well matched, and Fighter Command was never worn down to its last reserves.

The truth of it lay in the tactics with which the Battle of Britain was fought, with small, flexible, formations flung against large numbers of incoming raiders, RAF commanders and sector controllers juggling the need for executing maximum damage to the enemy while preserving their own forces, especially when fighting over the sea. Fighter Command's strength was dispersed around the country, not simply concentrated in southern England, because the whole of the British Isles lay within range of German bombers and Air Chief Marshal Dowding had a responsibility to defend the entire country. This, though, provided for battered squadrons to be withdrawn to quieter sectors and replaced in the line by replenished and refreshed units, while maintaining a vigilant all-round defence. So the RAF aircrew engaged in the main combat area of southern England, fighting in small penny-packet formations, really were facing overwhelming odds – despite statistics of overall aircraft and aircrew numbers.

A 152 Squadron combat report:

> At 1025 hrs a Do 215 was sighted and Yellow Leader was about to attack when Dornier flashed a white signal. Yellow Leader moved slightly to port to identify then gave a burst from almost astern. Yellow 3 (Pilot Officer Richard Hogg) then warned that two Me 109s had passed either side of him and heard an explosion as his port wing was hit. He turned and lost sight of his Section.
>
> Using cloud cover he returned to protect the convoy until relieved by Green Section. Yellow 2 (Pilot Officer Charles Warren) prepared to follow Yellow Leader into the attack, heard Yellow 3's warning and saw three Me 109s above and to his right. He took evasive action but E/A got on his tail and fired a short burst; Yellow 3 easily out-turned him. E/A broke off and climbed.
>
> Yellow 2 followed to 12,000ft but could not catch him and returned to the convoy, looking for Yellow Leader. Yellow 3 was attacked by another Me 109, which he evaded.
>
> Yellow 3, seeing Yellow 1 and 2 breaking away right and left, and no enemy fighters, attacked the Do 215 from astern and fired all his ammunition, opening at 300 and closing to 150ft, saw no return fire or damage to the E/A, which did a gentle turn into cloud and was lost.

Pilot Officer Hogg had, in fact, fatally hit the Dornier, of *Stab*/StG 77, which failed to return to base and the crew of which all remain missing.

KANALKAMPF DIARY, 10 JULY – 31 JULY 1940

Like the earlier *Luftflotte* 2 fighter sweep over the Channel, which had caught 610 Squadron unawares, this incursion by *Luftflotte* 3 was a similar *Freie Hunt*, excepting the lone Do 17 reconnaissance bomber, by JG2. Although the Spitfires of Pilot Officers Bayles and Warren were damaged in the skirmish, both pilots lived to tell the tale, although *Oberleutnant* Karl-Heinz Greisert of 2/JG2 claimed at Spitfire destroyed over the Isle of Wight at 11.20 hrs (Continental time).

Across the Channel, at 10 15 hrs *Hauptmann* Rubensdörffer led Me 110s of his *Erprobungsgruppe* 210 up from St Omer, heading for the Thames Estuary seeking targets of opportunity. Crossing the Channel at 0ft, off Lowestoft the raiders attacked a convoy of ten ships, which reacted with only light anti-aircraft fire. The Germans hit two ships, estimated to be 1,000 tons each, which were seen ablaze and claimed as sunk, although no such losses can be traced in mercantile marine records. The Me 110 pilots also claimed to have been attacked themselves by two Blenheims, one of which was subsequently shot down into the sea.

More likely, this was actually a pair of Detling's 500 Squadron Ansons, Sergeant Barr and crew (Anson MK-G) later reporting having engaged and shot down an Me 110 into the sea. No record exists, however, of either a relevant Me 110 or RAF loss. Some accounts have accredited this action to a 15 Squadron Blenheim, but it is written that *Erprobungsgruppe* 210 had returned to base by midday, whereas the potential Wyton-based 15 Squadron aircraft did not take-off until 14.05 hrs; the squadron's diary entry for the day is intriguing:

> Two aircraft left today on individual bombing raids on Sterkrade Holten. The first, with Flight Sergeant St John, Sergeant Sargent and Sergeant Beggs, returned through lack of cloud cover, but on the way back they made a photo recco of canals in Holland and Belgium.
>
> The second aircraft, with Pilot Officer Mahler, Sergeant Paveley and Sergeant Baker, left at 1405 hrs on the same raid but after they had crossed the coast and were some ten miles out to sea, three Me 110s broke formation. Two dived towards our aircraft, bursts were exchanged. The first Me 110 broke off the engagement. The second then forced an attack.
>
> Our aircraft put in a burst at close range. It is presumed that this aircraft crashed into the sea. The third aircraft attacked and our aircraft was damaged considerably. The Air-Gunner and Observer reported inner tanks ablaze. By this time our aircraft had made a landfall two miles from the coast and the pilot dived to make a forced-landing on the beach. This was successful.
>
> The crew ran for cover, no sooner had they done so than the aircraft blew up. An army officer reported that he saw the second Me 110 go down into the sea. [ORB]

No German casualty can be identified relating to this crash. However, a pair of 235 Squadron Blenheims, based at Bircham Newton, had become separated in bad weather while patrolling a convoy, one of which failed to return. Could this have been the aircraft the eye-witness had seen crash?

No such ambiguity surrounds the loss of two 236 Squadron Blenheims lost this day, though. At 11.20 hrs, three of the squadron's Blenheims left Thorney Island to escort a reconnaissance aircraft to photograph the port of Le Havre:

> Weather was bad with rain and thick cloud. Intense and accurate black AA fire from Cap de la Hague and light AA from South edge of harbour. On turning to keep in touch with escorted machine the leader (Flight Lieutenant Power) lost sight of Flying Officer Thomas and Pilot Officer Rigby due to heavy cloud and they were not seen again. They failed to return and have since been posted as missing.

Without doubt, the two missing Blenheims had been picked off by Me 109s scrambled in response, *Hauptmann* Wolfgang Schellmann of *Stab* II/JG2 claiming one destroyed North of Le Havre at 13.15 hrs, *Unteroffizier* Willi Meichert of 5/JG2 following suit ten minutes later. Indeed, likewise the fate of Detling's 53 Squadron's Flying Officer Mahoney and crew was never in doubt: on a reconnaissance sortie to the port of Flushing, this Blenheim was shot down into the North Sea off Vlissingen by *Feldwebel* Georg Kiening of 6/JG54.

At 13.00 hrs, 'B' Flight of Tangmere's 145 Squadron was ordered up to patrol base at 10,000ft, then told to make 'Vector 240°, Angels 10'. Fifteen miles South of Selsey Bill, the Hurricanes sighted and attacked a He 111.

Pilot Officer Parrott subsequently reported that:

> I led Green Section below the cloud, which was at 600ft. The E/A dived below cloud and I went into a beam attack; No 2 came in on a beam attack on my right. As I broke away, I saw the E/A dive into the sea and break up. There were two survivors, one of whom sank almost immediately. I gave Control a 'fix' on the remaining survivor, who was still swimming when we returned to base. No return fire was observed when he came below cloud, although two of Blue Section were hit by enemy machine-gun.

The raider belonged to *Stab*/KG27; three crew-men were killed, including the *Geschwaderkommodore*, *Oberst* Georgi.

Just as 145 Squadron's Hurricanes scrambled from Tangmere, at 13.00 hrs the Spitfires of 609 Squadron, based at Middle Wallop, touched down at Warmwell, operating from that forward airfield, just inland of Weymouth, for the rest of the day. At 15.15 hrs, Red Section – Flight Lieutenant Frank Howell, Flying Officer Alexander Edge and Sergeant Alan Feary – engaged a Ju 88 South-east of Swanage.

All three pilots made two attacks, but not without mishap. The Ju 88 had suddenly appeared out of cloud directly in front of Howell, who detailed Edge and Feary to cover him from attack by any German fighters. Sighting the danger, the Ju 88 jettisoned its bombs and dived towards the sea at over 350 mph.

The Spitfires then attacked but Howell's aircraft was hit by return fire in the coolant system:

> White fumes began pouring back into the cockpit, so that I was really not good enough. The poor old motor began seizing up ... I called 'Bandy' (Control) and said I was baling out four miles off Poole ... and stepped smartly from the aircraft. Everything was lovely ... chucked my helmet away but kept the goggles.
>
> Undid my shoes, blew up my Mae West, and leaned back and admired the scenery. The water quite suddenly became very close – a swish, and then I began my final swim of the season.
>
> I set out with a lusty crawl for Bournemouth, thinking I might shoot a hell of a line staggering up the beach with beauteous barmaids dashing down the beach with bottles of brandy – instead the current was taking me out to sea, and I was unceremoniously hauled aboard a 12-ft motorboat.
>
> Still, the Navy pushed the boat out and the half tumbler of whisky went down with a rush!

Having found no enemy fighters, Flying Officer Edge had joined the pursuit after Howell's initial attack and the Ju 88 jettisoned its bombs:

> Finding the speed of the diving E/A exceedingly high, I used the emergency boost cut-out and overtook it at approximately 400 mph. Owing to the controls being almost immovable, I found it impossible to do any attack other than astern. I closed to within 100ft or less, firing for about five seconds, and observed two streams of tracer which appeared to be parallel and about 20ft apart, passing my machine on each side.
>
> I then broke away and watched Red 1 make another attack, after which I made an attack from the quarter, closing to dead astern, owing to the excessive speed. I again observed the parallel streams of return fire. The E/A now levelled out about 10ft above the sea and I attacked from the starboard quarter and above, expending all ammunition.
>
> The port motor of E/A, which had been emitting white smoke after Red 1's initial attack, now appeared to be functioning normally. When last observed the E/A was flying steadily towards the South about ten miles offshore. I turned towards the coast, flying at about

> 100ft, until I noticed my glycol temperature was off the clock. I succeeded in climbing about 1,000ft when the cockpit filled with the glycol fumes and similar fumes streamed from the engine cowling. I succeeded in forcing the machine as far as the beach at Studland Bay, by which time, owing to the excessive fumes, it was difficult to see anything from the cockpit.
>
> I turned into wind and carried out a forced-landing with wheels retracted, the machine being very little damaged. On examining the aircraft I found a bullet hole through each wing; that in the starboard having apparently pierced the coolant pipes. I recovered the cine-camera magazine and placed a military guard on the aircraft, which was covered by the sea at high tide.

Some years later, Wing Commander Edge, as he became, recalled more of this forced-landing:

> Before I could get out, the Army appeared higher up the beach, yelling that I should stay where I was, as the beach was mined. Eventually I was conducted along an approved route and given the hospitality of their Mess in a seaside bungalow. They were extremely helpful and got hold of a local farmer who brought a pair of cart horses and made a valiant attempt to drag my kite out of the water. Not surprisingly they failed even to move it and the aircraft was engulfed by the incoming tide.

The Spitfire, R6636, was later recovered. The enemy rear-gunner had certainly performed well, shooting down two Spitfires, the action highlighting yet again just how vulnerable crucial systems were to fatal damage – often by just a single round.

The Ju 88, however, is not believed to have escaped; according to the 609 Squadron ORB, three sources reported it down in the sea, although unconfirmed. One II/LG1 Ju 88 returned to base damaged by RAF fighters, with a dead crewman aboard, while another crew was reported missing, so it is possible that the Ju 88 engaged by Red Section was one of these bombers.

At 18.00 hrs, 609 Squadron's Yellow Section caught a Ju 88 attacking a convoy off Portland, the intruder being promptly attacked and damaged by Pilot Officers John 'Bish' Bisdee and Charles 'Teeny' Overton (again, probably one of the II/LG1 machines referred to above). Afterwards, the Section,

> intercepted a long-nose Blenheim [the Mk IV bomber version] at 12,000ft over Warmwell. It looked very new and had the ordinary British markings on it. It aroused suspicion by taking violent evasive action, and Yellow 3 did a feint attack on it, but no one liked to fire at it. Blenheim last seen going due South, out to sea.

Pilot Officer Michael Appleby:

> On 18 July 1940 I did five sorties, on one of which, a patrol of Lyme Regis, Swanage and Weymouth, I acted as Section Leader, that is the leading aircraft of a section of three, but nothing of any event occurred so as the weather closed in we returned and patrolled base for half an hour before landing.
>
> The strain of waiting at dispersal, however, I will never forget, was greatly emphasised by the field telephone; every time it rang everyone would just stop until the operator answering would call out, perhaps, 'Sergeant so and so required in Sick Quarters', at which point we all promptly relaxed.
>
> On the other hand, when it was a scramble, we all rushed to our aircraft, preceded by the fitter and rigger, popped into the cockpit, set our parachute and safety harnesses, quite tight too, and having got the throttle mixture control and airscrew pitch controls set, the fitter operated the starter battery and the engine started. Then off we would go, taking off in formation, and after that, who knew what would happen?

On this day, Bomber Command sent forty-one Blenheims to attack Belgian and Dutch ports. Late that afternoon, the fighters of 111 Squadron left Croydon, and those of 615 from Kenley, and headed to Hawkinge, from which coastal airfield the Hurricanes escorted eighteen Blenheims to attack Boulogne harbour, and, as the 111 Squadron ORB notes, 'they all returned, after dropping bombs on jetties and docks. Balloon barrage was close hauled on barges and no E/A were seen'.

Certainly no enemy fighters were encountered, but 111 Squadron's Blue Section engaged and badly damaged a Henschel Hs 126 communications aircraft. According to 615 Squadron, the raid was 'highly successful'. One aircraft of the overall Blenheim force was lost; 101 Squadron's Flying Officer F.E.R. Ducker and crew, who failed to return from raiding enemy airfields in France and remain missing.

By night, Bomber Command despatched sixty-eight Hampdens and Wellingtons to six targets, losing one Wellington, while in a new feature of the night-bombing war, three crews approaching the end of their conversion courses at 15 OTU, Harwell, carried out propaganda leaflet drops over France, and one of these aircraft bombed an airfield.

FRIDAY, 19 JULY 1940

Although still cloudy and showery, the nine convoys steaming off the British coast prompted Air Vice-Marshal Park to move more fighters than usual to operate from coastal airfields, in anticipation of increased enemy air activity. Inevitably, the first intrusions were by German reconnaissance bombers.

Early on, a Do 17 of 4(F)/121 slipped undetected through to Croydon, being reported by the Observer Corps as 'Raid 15'. In response, Yellow and Red Sections of 145 Squadron, led by Squadron Leader John Peel, were scrambled from Tangmere at 06.03 hrs and vectored towards the bandit.

The Hurricane pilots found 9/10ths cloud between 2,000–6,000ft, which broke up close to the coast. North-west of Redhill the raider was sighted ten miles ahead of Peel's fighters, which were passing North-north-west over Staines. The bandit dived for cloud cover and the Hurricanes gave chase. During the subsequent game of cat and mouse, the Hurricanes became separated, but when Squadron Leader Peel contacted the Do 17 again, he was joined by the three Hurricanes of 257 Squadron's Green Section, which had scrambled from Northolt at 06.30 hrs and also vectored towards Raid 15.

At 06.54 hrs, according to Flying Officer Lancelot Mitchell, Green 1 of 257 Squadron, and 07.00 hrs as reported by Squadron Leader Peel, the bomber was shot down into the sea, twenty miles South of Brighton. As 145 Squadron's CO flew low over the crash, he saw an enemy airman among the debris.

At this time, a small number of aircraft in each unit were fitted with a navigational aid called 'Pip-squeak', the device automatically switching the TR9D radio's channel for fourteen seconds of every minute to transmit a homing signal to ground direction-finding stations, enabling the exact position of the aircraft to be fixed. Peel's Yellow 2, the New Zealander Pilot Officer Robert Yule, was flying the Section's 'Pip-squeak' aircraft and so was ordered by Peel to orbit the spot and fix the position, in the hope of the German airman being rescued. Unfortunately there would be no survivors; the victory was jointly shared by 145 Squadron's Yellow Section, and 257 Squadron's Green Section.

Sadly, however, this would develop into a black day indeed for Fighter Command, as Air Chief Marshal Dowding's grave concerns regarding the Defiant were tragically proved correct.

Fighter Command possessed two squadrons of the Boulton-Paul Defiant turret fighter, Nos. 141 and 264, the latter which had seen action, with a degree of success offsetting losses, during the Dunkirk fighting.

No.141 Squadron, doubtless inspired by 264 Squadron's performance, was keen to enter the fray, and on 9 July 1940 had been sent South from Turnhouse to 11 Group. Squadron HQ was to be established at Biggin Hill, while the Defiants were to operate from West Malling, near Maidstone, an advance airfield for both Biggin Hill and Kenley. By 13 July 1940, the move was complete. The following day, 141 Squadron's CO, Squadron Leader William Richardson, led a flight of six Defiants on their first operational sortie in 11 Group, a patrol of West Malling at 8,000ft. Further, similar, patrols were made over the next few days without meeting the enemy. On 18 July 1940, 141 Squadron flew further South, from West Malling, to operate, uneventfully, from Hawkinge, returning to West Malling that evening.

At 08.45 hrs on 19 July 1940 – coincidentally Squadron Leader Richardson's thirty-seventh birthday, an old man by fighter pilot standards – 141 Squadron again left West Malling for Hawkinge, being among the fighter squadrons Air Vice-Marshal Park was moving forward in anticipation of trouble.

The pattern of enemy air operations during the period 12 to 19 July 1940, certainly on five out of the eight days, was to operate in strength, deploying formations of mixed bomber types with strong fighter cover. Having rapidly reached their targets – Channel shipping – bombers would immediately turn for home, which was a comparatively short distance away.

The German fighters would remain, however, ready to pounce on any RAF fighters. Due to speed, distance and time, the defending fighters generally arrived as independent flight or squadron formations, often too late to prevent ships being bombed, but on two occasions out of the eight, both large-scale raids, German bombers were intercepted while retiring. Invariably, the German fighters, loitering over the sea, eager for action, enjoyed the height advantage, having climbed from their French bases to 10,000–20,000ft, with the bombers approaching their targets some distance below. This would be a significant factor in the tragedy about to unfold.

On 19 July 1940, *Oberst* Theo Osterkampf's JG51 was based in the Pas-de-Calais, the *Geschwader*'s various units dispersed around largely temporary airfields inland of Cap Blanc Nez and Wissant, and around St Omer. No. III/JG51's *GruppenKommandeur* was a very experienced fighter leader, *Hauptmann* Johannes Trautloft, who had become an ace in 1936, fighting over Spain with Germany's Legion *Kondor*, destroying five republican aircraft before later destroying a Polish fighter on 5 September 1939, and two Spitfires over Dunkirk in May 1940.

Unlike the RAF, a comparatively small peacetime air force, the ranks of which had been substantially swelled by the amateur volunteers of the AAF and RAFVR, *Luftwaffe* personnel were all professional airmen. Trautloft, born near Weimar on 3 March 1912, had learned to fly in 1931, spending four months the following year at the secretly reborn *Luftwaffe*'s training base in Russia. Already an experienced officer, he was one of the first six German pilots to arrive in Spain, and jointly recorded the first German victories in support of Franco. Although he initially flew He-51 biplanes in Spain, these were replaced by the Me 109, which proved itself in Spanish skies. Trautloft, in fact, became responsible for developing fighter tactics with the 109, so all of his experience to date made him a most dangerous foe indeed.

Trautloft himself described the scene across the Channel, on the day in question:

> Just as we were sitting down for lunch in our tent, a mission order from the *Geschwader* (Fighter Group 51 HQ) arrived: 'At 1300 hrs [Continental time] III *Gruppe* [third wing, comprising three squadrons, of JG51] will escort, with all available aircraft, a *Zestörergruppe* [destroyer wing] of Me 110s, which will make a dive-bombing attack on a British freighter, equipped with AA guns, north-east of Dover.

I had the *Staffel* [squadron] leaders report to discuss the *Gruppe* mission. In the meantime, *Hauptmann* Rubensdörffer, commander of the Me 110 *Zestörergruppe Erprobungsgruppe 210* [an experimental, precision, bombing unit], telephoned and told me how he was going to approach and attack the target. Soon we agreed on measures for the protection of his unit's outward and return flights.

At exactly 1300 hrs, the *Zestörergruppe* appeared over our airfield at St Omer. We took-off and one *JagdStaffel* [fighter squadron] positioned itself to the left, one to the right and one above the Me 110s.

Immediately after taking-off I could see the English coast. Never before had the weather been as clear as it was that day. Until reaching the French coast we flew at 500 metres under scattered cloud. At the coast, the clouds cleared and a clear, blue, sky extended before us. We climbed to 3,000 metres and set course for the target, which we could already see from the French coast. When we got closer, the enemy spotted us; the ship began zig-zagging at high speed.

Exactly eighteen minutes after take-off we were over our target, which the *Zestörers* dive-bombed, dropping their bombs at 800 metres before pulling out of their dives and climbing again. They then flew home, so we escorted and shepherded them to safety.

As we still had sufficient fuel remaining, I decided to do some 'free-hunting' with the *Gruppe* – the British fighters must be somewhere. Maybe they had not been alerted quickly enough and were on their way? In anticipation of this, we headed back out over the Channel again. I flew with my *Stabsschwarm* [wing staff section, of four Me 109s] at 3,000 metres. My three *Staffeln* were in loose formation, some 1,000 metres higher. Visibility was so good that one could see any aircraft taking-off from the airfields near the coast.

Trautloft knew that a small number of fighters were more likely to effect a successful ambush; the Germans, playing to the technical advantages of their aircraft, often attacking in high-speed, diving, passes – and away. Several thousand feet above, over thirty Me 109s provided a protective umbrella for their leader.

Thus, the scene for battle was set.

Just after midday, radar stations provided early warning of enemy formations assembling over the Pas-de-Calais, and German dive-bombers were reported attacking shipping off Dover at 12.15 hrs. With a surprising delay, it was not until 12.20 hrs that the Hurricanes of 111 Squadron's 'B' Flight were scrambled from Hawkinge, led by Squadron Leader John Thompson, to 'intercept enemy aircraft in the vicinity. Squadron was ordered North, as far as Deal, at 10,000ft.'

At 12.30 hrs, 141 Squadron was also scrambled from Hawkinge, with orders, the ORB states, 'to patrol twenty miles South of Folkestone at 5,000ft. Three aircraft fail to leave the ground in time, nine only carry out the patrol.'

KANALKAMPF DIARY, 10 JULY – 31 JULY 1940

Trautloft had correctly guessed that although the RAF had been slow to react to the attack on shipping, defending fighters would, in due course, arrive on the scene. With the advantage of height and concealed by the sun's dazzling glare, *Oberleutnant* Herbert Wehnelt, the *Gruppe* Communications Officer and Trautloft's wingman, also flying in the *Stabschwarm*, reported to his leader: 'Down below, to the right, several aircraft just crossing the English coast.'

Wehnelt had espied 141 Squadron, shortly after Squadron Leader Richardson had led his Defiants off from Hawkinge.

Trautloft continues:

> I looked towards the spot and located the aircraft, counting three, six, nine of them. They seemed to have only just taken-off. They climbed rapidly, making a large turn towards the middle of the Channel, coming straight at us. They hadn't spotted us yet, so we headed towards them, out of the sun. When I was only 800 metres or so above the formation I noticed the aircraft had turrets behind their cockpits. The aircraft were neither Hurricanes or Spitfires – Defiants – suddenly went through my head, heavily armed two-seaters whose rear-gunner had four heavy machine-guns with enormous firepower [this account, although accurate, was written for propaganda purposes and this is rather an exaggeration: the Defiant's armament was four .303 Browning machine-guns, with which the Hurricane and Spitfire was also armed, and were the same calibre as the Me 109E's pair of nose-mounted machine-guns; the 109, however, had the distinct edge in firepower, considering its two wing-mounted 20mm Oerlikon cannon]. They had obviously been sent up to attack our bombers.
>
> The enemy formation was still flying tightly together, as if on an exercise, when it suddenly turned back toward England. I didn't understand at all what the manoeuvre was for. After checking once more for signs of Hurricanes or Spitfires, I gave the order to attack. The clock on my instrument panel stood at 1343 hrs. I peeled over and dived towards the rearmost Defiant with my *Schwarmflieger* [fellow section pilots]. *Oberleutnants* Wehnelt, Otto Kath [*Gruppe* Adjutant], and Werner Pichon-Kalau von Hofe [*Gruppe* Technical Officer, referred to hereafter as Pichon], following behind. I aimed for the right-hand Defiant.

The commonly accepted narrative is that because the Defiants had no fixed forward-firing armament, once the Germans had recovered from their initial experience – and surprise – when attacking 264 Squadron from astern, future attacks were made head-on.

Clearly, Trautloft's account indicates that the Defiants had turned North towards home, and that he attacked from their rear. Trautloft had the immeasurable advantages of height, sun – and surprise. In such tactical circumstances, Spitfire and Hurricane squadrons would have also suffered, if not equally certainly with heavy losses, as the outcome of such combats during the Battle of Britain indicates. No.141 Squadron had been sent off to patrol over the sea at a dangerously low altitude, inviting attack from above – and paid the price.

Trautloft continues:

> Suddenly all hell broke loose. The Englishmen had seen us. Defensive fire from a number of turrets flew towards me – fireworks all over the place. I could see bullets passing by on either side and felt hits on my machine, but pressed home my attack. 200 metres, 100 metres – now was the time to fire and my machine-guns and cannon hammered away.
>
> The first volley was too high but the second was right in the middle of the fuselage; parts of the Defiant broke away and flashed past me. I saw a thin smoke trail appear below the fuselage and suddenly the aircraft exploded in a huge red ball of flames, which fell towards the sea.

A massacre ensued.

Oberleutnant Pichon claimed three of the hapless Defiants destroyed:

> We dive steeply. My commander attacks the nearest aircraft. Then everything happens at the speed of lightning. I fire a short burst. The Tommy emits a white stream of leaking fuel. Then it slowly turns over the right wing and descends vertically. I turn around quickly only to see Kath and Wehnelt finish off one enemy aircraft each.
>
> I swing in behind the British on the far right and open fire from a distance of 20 metres. My tracer disappears into the fuselage and wings. I give him only a short burst. The same thing is repeated: first, a white stream, and then the plane turns over. I got him! By this time I have shot down four [Pichon claimed three, officially] and still the British cling to their close formation and rearward firepower.
>
> I place myself behind the next aircraft and again fire a short burst. After my second burst the plane drops like a stone. Ten metres next to me, another Me 109 is firing at a Defiant in the next section of three. I see the burst hit one of the enemy's wings, and the next moment the aircraft is torn to pieces in a huge fireball.
>
> Now we had to be careful with ammunition. I selected the plane that flew to the far right. Meanwhile, we had gone down from 3,000 to 1,000 metres. I blast away with all my guns, but he doesn't fall. This is it! I fire with large deflection while turning, and see tracers hit

the fuselage and wings. Finally, he goes down. A yellowish-white streak marks his descent, which ends in a frothy water fountain in the Channel, not far from the English coast.

Squadron Leader Richardson (Defiant L6999) later reported that, having initially been ordered to patrol the Channel, South of Folkestone at the suicidal height of 5,000ft, at 12.35 hrs he was further instructed to,

> sweep Cap Gris Nez at 5,000ft. The Squadron was attacked out of the sun by twenty – twenty-five Me 109s [which Richardson records as having rained down from 20,000ft]. I immediately turned to port, completing a steep turn of 360°. This proved ineffective as aircraft attacked from below and on the outside. I then carried out 'S' turns, turning always towards the attack; this proved effective. After five minutes, Red 2 and myself, Red 1, were the only two Defiants left, so I decided to break off the combat and returned to base.

Squadron Leader Richardson's air gunner, Pilot Officer Antony Halliwell, reported the following:

> Me 109s came down out of the sun. As they came to deliver attack I had one in sights until well within range and opened fire while still astern (slight deflection). Tracer bullets were seen to hit the enemy aircraft, which dived down into the sea, leaving a large, round, patch of foam.

Pilot Officer Hugh Tamblyn (Defiant L7014) was flying to Squadron Leader Richardson's right, in the lead section, when the 109s attacked from astern; his air gunner, Sergeant Sydney Powell, reported that:

> I kept the enemy aircraft in my sight and opened fire at 200 yards. My tracer bullets were seen to hit aircraft which dived into the sea. This aircraft was the same one fired at by Pilot Officer Halliwell. Before this, another Me 109 delivered a similar attack. I was unable to fire as it attacked but as it pulled away to my right I was able to get it in my sight and fired twenty-five rounds. This aircraft dived towards the sea but I was unable to see it go in.

Hauptmann Trautloft, however, had not had everything his own way:

> I had gained speed in my dive and used it to curve into the attack again, to the right. While in the turn I saw another Defiant going

down behind me and to my left. By this time all my pilots were attacking, and then suddenly my engine vibrated and began running unevenly. I could smell burning oil in the cockpit and my coolant temperature indicated 120° with oil temperature also rising steadily. For the first time I noticed several hits on my left wing and a trail of smoke underneath it. I felt uneasy – I didn't want to bale out over the Channel.

Then Kath appeared on my left, his aircraft also trailing smoke. 'I've got to make an emergency landing,' he told me over the radio, and, like me, headed towards the French coast.

It's a damned uneasy feeling flying so slowly over the sea in a shot-up crate, all the more worrying when one's flying height was diminishing steadily – and all the while the coast didn't seem to be getting any closer. Luckily there weren't any enemy fighters about, otherwise we'd have been easy meat.

At last there was land below and I scraped over Cap Blanc Nez at 200 metres, finally landing on the airfield at St Inglevert with my propeller feathered. I didn't know where Kath had gone – I'd had my hands full during the forced-landing and hadn't been able to follow his progress. During the flight back I'd heard the voices of my pilots over the radio, 'I'm attacking' … '*Abschuss*' [aerial victory], and then I heard '*Achtung* [danger], Spitfires!', from which it was obvious that British fighters had joined the battle.

It was not 'Spitfires' that had suddenly appeared but the Hurricanes of 111 Squadron, and just the three of 'B' Flight's Green Section, to be exact; Flight Lieutenant Stanley Connors DFC:

Green 2 (Pilot Officer Jack Copeland) saw E/A off the coast after we were ordered on an interception … He informed me on the R/T and I attempted to inform the squadron Leader, then led my Section into the attack. I made an attack from abeam at short range on some Me 109s attacking a squadron of Defiants, and saw my bullets entering cockpit and fuselage of one E/A, which burst into flames and dived into the sea.

I made a further attack on an Me 109, which was followed up by Green 2, but was then attacked by several Me 109s, which I shook off by evasive turns and returned to base where I landed at 1330 hrs. I saw ten enemy aircraft dive into the sea, four of them in flames.

Flight Lieutenant Connors, however was mistaken; not all of the crashing aircraft were enemy.

Pilot Officer Copeland:

> I wanted until my Section Leader broke away and then attacked a 109 from astern at 250 closing to 150 yards. I fired 800 rounds into him and saw both wings smoking, and he was obviously seriously damaged. I broke off and returned to base as I was approaching the French coast and had lost contact with the rest of my Section.

Pilot Officer Peter Simpson:

> I followed my Section Leader into a formation of about twenty Me 109s and attacked one from astern. I fired a long burst, the E/A dived and I followed, giving several bursts from short range. Smoke started to pour from the E/A and my windscreen became covered in oil. E/A turned over slowly and started to dive. My Section Leader saw it fall into the sea.

Without 111 Squadron's intervention, it is likely that none of 141 Squadron would have made it home – thankfully, however, at least Squadron Leader Richardson's and Pilot Officer Tamblyn's Defiants returned to Hawkinge unscathed. The remainder of Squadron Leader Richardson's formation, though, met the following fates:

Pilot Officer Ian MacDougall (Defiant L6983) was crewed that day with Air Gunner Sergeant John Francis Wise, and reported that:

> Owing to the fact that Green 1 and Yellow 2 did not take-off, I assumed Yellow 2's position. I followed the squadron at 5,000ft – I never saw any of the enemy planes at all during the first two attacks, but bullets were being fired from all angles. After the third attack, my engine cut and believing that I had been shot down, ordered the Air Gunner to jump – but as I got no answer assumed him killed, so decided to come down to sea-level to land.
>
> On my way down my engine restarted and I was able to proceed to my base, where I found the turret empty, the Air Gunner having obviously baled out previously.

Sergeant Wise, aged 20, was the most experienced of all 141 Squadron's aircrew in action this day, having previously seen action over Dunkirk with 264 Squadron. He was never found.

Flight Lieutenant Malcolm Loudon's Defiant (L7001) was sufficiently badly hit for him to also order his gunner, Pilot Officer Eric Farnes, to bale out over the sea – Farnes was lucky to be rescued from the waves. Loudon, wounded, managed to nurse his shot-up aircraft back over the Kentish coast to crash-land 200-yards short of Hawkinge aerodrome, coming to rest against a hedge, which caught fire, although fortunately the pilot was rescued from the flames by the local farmer.

Flying Officer Ian Grahame Donald, the son of Air Marshal Sir D.G. Donald, was shot dead in his Defiant (L7009), and crashed, with his air gunner, Pilot Officer Arthur Charles Hamilton, into a cornfield North of Elmsvale Road, Dover. Hamilton, who did not bale out as per certain records, had actually been due to marry later that day.

Pilot Officer Rudal Kidson, a New Zealander from Wellington, and Sergeant Fred Atkins were shot down into the sea (Defiant L7015); Kidson remains missing, while Atkins was later washed up on the French coast.

Pilot Officer John Rushton Gard'ner, a New Zealander from Dunedin, was flying Defiant L7016, as one of 141 Squadron's four rearmost aircraft. Although shot down virtually immediately, Gard'ner's aircraft, unlike the other three Defiants, did not catch fire. Although injured, Gard'ner ditched in the sea four miles off Dover and managed to escape the doomed aircraft – which sank, presumably taking his gunner, Pilot Officer Dudley Malins Slatter, to a watery grave, as he was never found. Fortunately, Gard'ner was rescued from the sea just fifteen minutes after he came down.

Pilot Officer John Richard Kemp, also a New Zealander, from Napier, and his air gunner, Sergeant Robert Crombie, crashed into the sea, never to be seen again (Defiant L6974).

Pilot Officer Dick Howley and Sergeant Albert Curley (Defiant L6995) also went down in the Channel – and also remain missing to this day.

Back at Hawkinge, Squadron Leader Richardson immediately flew to RAF Northolt, from where he was conveyed to Fighter Command HQ at Bentley Priory to de-brief the disaster – which, appropriately, became known forevermore as the 'Slaughter of the Innocents'.

The folly of using the Defiant as a day-fighter had been confirmed with tragic consequences. No.141 Squadron was released from further operations, and although seven replacement Defiants were delivered on 20 July 1940, the following day the unit was ordered back to Prestwick. The Squadron would see no further action during the Battle of Britain, having already lost ten aircrew either killed or missing.

The day's action, though, was far from over.

Flight Lieutenant 'Sailor' Malan:

> I was leader of 74 Squadron when at about 1545 hrs the squadron was sent off [from Manston] to Deal to intercept enemy bombers at 6,000ft, and layers of fighters at 10,000ft and 12,000ft. I saw salvoes of bombs falling in Dover harbour at the same time as information was received that the raid had turned south. Squadron climbed towards Dover, in sections astern, towards numerous groups of fighters above.
>
> Red Section, with me leading, broke off towards the left and onto a group of three at 13,000ft which proved to be two Me 109s and a Hurricane in a tight circle. I delivered one 2-second burst at a

109 at 100 yards range, which was trying to turn onto the tail of the Hurricane. After my first burst the Hurricane immediately broke off and I applied full starboard bank and turned onto the 109's tail. I got in two two-second bursts at 75 yards range. E/A emitted smoke from starboard side and straightened up into a staggering dive.

I then climbed steeply to starboard as the other 109 was turning into my starboard quarter, and met groups of fighters above me which in all cases proved to be Hurricanes. During my climb I noticed the second 109 being pursued at close range by a Spitfire, which proved to be Red 3 (Pilot Officer Stevenson). The remainder of the squadron were not engaged as all remaining fighters in the vicinity proved to be Hurricanes.

Pilot Officer Hastings, Yellow 3:

> At approx. 1550 hrs I saw Red 1 attack one Me 109 and fire two bursts while climbing. I saw smoke pouring from the E/A which was diving steeply towards the sea, his wings rocking laterally as if out of control. Camouflage and markings appeared to be normal. I was then obliged to turn sharply to the right to avoid a Hurricane.
>
> When I had avoided the friendly fighter I turned to the left and looked for the E/A but only saw a round white patch of foam in the sea where previously there had been no such disturbance.

The Me 109 attacked by 'Sailor' Malan was accredited as a 'probable'. Pilot Officer Stevenson likewise claimed a 109 probably destroyed, last seen descending towards the French coast trailing smoke. According to German loss records, 109 listed on this day was a machine of II/JG51 which 'crashed near Chartres'.

Because the Me 109 had a fuel-injected engine and was therefore able to lose a Spitfire or Hurricane in the dive, diving away when attacked by an RAF fighter became the enemy's standard evasive tactic. Diving vertically with the throttle rammed forward for maximum power generated a substantial emission of black smoke from the 109's exhausts – giving the appearance that the enemy aircraft was fatally hit and going to crash. Owing to the presence of other enemy fighters and heights involved, rarely could a pilot watch his victim all the way down to confirm whether or not the machine crashed.

In reality, and all too often, the German fighter was not so badly damaged, and levelled out, unseen, returning safely to base. These claims were made in good faith by RAF pilots, as in this case, where both Malan and Stevenson were credited with a 'probable'. In this way, however, a single German casualty could become exaggerated on the scorecard, as the same aircraft could be claimed and accredited to multiple pilots, thereby providing a false impression of combat successes. This also emphasises the gulf of difference between a combat claim and an actual enemy loss.

It is worth adding that a 109 streaming a plume of white smoke was a different matter, and more likely to result in the damaged machine not making it home, because this was coolant, without which the engine would overheat and seize. In this case, unfortunately, neither Malan nor Hastings mention the colour of the smoke emitting from Malan's target. Whether the 109 which crashed at Chartres with a wounded pilot aboard was that claimed by Malan or Stevenson we will never know, and likewise what had crashed into the sea cannot be confirmed.

With 141 Squadron virtually annihilated, the Biggin Hill Sector Controller had recalled 32 Squadron from a rare day off and sent Squadron Leader John Worrall's Hurricanes down to Hawkinge; they were soon in action.

Sergeant Bernard Henson:

> While on patrol over Dover at 1600 hrs, I saw three puffs of AA fire above Dover harbour, followed by bombs being dropped in harbour. Following my Yellow Leader I turned towards harbour (we were then three miles South of Dover at 9,000ft) when a machine marked with crosses came from above and got on my leader's tail.

Dover harbour was being attacked by *Erprobungsgruppe* 210, and 32 Squadron had been bounced by Me 109s of II/JG51. Henson continues:

> I gave him a short burst in his side at about 40ft range, but I could not turn fast enough to follow him, but I noticed that the enemy (most likely an Me 109) turned steeply away and dived from Yellow 1.
>
> I saw a Ju 87 dive towards the harbour dived after him, keeping above him, and as he pulled up in front of me I opened fire at 300 yards (one burst of about six seconds), he turned to port in a fairly steep turn. I throttled back, turning inside his turn and gave him a 15-second burst. Clouds of smoke came from his engine, he then slowly glided towards the French coast. I closed in to about fifty yards and was giving him another burst when bullets coming from behind me passed my starboard wing.
>
> I tightly turned, completing a circle to port, and noticed a machine climbing away from me. I then looked for my victim and saw a terrific splash in the sea about eight miles from the French coast. I switched on the camera just before the attack.

Henson claimed the Ju 87 confirmed, and the 109 unconfirmed. Other 32 Squadron pilots also claimed successes: Flight Lieutenant Peter Brothers a 109 destroyed, while Squadron Leader John Worrall, Pilot Officers Keith Gillman and Rupert Smythe, all claimed 109s 'unconfirmed'. *Erprobungsgruppe* 210 suffered no losses in what was a successful attack, during which the Royal Fleet Auxiliary ship *War Sepoy* was hit in the engine room, catching fire, the resulting damage making repairs impractical (this ship was later filled with concrete and deliberately sunk on 7 September 1940 to block Dover harbour's western entrance).

The destroyer HMS *Griffin* was also damaged, as were two other vessels. Moreover, 32 Squadron lost Flight Sergeant Guy Turner, shot down in flames over Hougham at 16.25 hrs. Turner baled out, badly burned, was admitted to Dover Hospital and placed on the 'danger list'.

At 15.30 hrs nine of 64 Squadron's Spitfires scrambled from Kenley and vectored towards Dover. Off the coast there, at 16.00 hrs, battle was joined with the Me 109s, Flying Officer Herbert Woodward and Pilot Officer James O'Meara both claimed Me 109s destroyed, although the former collided with a German fighter, safely returning to Kenley with a damaged wingtip. O'Meara's cockpit hood was also damaged when the starboard aileron of the 109 he attacked broke off and hit his Spitfire.

Flying Officer Alistair Jeffrey, also of 64 Squadron, reported that as Yellow 1 at 16.15 hrs that afternoon,

> I was on patrol over Hawkinge when I saw two aircraft which I took to be Me 109s going towards France. I followed them but did not close appreciably. When about three miles off the coast of France I saw two floatplanes, one flying in an easterly direction at approximately 200ft, the other taxying in a westerly direction. I dived on the first and after firing a short burst saw him spin in. I broke away upwards and attacked the other, which was just taking off, from the beam and followed into the astern position.
>
> I saw him fall into the sea, to starboard. I experienced some AA fire so pushed my nose down and came home. I continued patrol over forward base but saw no activity, so returned to base, landing at 1645 hrs.

The 'floatplanes' were He 115s, one of which, from 3/KüFlGr 906 was destroyed.

At 15.55 hrs that afternoon, Squadron Leader David Bayne, a Cranwellian, had led two sections of 257 Squadron Hurricanes off from Northolt, heading for the action over Dover, but no contact was made. Bayne had formed 257 Squadron, equipped with Spitfires, at Hendon on 17 May 1940, although the new unit soon re-equipped with Hurricanes. Bayne was remarkable in that he had suffered the amputation of a leg as the result of a flying accident in 1935, so was among the small number of pilots missing limbs who flew operationally during the war. This particular sortie represented his first operational patrol of the Battle of Britain, qualifying him for the coveted Battle of Britain Clasp; he would fly two more similarly uneventful scrambles on 21 July 1940, before being posted away to HQ Fighter Command the following day.

Down at Tangmere, Flight Lieutenant John Simpson of 43 Squadron scrambled with his 'A' Flight Hurricanes at 16.55 hrs. Fifteen minutes later, Simpson's formation was patrolling over Selsey Bill at 10,000ft when attacked from above by III/JG27 Me 109s.

A short but sharp fight developed, during which Simpson claimed a 109 destroyed before being shot down himself. Taking to his parachute, as Simpson floated down he became understandably anxious when an Me 109 appeared and circled round him. Defenceless and fearing he would be machine-gunned, Simpson was somewhat relieved when the enemy pilot simply opened the Perspex panel in his canopy and gave a friendly wave. The Hurricane pilot's adventures were not yet over, however, as he broke a collar bone when landing on a roof in West Worthing and falling off it into the garden below.

Pilot Officer Frank 'Chota' Carey also claimed a 109 destroyed in this combat, before he,

> noticed a Hurricane on its back below me and an opened parachute. I went down to watch the parachute but noticed another E/A in the vicinity. I engaged him with about three short bursts, the last one being from below and astern at about 150 yards range. Fire appeared to be hitting the E/A but after twisting and diving, E/A headed South, low over the sea.
>
> I endeavoured to search for the pilot who had jumped by parachute but was unable to find any trace of him. Two large patches of oil and wreckage also observed about quarter of a mile apart about two miles South of Felpham. After vain search I returned to base to refuel and rearm at 1736 hrs.

The pilotless Hurricane Carey had seen, and the pilot descending by parachute, was 24-year-old Sergeant James Buck, a Mancunian reservist, who was sadly drowned.

At 17.30 hrs, Squadron Leader David Pemberton, CO of 1 Squadron at Northolt, led Red Section, comprising Pilot Officers Peter Matthews and Dennis Browne, on a patrol when:

> A He 111 was sighted approximately twenty miles North of Brighton and on emerging below cloud was engaged by Pilot Officer Browne, who exhausted his ammunition and continued to follow the E/A in order to advise, through his Pip-Squeak, the course of the raider. In so doing he was shot down with a bullet in his glycol tank. He brought his aircraft down while on fire and succeeded in extricating himself before the petrol tanks blew up. [ORB]

Browne, who had forced-landed near Brighton, was a lucky man. A few minutes later, the same raider was intercepted by 145 Squadron aircraft.

Flight Lieutenant Roy Dutton, 145 Squadron:

> I was leading Red Section ... left Tangmere at 1750 hrs – orders to patrol Brighton, 10,000ft. Later, on instruction, proceeded West

down coast to intercept one bandit at 2,000ft. When over Shoreham I sighted He 111 about five – six miles off, over sea, proceeding South. I ordered my Flight into line astern and gave chase at maximum boost. I was still to deliver my attack before bandit reached clouds.

Following three long bursts I noticed starboard engine smoking heavily, and port motor stopped dead. Bandit glided down towards sea on southerly course but after a couple of minutes or so turned back towards the English coast and finally alighted on sea ten – twelve miles off Brighton. E/A sank quickly, leaving three survivors without rubber boat.

After half an hour, two of them sank. I circled for another half hour in the hope of obtaining assistance, but at the end of this time I returned to Tangmere, owing to lack of petrol, landing at 1925 hrs.

Destruction of the He 111, of 7/KG77, was shared between Flight Lieutenant Dutton, the Polish Flying Officer Antoni Ostowicz, and Pilot Officer Michael Newling, the latter's glycol tank and hydraulic system being damaged in the action, forcing the pilot to land wheels-up at Shoreham before being admitted to the local hospital. Three of the Germans were killed, and two captured.

Here, however, is a paradox: while RAF fighter pilots destroyed German Red Cross seaplanes, they still felt a duty to try and effect the rescue of a downed foe.

At 18.45 hrs, 87 Squadron's Flying Officer Roddy Rayner led his Section, comprising Pilot Officer Christopher Darwin (coincidentally son of Major C.J.W. Darwin, who had formed the squadron in 1917) and Sergeant Laurence 'Rubber' Thorogood, up from Exeter to patrol Portland. The latter, however, somehow became separated and, as the ORB note, 'ran into about eight Ju 87s West of Portland. He attacked one and killed the rear gunner, but then found it advisable to take evasive action.' The *Stuka* was recorded as damaged, at 19.00 hrs.

Just after dusk, at 22.30 hrs, 603 Squadron's Sergeant James Caister engaged a Ju 88 ten miles off Aberdeen, claiming the nuisance raider as 'unconfirmed'. During the exchange of fire, Caister's Spitfire was damaged, although fortunately the pilot returned safely to Turnhouse.

Earlier in the day, Coastal Command located two German cruisers and six destroyers in the Skagerrak, which were monitored by Hudsons, and that night Coastal Command aircraft attacked enemy shipping off Emden. Poor weather conditions over the Continent, however, thwarted Bomber Command's sixteen Blenheims sent to attack various targets, only one finding and bombing a railway viaduct near Dortmund. Neither Bomber Command nor Coastal Command suffered any losses.

This day, 19 July 1940, was also, of course, the long-awaited day of Hitler's 'last appeal to reason'. In the Kroll Opera House that evening, the empty seats of six deputies who had fallen in the fighting against the Allies were garlanded with laurel wreaths, but the atmosphere was triumphal, charged with Nazi pomp and ceremony. Hitler's first act was to hold an investiture and elevate twelve high commanders to the rank of *Feldmarschall*, including both Hugo Sperrle, commander of *Luftflotte* 3, and 'Smiling Albert' Kesselring, commanding *Luftflotte* 2. The latter recalled that the promotions and Hitler's subsequent speech,

> made our minds easy. We regarded Hitler's peace offer as seriously meant, and reckoned on the possibility of England accepting it.

In addition to the batons handed out to his new field marshals, many other promotions followed. Significantly, Hitler elevated *Luftwaffe* chief Hermann Göring to the unique and unprecedented position of *Reichsmarschall*, a new and unsurpassable rank. The justification for this, Hitler wrote, was because the 'Iron Man' had 'created the preconditions for victory'.

Of the event, Count Ciano recalled, 'It is solemn and theatrical'. He went on to add that, 'Hitler speaks simply and, I should say, in an unusually humane tone. I believe that his desire for peace is sincere.'

Also in the audience was the American journalist William Shirer:

> The Hitler we saw in the *Reichstag* tonight was the conqueror, and conscious of it, and yet so wonderful an actor, so magnificent a handler of the German mind, that he mixed superbly the full confidence of the conqueror with the humbleness which always goes down well with the masses when they know a man is on top ... His oratorical form was at its best.

Hitler's speech lasted nearly three hours, towards the end of which he said:

> Mr Churchill has repeated the declaration that he wants war. About six weeks ago now, he launched this war in an arena in which he apparently believes he is quite strong: namely, in the air war against the civilian population, albeit beneath the deceptive slogan of a so-called war against military objectives. Ever since Freiburg, these objectives have turned out to be open cities, markets, villages, residential housing, hospitals, schools, kindergartens, and whatever else happens to be hit.
>
> Up to now I have given little by way of response. This is not intended to signal, however, that this is the only response possible or that it shall remain this way.
>
> I am fully aware that with our response, which one day will come, will also come the nameless suffering and misfortune of many men. Naturally, this does not apply to Mr Churchill himself since by then he will surely be secure in Canada, where the money and the children of the most distinguished of war profiteers have

already been brought. But there will be great tragedy for millions of other men. And Mr Churchill should make an exception and place trust in me when as a prophet I now proclaim: a great world Empire will be destroyed.

A world Empire which I never had the ambition to destroy or as much as harm. Alas, I am fully aware that the continuation of this war will end only in the complete shattering of one of the two warring parties. Mr Churchill may believe this to be Germany. I know it to be England. In this hour I feel compelled, standing before my conscience, to direct yet another appeal to reason in England. I believe I can do this as I am not asking for something as the vanquished, but rather, as the victor, I am speaking in the name of reason. I see no compelling reason which could force the continuation of this war.

I regret the sacrifices it will demand. I would like to spare my *Volk*. I know the hearts of millions of men and boys aglow at the thought of finally being allowed to wage battle against an enemy who has, without reasonable cause, declared war on us a second time.

But I also know of the women and mothers at home whose hearts, despite their willingness to sacrifice to the last, hang onto this last with all their might.

Mr Churchill may well belittle my declaration again, crying that it was nothing other than a symptom of my fear, or my doubts of the final victory.

The content of and language used in Hitler's 'appeal' was entirely predictable: essentially, Churchill was accused of being responsible for enthusiastically prosecuting an unjust war against Germany, which would end in destruction for Britain and its Empire, and Hitler therefore laid the blame for the suffering of countless people as a result of the war firmly at Churchill's door.

Surprisingly, after the big build up, this was nothing more than bluster, without even anything to encourage those who opposed Churchill's steadfast views to petition for peace. In truth, Hitler had completely misunderstood the defiant mood in Britain, and reasons for it, and soon found that the leaflets reproducing his speech, dropped over England in droves, represented nothing more than a waste of ink and paper.

The immediate effect of Hitler's poor judgement was documented by Count Ciano:

Late in the evening, when the first cold British reactions to the speech arrive, a sense of ill-concealed disappointment spreads among the Germans.

Ciano also wrote that he reported his 'impressions' of Hitler's speech to the *Duce*, and noted the following:

> He, who had been against Hitler speaking, describes it as 'a much too cunning speech'. He fears that the English may find in it a pretext to begin negotiations. That would be sad for Mussolini, because now more than ever he wants war.

Hitler, however, had long been attracted to the idea of a peaceful victory; in 1932, he is recorded as having said that 'wars will in fact be fought before military operations begin. I can quite imagine that we might control Britain in this way. Or America.'

If Hitler, though, expected a response from Churchill he would be bitterly disappointed. That evening, having read a translation of the 'appeal', Churchill remarked to his Private Secretary, Jock Colville, that, 'I do not propose to say anything in reply to *Herr* Hitler's speech, not being on speaking terms with him.'

That night, however, Bomber Command sent Hitler a clear message: a force of eighty-nine Wellingtons, Whitleys and Hampdens attacked *Luftwaffe* airfields in the Netherlands and industrial targets in Germany.

SATURDAY, 20 JULY 1940

The day after Hitler's 'last appeal to reason', the Daily Home Intelligence Report documents that:

> Morale is high ... Reactions to the expected 'Peace' speech: 'Hitler speaks – in vain'. On the whole, people have treated the speech less seriously than the press have done. People laughed and jeered.

Indeed, having failed through 'Air Fleet Diplomacy' to frighten Britain into accepting his final offer, Hitler now had a serious problem: unable to win the day without a bitter fight, fully aware that a seaborne invasion was little more than a pipe dream, he would soon have to commit to battle or lose face. Still, he faltered and Goebbels's documented that his leader 'thinks of waiting a bit', still in the vain hope that Britain would see 'reason'.

At a conference this morning, Count Ciano recorded in his diary that Hitler 'confirms my impressions of yesterday. He knows that war with the British will be hard and bloody, and knows also that people everywhere today are averse to bloodshed.'

Ciano's diplomatic papers record that Hitler was preparing to strike against Britain through intensified aerial attack, which to date had not been seriously

KANALKAMPF DIARY, 10 JULY – 31 JULY 1940

affected by British defences. Göring – his enormous ego duly inflated now he was *Reichsmarschall* – remained entirely confident that his *Luftwaffe* would prevail in any decisive contest against the RAF.

On 12 January 1940 – Göring's forty-seventh birthday – the Italian king had conferred upon the German air chief Italy's highest civilian decoration, the opulent, bejewelled, Collar of the *Annunziata*.

Count Ciano:

> In the afternoon a visit to Göring. He looked feverish, but as he dangled the collar of the *Annunziata* from his neck he was somewhat rude and haughty towards me. I was more interested in the luxurious decoration of his house than in him and his variable humours. It is an ever-increasing show of luxury, and it is truly incomprehensible how, in a country which is socialistic, or almost so, people can tolerate the extraordinary pomp displayed by this Western satrap.

Without doubt, as the summer of 1940 progressed, from the German perspective the vanity and delusion of the narcissistic *Reichsmarschall* would have an enormous impact on the ultimate outcome.

With the prospect of having to actually launch a seaborne invasion of southern England now appearing a real possibility, the German naval and army high commands were of a divided opinion. The OKW had ordered thirteen divisions to the Channel coast, which would be first-wave troops. Under the overall command of *Feldmarschall* von Runstedt, six 16th Armee divisions were to embark from ports around Calais and land between Ramsgate and Bexhill, while four 9th Armee divisions were to set sail from Le Havre, bound for landfall between Brighton and the Isle of Wight. From Cherbourg, three 6th Armee divisions were to land between Weymouth and Lyme Regis.

This first wave was to comprise 90,000 men, who would be supported by airborne forces. The plan was that by day three, the number of troops landed in Britain would number 260,000 men, the original force having rapidly been supplemented by armour and motorised divisions. In total, forty-one divisions, including two airborne, were to be committed. Strong bridgeheads would provide for safe reinforcement and the ability to direct heavy artillery fire, which, in concert with guns in France, would dominate the all-important Dover Strait. Mobile troops were to advance and seize the Gravesend – Southampton line, while *Feldmarschall* von Richenau's 6th *Armee* made for Bristol.

The OKW and OKH planners were confident, in fact, that the second objective, the Maldon-Severn line, would be achieved without difficulty, while concurrently London was first isolated, then occupied. Then, the industrial Midlands and the North would be quickly overrun by motorised divisions. Astonishingly, *Feldmarschall* Walther von Brauchitsch, Commander-in-Chief of the German army, considered the whole undertaking straightforward and anticipated the operation being completed within a month. The *Kriegsmarine*, however, thought much differently and did not share the army's optimism.

Grand-Admiral Erich Raeder, *Kriegsmarine* chief, had given preparations for Operation *Seelöwe* full priority, the Naval Staff, according to its war diary, being ordered 'to take up this new task with energy and vigour'. Raeder, however, fully recognised the enormous risks involved and had made clear to von Brauchitsch on 17 July 1940 that if things went awry, the invasion armies could be completely lost.

On the day of Hitler's 'final appeal to reason', Raeder's staff reported to him their considered opinion that the task ahead was disproportionate to the *Kriegsmarine*'s strength. Moreover, the ports available and even inland waterways had been damaged during the campaign to date, compounding logistical and practical difficulties – but the sea itself was potentially the greatest concern, given the unpredictable weather and currents in addition to tides. The first wave of troops needed to be transported in suitable vessels, but there were no dedicated amphibious landing craft up to the job or available in sufficient numbers. Clearing minefields was almost impossible, owing to Britain's ability to sow minefields at any time.

The practical difficulties and weakness of the *Kriegsmarine*, however, could be overcome through air power – but, even so, the OKM doubted that the *Luftwaffe* could effectively deal with defending troops without the support of naval bombardment, which may be impossible. Moreover, if, after the first landings, the RN counter-attacked, future crossings may be prevented, because minefields were not infallible, and because the *Luftwaffe* was dependent upon good weather, air cover for the proposed invasion task force was not a given. As far as the OKM was concerned, therefore, the proposed landings involved 'exceptional difficulties' – which were communicated to Hitler.

In terms of the air fighting was concerned on 20 July 1940, although 'B' Flight of 54 Squadron was scrambled from Rochford at 05.21 hrs, the ORB states, to intercept 'a large enemy raid off the estuary, no interception took place and the squadron landed at Manston'. The next engagement would involve the Hurricanes of 56 Squadron.

During the Fall of France, Flying Officer Steve 'Squeak' Weaver, who had previously served with 56 Squadron pre-war, was posted to controller duties at North Weald – much to his frustration. On 20 June 1940, he was returned to 56 Squadron, which required replacement pilots after action in France and during the Dunkirk evacuation – and already being operational on the Hurricane, 'Squeak' Weaver was an experienced pilot.

Back with the squadron, he joined 'B' Flight, in which served Pilot Officer Geoffrey Page, a name later to become synonymous with the Battle of Britain, commanded by Flight Lieutenant Edward 'Jumbo' Gracie. After the Battle of France, the squadron's long-serving CO, Squadron Leader E.V. Knowles, was posted away to the Air Ministry, his replacement Squadron Leader G.A.L. 'Minnie' Manton, not arriving until 28 June 1940. Having initially joined the RAF on an SSC in 1931, Manton had been permanently commissioned in 1936, his flying experience having been flying biplane fighters and as a pre-war flying instructor. Since 1937, however, he had flown a desk, being refreshed and converting to monoplane fighters at 5 OTU, Aston Down, the same month he took over 56 Squadron. While Manton lacked experience on modern fighters, and was without combat experience, he was an experienced officer and leader who sensibly deferred to his able flight commanders until sufficiently acclimatised to take 56 Squadron's operational reins.

Flying Officer Weaver's first taste of action came on the dawn patrol of 20 July 1940, when the Controller perfectly guided Blue Section, comprising Flight Lieutenant Gracie, Pilot Officer Page and Flying Officer Weaver, to intercept a Ju 88 at 05.45 hrs off Burnham. The enemy pilot dived for cloud, but failed to reach it before Gracie emptied all of his ammunition into the lone reconnaissance aircraft, at which Page also fired. The Ju 88 then entered and passed through cloud, when it was picked up and attacked by Flying Officer Weaver, who chased his target North-east.

The German then began weaving from side to side, allowing the Hurricane pilot to catch it. From 250 yards, Blue 3 then emptied his ammunition into the bomber. Both Weaver and Page's Hurricanes, however, were damaged by return fire, forcing both to break away, losing their quarry. Nonetheless, this reconnaissance machine of 4(F)/122, crash-landed in flames at Cocket Wick Farm, at 05.50 hrs, its four-man crew being captured. For Weaver, it would be the start of what would be an august – but sadly short-lived – combat career.

Throughout the morning, more lone German reconnaissance aircraft continued to be active. At 09.20 hrs, Squadron Leader James 'Prof' Leathart, CO of 54 Squadron, fired upon a Do 17 over Dover, but lost his target in cloud. At the same time, further West, South of Selsey Bill, Flight Lieutenant Thomas Hubbard, commanding 601 Squadron's 'B' Flight, was up from Tangmere with Flying Officers Michael Doulton and Thomas Grier, when they too encountered and damaged a prowling Do 17.

Then, at 12.05 hrs, Blue Section of 603 Squadron, namely Flight Lieutenant John Cunningham, Flying Officer Robin 'Bubbles' Waterston and Pilot Officer Basil 'Stapme' Stapleton, destroyed a Do 17 of 1(F)/120 thirty miles off Aberdeen; the bomber crashed into the sea with no survivors.

So far, the day was typical, with lone reconnaissance aircraft playing cat and mouse from Scotland to Sussex with the RAF fighters. The next action, however, involved a fighter sweep in strength by I/JG27 over Lyme Bay – and were met by Hurricanes of Middle Wallop's 238 Squadron.

Flight Lieutenant Donald Turner:

> Red Section 238 Squadron went on convoy patrol at 1303 hrs, picked up convoy at 1320. I called Blue 1 and got an answer. Position fifteen miles South of Swanage. I was on patrol for five minutes when I saw several aircraft dogfighting below. I waited several minutes to see if there were any E/A above and during this time I saw suddenly first

an aircraft going down in flames, and pilot baling out, also an aircraft going down from which pilot also jumped, and an Me 109 passed beneath me, heading south-west, about 2,000ft below.

I was at about 12,000ft. I immediately dived on his tail and gave him one short burst, and he went straight into the sea. I circled round and saw a large patch of oil and a lot of foam, but no sign of the aircraft or pilot. I then tried to get in touch with the Section but could get no reply, so I climbed straight into the sun at about 18,000ft and patrolled convoy on my own. Was then ordered to pancake, which I did at 1422 hrs.

Turner had shot down and killed *Oberfeldwebel* Beushausen of 3/JG27. Meanwhile, Red 2, Pilot Officer Charles Davis, was also engaged:

I saw a Hurricane (Red 3, Sergeant Parkinson) shot down in flames by an Me 109, and dived on this E/A and fired two or three short bursts of two seconds each. My dive was for about 2,000ft, from 14,000ft, and I made a stern attack. The Me 109 went into a vertical dive and flattened out about 5ft above the sea.

I dived down onto him again and fired several long bursts which went into the Me 109 from astern – it started to burn furiously, with clouds of black smoke, but I did not see the aircraft crash as I was then attacked by two other Me 109s. I broke off the engagement by doing a steep diving turn to the right. The E/A made no attempt to follow me but made straight for home. The enemy shooting was very bad and I had no ammunition left.

Flight Lieutenant Stuart Walch, an Australian, had been leading 238 Squadron's Blue Section, arriving over the convoy at 12.20 hrs, fifteen miles South-east of Portland. The situation was confusing, however; Walch lost his numbers 2 and 3 by 13.00 hrs, having investigated the appearance of other aircrafts, which transpired to be Hurricanes.

Switching to his reserve fuel tank, Walch turned for home; five miles off Swanage, he saw fifteen aircraft approaching the convoy – codenamed *Bosom* – from the South, and given their direction of travel assumed these newcomers to be hostile. Returning to the convoy, climbing into the sun, Walch watched bombs explode around an escorting destroyer, at 9,000ft the Hurricane pilot encountered three Me 109s – and immediately attacked the port machine, closing from 200 to fifty yards:

Black smoke poured from under the engine of the E/A and he turned right and made a vertical dive for towards the sea. I did not follow as the other aircraft were trying to get astern of me. I pulled up in a steep stall turn and made for home as petrol was very low.

That day, 3/JG27 also lost *Leutnant* Scherer, whose 109 was that attacked by either Pilot Officer Davis or Flight Lieutenant Walch. In response, *Oberleutnant* Gerhard Homuth of 2/JG27, claimed two 'Spitfires' West of Swanage at 14.25 and 14.28 hrs respectively (Continental time); no Spitfires were engaged or lost, just one Hurricane: Sergeant Cecil Parkinson, who Flight Lieutenant Turner and Pilot Officer Davis both reported having seen shot down.

Although Parkinson was picked up from the sea by HMS *Acheron*, sadly he died of wounds before reaching land. He was the first NCO pilot to be lost by 238 Squadron, and, notes the ORB. 'one who was of great resource and daring'.

At 13.30 hrs, Flight Lieutenant Mike Crossley of 32 Squadron was patrolling with his Red Section twelve miles South-east of Dover when an Me 110 'Jaguar' was sighted, which, upon seeing the danger, dived from 8,000ft, releasing its bomb at 2,000ft before taking evasive action, zig-zagging, at 300ft. Crossley, and his Red 2, Pilot Officer John Proctor, fired several bursts at the 110, until a second 'Jaguar' prepared to attacked Crossley, which in turn was briefly engaged by Proctor.

Crossley broke to starboard, in a tight turn, while Proctor, finding himself just 15ft above the waves, broke sharply upwards, to gain height. Both pilots, upon completing their evasive manoeuvres, saw the second Me 110 heading for France, although according to Crossley, during his turn he 'saw the first aircraft go into the sea'.

That day, *Oberleutnant* Otto Hinze led the Me 110s of 3/*Erprobungsgruppe* 210 on the first of the thirteen raids the unit would fly over the next week, flying such operations himself on the day in question. It is likely that the 'Jaguars' encountered by 32 Squadron were from this enemy unit, although no Me 110 loss appears to match Crossley's claim, which was shared with Pilot Officer Proctor.

To the West, at 14.00 hrs, three sections of 238 Squadron were up and patrolling over *Bosom*, the convoy still chugging eastwards. At 15.15 hrs, the ORB reports, Pilot Officer Jack Urwin-Mann of Green Section 'engaged a He 59 (seaplane), firing several bursts and put starboard engine out of action. Pilot Officer Urwin-Mann was within three miles of the French coast and returned. The enemy appeared discomfited immediately firing began and was desirous of making off'. This Red Cross emblazoned seaplane was credited as 'damaged' – but was in fact destroyed, with four crewmen reported missing.

At 16.00 hrs, Squadron Leader Harry Hogan, a Cranwellian recently converted to Hurricanes and posted to command 501 Squadron on 29 June 1940, led his Hurricanes off from Middle Wallop, heading for Convoy *Bosom*:

> The Squadron was ordered to patrol convoy approximately twenty miles South of Swanage. Twenty miles South of Weymouth Bay I observed a destroyer being bombed but could not see E/A, owing to glare and haze. My height was 8,000ft. The Squadron approached a destroyer which did not appear to be hit. I had glimpses of E/A below me and gave chase.

> I saw two Do 17s and a Ju 87 on the water, and 4,000ft above them seven Me 109s. I attacked a 109 with a 3-second burst from dead astern and no deflection. Immediately black smoke poured out of E/A which dived steeply towards the sea. The other 109s drew ahead and dived vertically for the sea head of the two Do 17s. I dived on a Do 17 and loosed off more ammunition from above and behind. My shooting was not accurate and as we were almost over the coast I returned home.

The combat occurred, Hogan reported, 'half way between Warmwell and Guernsey', some thirty miles North of Sark, at 16.15 hrs. This was the 501 Squadron CO's first combat. Among his pilots also engaged was Sergeant James 'Ginger' Lacey – destined to become a leading ace of the Battle of Britain. Lacey, Yellow 2, was flying with Flight Lieutenant P.A.N. Cox, who dived to attack a 109:

> Sergeant-Pilot Lacey picked on the third Me 109, closed to 150 yards, fired a burst of ten seconds. The E/A turned on its back and dived vertically into the sea. There were no signs of fire and Sergeant Lacey then followed Me 109, fired a short burst at 150 yards, full deflection, no obvious results. He broke away as Flight Lieutenant Cox was on this aircraft's tail. Watched this machine dive into the sea, trailing white smoke. Sergeant Lacey returned to base at 15ft as he had no ammunition left. [Combat Report]

Cox and Lacey had shot down *Major* Riegel, the *Kommandeur* of I/JG27, who remains missing – although the combat was not without loss to 501 Squadron: *Leutnant* Igor Zirkenbach, 1/JG27, shot down Pilot Officer Edmund Sylvester, a veteran of the fighting over France, who also remains missing.

As *Bosom* passed into 11 Group's area of responsibility, the six Hurricanes of 43 Squadron's 'A' Flight left Tangmere at 16.35 hrs. At 18.00 hrs, Yellow Section went to investigate a He 115 red cross seaplane off the Needles, but Flying Officer Joseph Haworth 'was last seen to approach E/A, pull away and bale out. Missing, believed killed in action'. Like so many others, Haworth was never found.

Given the fighting to date on this day and good weather, Air Vice-Marshal Park rightly anticipated more action over *Bosom*. Between 17.40 and 17.55 hrs, the Biggin Hill Sector Controller scrambled two sections of 32 Squadron Hurricanes, which were as usual operating from the forward base at Hawkinge, which joined in the air with nine 610 Squadron Spitfires sent up from Biggin Hill at 17.45 hrs. Five minutes later, the Kenley Controller scrambled eleven 615 Squadron Hurricanes from Kenley, and the Spitfires of 65 Squadron from Manston. Compared to previous reactions by Fighter Command's controllers, this represented a response in strength.

By 18.00 hrs, *Bosom* was off Folkestone and under attack by Ju 87s, escorted by Me 109s and Me 110 'Jaguars'.

Flight Lieutenant Mike Crossley, 32 Squadron:

> I took off with Red Section and joined Green and Blue at 10,000ft, and immediately sighted about twelve Me 109s to the South. I turned towards them but my attention was diverted by a string of Ju 87s in the act of bombing. I turned towards them and fired a burst at one at close range as he went past but did not observe the result as I saw an Me 109 coming round in front of me.
>
> I tacked on and got a deflection burst at close range, about 1,000ft up. He went straight down into the sea about one-mile South of Dover harbour. During this engagement I also saw a Ju 87 crash into the sea about two miles south-east of Dover.

Flight Lieutenant John Humpherson, also of 32 Squadron, had destroyed the *Stuka* Crossley had seen crash, reportedly 'three miles off Dover':

> The E/A was apparently returning to France and it was flying just above the surface of the water at about 30ft. I approached from behind and at same height as E/A. I closed to about 200 yards and opened fire. After a very short burst the E/A dived straight into the sea and disappeared below the surface.

A Me 110 was claimed by Crossley's Red 2, Pilot Officer Proctor:

> At about 4,000ft I spotted five Jaguars approaching convoy from the south-east, about 500ft below me. I rolled over and attacked the nearest one; the E/A rolled over onto its back and went straight into the sea. I followed it down but could see no trace of survivors or wreckage. I returned to base chased by a 109 which soon broke off his attack as I neared the cliffs at Folkestone Warren

The German formation numbered around fifty aircraft, and a great mêlée was now in progress just off Dover. In this engagement, Park's pilots for once enjoyed the element of surprise, attacking from the sun; in total, 32 Squadron claimed three Me 109s, three Me 110s and one Ju 87 destroyed, in addition to three more *Stukas* and a 109 damaged. In this hectic action, *Hauptmann* Horst Tietzen of 5/JG51 shot-up Sergeant William Higgins, who was 'slightly wounded in face by splinters from bullets which hit protecting armour' [ORB].

Similarly, *Oberfeldwebel* Johann Illner, 4/JG51, claimed a Hurricane '8 km NE Dover', which may have been Squadron Leader John Worrall, whose Hurricane was written-off in a forced-landing near Hawkinge. Not so lucky, sadly, was

Sub-Lieutenant Geoffrey Bulmer, on loan to Fighter Command from the FAA; shot down by *Oberleutnant* Josef Priller of 6/JG51, off Folkestone, the 20-year-old Hurricane pilot baled out into the sea but remains missing.

No.65 Squadron's Spitfires were also on the scene at 18.20 hrs, as the Australian Flight Lieutenant Gordon Olive, leading Yellow Section, reported, 'mid-Channel, off Folkestone':

> We were on the lookout for E/A supposedly bombing a convoy but none were visible near the convoy and no bombs were dropping. I then noticed an E/A on a Hurricane's tail, the Hurricane apparently unaware that E/A were about. E/A opened fire and blew off part of Hurricane's tail off. Hurricane dived vertically and pilot jumped out at 9,000ft. I chased Me 109 across Channel and fired all my rounds at about 150 yards.
>
> Towards end of burst E/A caught fire and crashed in sea about two miles West of Cap Gris Nez. Several E/A observed patrolling but as I was out of ammunition I returned and joined Red Section over convoy. Yellow 2 and 3 remained with convoy. I returned to rearm but noted position of parachute, which had landed one-mile SW of Shepherdswell and four–five miles NE of Dover.

Olive had shot down a II/JG51 Me 109, confirmed by Sergeant Orchard, the unknown pilot of which was rescued by the *Seenotdienst*. The Hurricane he had seen attacked was that of Sub-Lieutenant Bulmer, although the description of his parachute alighting inland is confusing, given that Bulmer remains missing.

No.610 Squadron's Spitfires were also engaged:

> Green 2 [pilot's identity unknown] attacked an Me 109 and saw smoke coming from it. Red Section saw six Me 109s near Folkestone and climbed inland, towards Ashford, to attack out of the sun. Turned and attacked three Me 109s, which had followed, but did not appear to damage any E/A. Pilot Officer Geoffrey Keighley baled out after being hit in the leg and with his aircraft out of control. He landed at Lydden, near Canterbury. [ORB]

Keighley, who survived the experience, had been shot down by *Leutnant* Michael Sonner, of 3/JG51, and represented the German pilot's third victory.

No.615 Squadron joined the action between Folkestone and Dover, at 18.20 hrs:

> Flight Lieutenant L.M. Gaunce chased an Me 109 to Cap Gris Nez and saw it catch fire and crash on French land.
>
> Pilot Officer Hugo (Red 2) attacked an Me 109, saw smoke pouring out and E/A went into a spin. He saw a parachute going down.

He then attacked another Me 109 which appeared to be gliding down to the sea with engine stopped. He did not see the aircraft crash.

Pilot Officer Madle (Yellow 3) attacked an Me 109 close to the sea. Result inconclusive.

Pilot Officer Eyre brought down an Me 109 ESE of Dover. This was confirmed by observers from the land.

The day's final combat was fought at 19.20 hrs, twenty-five miles South of Selsey Bill, when the three Hurricane pilots of Green Section, 601 Squadron, up from Tangmere, recorded their second success of the day: a He 59 seaplane. Having initially tried to shepherd the enemy red cross machine towards England, when the German pilot turned South, for home, he was shot down in flames. The crew of four, belonging to *Seenotflugkommando* 1, baled out but are all still missing.

Although not without loss, it had been a successful day for Park's pilots.

During the day, Coastal Command and the PRU flew various reconnaissance sorties, without incident, until early evening, when Blenheims fighters of 236 (F) Squadron, operating from Thorney Island, escorted a 59 Squadron Blenheim Mk IV on a reconnaissance of Cherbourg:

> At 1745 hrs, Pilot Officer Cotes-Preedy leading Pilot Officer Peachment and Sergeant Lockton (Air-gunner Sergeant Corcoran) left to escort reconnaissance machine to Cherbourg in brilliant sunshine. Outside Cherbourg, when flying at 13,000ft, three E/A approached from the SE while three more stood off at about 25,000ft. Our aircraft turned NW into the sun, forming line astern and dived down to 6,000ft, but Sergeant Lockton failed to close up into line astern and remained at 13,000ft, and was attacked by two Me 109s who dived from astern.
>
> Pieces were seen to fly from the port wing by the other two pilots who saw the Me 109s dive under Sergeant Lockton and circle to starboard when they repeated the attack. With smoke pouring from both engines, Sergeant Lockton was seen to spin steeply into the sea. This occurred about 1820 hrs. Pilot Officer Cotes-Preedy and Peachment returned to Thorney Island with the reconnaissance machine where they landed at 1850 hrs without further incident.
> [ORB]

Sergeants Eric Lockton and Henry Corcoran are remembered on the Runnymede Memorial, and were the first victory recorded in the Second World War by *Hauptmann* Eduard 'Edu' Neumann of *Stab*/JG27, who became *Kommandeur* of I/JG27 the following day.

That night, Coastal Command remained active, attacking oil storage facilities and claiming a U-boat sunk off Bergen.

The lack of cloud cover over the Continent during the day led to twenty-three of the twenty-five Bomber Command Blenheims that had been despatched to attack airfields and other targets in enemy occupied Europe being forced to abort.

One, however, pressed on and attacked Flushing airfield, but the 110 Squadron Blenheim of Squadron Leader J.F. Stephens was intercepted off Rotterdam at 13.30 hrs and destroyed by JG54 Me 109s – the bomber crashed into the North Sea. Stephens and another crewman, Sergeant J.V. West remain missing, while Sergeant E.C. Parker was rescued and captured by the Germans.

That night, Bomber Command sent ninety-five aircraft to bomb six targets in Germany, airfields in the Netherlands and to sow mines. Four Hampdens in total were lost while another crashed on the Norfolk coast after running out of fuel returning from minelaying in the Baltic; two Wellingtons also failed to return. Of interest is that four Hampdens attacked *Tirpitz* and *Admiral* Scheer from low-level – 30ft to 100ft – at Wilhelmshaven with 'special bombs', which were actually parachute mines designed to explode on the seabed, thereby causing damage to a warship's less well protected hull. Only one of these brave Hampden crews returned, the other three all victims of heavy flak.

This day and night certainly showed Hitler just how unreasonable the British could be.

SUNDAY, 21 JULY 1940

It was on his day that Churchill told the people that, 'We cannot be clear what lies ahead. It may be that greater ordeals lie before us. We shall face whatever is coming to us. We are sure of ourselves and of our cause and that is the supreme fact that has emerged in these weeks of trial.'

Prophetically, Edward Hulton's *World Review* opined that:

> We, who live in 1940, are the fortunate people. Those who come after us will look back on our generation and our opportunities, for we are watching the birth of the new world. This is our great moment. The future of the world is in our hands.

If Hitler was confused as to the position in Britain, and the country's refusal of his terms in spite of an apparently hopeless situation, the British were equally so as to why there was no major attack or invasion. 'Why doesn't *he* come?', the people asked, although a Dover housewife, Mrs Knoyes, remarked: 'I don't mind him coming so long as he doesn't come just when the meals are ready.'

> Mr Tilbroke, Manager of Dover's Esplanade Hotel: We are still on the front with a fine view of the sea. There is no charge for watching dogfights.

KANALKAMPF DIARY, 10 JULY – 31 JULY 1940

The poet Edward Shanks wrote that 'the battle was not ended and the ending might be death'.

On this day, Hitler held a conference with his OKW chiefs in Berlin. The *Führer* was confused. Von Brauchitsch later reported to Halder on Hitler's view that he had 'No clear picture on what is happening in England', adding that 'Preparations for a decision by arms must be completed as quickly as possible'.

Hitler was conscious that Britain hoped for American or Russian intervention, but was confident that America's neutrality would remain steadfast, and that Russia would 'make no attempt to enter the war against Germany of her own accord'. Hitler genuinely still believed Britain's position to be hopeless: 'The war has been won by us and reversal of the prospect of success is impossible.'

All involved knew just how high the stakes were. Hitler knew that a quick conclusion to the fighting was in Germany's interest, but this was not an urgent necessity, considering Germany's strong economic position. Nonetheless, Hitler considered Operation *Seelöwe* 'the most effective means' to effect a swift and successful outcome for Germany, but was well aware of the difficulties, describing the proposed seaborne invasion as,

> an exceptionally daring undertaking ... This is not just a river crossing, but the crossing of a sea dominated by the enemy. This is not a case of a single crossing operation as in Norway; strategic surprise cannot be expected ... forty divisions will be required ... the most difficult part will be the continued reinforcement of equipment and stores.

Still, however, he saw the operation as the last option, 'if no other means are left for settling with Britain'. Hitler was also acutely aware that time was moving on: 'The time of year is an important factor, since the weather in the North Sea and in the Channel is very bad during the second half of September and the fogs begin in the middle of October.'

Hitler ordered Raeder to prepare a report regarding to what extent the *Kriegsmarine* could guarantee protection for the crossing, and a prediction as to when preparations would be complete. If this was not by the beginning of September, it may be necessary to postpone the invasion until the following spring. Because of the weather, Göring was given until 15 September 1940 to achieve the prerequisite aerial superiority.

This conference also provided the first definite evidence of a projected attack by Germany on the Soviet Union. Hitler did not fear an attack by Russia, but remained hell-bent on prosecuting an all-out war on this ideological enemy and expanding *Lebensraum* – 'Living Space' for the German *Volk* – in the process. There were now significant strategic reasons for commencing a war on two fronts: in spite of the unholy alliance between Hitler and Stalin currently in force, Britain still hoped that this match would not last and that Russia would enter the war against Germany. By conquering Russia, however, Hitler would quash this hope and substantially assist forcing Britain to accept that continued resistance was futile.

Hitler and the OKW knew just how difficult an invasion of Britain would be, which the German people, owing to Hitler's threats and rhetoric, now expected. An invasion of Russia, however, would be 'child's play', or so Hitler had told OKW head, *Feldmarschall* Wilhelm Keitel, and his operations chief, *Generaloberst* Alfred Jodl. With a successful seaborne invasion of, and campaign against, Britain far from certain, while preparations for Operation *Seelöwe* went ahead, it is clear that already, before this mighty undertaking had even been attempted, Hitler and the OKW were already contemplating what was perceived to be a less hazardous operation – a quick campaign against Russia, a less dangerous enemy, which in itself would help neutralise Britain.

On the same day, Göring met with his *Luftflotten* commanders and charged them with working out their strategies for defeating the RAF. The OKL defined the task of *Luftflotten* 2 and 3 thus:

1. To eliminate the RAF both as a fighting force and general organisation.
2. To blockade Britain through attacking ports and shipping.

The first objective was to be achieved in two stages:

A. Defeat of Fighter Command South of the London to Gloucester line.
B. Northward extension of the air offensive until all RAF airfields were under attack.

The plan also included an offensive against the British aircraft industry, by day and night. From now onwards, enemy formations engaged over the Channel, attacking ports and shipping, would increase in size. The *Stukas* of *Fliegerkorps* VIII, which had performed so well during land battles, essentially providing a dynamic artillery barrage ahead of advancing German troops, were tasked with closing the Channel to British shipping by day. Heavier bombers were to make the movement of shipping and port activity impossible, and sow minefields in the shipping lanes.

This offensive, which would test the British defences and begin the process of wearing down Fighter Command, was the prelude to a major offensive planned for August 1940 – *Adler Tag* (Eagle Day) – during which the *Adlerangriff* (Eagle Attack) would eliminate the RAF and British aircraft industry. The *Luftwaffe* was confident; destruction of the RAF in southern England was predicted to take four days, and the overall objective achieved in four weeks. Thereafter the invasion fleet could set sail, unmolested by the RAF, and land between the Isle of Wight and Dover. Given Germany's undefeated battlefield record to date in the Second World War, and how well the *Luftwaffe* had performed supporting the army, the level of confidence was understandable – but it was much more complex than that.

KANALKAMPF DIARY, 10 JULY – 31 JULY 1940

As is well-known today, the Nazi state was Machiavellian, the dysfunctional administration comprising innumerable departments, each vying for the *Führer*'s favour in an environment where knowledge was political power – and knowledge was only shared at the highest level. In terms of intelligence work, there were over a dozen such agencies outside of the *Wehrmacht*, all of which were insular and mistrustful of each other, meaning that there was no shared approach to intelligence work – and 'intelligence', which is to say information on the enemy's strength, deployment, weapons and operational intentions, and much else besides, is crucial to properly informing strategy and tactics.

Unfortunately, within the *Luftwaffe* intelligence work was not viewed as a priority and the 5th *Abteilung* of the OKL, which dealt with air intelligence, was subordinate to the operations department. Within the *Luftflotten*, therefore, it was frequently operations officers who prepared intelligence reports, because the Germans evaluated all scenarios from the perspective of their own operational intentions and objectives, rather than the enemy's situation – which is what should really have driven operational planning. Such low status, in fact, did *Luftwaffe* intelligence officers have that their role included responsibilities such as welfare, propaganda and censorship.

All of this contrasted sharply with the Air Intelligence Branch (AIB) of the Air Ministry, which was sub-divided into sections dealing with a specific country, and was a separate Directorate within the CAS's department. Moreover, the Director of AIB had equal status to the Director of Plans, and AIB produced independent reports on the German military. Intelligence officers had status and were even attached to squadrons – unlike the *Luftwaffe* which failed to have intelligence officers represented at formations smaller than a *Fliegerkorps* (a sub-division of a *Luftflotte*) until 1944. *Luftwaffe* Intelligence was one of at least four *Wehrmacht* intelligence services, and the fifth-ranking department within the OKL; additionally, there was a General of Reconnaissance, an aerial photography branch, and the Air Signal Communications Chief Wolfgang Martini with his Cipher Office.

Within the *Luftwaffe*, however, the intelligence role did not enjoy high prestige, the most promising officers being assigned elsewhere. The long-standing *Luftwaffe* intelligence chief, *Oberst* Josef 'Beppo' Schmid also worked as Göring's Ministerial Officer, so was not even a dedicated intelligence specialist. Indeed, Schmid had a demonstrable habit of embellishing reports to his chief and Hitler; to please his masters he told them what they wanted to hear rather than actual facts, especially about enemy strength and losses.

For example, on 31 March 1939, Schmid reported that the Western powers' aircraft production was 'inadequate to catch up with the major advance in the expansion of the air forces achieved by Germany in the next one to two years'. In 1939, Germany produced 8,295 aircraft, 10,826 in 1940, and 11,776 the following year. Correspondingly, Britain's factories saw 7,940 in 1939, rising to 15,049 in 1940, and 20,094 in 1941. In January 1940, Schmid estimated that the air forces of Britain and France were 'definitely inferior to the *Luftwaffe* in terms of numbers and equipment', and opined that no decisive improvement could be 'immediately' expected in 1940. Schmid also maintained that the RAF fighters would have little chance against the heavily armed Me 110 twin-engine heavy fighter, which, he said, had 'better dogfight performance'.

Again, this was a flawed assessment, based upon the performance of German fighters against unescorted RAF bombers during the Battle of Heligoland Bight. In the event, the Me 110 was found significantly lacking when facing Spitfires and Hurricanes, but because of Schmid their production increased at a cost to the superior Me 109. In a report of 16 July 1940, Schmid considered both Hurricanes and Spitfires inferior to the Me 109, and the Me 110 superior to the Hurricane but inferior to Spitfires. The fact was that the Me 110 was no match for either British fighter, but because Göring personally favoured the twin-engine *Zerstörer* concept, Schmid – as so often happened – had dumbed down his assessment so as not to upset his volatile and vain chief.

Furthermore, the German success in Scandinavia and in the West had given Hitler and the OKW a false impression of the *Luftwaffe*'s actual capability, this optimism and over-confidence being shared by the OKL, including *Generalmajor* Hans Jeschonnek, the OKL Chief of Staff. These deficiencies in the German intelligence system, coupled with inadequate incoming intelligence and inaccurate analysis of available information, would soon manifest itself in poor target selection and ever-changing battle plans.

If air intelligence was lacking, so too were defined orders from on high; things were still not entirely clear to the German *Luftflotte* commanders.

Albert Kesselring:

> The central purpose was lacking. During the weeks of preparation I became more than ever convinced that the operation would not be started. In contrast to our preparations for previous campaigns, there was not one conference within the *Luftwaffe* at which details were discussed with group commanders and other services, let alone with the High Command or Hitler himself.
>
> The conversations I had at my battle headquarters on the Channel coast with Göring and the military commanders appointed to *Seelöwe* were informal talks rather than binding discussions. I was even left in the dark about the relation of the current air raids on England and the invasion plan; no orders were issued to the Chiefs of Air Commands. No definitive instructions were given to me about what my *Luftflotte* was to expect in the way of tactical assignments or what provision had been made for cooperation of army and navy.

And so, at least being aware of the required end result, the *Luftflotten* commanders, Kesselring, Sperrle and Stumpff, were left to work out for themselves the best tactics and battle plan to achieve this. That there was no high-level meeting with

KANALKAMPF DIARY, 10 JULY – 31 JULY 1940

Hitler adds further weight to the argument that the *Führer* was still less than enthusiastic regarding the prospect of an all-out war with and invasion of Britain.

There was a development in *Luftflotte* 2 this day when *Major* Gottard Handrick, an Olympian and 'Spaniard', led the 121 Me 109s of his JG26 from its bases in Germany to the Pas-de-Calais. The airfields were French cornfields around Calais, but were selected on the basis of being sufficiently flat and sizeable. The three *Staffeln* of I/JG26 made ready at Audembert; the three of II/JG26 at Marquise-Ost, and III/JG26's three *Staffeln* at Caffiers (by 30 July 1940, the *Geschwaderstab* was also operating from Audembert). Operational business and administration were carried out in trailers (although by 30 July 1940 a *Geschwader* operations room had been set up in a building at Le Colombier), while personnel were billeted in tented accommodation on the airfields or, if lucky, in nearby dwellings. The aircraft were hidden beneath vast sheets of camouflage netting, raised up on long poles to facilitate ground movement.

Handrik's pilots were keen to join the fray over England. In the weeks ahead they would be heavily engaged. Assembling over France at 15,000–18,000ft, these Me 109s would climb much higher still while approaching the English coast, typically to between 20,000–25,000ft, but range was a problem. Like the Spitfire and Hurricane, the Me 109 was designed as a short-range defensive interceptor, but now it was being deployed as a long-range offensive fighter, a role it had not the range to fulfil.

Fuel endurance was around ninety minutes, providing for thirty minutes combat time, twenty if the action was over London. Faced with two sea-crossings every sortie, the German fighter pilots anxiously monitored their fuel gauges, disengaging and heading homeward whenever the cockpit's red lamp illuminated, warning that fuel was getting low. In time, the German *jagdflieger* would come to hate the English Channel – *Der Kanal* – soon dubbed the '*Schiesskanal*' ('Shit Sewer').

Returning to the events of 21 July 1940, given the previous day's success, both 10 Group and 11 Group mounted convoy protection patrols in squadron strength. The morning was surprisingly quiet.

From 09.00 hrs onwards, two convoys were patrolled off the Thames Estuary by four sections of 54 Squadron Spitfires up from Manston in turn, but there was no reaction from the *Luftwaffe*. Flying Officer John Kemp suffered a dead engine fifteen miles off Clacton and was forced to bale out; fortunately he landed by parachute close to a destroyer, which picked him up. The ship was bound for Rosythe, from where the RAF pilot returned to base two days later.

As ever, the morning featured German reconnaissance aircraft droning over England.

At 10.05 hrs, Red Section of 238 Squadron scrambled from Middle Wallop following the Observer Corps reporting sight of a 'bandit'. In fact, this Me 110, of 4(F)/14, had already shot down a Fairey Battle engaged on a training flight at Stockbridge, and a Hawker Hart over Old Sarum.

Flight Lieutenant Donald Turner reported that:

> At approximately 1013 hrs I saw a single E/A which I identified as an Me 110 at 6,000ft, approximately ten miles SE of base. I ordered line astern and dived to within 500 yards and got in a 2-second burst just as the E/A was disappearing into cloud. I followed E/A, having ordered Red 2 and 3 (Flying Officer Charles Davis and Pilot Officer John Wigglesworth) above cloud. Running fight ensued eastwards with E/A darting in and out of cloud using very unusual tactics.
>
> Finally it disappeared into a large cloud with smoke pouring from starboard engine. I had used all ammunition, firing short bursts, whenever E/A appeared out of cloud, going towards Goodwood where I subsequently learned it had crashed... The E/A ceased firing early in the action, the rear gunner being certainly disabled. I received a bullet through my propeller.

This Me 110, of 4(F)/14, successfully forced-landed at Home Farm, Goodwood, at 10.25 hrs, both crewmen being captured.

For the rest of the day, 238 Squadron patrolled from Warmwell. Since 15 July 1940, the unit had been commanded by Squadron Leader Harold Fenton, an experienced pre-war pilot but lacking both operational and combat experience on fighters. Sensibly, Fenton chose to allow his more experienced 'A' Flight Commander, Flight Lieutenant Donald Turner, to lead as Red 1, when five Hurricanes of Red and Yellow Sections, including Fenton himself, took off at 14.20 hrs to patrol at 20,000ft.

At 14.40 hrs, West of Shaftesbury, a Do 17 was sighted at 18,000ft, and attacked by all five RAF pilots. A burst from Turner caused a fire behind the pilot, whose starboard engine was already disabled. The Do 17 forced-landed at Nutford Farm, Blandford, where the crew, all of whom were wounded, were captured. The victory was equally shared between 'A' Flight.

A westbound convoy, OA178, had safely passed through the Dover Strait under cover of darkness, but, ten miles South of The Needles and in plain sight, was attacked at 14.30 hrs by a *Gruppe* of Do 17s, escorted by some fifty Me 109s and Me 110s.

This formation, numbering eighty enemy aircraft in total, had been reported to Fighter Command as numbering only nine aircraft, leading the 11 Group Controller to despatch just three flights of fighters to intercept. 'B' Flight of 43 Squadron was already up from Tangmere and patrolling over the convoy, as Squadron Leader John Badger, the CO, reported:

> I was leading 'B' Flight on convoy patrol as Green 1. Blue Section was behind and above. The convoy was steaming West and we were flying South across its bows when I heard Blue 1 give 'Tally Ho!'.

Simultaneously I saw the hostile formations. I closed my Section up in line astern.

The enemy were in echelon, stepped up. I decided to attack from the inside of the circle of bombers as they swept round to attack. I attacked one Do 17 and got in a short burst using full deflection. I had to pull away immediately because I was in close line abreast with the succeeding Do 17.

I returned to attack another Do 17 and had just opened fire when tracer started whipping past me. I took immediate avoiding action but my starboard aileron was badly hit and partially jammed, and the aircraft was difficult to control. I then returned slowly to base and pancaked. It was impossible to see the results of my fire because of the great numbers of E/A diving on the convoy.

Flight Lieutenant Thomas Dalton-Morgan became embroiled with Me 109s, claiming one destroyed and another damaged, but Pilot Officer Ricardo de Mancha collided with the Me 109 of *Leutnant* Heinz Kroker of 7/JG27; both pilots remain missing.

Blue Section of 238 Squadron then arrived on the scene, as Flight Lieutenant Stuart Walch:

When approaching The Needles (1550 hrs) I saw the convoy being attacked by fifteen Me 110s. These aircraft were flying in wide line astern, attacking convoy by dive-bombing attacks from the northern side. I put my Section into line astern and gave order to Blue 2 and 3 to select a target each and attack independently. I dived from 22,000ft to 8,000ft, following the last aircraft in the enemy formation, which was now flying away from the convoy, south-east, apparently returning to France. I closed to about 500 yards before I was sighted.

The formation then went into a right-hand turn, aircraft still in line astern. The aircraft I was following swung out on its turn and was on the outside of the circle. I opened fire at 250 yards, closing to fifty. No 2 attacked the enemy aircraft on my right. The aircraft I attacked tightened his turn and dived towards the sea. I broke off the attack and the starboard engine of the E/A was omitting black and white smoke. I lost sight of the E/A in the dive, as I pulled away in a slight left-hand turn.

A few seconds later I saw an Me 110 flying at sea-level. It went straight for a mile then dived straight into the sea. I cannot say whether this was the E/A which I attacked or the one Blue 2 attacked. I then saw three Me 109s in line astern formation coming towards me on the beam at about 10,000ft. They did not attack me but turned away in a south-east direction and dived. I started to follow but saw an aircraft I thought to be an Me 109 flying at sea-level towards the convoy. I broke off following the three Me 109s and dived to attack the aircraft I had just seen. On getting within range it turned out to be Blue 2. By the time I had climbed up to 10,000ft again all hostile aircraft had disappeared.

Walch claimed one Me 110 destroyed and confirmed, and a second unconfirmed, while Pilot Officer Brian Considine, Blue 2, also claimed a 110 – destroyed but unconfirmed. This enemy aircraft, of 14/LG1, was in fact severely damaged and crash-landed at Theville, one crewman being killed.

For their efforts, the German sank just one ship, the SS *Terlings*, a cargo vessel of 2,318 tons, in transit from London via Southampton for Milford Haven and Sydney, in ballast. Nine of the crew were lost.

It was also a busy day for Coastal Command, which flew seventy-five patrols and escort sorties, two Hudsons being lost attacking shipping off the Lister Light, both shot down by Me 110s, while an Me 109 of 8/JG77 accounted for a 204 Squadron Sunderland engaged on a reconnaissance of Trondheim.

By night, all six 53 Squadron Blenheims attacking petrol stores at Ghent were hit by flak, although all returned, while three 235 Squadron Blenheims inconclusively engaged a 109 while on reconnaissance over Le Havre. By day, a lack of cloud cover prevented Bomber Command operating over the Continent, but by night targets in Germany were hit. For the first time, Fairey Battles were deployed in the Battle of Britain: three aircraft of 103 Squadron were tasked with attacking oil storage tanks at Rotterdam, but, unable to locate the primary target, one aircraft bombed an airfield near Goeree, while another hit a chemical plant; the third aircraft was forced to abort owing to a faulty directional gyro. Wellingtons, Whitleys and Hampdens attacked various aircraft factories in Germany and laid mines; just one aircraft of this force, a 78 Squadron Whitley, failed to return, having fallen victim to a night-fighter on a raid to marshalling yards at Hamm.

MONDAY, 22 JULY 1940

As has previously been discussed, when the Battle of Britain actually began remains a moot point. If we are to accept that this unprecedented aerial conflict was fought to deny Germany the aerial supremacy over southern England required for a seaborne invasion, then surely the start-date is dictated by the aggressor, not defender? Most importantly, the start and finish must align completely to German invasion plans. We have seen that the lull after Dunkirk concluded on the night of 18/19 June 1940, when some seventy German bombers attacked various targets in England after dark.

KANALKAMPF DIARY, 10 JULY – 31 JULY 1940

Another lull ensued, which broke on 2 July 1940 with fighting over Channel-bound convoys. Over the next week or so the tempo of fighting and size of enemy formations increased, leading to Air Chief Marshal Dowding 'somewhat arbitrarily' choosing 10 July 1940 as the official start-date. At that time, however, Hitler's policy toward the prosecution of the ongoing war was blockade, not invasion, and the hope of a diplomatic conclusion, with Britain accepting Germany's peace demands.

Throughout this time, Hitler had played 'Air Fleet Diplomacy' in an attempt to frighten Britain – the level of threat increased on 16 July 1940 with his '*Führer Directive*', expressing intentions to carry out a seaborne invasion 'if necessary'. Our study has shown, however, that the *Wehrmacht* was, in reality, under-resourced and unprepared for such an ambitious undertaking – which Hitler knew full-well. Hitler's hopes were not for invasion, but rather for Britain to accept his 'last appeal to reason' of 19 July 1940. With no formal response forthcoming, except a continuation of the Bomber Command offensive and defence of Britain, Hitler was approaching the time when he would have no choice but to abandon Brinkmanship and instead carry out his threats – and had held a high-level conference to discuss invasion plans on 21 July 1940. The following day saw things reach a head.

Churchill had, rightly, refused to respond to *Herr* Hitler's appeal for peace, so as not to dignify the 'last appeal to reason'. The War Cabinet, however, decided that there should be a response – and that this should be given by the Foreign Secretary Lord Halifax. The choice of speaker was significant – and in itself sent a strong message to Hitler. As we have explored, Halifax had previously been an appeaser, but now left Hitler in no doubt that Britain would never accept terms, nor back down.

On 22 July 1940, Halifax made a radio broadcast from London. Called 'Great Britain Shall Go Forward: We Remain Unmoved by Threats', the full text of it read as follows:

> MANY of you will have read two days ago the speech in which *Herr* Hitler summoned Great Britain to capitulate to his will. I will not waste your time by dealing with his distortions of almost every main event since the war began.
>
> He says he has no desire to destroy the British Empire, but there was in his speech no suggestion that peace must be based on justice, no word of recognition that the other nations of Europe had any right to self-determination, the principle which he has so often invoked for Germans.
>
> His only appeal was to the base instinct of fear, and his only arguments were threats.
>
> His silence as to the future of nations whom on one false pretext or another he has subjugated is significant.
>
> Quite plainly, unless the greater part of the world has entirely misread his speech, his picture of Europe is one of Germany lording

it over these peoples, whom he has one by one deprived of freedom. Our picture, drawn once again in bold outline by the President of the United States and General Smuts, is quite different. With them we see Europe a free association of independent States; and because of that contrast we remain unmoved by threats.

Hitler has now made it plain that he is preparing to direct the whole weight of German might against this country. That is why in every part of Britain, in great towns and villages alike, there is only one spirit of indomitable resolution.

Nor has any one any doubt that if Hitler were to succeed it would be the end, for many besides ourselves, of all those things which, as we say, make life worth living.

We realise that the struggle may cost us everything, but just because the things we are defending are worth any sacrifice, it is a noble privilege to be the defenders of things so precious.

We never wanted the war; certainly no one here wants the war to go on for a day longer than is necessary.

But we shall not stop fighting till freedom, for ourselves and others, is secure.

What do we mean when we say that we are fighting for freedom?

We want to be able to live our own lives as we like, and not have to look over our shoulders all the time to see if the Gestapo is listening.

We want to worship God as we like, and this religious freedom based on conscience we will not let go. For conscience is not something that you can hand over to anybody else.

But in Germany the people have given their consciences to Hitler so the people have become machines. And what has been the effect on Hitler?

When he first gained power he was at pains to explain that his aims were strictly limited. He was only concerned with the welfare of Germany. He had no claims against her neighbours. But steadily his appetite grew, until today he assumes the role of a supreme protector.

Already we see him ruling through creatures, pale shadows of himself, that he has established in central and northern Europe. Further south, Mussolini, flushed by his triumphs over a France whom he has not fought, may be allowed the role of master of a Mediterranean which he has not conquered.

For Hitler, force has become the final rule of the destinies of men and nations. Germany has the force. Hence Germany must alone decide how the nations are to live together. What matter if they do not like it?

Man, in his view, is a frail creature, fallible and made to obey, and will soon learn to obey his master. According to Hitler, old-fashioned respect for the pledged word is a sign of weak fibre, and unworthy of robust masterminds.

He would have no nonsense about equality before the law which is an outrage against reason and the all-powerful State. Bad faith, cruelty, crime become right by the fact that it is he, Hitler, who ordains them. That is the fundamental challenge of anti-Christ which it is our duty as Christians to fight with all our power.

The peoples of the British Commonwealth, along with all those who love the trust and justice and freedom will never accept this new world of Hitler's.

Free men not slaves. Free nations, not German vassals. A community of nations freely cooperating for the good of all these are the pillars of the new and better order that the British people wish to see.

And I hope that our country which leads the fight today to prevent the immeasurable human tragedy which Hitler's victory would mean will be the one to point the way for all peoples to a better life.

We can be of good heart when we survey the prospect. Hitler may plant the swastika where he will, but unless he can sap the strength of Britain, the foundations of his empire are built on sand.

In their hearts the peoples that he has beaten down curse him and pray that his attacks may be broken on the defences of our island fortress.

They long for the day when we shall sally forth and return blow for blow.

We shall assuredly not disappoint them. Then will come the day of final reckoning when Hitler's mad plans for Europe will be shattered by the unconquerable passion of man for freedom. And beyond the bounds of Europe, across the wide Atlantic, there are mighty nations who view his works with growing detestation.

The people of the United States did not build their new home in order to surrender it to this fanatic. They have judged his narrow and twisted vision. They see that his gospel is a gospel of hate, that his policy is the policy of brute force, his message to mankind the enthralment of the human spirit under ruthless tyranny.

We may take heart from the certain knowledge that that great people pray for our victory over this wicked man and his ways as fervently as any of his present victims. The foundations of their country, as of ours, have been Christian teaching and belief in God.

For this reason, I have no doubt that the King's broadcast last Christmas, when he spoke of putting our hand in the hand of God, went home to them as it did to us.

Where will God lead us? Not, we may be sure, through easy or pleasant paths. That is not His way. He will not help us to avoid our difficulties. What He will do is to give to those, who humbly ask, the spirit that no dangers can disturb.

The Christian message to the world brings peace in war; peace where we most need it; peace of soul.

It is that same Christian message which makes its giver, who is God, the best friend with whom a man can share life or death. Those of us who cannot serve in the armed forces must all do our best in other ways to help them. I'm sure we shall and there is one thing we can all do, soldiers, sailors, airmen and civilians, men, women and children, all together, which may be much more powerful than we know. And this is to pray.

I heard the other day of a Yorkshire village where after all the talk about a fifth column the people had agreed to form a sixth column, in which they pledged themselves to try and give a few minutes each day in God's house to prayer. We shall naturally ask God to take care of those we love and to bless the cause for which our country is at war. We can ask this with confidence because we know that we are trying to resist things that cannot be according to God's will.

But prayer is not only asking God for what we want, but rather the way to learn to. trust Him, to ask that we may know His will and do it with all our strength. If we can really do our work, whatever it is, as well as we can in God's sight, it will become His work, and we can safely leave the issue in His hands.

This, then, is the spirit in which we must march together in this crusade for Christianity.

We and our great dominions overseas stand, and shall continue to stand, four square against the forces of evil.

We shall go forward, seeing clearly both the splendour and the perils of the task, but strengthened by the faith, through which by God's help, as we try to do His service, we shall prevail.

There was now absolutely no doubt: Britain would fight on. Halifax's speech made that clear enough, in addition to maintaining that public opinion in the USA was anti-Hitler. Home Intelligence, however, somewhat pompously and condescendingly reported that the 'high moral tone' of 'Lord Holy Fox's' speech was 'above the heads of a large section of the public'.

According to Count Ciano, the speech was 'inconsequential'. He was wrong. Hitler now knew that his gamble, his 'Air Fleet Diplomacy', and threats had failed.

It was, as Cajus Bekker wrote in *The Luftwaffe War Diaries*, 'the final blow to German illusions that the British might still come to terms'. It is surely from this date on, therefore, more than any other, that the Battle of Britain can truly be considered to have begun – because now Hitler had no other option but Operation

KANALKAMPF DIARY, 10 JULY – 31 JULY 1940

Seelöwe. From now on, *Luftwaffe* operations were no longer the bluff of 'Air Fleet Diplomacy', but genuinely appended to the serious prospect of invading Britain.
Daily Home Intelligence Report:

> People cheerful and optimistic at weekend when Hitler failed to invade Britain on Friday, as threatened. General feeling now that war will last a long time as invasion cannot succeed and we shall then settle down to hammering away at Germany by RAF.

Ironically, on account of minimal shipping activity in the Channel the air fighting on this most historically significant day was slight. Inevitably, though, German reconnaissance aircraft were ever-present.

During the Norwegian campaign, tragedy had struck 46 Squadron, operating Hurricanes from HMS *Glorious*, when the carrier was sunk by the German cruisers *Scharnhorst* and *Gneisenau*: only two of the fifty-nine RAF personnel aboard survived, both pilots of 46 Squadron.

Withdrawn to Digby in 12 Group, the squadron was rebuilt and declared operational by June 1940. From there, the replenished unit trained and flew convoy protection patrols off the East Coast. On the dawn patrol of 22 July 1940, Blue Section, comprising Pilot Officer Peter McGregor, and Sergeants Gerald Edworthy and Ernest Bloor, made 46 Squadron's first interception of the Battle of Britain.

Pilot Officer Peter McGregor:

> Blue Section took off at 0445 hrs to patrol convoy stated to be 78° from home base, thirty miles out to sea. At 0514 hrs convoy was sighted and several bursts of AA fire were seen. AA increased and one bandit was sighted, flying West at 3,500ft. Aircraft (bandit) climbed to 5,000–6,000ft, entered cloud and turned East. Blue Section followed and sighted bandit again, about ½ mile ahead which was now flying just below cloud. Blue 1 [Pilot Officer McGregor himself] attacked from port quarter, dropping into line astern. Bandit did a climbing right-hand turn and then dived almost vertically to sea-level. Fragments appeared to come from starboard engine, also small flames and smoke.
>
> Blue 1 broke away to left and Blue 2 fired five short bursts as bandit dived at the sea. No results observed. Blue 3 fired short burst before bandit levelled out and one burst 4–5 seconds dead astern at 200–300 yards. Each aircraft then carried out a No 1 Attack from dead astern. Cannon fire was experienced from top centre turret, which passed over and to port of Blue 1 and Blue 3 during the second attack. Blue 2, who carried out the final attack, did not observe any fire.
>
> During the first attack no fire was experienced. No fire was experienced from lower turret at any stage in the attack. When last

seen bandit was flying SE, just above water. Blue Section left bandit at 0525 hrs as estimated position was then 80° out to sea. The Section landed at 0600 hrs.

The 'bandit' was identified as a Do 17 and shared equally by Blue Section as a 'probable', although it appears this machine returned to France, damaged.

At 05.24 hrs, Squadron Leader Rupert 'Lucky' Leigh led 'A' Flight of his 66 Squadron up from Coltishall to patrol the Cross Sands lightship. The Flight comprised Red Section, 1, 2 and 3 being Leigh, and Pilot Officers John Mather and Crelin 'Bogle' Bodie, and Yellow Section, 1, 2 and 3: Pilot Officer Hugh Kennard, Sergeant Matthew Cameron and Pilot Officer Charles Cooke.

At 05.25 hrs, Leigh was re-vectored to patrol Convoy *Booty*, and, at 05.37 hrs, sighted two Do 17s entering cloud:

> He ordered Red Section below cloud and Yellow Section above cloud. Yellow Section was flying in line astern when at 0550 hrs Yellow 3 saw a Do 17 behind him as it came out of cloud, which was 10/10 at 8,000ft with a depth of 500ft. Yellow 3 immediately turned and chased it, at same time informing Yellow Leader. E/A immediately climbed back into cloud, but Yellow 3 managed to give it a short burst from astern. He saw his tracer entering E/A by top rear gunner.
>
> No fire was experienced from E/A. Yellow 3 followed E/A into cloud and on emerging from top of cloud could not see E/A. He then went below cloud and saw E/A but before he could attack again E/A had got back into cloud, and so Yellow 3 re-joined his Section patrolling convoy. Red Section and Yellow 1 and 2 did not have combat. [66 Squadron CR]

The combat was inconclusive.

The only confirmed victory that morning was scored by Blue Section of 'B' Flight, 145 Squadron, up from Tangmere, as Pilot Officer Nigel Weir reported on the combat, which took place between 07.00 to 07.15 hrs, twenty miles South of Selsey Bill:

> We had been vectored back from Beachy Head to Selsey Bill, where sundry bandits were allegedly flying around. I sighted one, a long way South of us, flying South, but by that time Blue Section Leader [Flight Lieutenant Archibald Boyd] had begun to dive on a Do 17 a few thousand feet below us, heading South. Green Section left us and as Blue Section dived flat out, the Dornier dived East.
>
> Blue Leader silenced the rear gunner and damaged the starboard engine. As soon as he broke away I, as Blue 2, opened fire from above at 300 yards, aiming ahead of the pilot. After a time, seeing

he was still flying on, I transferred my fire to the starboard engine, which caught fire just after I broke away. Blue 3 attacked and the Dornier finally landed in the sea. We signalled a motor boat to rescue the crew, and when this had been done we returned to base, leaving the rubber dinghy on the sea.

The Do 17 belonged to 4(F)/121. The crew were all captured by a Royal Navy Motor Torpedo Boat (MTB).

Much further North, bombs fell on Duff House, Banff, Scotland, shortly after 09.00 hrs – ironically this was PoW Camp No.5 and was accommodating German prisoners. Among them was one Paul Mengelberg, an electrician aboard *U-26*, captured on 1 July 1940 when his submarine was abandoned by the crew after being badly damaged off Ireland by HMS *Gladiolus* and a Coastal Command Sunderland:

> In the morning, at nine o'clock, the klaxon for roll call went. We were all lined up outside. We heard an aircraft and he came pretty low. He must have been coming out from Norway. I think it was a reconnaissance aircraft. They are loaded with bombs too. I think he was on a reconnaissance mission to explore northern Scotland, and he saw this camp down there. He saw the tents of the guards up on the hill, and he saw this building there with people outside and thought, 'let's give them a lesson', so to speak.
>
> Before we witnessed that it was over, the bombs fell. Miraculously, I wasn't hit by anything, but I lost six of my crewmates from U-26 during the air attack mistakenly made by Hermann Göring's 'Flying Circus'. Two bombs went into the elevator shaft as duds, they never blew up. But two guards outside, they were killed through the bombs Those who died were given a soldier's funeral by the British forces at the gravesite in Banff.

Eighteen Germans and the same number of British soldiers were wounded in the attack, while in addition to the six *U-26* crewmen, a British guard was also killed. The raider escaped without interception.

For Coastal Command it was a day of much effort, with 116 crews flying various patrols. On one of these, an Anson pilot, Pilot Officer Winter-Taylor of Dyce's 612 Squadron, was patrolling Convoy HX56A when he 'sighted and attacked a U-boat with bombs. The destroyers escorting the convoy subsequently carried out further attacks with depth charges. Two further sorties were flown to cooperate with the destroyers until the Senior Naval Officer signalled, "I think it is a wreck now".'

By night, Coastal Command Swordfish biplanes sowed mines, while Blenheims and a Hudson bombed the concentration of invasion barges at Amsterdam. Daylight operations by Bomber Command, however, were all cancelled owing to the clear weather over the Continent. After dark, sixty-eight Bomber Command aircraft, of all types, attacked various targets in Germany, airfields in France, barges in the Netherlands, and also laid mines. One Whitley and its crew of five was lost, having been hit by flak over Detmold.

There was, however, a potentially bitter-sweet success that night when a Blenheim of the Fighter Interception Unit (FIU) equipped with experimental Airborne Interception (AI) radar stalked and destroyed its prey, believed to have been a Do 17. This was the first aerial success recorded by an AI-equipped aircraft. Sadly the target may have been, according to some sources, a 107 Squadron Blenheim, which crashed into the Channel returning from a raid on Creil airfield, the crew being lost; other secondary sources identify the target as legitimately a Do 17 of 2/KG3.

TUESDAY, 23 JULY 1940

For Fighter Command, this would be the quietest day since the fighting began on 2 July 1940, doubtless owing to the still minimal shipping traffic off the British coast, and lack of a cohesive *Luftwaffe* plan.

During an hour's dawn patrol commencing at 05.10 hrs, Flight Lieutenant George Powell-Shedden, of Coltishall's 242 Squadron, engaged and damaged a Ju 88 off Yarmouth. Although no claim was made, this combat may well have concerned a Ju 88 of 4(F)/122, lost on a reconnaissance sortie to the Dover area.

The only other enemy aircraft lost on this day fell to the guns of 603 Squadron's Blue Section, which patrolled off Aberdeen between 14.47 and 16.00 hrs. At 15.30 hrs they engaged 'a Do 17, seventy-five miles off Aberdeen, confirmed, which crashed into the sea. No survivors.'

During this engagement, the Spitfires of both Flight Lieutenant Frederick 'Rusty' Rushmer (Blue 1) and Pilot Officer Noel 'Broody' Benson (Blue 3), although both pilots returned safely to Montrose, while Pilot Officer Ronald 'Raz' Berry (Blue 2) escaped unscathed.

Scotland was also the location for a flying accident at 12.35 hrs, when a Coastal Command Blenheim of 269 Squadron collided on take-off from Wick with a 3 Squadron Hurricane – the Blenheim crew were all killed; the Hurricane pilot, Pilot Officer Douglas Bisgood, survived but was badly injured.

Elsewhere, Coastal Command Hudsons were active, one of 269 Squadron shooting down a Do 18 seaplane off Karmoy, Norway, while a 224 Squadron Hudson was forced to abandon a combat with three Do 18s when its guns jammed.

After dark, 53 Squadron Blenheims, based at Detling, attacked the barges concentrated in Amsterdam's Spoorweg Basin, and six 59 Squadron Blenheims went to attack, the ORB records, 'oil wells at Flushing. One aircraft returned with engine trouble and another formatted on two stars and dropped his bombs in Germany. All aircraft returned safely.'

Again, unsuitable weather conditions over enemy-occupied Europe prevented eleven of 2 Group, Bomber Command's Blenheims from attacking oil refineries in Germany – unescorted and in daylight – but one hit docks at The Hague while three aircraft instead bombed *Luftwaffe* airfields in France. That night, eighty-five Bomber Command aircraft were briefed to attack various targets, including airfields and factories, but low-lying cloud and fog hampered operations. One Blenheim, of 110 Squadron, failed to return, crashing onto the North Sea off the Dutch coast, the crew all being reported missing.

On the Home Front, according to the Daily Home Intelligence Report, 'Morale is high. People are fully behind the war effort although small pockets of defeatism confined to certain localities, age or social groups are still present.' Lord Halifax's broadcast of the previous day remained a topic of conversation, these reactions being noted:

> 'Too much like a bishop. 'Depressing.' 'Disappointing.' 'Unsatisfactory.' 'He didn't explain anything.' 'Very nice and gentlemanly.' 'Old-fashioned diplomacy.' 'Too much like Chamberlain days.' 'It was a dull speech: I switched off.' 'I liked the high moral tone.' 'It's no use treating a mad dog like that.' 'An excellent sermon but lacking the directness the situation demands.' 'Any bishop could have done as much from his pulpit.'

Prior to the broadcast, Halifax had visited Churchill at Chequers, seeking the Prime Minister's approval over content. Explaining how 'cumbrous' he found mentioning all three services individually, Halifax later recalled that Churchill,

> thought for a moment or two, walking up and down the long room, and then said: "Why not say unless that man can sap the might of Britain?" Which Halifax did, adding 'what an example of language – and nearly all monosyllables'.

Beyond doubt, the Prime Minister was a highly skilled master of the English language – which found itself, along with the whole nation, fully mobilised.

WEDNESDAY, 24 JULY 1940

The Daily Home Intelligence Report on this day noted how, 'The lull in events is reflected in morale'. It went on to state:

> People are calm, not highly interested in the wider implications of war, critical of the Government's home policy but fundamentally

cooperative in all measures believed to indicate a vigorous war policy. Defence measures are approved and giving increased confidence. Factory employees are working at high pressure although there are signs of fatigue because of long hours and few holidays.

Most people continued working as normal, while the Minister of Supply, Herbert Morrison, enthused a veritable army of voluntary labour with his famous slogan, 'Go to it.' Churchill had defined his War Cabinet's aim in one word: 'Victory'. And this was, more than any other, a 'People's War' – because Britain's population was mobilised to a greater extent than any other nation throughout the Second World War.

The British people overwhelmingly supported the war effort, evidenced by the lack of a strong and popular peace lobby. Most importantly, the national effort, including conscription, taxation, requisitioning and rationing, affected everyone, cutting across the social classes and accelerating 'social levelling'. As Churchill often told the people during this 'good war', it was a case of going 'forward together'.

Nonetheless, there was an acute awareness, if not fear, of the threat of invasion: since June 1940, the ringing of church bells had been forbidden and were only to be sounded by the military or police to alert the population of an airborne landing. The War Cabinet agreed that the code word 'Cromwell' would be issued in the event of invasion either appearing imminent, or actually in progress. And so the nation went about its business – and continued waiting for what was 'to come'.

At his opulent home, Carinhall, *Reichsmarschall* Göring entertained a would-be peacemaker: Dr Albert Plesman, head of the Dutch airline. He offered to act as a mediator between Britain and Germany, and proffered his own ideas for a diplomatic solution, involving specific territorial interests for both parties. Göring apparently agreed to discuss the matter with Hitler, providing further evidence that regardless of the supposed 'last appeal to reason' of 19 July 1940, avenues for a non-military outcome were still being pursued behind the scenes. In this particular case, Lord Halifax would reject Plesman's plan the following month, by which time, in any case, the Battle of Britain was in full swing.

Wednesday, 24 July 1940 dawned dull and cloudy – and inevitably the *Luftwaffe*'s first incursions were early reconnaissance flights.

No.92 Squadron, based at Pembrey in South Wales, scored an early success:

A Section led by Flight Lieutenant Kingcome, with Pilot Officer Bryson and Flying Officer Paterson, encountered a Ju 88 this morning at about 0730 hrs over Porthcawl. They gave chase and brought it down at Ilfracombe on the Devon coast. One German baled out at twenty yards and was killed. The remainder of the crew of three got out of the burning machine but our pilots were unable to know if they were injured or not. Later, it was ascertained that one of the crew had been injured. [ORB]

The Ju 88, of 3/LG1, had been seeking shipping in the Bristol Channel, when attacked by the Spitfire pilots and, according to some accounts, Pilot Officer Roland Beamont, a Hurricane pilot of 87 Squadron up from Exeter (although no confirmation of this can be found in primary sources). Master Dalyn, 10 years old, was working in the fields of his family's farm, Killmington, near Lynton on Devon's Exmoor coast, when he saw a Ju 88 appear low overhead, pursued by the RAF fighters; the bomber crash-landed in flames just a few hundred yards from the farm house, smashing through a dry-stone wall before coming to rest. *Hauptmann* von Maltitz, the *Staffelkapitän* and *Feldwebel* Pliefke were captured unhurt, while *Feldwebel* Weilmaier was wounded; one man, *Feldwebel* Wachholz, was dead. Later, the three victorious Spitfire pilots visited the scene, removing and holding aloft the swastika from the Ju 88's tail, much to the delight of watching locals.

Red Section of 603 Squadron was also in action at 07.30 hrs, when Flying Officer John Haig, and Pilot Officers George 'Sheep' Gilroy and Bill Read intercepted and, as the ORB states, 'attacked a He 111 out to sea between Aberdeen and Peterhead. E/A's port engine was disabled and rear-gunner put out of action. E/A circled and lost height, but disappeared into low cloud and was not seen again.'

At 08.50 hrs, Blue Section of 64 Squadron's 'B' Flight, led by Sub-Lieutenant Dawson-Paul (Blue 1), was scrambled from Kenley with orders to patrol Dover, as enemy aircraft were approaching. Having somehow lost Blue 2, Blue 1 and 3 found a convoy North-east of the Goodwin Sands.

At 09.00 hrs, as Blue 1 later reported,

> six Do 215s in two vics, very tight, approached the convoy, their height was about 11,000ft. I dived towards them and positioned myself for a beam attack on their port side – fired three 3-second bursts at one aircraft and he broke away and fell in a spin. I fired the remainder of my ammunition into the enemy and then broke away downwards.
>
> In so doing I received a burst from the rear-gunner which holed my bottom petrol tank. I preceded to forward base and landed intact. The Do 215 has been confirmed as having crashed in the sea off the NE end of the Goodwins. These E/A bombed the convoy heavily but all their bombs fell short.

Dawson-Paul, however, did not personally see his adversary crash, and no Dorniers were actually lost on this day. More likely, the enemy bomber returned home damaged, and the aircraft reportedly down in the sea was an Me 110 of *Erprobungsgruppe* 210.

That day, the unit was again active in attacking convoys, claiming to have destroyed 20,000 tons of British shipping – but suffered its first fatality of the Battle of Britain in the process, when *Unteroffizier* Paul Hermann and *Unteroffizier* Heinz Meinhardt of 2 *Staffel* were shot down by AA fire while attacking a convoy some fifteen miles East of Harwich.

For 54 Squadron, operating from Manston, 24 July 1940 would prove to be a busy day indeed.

At 05.15 hrs that morning, 54 Squadron's Sergeant George 'Dick' Collett flew the dawn patrol with Pilot Officers John Allen DFC and Archibald Finnie. After just ten minutes the trio landed back at base, for some unrecorded reason, taking off again five minutes later for a further fifteen uneventful minutes. Dick also flew on the day's third patrol, taking off at 08.40 hrs.

A convoy passing through the Dover Strait had drawn an attack from two *Staffeln* of Do 17s, in two waves of six; the first wave reached the ships but missed their targets. No.54 Squadron's Green Section, led by Pilot Officer George Gribble, harried the second wave, which jettisoned its bombs and ran back to France. Sergeant Collett took no direct part in the action, and 54 Squadron claimed none of the bombers destroyed, but sighting the enemy for the first time must have been an adrenalin-inducing moment.

Then came, according to the 54 Squadron scribe, 'The Battle of the Thames Estuary'.

This time, a much heavier attack was mounted on a convoy steaming out of the Medway at 11.00 hrs, some eighteen Dorniers approaching the ships. On what was JG26's first mission against England, ten Me 109s II/JG26 swept ahead of the bombers while forty fighters of *Major* Adolf Galland's III/JG26 closely escorted the Dorniers.

At 11.12 hrs, Red, Blue and Green Sections of Biggin Hill's 610 Squadron were scrambled at patrol Dover, led by Flight Lieutenant John Ellis, and at 11.35 hrs engaged the incoming Me 109s ten miles South of Dover. *Hauptmann* Noack, however, of II/JG26 reported a large number of Spitfires (actually only the nine of 610 Squadron) over Dover, so aborted the mission and returned to France – where, ironically, he was killed while landing back at Marquise.

No.610 Squadron's ORB:

> Attacked three Me 109s flying at 3,000ft above and in the opposite direction. On attack E/A broke formation. Flight Lieutenant Ellis (Blue Leader) fired successive bursts at one E/A which dived vertically for the sea, belching forth black and white smoke, completely out of control. Nos 2 and 3 of this Section confirm that this E/A was destroyed. Flight Lieutenant E.B.B. Smith (Red Leader) flying at 14,000ft South of Dover sighted nine to twelve Me 109s below, approaching head-on in open formation, line abreast. He attacked one E/A, firing several short bursts, causing it to smoke heavily and dive vertically, out of control. Sergeant Chandler, who confirms this, met three unidentified aircraft below, wheeled round and delivered a No 2 Attack, and saw pieces falling away from E/A, and Red 2 was convinced that E/A was out of control, his attack having been delivered against centre of E/A. Red 3 (Sergeant

Parsons) confirms this and says E/A was destroyed. This E/A was subsequently identified as a Chance-Vought.

The reference to a 'Chance-Vought' was erroneous, but 610 had done well, claiming two Me 109s confirmed destroyed.

At 11.20 hrs, 54 Squadron, led by Flight Lieutenant Al Deere, had also scrambled towards the approaching trouble off Dover. Within minutes, Deere's Spitfires were embroiled with Galland's Me 109s. Sergeant Dick Collett again flew in a section of three with Pilot Officers Allen and Finnie, as he subsequently reported:

> I was flying in vic formation at 12,000ft, acting as rear guard, when I saw about nine E/A on our tails about 2,000ft above and immediately told my leader, who turned to port. I next noticed white smoke coming from the starboard side of a Spitfire, I think that of Yellow One. I turned left and right and got in a deflection shot on the 109 which was on the tail of this Spitfire; he came off Pilot Officer Allen's tail at once, and as the 109 came up I got in another burst, after which the E/A wobbled badly and his engine stopped.

This was a classic case of the vulnerable 'Tail End Charlie' section, weaving to and from slightly above and behind their squadron, being 'bounced' first by the ever-watchful high-flying Me 109s. Dick continued:

> As he dived down, I gave a final burst, after which he was obviously finished. I did not see him strike the sea as my attention was drawn to another 109 which I chased and finally got in my sights and pressed the button, but unfortunately all my ammunition was spent. I had to throttle back to about plus 4 boost to keep on his tail. This last E/A took no evasive action, since he probably didn't know I was there.

Galland himself later wrote:

> Over the Thames Estuary we got involved in a heavy scrap with Spitfires ... Together with the *Stabschwarm* [Staff Flight] I selected one formation as our prey, and we made a surprise attack from a favourably higher altitude. I glued myself to the tail of the plane flying outside on the left flank and when, during a right-handed turn, I managed to get in a long burst, the Spitfire went down almost vertically. I followed it until the cockpit cover came flying towards me and the pilot baled out, then followed him down until he crashed into the water. His parachute had failed to open.

There is no record, however, of an RAF fighter pilot baling out into the sea that day. The parachute of *Leutnant* Josef Schauff of 8/JG26, failed to open, though, after he was shot down by a Spitfire over Margate, but his aircraft crashed in Byron Avenue, the pilot's body falling in nearby playing fields. (It is impossible to say who shot Schauff down.) Both Sergeant Collett and Pilot Officer Colin Gray were credited with Me 109s destroyed, and unconfirmed kills were attributed to Flight Lieutenant Deere, Flying Officer Desmond McMullen, Pilot Officers Edward Coleman and Douglas Turley-George.

Furthermore, eight 109s were claimed as probably destroyed by Flying Officer McMullen, Flight Lieutenant Basil 'Wonky' Way (two), Pilot Officer Gray, Pilot Officer George Gribble (two), Pilot Officer Turley-George and Flight Sergeant Phillip Tew, in addition to two damaged by Pilot Officer Coleman and Pilot Officer Henry Matthews. In reality, Schauff's was the only Me 109 lost by III/JG26 in this action, confirming how, yet again, the confusion of air fighting, owing to the speed of combat, so often deceived the human eye. Little wonder, though, that the 54 Squadron diarist described 24 July 1940 as 'The biggest and most successful day since Dunkirk.'

While during the engagement Sergeant Collett had shot a 109 off the tail of Pilot Officer Allen, it would seem that the latter's Spitfire was already grievously damaged, as the 54 Squadron ORB reports:

> The action was marred by the unfortunate loss of Pilot Officer Allen DFC. He was attacked by an Me 109 near Margate; he was seen coming down with engine stopped and appeared to be making a forced-landing under perfect control. The engine came to life again, and he made for Manston, the engine cut a second time and Pilot Officer Allen apparently turned towards Foreness when he stalled and spun straight into the ground. The loss of Pilot Officer Allen, who had destroyed seven enemy aircraft, will be greatly felt by the whole Squadron.

Sergeant Collett's report continues: 'I tried by R/T to get a homing vector but could get no reply, so I set course about NW and made landfall close to where I landed. I had only five gallons left so could not try for an alternative landing.'

Collett had 'crashed' (his word), forced-landing Spitfire N3192, KL-V, at Sizewell, near Orfordness.

The following day, the Record Office at RAF Ruislip wrote to his father:

> I regret to inform you that according to a communication received from 54 Squadron ... your son No 745500 Sergeant George Richard Collett of the above unit was admitted to Ipswich Hospital and placed on the 'Seriously Ill' list on 24 July 1940.

> He was seriously injured when the aircraft of which he was the pilot and sole occupant crashed at Saxmundham, near Martlesham Heath, Suffolk, after an engagement with enemy aircraft.
>
> Should you propose to visit your son it is desirable that you communicate with the hospital authorities concerned to ensure that he has not, in the meantime, been transferred elsewhere.
>
> Any change in his condition will be notified to me, and you will be informed immediately.

This prognosis, however, was a mistake. Certainly, Dick Collett was a patient at East Suffolk and Ipswich Hospital's Churchman Annex Ward, from where, the same day, he wrote to his father and sister (his mother having already sadly died) clarifying the situation and alleviating their anxiety:

> Shall start by saying I am only slightly hurt, the chief thing being two stitches in the chin, the rest are really aches and pains, which will heal ... very rapidly. I should not bother about coming over to see me as it is not worth it, especially as I should be out in about three days. Am very comfortable with nice ward and other HM forces to keep me company.
>
> Perhaps you may have heard the news on the wireless that an air battle took place over the Channel with the result that we got five certs and nine probables with the loss of two Spitfires. Well, one of the two was me, and the other my Section Leader. We were busy from 5 o'clock in the morning but the big do was at 1 pm.
>
> I was not shot down but ran out of juice and had to make a forced-landing not far from Lowestoft, which was not a success owing to the engine coughing when just over the hedge, with the result that I hit the dirt rather hard. It was not a complete debit as I did get an Me 109, but wandering so far after another which, when I caught up with was only to find my ammo was used up. I had difficulty finding merry England and when I did only have five gallons left, so had to get a move on in the way of a landing. Not very good business trip but I hope it will improve later.
>
> As luck would have it I was to have 24 hours leave from 1 o'clock yesterday to 1 o'clock today, but that, of course, is knocked on the head and will have to wait a bit. Pity, especially as it is such a nice day today with sun streaming in through the windows.
>
> Well old things there is no more news I can think of at the moment but will write again giving you an update of my movements before very long. Be good, people, don't get into trouble and don't worry

about me as I have literally NOTHING wrong with me and am only here really under observation.

Heaps of love from old son and brother, Dick.

Back at Manston, 54 Squadron received a signal from 11 Group HQ:

> Air Officer Commanding has read with great interest the combat report of 54 Squadron and congratulates the leaders and pilots on their magnificent fight against superior numbers. He wishes 54 Squadron to know that 65 and 610 Squadrons were also despatched to intercept the same raid and were also engaged with enemy fighters and bombers.

While the end result, considering actual German losses, was not the body-blow 54 Squadron believed it had delivered to III/JG26, *Major* Galland, a leading German fighter ace and tactician, a veteran of Spain and the campaigns to date, concluded after the day's events that 'We were no longer in doubt that the RAF would prove a most formidable opponent.'

At dawn that morning, 65 Squadron had flown from Hornchurch to also operate from the coastal airfield at Manston, 'B' Flight being ordered up at noon to patrol a convoy in the Medway, so was also embroiled in the 'Battle of the Thames Estuary' with 54 Squadron.

While the latter engaged the Me 109 escorts, 'A' Flight of 65 Squadron attacked the bombers, which maintained a close formation and effective defensive cross-fire, making it difficult for the Spitfire pilots to get in close, which instead joined in fighting the 109s at 12.30 hrs:

> Squadron Leader Sawyer closed behind one and fired some short bursts at it. The E/A was seen to go into a dive with some pouring from it. Owing to the attention of other aircraft, Squadron Leader was unable to follow the Me 109 down and therefore only claimed an unconfirmed destroyed. He also damaged three others. Flight Sergeant Phillips claimed to have slightly damaged two Do 215s while Flying Officer Nicholas and Flight Sergeant McPherson claimed to have damaged one each. [ORB]

No.65 Squadron returned to Manston, and at 13.30 hrs was ordered off to spend the remainder of the day at Rochford. Until then, the squadron had been having a comparatively quiet time, the ORB recording that, 'This little shindy has eased that "browned off" feeling and put our tails up, and at least there will be a few Huns unserviceable for some time.'

When III/JG26 had been forced to disengage due to low fuel reserves, the Me 109s dived for the deck and skimmed over Kent at low-level, roaring over the Kentish coast and streaking back across the Channel to their Pas-de-Calais bases. This power dive was, in fact, the 109's standard evasive tactic; due to its Daimler-Benz 601A engine being fuel-injected, the flow of petrol to the engine was unaffected by gravity, meaning that it did not cut out in a dive – unlike the Rolls-Royce Merlin powering the British fighters, which did not enjoy the benefits of a direct fuel feed.

The 109, therefore, was always able to outrun a Spitfire in a dive. Ramming the throttle forward produced a sudden plume of black smoke, which is why, seeing their targets hurtling vertically earthwards and trailing black smoke, RAF pilots believed their adversaries destroyed – which was often not actually the case. This is also another reason for RAF fighter pilots overclaiming. During the late morning and lunchtime combats on this day, for example, Spitfire pilots claimed at least seventeen Me 109s either confirmed or unconfirmed destroyed; in reality, JG26 and JG52 lost six fighters destroyed in addition to *Hauptmann* Noack, who crashed and was killed back at base.

Enemy tactics on this day represented an important development: with the German fighter force on the *Kanalfront* reinforced by JG26, it was now possible for the enemy to coordinate fighter sweeps in advance of their main raids – intended to preoccupy and exhaust the defending fighters, leaving the way clear for bombers to attack convoys.

Sadly, there was a tragic accident at the North Weald Sector Station, as Squadron Leader Edward 'Teddy' Donaldson, CO of 151 Squadron recalled:

> That day the weather was appalling. I got an urgent telephone call from the AOC. He said 'The weather is bloody awful, but I have an unidentified aircraft circling Felixstowe at 10,000ft and I don't like it. As the weather is so bad I must ask you, not order you, if you can go after him.'
>
> I turned to my Red Two, Pilot Officer Jack Hamar, and said 'What about it?' Jack replied, as I knew he would, 'Let's get the bastard!'
>
> Air Vice-Marshal Park said 'Thanks a lot', so off we went.
>
> Visibility was down to about a quarter of a mile. The danger at North Weald was the international radio masts, which went up several hundred feet, and while the controllers could get pilots back to the field, to avoid the masts you had to see them in time.
>
> No sooner were we airborne with wheels up than Group identified the bogey as friendly. We turned around and, flying slowly at 120 mph and only some 60ft above the ground, I waited for North Weald to reappear, which it did in a few minutes. I ordered Jack to break. To my horror he broke upwards and commenced an upward role. In a Hurricane it was impossible to carry out such a manoeuvre at that low speed. As I saw him start his right-handed roll, I screamed 'Don't, don't!' down the R/T – but it was too late: Jack stalled and hit the deck upside down.

> I was on the ground and beside him within seconds. Jack had had his hood open to improve visibility in the awful weather conditions, which had caused massive head injuries. I was devastated.

Pilot Officer Hamar had crashed at 14.00 hrs in Hurricane P3316. His loss was a completely unnecessary waste of a young life, devastating family and friends. That fateful day, the Hamars were celebrating news of Jack's DFC, but within an hour of his letter arriving, informing the family of his well-deserved award, Jack's parents received the telegram notifying them of their eldest son's death.

Pilot Officer Hamar was given an impressive military funeral at Knighton Cemetery on 28 July 1940, receiving over a hundred floral tributes. Indicating the young fighter pilot's popularity, the firing party from North Weald, attended at their own request.

On 4 September 1940, Jack's father received a letter from Buckingham Palace:

> I have the honour to inform you that your attendance is requested at Buckingham Palace at 10.30 o' clock a.m. on Tuesday 17 September next, in order that you, as next of kin, may receive from the King the decoration of the late Pilot Officer Jack R. Hamar, which he would have received personally, had he survived.

At the investiture, Lord Clarendon, the Lord Chamberlain, was at the king's side, calling out the names of the heroes and then their relatives who were to step forward and receive decorations. Mrs Hamar proudly accepted her late son's DFC, returning with it to Knighton, a world away from London at the Battle of Britain's height. Naturally, the family was extremely proud of Jack's august achievements, but, as his brother Fred told me many years later: 'I don't think as a family we ever really got over it.'

Clearly, Air Commodore Donaldson, as he became, never 'got over' the death of his friend either. After a distinguished career in the service, 'Teddy' became the air correspondent for the *Daily Telegraph* until retiring in 1979. He died in 1992 and was buried at Tangmere, his regard for his wingman and friend as strong then as on that fateful day at North Weald in 1940. As Teddy said, 'Jack and I were extremely close; I loved the fellow.'

For Fighter Command, the final combat of the day involved 74 Squadron:

> At 1721 hrs, 'A' Flight took off from Manston to patrol the Channel and at 1724 hrs were detailed to intercept Raid 45 near Dover. On nearing objective they sighted three Do 215s flying at sea-level. On being spotted by our fighters the E/A immediately turned towards the French coast. The E/A opened fire at 2,000 yards range in an attempt to scare our fighters off, but Red and Yellow Sections closed to 300 yards and opened fire. One Do 215 was seen to be disabled when our fighters

broke away over the French coast. Pilot Officers Freeborn, Cobden and Hastings took an active part in this combat. [ORB]

Meanwhile in the Duxford Sector of 12 Group, 19 Squadron packed up its troubles and moved to operate from the nearby satellite landing ground at Fowlmere Farm, codenamed G1. This was a wise precaution, dispersing the sector's fighters so all were not concentrated on one airfield.

John Milne was an 18-year-old Halton-trained Flight Rigger LAC on 19 Squadron:

> When we first moved to Fowlmere there was no permanent accommodation. We slept in bell tents, feet to the central pole. A mobile cookhouse accompanied us – one day it caught fire! We dug latrine trenches and spent most of our time out of doors. Nobody seemed to mind. Fowlmere later had Nissen huts, never popular, as condensation dripped down from the underside of the cold steel roof, onto one's bedding and oneself.
>
> Flying from Fowlmere must have been fun! The airfield was far from level and dipped considerably in the corner closest to Duxford. Part of it was overlaid with a metal mesh decking to improve the surface. There were certain features of Duxford and Fowlmere which must remain forever recalled by everyone who served there: the sound of Merlin engines starting up, Spitfires taxying and flying low over the airfield, the smell of glycol coolant leaking onto hot metal, the smell of 100 octane petrol and attempting to strain the green dye from it.

For Coastal Command, 24 July 1940 saw the usual round of patrols, during which a pair of 269 Squadron Hudsons damaged a Do 18 seaplane off Norway, while another two of the squadron's aircraft inconclusively attacked a U-Boat. Again, the weather frustrated Bomber Command's 2 Group Blenheims, nine out of ten aircraft forced to abort their sorties, just one sole bomber able to press on and attack an airfield near Dieppe.

That night, the bad weather prevented twenty of twenty-seven Whitleys and Hampdens hitting their targets in Germany.

THURSDAY, 25 JULY 1940

At a conference with Hitler on this day, *Grand-Admiral* Raeder was optimistic regarding Operation *Seelöwe*. Many technical issues referred to in a previous naval assessment could be resolved: if air superiority could be gained soon, it would then be possible to clear the invasion route of sea mines and sow protective fields on both flanks; barges could be assembled and converted to carry troops across the Channel; the necessary port administration and logistics could be organised; heavy artillery would be ready in the Pas-de-Calais by mid-August, although it was uncertain regarding how many steamers would be available and how long their conversion would take.

The *Kriegsmarine* chief expected to have answers by 31 July, and so another conference with the *Führer* was arranged for then. In the meantime, feverish preparations went ahead while the war in the air increased in intensity.

Shortly after dawn, Pilot Officer Tim Vigors of 222 Squadron's 'A' Flight, based at Kirton-in-Lindsay in 12 Group, led Red Section up on a convoy patrol. Then, at a point about sixty miles East of Mablethorpe:

> At 0700 hrs I was about to return from a convoy patrol when I sighted two He 111s 500ft below heading westward towards the convoy ... The enemy sighted my Section and immediately dived eastwards to sea-level, splitting up formation. I dived after enemy at full throttle, opening fire at 200 yards from astern and closing to 100 yards. I experienced accurate machine-gun fire from the top rear-gunner who scored two hits in my mainplanes, near the fuselage.
>
> My second attack was diving from the port beam at about 45°. Rear-gunner was silenced. Third attack was from the starboard beam, opening fire at 100 yards. Large white puffs of smoke came from starboard engine and after another attack the engine practically stopped. Closing to twenty-five yards I saw my tracer entering wings and fuselage of *Heinkel*, whose speed had decreased appreciably. No 3 of my Section made one long attack after I had broken away, while No 2 was attacking second *Heinkel*.

Pilot Officer Vigors landed safely back at base with Pilot Officer William Assheton, but Pilot Officer John Cutts ran out of petrol and so forced-landed his Spitfire in a cornfield four miles North-west of the airfield. Although the bomber was jointly shared by Red Section as 'unconfirmed' but destroyed, it appears that both enemy aircraft made it home, albeit damaged.

Much further North, at 07.10 hrs, the two Hurricanes of Red Section, 'A' Flight, 3 Squadron, scrambled from Wick to intercept a bandit reported over Scapa Flow. At 07.35 hrs, Flying Officer Denys Jones and Pilot Officer John Lonsdale engaged the raider, a He 111, above 10/10ths cloud covering the anchorage.

Although the *Heinkel*, of *Wettererkundungsstaffel* 1, escaped from the RAF fighters by flying into cloud, it crashed into the Pentland Firth. Four of the enemy crew were missing, but one was rescued from a dinghy twelve miles off Rora Head. Jones and Lonsdale returned safely to base, their victory being 3 Squadron's first success since arriving at Wick on 23 May 1940.

To the South-west, at 10.50 hrs, Squadron Leader Devitt led his Spitfires of 152 Squadron off from Warmwell in 10 Group to patrol Portland. Twenty-five minutes later,

> a large number of E/A, estimated to be eighteen Ju 87, twelve Me 109s and a Do 17 were spotted about twenty miles South of Portland, flying north-west at 10,000–11,000ft. The aircraft of the squadron operated in pairs. When getting within range, 'B' Flight attacked the formation of Me 109s, which was above and acting as a rear-guard to the Ju 87s and Do 17. 'A' Flight intended to attack the bombers but were immediately attacked by the Me 109s.
> A dog-fight followed. Flying Officer Deansley, Pilot Officer Hogg and Sergeant Wolton attacked the Do 17 (No 1 Attack). Cannon fire was experienced from the rear gun. Flying Officer Deansley fired all his rounds but was brought down in the sea. He was picked up by a trawler and landed at Lyme Regis. Sergeant Wolton and Pilot Officer Holmes also fired at this E/A which came down near Fleet. Sergeant Wolton and Pilot Officer Hogg also attacked a Ju 87 at which they both fired the rest of their ammunition.
> The E/A dived steeply at 110 Searchlight Battery at Portland reported that a Ju 87 crashed nearby into the sea at the time of the combat. Pilot Officer Innes attacked an Me 109 from above and the quarter. He climbed after the E/A for 1,000ft, firing again at 100 yards. The E/A dived vertically down, but Innes could not follow as he had to take evasive action from two Me 109s which dived on his tail. Squadron Leader Devitt attacked an Me 109 but he himself was attacked from the rear and the tail of his aircraft was hit by cannon shot. He turned sharply and was unable to see what happened to the 109. [ORB]

In what was its first major action, 152 Squadron had run into *Stukas* of StG1, escorted by Me 109s of III/JG27. The Do 17 shot down by Flying Officer Christopher Deansley, Pilot Officer Edward Hogg and Sergeant Ralph Wolton was from the *Stab* of StG1; the reconnaissance bomber crashed and burnt out at East Fleet Far, Fleet, one crewman being killed while the other two were captured. In turn, Deansley had been shot down by *Hauptmann* Joachim Schlichting of *Stab* III/JG27.

The next action was also off the South-west Coast, when, at 11.30 hrs, Flying Officer Roddy Rayner of 87 Squadron's 'A' Flight, up from Exeter, was patrolling at 17,000ft twenty miles South-east of Portland when three Me 110s emerged from cloud. Rayner immediately attacked the starboard machine, setting its starboard engine ablaze. The enemy leader half-rolled and dived away, but his No.3 at least tried to present his gunner an opportunity to return fire before also disappearing. The damaged Me 110 made it back to France.

Now, the action shifted to the south-east.

Lunchtime found 65 Squadron up from Manston and patrolling over convoy CW8 in the Dover Strait. At 12.10 hrs, the squadron was ordered by the Sector Controller to intercept raiders off Dover.

Arriving over the coast at 14,000ft, the Spitfire pilots noted AA fire to the East, and later sighted five Me 109s; Sergeant William Franklin reported that at 12.45 hrs he sighted,

> a large number of E/A high above me on our right, near Dover. I became separated from my Flight and climbed to 25,000ft over Dover. I saw five Me 109s below me, over the Channel; I attacked from above, but before getting in range the E/A dispersed. In the ensuing fight I pursued one E/A towards Calais, just over the water. I glanced in the mirror and saw a second E/A diving on me from above. I pulled away and saw this machine crash into the sea for no apparent reason. I then returned home as I was very close to the French coast.

At the same time as Sergeant Franklin's shot-less victory, Flight Lieutenant Mike Crossley DFC was leading 32 Squadron's Hurricanes, operating from Hawkinge, and patrolling Convoy CW8, which was proceeding westwards through the Dover Strait:

> We observed eight 109s approaching from the South on a level with us, 22,000ft. We wheeled round to the left to engage them, their leader turned and opened fire with cannon at me, out of machine-gun range, head-on. I waited until I could open fire and did so at about 400 yards, pulling sharply up as he went over my head. I observed white plumes of petrol or glycol pouring from the wings, near the fuselage. This was confirmed by Yellow 3, Pilot Officer Gillman, who saw the two streams of smoke or liquid and he saw the E/A yaw away to starboard, to the North, over our coast and go down fairly steeply; neither of us saw it crash.

Meanwhile, Pilot Officer Victor Daw was badly shot-up by a 109, causing him to crash-land near Dover. Slightly wounded in a leg, Daw was admitted to Dover Hospital.

At noon, eleven Hurricanes of 615 Squadron were scrambled from Kenley,

> to intercept mass enemy raid near Dover. Red Section saw the raiders but the others did not ... Flight Lieutenant Gaunce shot down one

Above: The first phase of the Battle of Britain opened with attacks on shipping in the Channel – here, a merchantman is under attack by a *Stuka* dive-bomber.

Below: The convoy being attacked off Folkestone on 14 July 1940 – inspiring Charles Gardner's controversial BBC broadcast.

Left: Dover Harbour being attacked by *Stukas* on 29 July 1940.

Below: HMS *Sandringham* burns in Dover Harbour.

Above: Hurricane pilots of 32 Squadron await their next scramble at Hawkinge, a forward airfield inland of Folkestone.

Below left: Squadron Leader Mike Crossley, the commander of 32 Squadron, whose efforts were recognised with an early 'double' of both DSO and DFC.

Below right: Pilot Officer Rupert Smythe of 32 Squadron had a lucky escape in July 1940 when a bullet grazed his leather flying helmet – Smythe survived unscathed to show Flight Lieutenant Peter Brothers the damage back at Hawkinge.

Life goes on: in the manner of Sir Francis Drake, a game of bowls.

The Prime Minister, complete with 'Battle Bowler', visiting Ramsgate in July 1940.

Inside a typical Observer Corps hut.

Men of the Observer Corps at their post on a London rooftop.

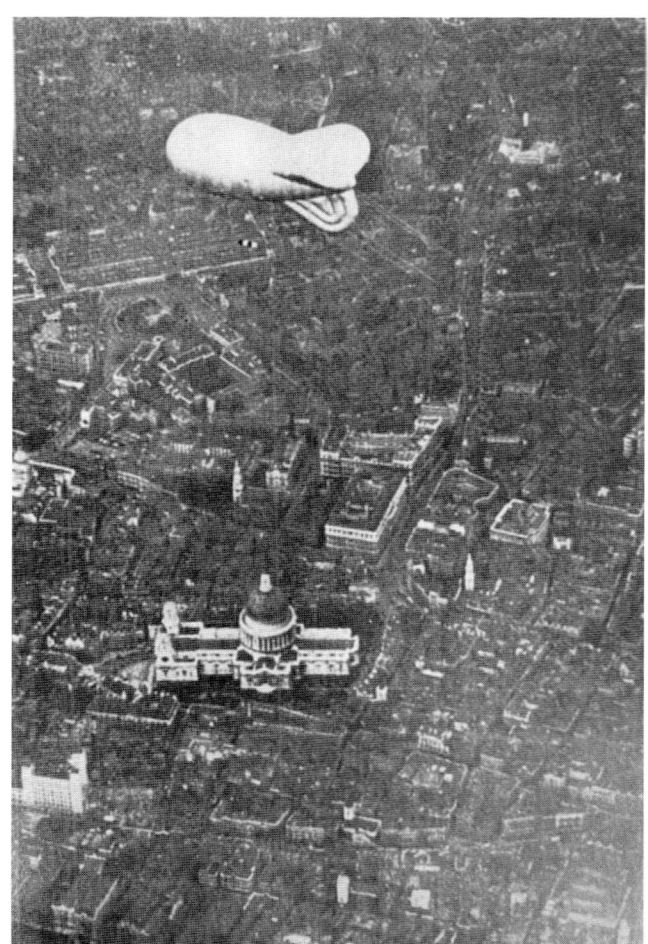

Right: A barrage balloon – commonly known as a 'Blimp' – flying over St Paul's.

Below: A Short Sunderland of Coastal Command patrolling a convoy.

Above: An Armstrong-Whitworth Whitley of Bomber Command takes-off for a nocturnal raid.

Left: A section of 56 Squadron Hurricanes scramble from North Weald in July 1940.

Pilot Officer Jack Hamar DFC of 151 Squadron, a successful fighter pilot during the Battle of France and *Kanalkampf* – killed in a tragic flying accident at North Weald on 24 July 1940.

Right: Kemble-based Pilot Officer Alec Bird, who was killed in action over Gloucestershire on 25 July 1940. However, being a ferry pilot, his name is not included amongst those of the fabled Few.

Below: Flight Lieutenant Ian 'Widge' Gleed leading a section of 87 Squadron Hurricanes on patrol over the West Country in July 1940.

Bottom: Pilot Officer David Crook taxies his 609 Squadron Spitfire at Warmwell in August 1940.

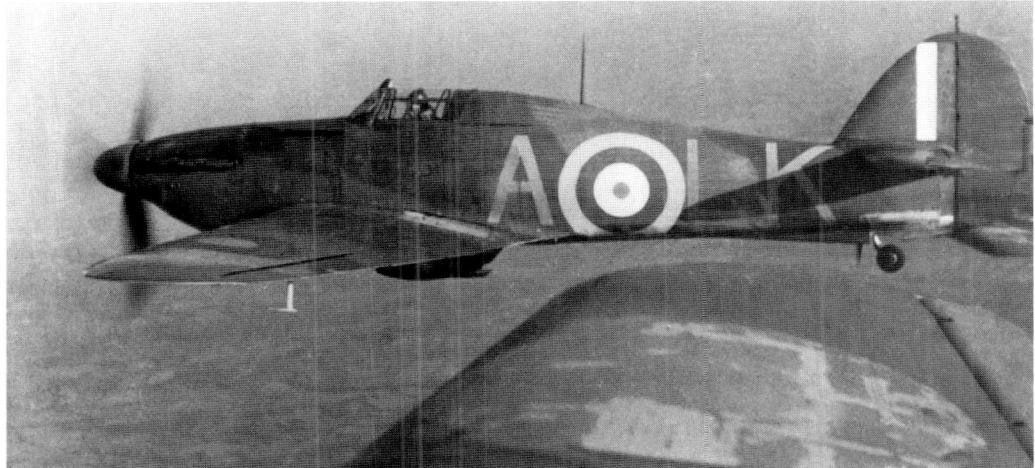

Above left: 609 Squadron's Pilot Officer David Crook (right) scribbling notes in his diary, whilst Pilot Officers Geoffrey Gaunt (centre) and the American volunteer Pilot Officer Andy Mamedoff relax whilst awaiting the next scramble from Warmwell. None of the trio would survive the war.

Above right: Ray Johnson was an armourer on 152 Squadron at Warmwell – whose tape-recorded memoir provides a colourful account of those dark days.

Below: Exhaustion – Flight Sergeant Frederick 'Taffy' Higginson, 56 Squadron.

Above: Sergeant Gordon Batt was involved in the Channel fighting and action over Portland whilst serving with 238 Squadron.

Right: On 8 August 1940, 152 Squadron's Sergeant Denis Robinson was shot down by a Me 109 off Swanage and forced-landed near Langton Matravers – although his Spitfire ended up on its nose, the pilot was unhurt.

Above: A Me 109E-1 of Luftflotte 3's JG2 *Richthofen*.

Right: The strain of combat flying clearly shows on the face of leading Luftwafe ace Helmut Wick, of JG2.

Above: A Blenheim of Bomber Command's 2 Group preparing for a raid on either an enemy airfield or one of the invasion ports.

Above: Me 110s taking off for a raid.

Left: The *Jagdfliegerführer* on the *Kanalfront*, 'Oncle' Theo Osterkamp (centre), responsible for coordinating the fighter operations of both *Luftflotte* 2 and 3.

Above left: *Generalfeldmarschall* 'Smiling Albert' Kesselring, chief of *Luftflotte* 2 – a hands-on commander, Kesselring is seen here visiting the *Stab* of JG51; behind him is the ace *Major* Werner Mölders.

Above right: The imposing commander of *Luftflotte* 3: *Generalfeldmarschall* Hugo Sperrle.

Below: A Do 17 and crew before a raid on England.

Above left: Pilot Officer Alexander Osmand, a Hurricane pilot based at Exeter with 213 Squadron – who saw action over Portland in July and August 1940. Sadly, a married man and father, he would not survive the war.

Above right: Tony Osmand proudly displays his father's log books and medals.

Below left: Pilot Officer Richard Demetriadi of 601 Squadron, a Hurricane pilot shot down and killed during the furious combat off Portland on 11 August 1940 – the day on which Fighter Command lost twenty-five pilots killed or missing, the highest number of any day throughout the entire sixteen-week conflict.

Below right: Tessa Houghton with her family archive and proudly displaying her uncle's, Richard Demetriadi's, portrait. Sadly, Pilot Officer Demetriadi would not be the only family-member killed in action during the Battle of Britain.

Above left: In July 1940, Michael Wainwright was a pilot officer flying Spitfires with 64 Squadron at Kenley; he died in 2015.

Above right: Squadron Leader Ronald 'Boozy' Kellett was a stock-broker and auxiliary airman tasked with forming and commanding the Polish 303 Squadron, the second Polish squadron to be formed and which would in due course see much action.

Volunteers from the Fleet Air Arm reinforced Fighter Command during the Battle of Britain, this pair being Sub-Lieutenants Richard 'Dickie' Cork (left) and Richard Gardner, both of whom flew Hurricanes in Squadron Leader Douglas Bader's famous 242 Squadron. Cork was a professional, indicated by his sleeve rank ring being a straight line, whereas Gardner was a reservist of the so-called 'Wavy Navy', owing to the zig-zag sleeve ring of the RNVR. Both became successful fighter pilots, but only Gardner survived the war: Cork was killed on 14 April 1944 in a flying accident whilst serving in the Far East on HMS *Illustrious*.

Left: A snapshot taken at North Weald of 257 Squadron's Flying Officer The Hon David Coke. On 12 August 1940, Coke was shot-up over Portsmouth and wounded, as a result of which a finger on his right hand was amputated. He was later shot down and killed over the western desert on 9 December 1941.

Below: An illustration of the ill-fated Boulton-Paul Defiant turret-fighter that appeared in *Britain's Wonderful Air Force* in 1942.

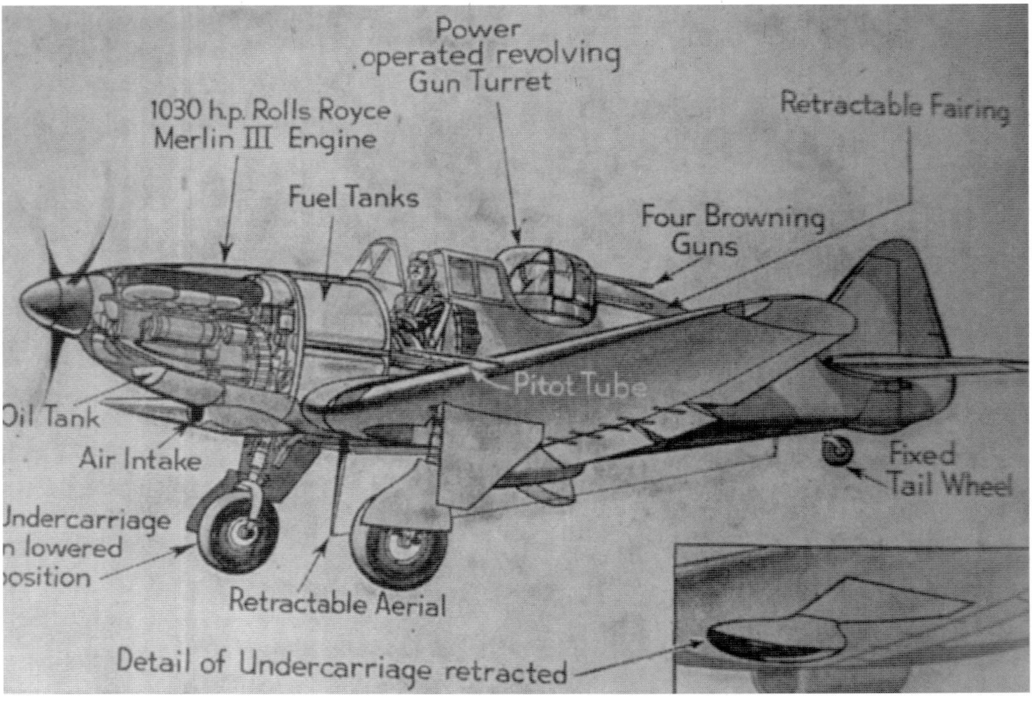

Above left: Pilot Officer Richard Howley, a Newfoundlander, lost when the Defiants of 141 Squadron were massacred by Me 109s on 19 July 1940.

Above right: Killed with Pilot Officer Richard Howley in what became known as the 'Slaughter of the Innocents' was his air-gunner, Sergeant Albert George Curley. (via Elizabeth Callow Worth)

Right: The huge pylons of a Chain Home radar station.

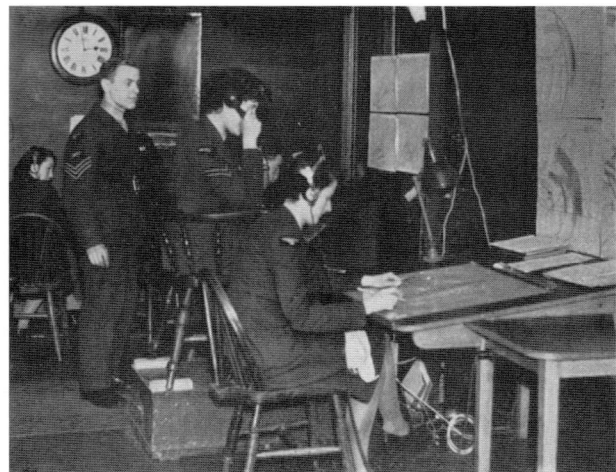

Left: Interior of the Dunkirk Chain Home Station's Receiver Hut – one of *Erprobungsgruppe* 210's targets on 12 August 1940.

Below: The KG54 Ju 88 which crash-landed on Portland Head on 11 August 1940, being dismantled by RAF technical experts.

Bottom: Luftwaffe meteorological experts – adverse weather would delay *Adler Tag* until 13 August 1940, bringing the *Kanalkampf* to a close.

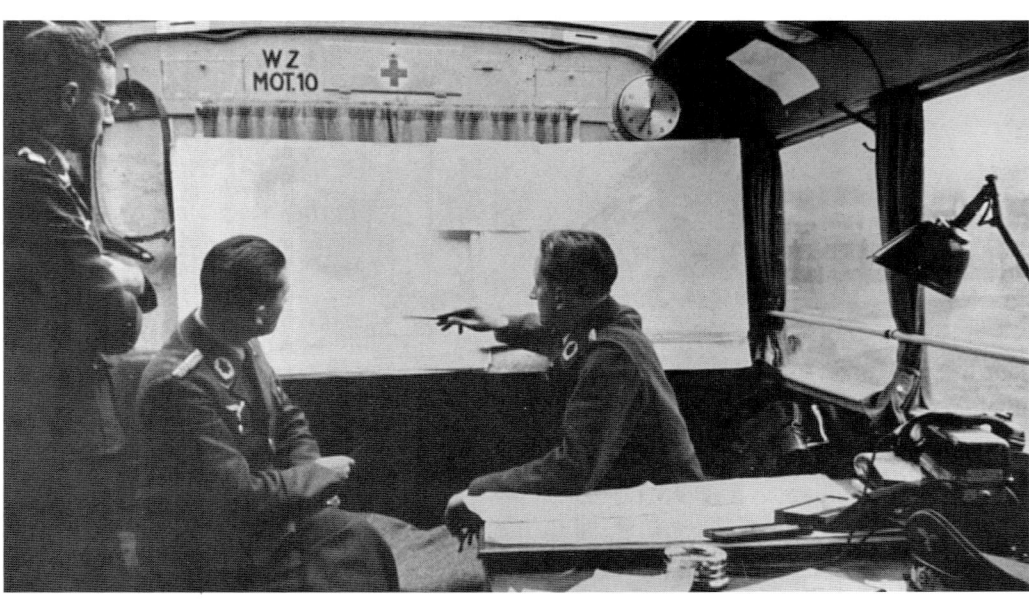

Unless otherwise indicated, all photographs Dilip Sarkar Archive.

KANALKAMPF DIARY, 10 JULY – 31 JULY 1940

> Me 109 which crashed into the sea in flames (confirmed by Red 2). Pilot Officer Hugo attacked another from which grey vapour issued and engine appeared to stop. [ORB]

This, however, was just the beginning.

Convoy CW8 was now to become the focus of fierce fighting, as *Oberst* Johannes Fink, the *Kanalkampführer*, unleased three waves of *Stukas*, each escorted by a whole *Gruppe* of the newly arrived JG26. Five Spitfires of 'B' Flight, 54 Squadron, were up from Manston, encountering 'hordes of Ju 87s, with the usual escort of Me 109s', approaching from a direction of Cap Gris Nez.

Pilot Officer Colin Gray, a New Zealander, reported that at 14.40 hrs:

> On sighting the Ju 87 dive-bombers we immediately attempted to engage, but were ourselves attacked by Me 109s, fifty–sixty in number. I, Blue 2, was engaged by about a dozen of these for about fifteen minutes at a height varying from 10,000–19,000ft, but being rather outnumbered found it difficult to get in a burst. Fired at one Me 109 which immediately rolled over and over in the horizontal plane, apparently completely out of control. I observed a Spitfire spinning apparently out of control from 10,000ft.

Gray's 109 was claimed as a 'probable', while Squadron Leader 'Prof' Leathart claimed another, and Flight Lieutenant Basil 'Wonky' Way was seen to destroy one. Unfortunately, it is likely that it was his Spitfire that Gray had seen spinning out of the fight, having fallen to the guns of *Major* Adolf Galland, *Kommandeur* of III/JG26. Way crashed into the sea near Dover harbour and was reported missing.

Having lost Pilot Officer Johnny Allen DFC the previous day, this was a blow to 54 Squadron, the ORB of which recorded that 'The loss of Flight Lieutenant Way in this action was a great tragedy. That he accounted for an enemy aircraft before meeting his unknown fate is typical of his keenness and great courage in the face of odds great or small.'

Pilot Officer Turley-George was also shot down in this engagement, surviving a forced-landing near Dover. Truly, the Spitfire pilots involved had faced overwhelming odds – which would be the shape of things to come.

Pilot Officer Michael Wainwright, 64 Squadron, Kenley:

> Having lost our CO on a dreadful patrol over the French coast on 29 May 1940, we carried on without one. Our two flight commanders were Flight Lieutenants Henstock and Hobson, but I found neither that inspiring. Each flight just did its own thing, independent of the other. There was another chap who claimed a lot of enemy aircraft destroyed, but his gun cameras showed absolutely nothing; he was killed. Squadron Leader MacDonell,

the Laird of Glengarry and a Cranwellian, was posted to command. Although he hadn't seen combat personally he tried to tell us what was what, which failed to impress. We thought 'We've been through a lot, and seen action – who the hell is he to tell us?' He said we were a 'Bolshy' lot and badly disciplined; 'Bonnie Prince Charlie' we used to call him!

Squadron Leader Aeneas Ranald Donald 'Don' MacDonell, however, found that:

Morale was low ... there was no corporate spirit ... One flight commander had recently returned from hospital with wounds to the head from a cannon strike; the other was suffering from nervous exhaustion. One or two of the junior officers were showing signs of bloody-mindedness. One was insolent, bordering on insubordinate ... I had one hell of a job to do to pull the team together before the real fighting began.

Pilot Officer Richard Jones:

I was a VR pilot, and late in July 1940, after operational training, joined 64 Squadron, a regular RAF squadron, at Kenley. Upon arrival I remember being met by the CO, an absolutely charming man and a real gentleman in every sense of the word, Squadron Leader A.R.D. 'Don' MacDonell, who was also the Laird of Glengarry. He immediately made us new pilots feel at home, calling us his 'chicks'. We found him to be a quiet but determined leader and an excellent fighter pilot. He looked after the best interests of all who served under him and he had the respect of all.

To give us battle experience as quickly as possible, whenever the time allowed, we were paired off with a senior battle-experienced pilot to practice dog-fighting and yet more dog-fighting, to give us both experience and confidence in the Spitfire and combat conditions. We were lucky to have that extra-curricular training, which would have been impossible had we been posted to 64 Squadron later on that summer, and for obvious reasons.

One incident I particularly remember was when we of 64 Squadron were visited by the Air Minister, Sir Archibald Sinclair. We were all lined up to meet him, standing in front of our Spitfires. He congratulated us on the work that we were doing and in his opening words thanked us as Hurricane pilots of 12 Group! Clearly the Air Minister knew not the difference between a Spitfire or a Hurricane, much less the disposition of Fighter Command's fighter groups. We were not impressed.

At 14.30 hrs on the afternoon of 25 July 1940, Squadron Leader MacDonell had led seven other 64 Squadron Spitfires up from Hawkinge, from which forward airfield the Kenley-based unit was operating, Dover bound.

The Spitfires almost immediately ran into thirty Ju 88s of III/KG4, 'Bonnie Prince Charlie' destroying one, while Sub-Lieutenant Dawson-Paul claimed one of the many escorting Me 109s. MacDonell's Spitfire, however, was damaged by return fire, causing him to make a safe forced-landing at Hawkinge, but 22-year-old Flying Officer Alistair Jeffrey failed to return.

With the action clearly hotting up, more 11 Group squadrons were brought forward to operate from coastal bases in South-east England, Squadron Leader John Thompson's Hurricanes flying down from Croydon to be at Hawkinge and available in fifteen minutes. At 14.50 hrs, fourteen minutes after receiving the order, as the ORB proudly recorded, Thompson led off ten other Hurricanes and raced towards the action over Dover. By now, with 64 Squadron's Spitfires already engaged, it was a confused fight, the sky full of aircraft:

> Interception of enemy fighters occurred off Dover at 17,000ft. Operations were to some extent interfered with by Spitfires which twice approached Squadron Leader Thompson and made attack approaches on Flight Lieutenant Powell DFC and Pilot Officer Wilson. Pilot Officer Wilson made three attacks on E/A. One from astern which he closed to 100 yards and saw it strike the water, one deflection attack, where glycol was seen to issue from E/A, and one head-on attack, result not observed.
>
> Flight Lieutenant Connors DFC, Green 1, and Sergeant Carnall, Green 3, attacked an Me 109 from head-on and astern, and Green 2, Pilot Officer Simpson, considered it so badly crippled that he thought it unnecessary to attack further. Flight Lieutenant Powell DFC, Red 1, attacked an Me 109 head-on, and saw pieces of the E/A fall off, and marks of bullet holes in E/A's centre-section as it broke off. Sergeant Craig, Yellow 3, also attacked an Me 109 head-on over Dover, but was unable to see any damage as E/A disappeared. [ORB]

Without loss, Thompson's aggressive and highly successful pilots returned to Hawkinge to rearm and refuel, as both sides withdrew. While the fighting was now very much focused on Convoy CW8, that afternoon Me 109s also swept over Portland, high over which they were intercepted by Hurricanes of 1 Squadron:

> At 1520 hrs Blue Section, 'B' Flight, Flight Lieutenant H.B. Hillcoat, Flying Officer H.N.E. Salmon and Pilot Officer G.E. Goodman, encountered enemy escort fighters, type Me 109. In the ensuing dogfight Flight Lieutenant Hillcoat emptied his guns without visible result. Flying Officer Salmon fired approximately half his

ammunition and followed the E/A, which was in an uncontrolled spin, from 10,000–2,000ft, when he was forced to break away. He blacked out and did not see the Me 109 hit the water but there could be little doubt that the enemy was incapable to getting out of his spin. Pilot Officer Goodman was attacked at close quarters on the beam by an Me 109 which, on breaking away, stalled, dived and was seen to hit the water. [ORB]

This was, remarkably, the second Me 109 of the day destroyed without a shot; *Oberleutnant* Kirstein of *Stab* III/JG27 was killed when his Me 109E-4 crashed into the Channel ten miles South of St Catherine's Point.

Returning to CW8, Flight Lieutenant John Ellis had led eight 610 Squadron Spitfires off at 14.58 hrs, the formation including the CO, Squadron Leader Andrew Smith. Once airborne, Ellis was ordered to join the fray over the convoy, now between Dover and Folkestone and being dive-bombed by twenty *Stukas*. Fifteen Me 109s provided top cover at 12,000ft, which 610 Squadron's pilots engaged at 16.05 hrs:

Flight Lieutenant Ellis, acting as leader of the squadron, attacked an Me 109 and shot it down in flames. This was confirmed by Blue 2 and 3. Sergeant Else (Blue 3) engaged an Me 109 at 200 yards, closing to about 25 yards, causing it to fall out of control. Flying Officer Gardiner (Blue 2) attacked an Me 109, fuselage of E/A was obscured by heavy smoke, but was wounded in the arm and his aircraft was unserviceable on landing. Pilot Officer Norris attacked one of same type and aircraft turned over on its back, emitting black smoke and giving every indication of being out of control. [ORB]

During the action, Squadron Leader Smith,

was seen by his Section attacking an enemy plane. He was next seen some thirty minutes later, circuiting Hawkinge aerodrome, with his aircraft smoking and the pilot in obvious difficulty. On making an approach to land, the aircraft appeared to stall and crashed into a disused engine testing shed. The aircraft caught fire and was burned out. [ORB]

No.610 'County of Chester' Squadron was an AAF unit, and Smith – who was killed – had been commissioned into the part-time squadron in 1936, later taking command during the Dunkirk fighting; he was 34. The following day, command of 610 Squadron would pass to the exceptional John Ellis, who was promoted to Acting Squadron Leader.

KANALKAMPF DIARY, 10 JULY – 31 JULY 1940

The cloudy conditions over Britain were perfect for *Störflug* operations (harassing attacks) by single aircraft directed primarily against targets connected with the British aircraft industry. Ju 88s were especially used for these nuisance raids, being the fastest German bomber, and crews would use cloud cover to escape detection before attacking their target and escaping back into the clag.

On this day, Ju 88s were active over Britain on such sorties, and at 16.20 hrs Blue Section of Pembrey's 92 Squadron, patrolling Tenby and Pembroke in South Wales at 11,000ft, sighted one such at 22,000ft over Tenby. The Spitfire pilots, namely Flight Lieutenant Robert Stanford Tuck, and Pilot Officers Robert Holland and Robert Mottram, immediately gave chase, engaging the bandit ten miles East of Fishguard. After several attacks by the section, Pilot Officer Holland reported: 'The last I saw of E/A it disappeared into cloud well out to sea and I saw black smoke coming from its starboard engine.' The bomber was shared between the three pilots as 'unconfirmed', but appears to have made it home.

At 16.21 hrs, off Dover, 'A' Flight of 54 Squadron, up from Hornchurch, reported a number of E-boats off Calais, as a result of which HMS *Boreas* and HMS *Brilliant*, both of the Dover-based 1st Destroyer Flotilla and which were escorting Convoy CW8, were despatched to,

> deal with them and resulted in the second big air battle of the day, when nearly 100 enemy fighters and bombers descended on the destroyers. Our Squadron (ten aircraft) went to their assistance, encountering Ju 88s, Ju 87s and the ever-attendant Me 109s. The Squadron, finding themselves heavily outnumbered, evaded enemy attacks, looking for the straggling Me 109 which did not materialise on this occasion. [ORB]

Me 110s were also involved in the attacks on the destroyers, most likely from *Erprobungsgruppe* 210. The commander of HMS *Boreas*, Lieutenant Commander Michael Tomkinson, reported:

> I was attacked from ahead by eight Me 110 dive-bombers. They were sighted and engaged one minute before they turned to their attacking dive. As the first one turned I ordered starboard 20 with the idea of keeping my 3-inch and Pom-Pom in action and putting off the attackers.
>
> No hits were obtained by the enemy during this attack, nor were there any casualties but there were a number of near-misses which caused considerable damage and the ship was stopped for a short time. Perhaps the most remarkable of the near-misses was two bombs which fell some ten yards ahead. Steaming at high speed into the resulting column of water was an astonishing sensation.

Then, HMS *Boreas* was attacked by *Stukas*:

> Both attacks were from ahead and pressed right home. When first sighted the enemy were, in both cases, in loose formation but formed in line ahead just before they turned to dive. They dived at an angle of 50°, well above the maximum elevation of the 4.7-inch guns, and followed each other in quick succession. After dropping their bombs they retired low over the sea.

Twenty-two of HMS *Boreas*'s crew were killed, the ship out of action until January 1941. HMS *Brilliant* was also damaged and put out of commission until September 1940, although there were no casualties.

Having already lost the popular Flight Lieutenant 'Wonky' Way earlier in the day, 54 Squadron, desperately fighting above the destroyers, would remember 25 July 1940 as 'Black Thursday':

> In the initial stages of the attack our cup of woe was filled with the loss of Pilot Officer Finnie, shot down and killed near Dover. No enemy casualties were claimed but our attack so dispersed the fighters that other squadrons coming into the fight were able to take toll of the enemy bombers.

With only six survivors of the Dunkirk fighting left, and having now lost two pilots killed during this opening stage of the Battle of Britain, the following day 54 Squadron would be relieved at Hornchurch by 41 Squadron, and flying North to rest and refit at Catterick.

At 16.30 hrs, eight Spitfires of 64 Squadron had scrambled from Kenley towards the trouble off Dover, CW8 now passing through West of Folkestone. At 16.50 hrs, Flight Lieutenant Lawrence Henstock led Blue Section towards German bombers sighted over the Channel, but before the interception was made the Spitfires were attacked by Me 109s. Henstock damaged a 109, which fell away from the fight, but was forced to break off the engagement owing to an overheating engine, landing at Lympne.

During the combat Henstock saw his Blue 2, Sub-Lieutenant Dawson-Paul, attacking another 109 – but the FAA pilot failed to return. Possibly shot down by *Hauptmann* Horst Tietzen of 5/JG51 off Dover, Dawson-Paul, described by his CO, Squadron Leader MacDonell as 'One of the mavericks', baled out and was picked up, badly wounded, by a German E-boat; sadly the 24-year-old succumbed to his injuries five days later.

Pilot Officer Michael Wainwright, 64 Squadron:

> We did many convoy protection patrols, and were pretty busy when the Battle of Britain began. On July 25, we engaged the enemy over

the Channel, but Sub-Lieutenant Dawson-Paul, on secondment from the Fleet Air Arm and a very gallant officer, was killed. I damaged an Me 109 but my guns suffered an inexplicable stoppage.

At 18.27 hrs, Flight Lieutenant John Ellis was scrambled from Hawkinge and vectored towards CW8. Mid-Channel, West of Folkestone, the Spitfire pilots sighted the two destroyers under attack. Before they could reach the dive-bombers, however, twenty-four escorting Me 109s pounced on 610 Squadron and at 18.40 hrs a general dogfight developed at 10,000ft:

> Pilot Officer Norris shot down an Me 109 in flames, and saw it hit the sea. Sergeant Chandler chased an Me 109 for five minutes and saw it go down burning. Sergeant Else chased an Me 109 which flew over Hawkinge aerodrome at 500ft, he engaged the E/A and it was seen to go down in the sea off Folkestone by soldiers. Sergeant Parsons placed himself on the tail of an Me 109 at about 300 yards, opened fire for about two seconds. E/A went down vertically, apparently out of control.
> Pilot Officer Wilson engaged an Me 109, after two bursts E/A caught fire, our pilots seeing it crash into the sea. Flight Lieutenant Ellis and Sergeant Chandler confirm this. Flight Lieutenant Ellis attacked the rearmost of a section of four Me 109s in line astern, causing it to spin down out of control. He then attacked another Me 109 from below, which gave out clouds of smoke and fell over, burning furiously. Sergeant Else confirms both these victories. Flight Lieutenant Smith attacked an Me 109 which broke away emitting black smoke. He then attacked another single-engine E/A, larger than a fighter, without visible effect. [ORB]

This was a brilliant result for 610 Squadron, which claimed five Me 109s confirmed destroyed and three more unconfirmed. The Spitfires had fought III/JG52, which actually lost four machines in the action, with three pilots missing and one captured.

At 18.50 hrs, Squadron Leader 'Minnie' Manton and 56 Squadron, up from North Weald, arrived over Dover and sighted the dive-bombers bearing down on *Boreas* and *Brilliant*. The Hurricanes immediately charged, some becoming embroiled with the escorting fighters while others made it through to the *Stukas*.

Pilot Officer Barry Sutton:

> I ... dived towards a cluster of Ju 87s. They dispersed and I singled one out. I chased E/A out to sea and got on its tail, firing a long burst at about 300/290 yards. E/A broke away and I was unable to see what effect my fire had. I then noticed another Ju 87 and gave chase. I got in a long burst at about 500–50 yards and silenced the rear-gunner

who had been firing at me. E/A then took violent evasive action by a number of steep turns. This enabled me to get in two further bursts with deflection at very short range and after second of these E/A turned on its side and dived into the sea ... I can confirm Pilot Officer Page's successful attack on another Ju 87, which I witnessed just after my own success.

In addition to the two *Stukas* of II/StG1 destroyed by Pilot Officers Sutton and Page, 'unconfirmed' dive-bombers were claimed by Flight Lieutenant 'Jumbo' Gracie and Pilot Officer Maurice Mounsden, while Flight Lieutenant Richard Broker damaged an Me 109. After the engagement, the pilots landed variously at Manston and Rochford, Brooker at the latter 'with only ten gallons in my tank'. Squadron Leader Manston had been shot-up, however, and slightly wounded, but made it safely back to North Weald.

And so closed the fighting that day over CW8 and HMS *Boreas* and HMS *Brilliant*, which had seen the greatest *Luftwaffe* effort and largest formations thus far. The convoy, however, had been shattered. Of the twenty-one colliers and coasters that had sailed that morning from Southend, bound for Southampton, only eleven passed safely through the Dover Strait – and just two arrived at their destination without damage.

With so many maritime losses, Coastal Command was busy looking for survivors and seeking enemy shipping. Five Thorney Island-based 59 Squadron Blenheims flew one such sortie off Portland Bill that afternoon, but Flying Officer H. Haswell's Blenheim was shot down by *Unteroffizier* Karl Born of 7/JG27, the crew being lost.

That evening, another 59 Squadron aircraft was lost, this one shot down off Cherbourg by *Feldwebel* Karl Schmid, also of 7/JG27. No.53 Squadron, based at Detling, also lost a Blenheim, this probably being the Bréguet 690 erroneously claimed forty kilometres East of Margate by *Unteroffizier* Edmund Rossmann of 7/JG52.

By day, the Blenheims of 2 Group, Bomber Command, were largely frustrated again by adverse weather over the Continent, but Pilot Officer Short and crew of 101 Squadron, were flying a weather recce when intercepted off Cherbourg and shot down by *Leutnant* Herbert Wasserzier in what was a successful day for his 7/JG27. Perhaps surprisingly, given the bad weather, that night saw 166 Bomber Command aircraft attack seven targets in the industrial Ruhr Valley, and airfields in the Netherlands. Three Hampdens, two Blenheims and two Wellingtons were lost.

Before departing 25 July 1940 completely, there was an all-but forgotten action fought over Gloucestershire that afternoon, which is not part of the main Fighter Command narrative...

A Ju 88 crew of 5/KG51 based at Paris-Orly airfield, was briefed to carry out a *Störflug* to attack the Gloster Aircraft Factory at Hucclecote in Gloucestershire. The crew concerned comprised the pilot, *Unteroffizier* Friedel Dörner, the pilot, a

25-year-old from Gruiten in the Rhineland, *Unteroffizier* Wilhem Hugelschäfer, the navigator and observer, aged 23 from Kleinlangheim, *Unteroffizier* Walter Theiner, the flight engineer, aged 26 from Breslau, and *Gefreiter* Gottfried Treue, the wireless operator, aged 19, from Bielefeld.

Before lunch, Dörner took off, Hugelschäfer later recalling that the crew were in high spirits, singing aloud as their bomber headed for action. Passing over the Isle of Wight at 18,500ft, he also remembers that weather was fine, unsuited, in fact, to the nature of their solo mission owing to the distinct lack of cloud. East of their target, the Ju 88 turned to pass directly over the Gloster Aircraft Factory. Hugelschäfer was concerned that the aircraft could so clearly be seen, and unsurprised when Theiner suddenly shouted the warning *Achtung! Jäger!* [danger hunter].'

As Hugelschäfer had correctly anticipated, the Ju 88's unwelcome presence had not gone unnoticed by the defenders.

> Pilot Officer Ernest 'Bertie' Wootten, a pilot at 4 Ferry Pilots' Pool (FPP), RAF Kemble: We were lying sprawled out on the airfield on what was a lovely day, when we heard the unmistakable *umph-umph* of the Ju 88's unsynchronised engines passing overhead.

Kemble's response was to immediately scramble two Hurricanes, flown by Pilot Officers Richard Manlove and Alec Bird, also of No.4 FPP. Climbing northwards to 12,000ft, the pair then turned South, Bird's aircraft, P3271, fitted with the superior Rotol Constant Speed propeller, overhauling Manlove's. As Pilot Officer Bird closed in and Theiner shouted his warning, Hugelschäfer, the aircraft's captain, jettisoned the bombs as Dörner turned South-south-west, racing for the far-off coast and home.

Anti-aircraft fire then burst between the two Hurricanes, Manlove, slightly behind, watching his comrade close in for a stern attack on the Ju 88, level with the bomber at 18,000ft. As the bombs were jettisoned, Dörner changed course abruptly and dived for the nearest patch of thin cloud. No sooner had he done so that Hugelschäfer felt 'a severe jolt in the back'. While converging from the port side, Manlove saw Bird 'close right in and deliver his attack from very close quarters before turning away upwards and to port'. At the top of the break, Manlove watched Bird's Hurricane suddenly go into a spin.

Alone, Pilot Officer Manlove then opened fire from long-range, some 500–600 yards, at which point the Ju 88's starboard engine broke up and a parachute left the aircraft. Inside the bomber was chaos. At 12,500ft, Dörner lost control, ordering the crew to bale out. Manlove had followed the bomber's downward spiral, observing Pilot Officer Bird's Hurricane still spinning but down to only 500ft. Then, he saw 'a flock of Spitfires arriving', which orbited the burning Hurricane. Reluctantly accepting that Alec Bird's fate was sealed, Manlove returned to Kemble.

The Spitfires were from nearby 5 OTU at Aston Down – actually Flight Lieutenant Peter Prosser Hanks DFC in Spitfire P9501, and a pupil in a Hurricane. The pair were engaged on dogfight practice when informed by the Duty Controller of the Ju 88's presence. Hanks, who was already an ace, having scored eight confirmed victories during the Battle of France while flying Hurricanes with 1 Squadron, remembered:

> When I first saw the Ju 88, he was well above me, being chased by a Hurricane, presumably Bird's. I went after them, leaving my pupil a long way behind. When the 88 entered cloud, Bird's Hurricane was about 800 yards astern of it and followed the bomber into the cloud. I was still about a thousand feet below.
>
> I carried on below cloud in the general direction of the Ju 88, which after only a short while broke cloud about a thousand yards ahead of me. It looked to be flying quite normally and I saw no damage or pieces falling off. I closed with it and started firing. I must admit to having been surprised to have received no return fire, and almost immediately the crew began baling out.

At 14.15 hrs, Albert Stephens had the shock of his life while hedge-cutting when the Ju 88 crashed into Bidcombe Bottom, between Oakridge and France Lynch, near Stroud. High above, the close proximity of the newly arrived British fighters, as he descended by parachute, was perturbing for Hugelschäfer, and the descent seemed to take forever. Suddenly the ground was rushing up towards the young German, who landed heavily in a cornfield:

> After only a short time, I saw some people, land workers carrying scythes and pitchforks, hurrying towards me. At the same time, a car carrying some policemen also arrived. They spoke to me but I could not understand the language. They put me in a car and drove to a nearby airfield.

Gefreiter Gottfried Treue had landed in the Cotswold garden of a Mrs le Bailley: 'For a moment, I thought that the airman would strike the holly tree but he missed it and landed on the lawn, striking his mouth on the sundial.'

Mrs le Bailley, together with her maid, 19-year-old Mavis Young and her brother, Ray, the gardener's 'boy', approached the enemy airman. Propping the shaken Treue against a tree, Mavis handed the German a whisky. With Teutonic manners, the wireless operator, also 19, clicked his heels together, said 'Thank you', and kissed the blushing maid's hand. Mrs le Bailley's neighbour, the local schoolmaster Mr Watson, then took charge and called the police.

At nearby Miserden, the church bells rang in alarm, mobilising the Local Defence Volunteers – otherwise known as the 'Home Guard' – who arrested *Unteroffizier* Dörner, who had landed on top of a house. Captain Guise, the unit's CO, reported that the German 'seemed very frightened. I think the Germans must have told their people that we ill-treat or kill our prisoners, but he cheered up when we gave him a cigarette.' Guise then went on to take Hugelschäfer into custody, who continues the story:

> Upon arrival at the airfield I was taken to a barracks and inside were two of my crew, Dörner and Treue. A nurse gave us some tea and gave me an old gym shoe to replace the flying boot I'd lost. We sat for a few hours but it was difficult for us to converse. In the evening a lorry came to take us away. It was a frightening moment – we were led to the lorry along an aisle of soldiers with fixed bayonets.
>
> We spent that night in a prison, in single cells. We were in some sort of basement and on the ground was an old, dirty, mattress and a single blanket. The window was covered by an iron plate with small holes in it. In the iron door there was a peep-hole through which a guard peered every hour or so. Next morning, we were taken to London by train, guarded by armed soldiers. I was placed alone in a room at a building in Hyde Park and remained there for about a week.
>
> Throughout, I was handled in a very correct manner. Eventually I was taken to a prisoner of war camp at Oldham where I remained until January 1941, when I shipped out to Canada, returning to England in the spring of 1946, remaining there until repatriation in 1947.

Unteroffizier Theiner was not so lucky. Hit by machine-gun bullets during Pilot Officer Bird's attack, he was thrown out of the Ju 88 as the Hurricane smashed into it. Several hours later, his body was discovered by the Brimscombe Home Guard, who had formed a line to comb the hills after previous attempts had failed to locate the fourth airman. Just 10 yards into Oldhills Wood, Theiner was found hanging head-down from a tree, his parachute unopened. With great chivalry not uncommon during this early war period, he was subsequently buried with full military honours at Brimscombe Church (later being reinterred at the *Soldatenfriedhof* at Cannock Chase).

Pilot Officer Bird's Hurricane crashed at Bournes Green, Oakridge, on the Bisley Road. Soon after, a posse of special constables arrived on the scene, finding the fighter burnt out and the pilot's remains being removed by a Mr P. Handy of Painswick. What, though, had caused the crash?

Unteroffizier Hugelschäfer, an experienced combat flyer, remained convinced to the day he died that his aircraft had been deliberately rammed by Bird. Certainly, in the opinion of Pilot Officer Manlove, 'there is no doubt that the aircraft (Ju 88) was destroyed by Pilot Officer Bird', although his combat report does not provide an explanation for Alec going into a spin, or mention seeing his Hurricane collide with the Ju 88. Upon hearing of Pilot Officer Bird's involvement and fate, Flight Lieutenant Hanks retracted his claim for the raider's destruction.

Whatever happened that day, war came abruptly to the peaceful Cotswolds, the destruction of Hugleschäfer's aircraft was accredited to Pilot Officer Bird.

The story of Pilot Officer Bird, who made the ultimate sacrifice between the officially defined dates of the Battle of Britain, raises an important point: although he gave his life in action against the enemy, Alec Bird's name will not be found among those of the fabled Few. Nor will that of Flight Lieutenant Peter Prosser Hanks or Pilot Officer Richard Manlove. Why? Simply because none served with one of the fighter squadrons and appended units accredited by officialdom as having fought in the Battle of Britain.

When considering that a pilot with one of those units could qualify for the coveted Battle of Britain Clasp to the 1939–45 Star simply through having flown one uneventful operational patrol of whatever duration, between 10 July and 31 October 1940, this does seem unjust. Perhaps more appropriately, the Air Ministry could have considered aircrew for inclusion from non-accredited units on a case-by-case basis, the criteria being that they actually saw action in the defence of England during the sixteen weeks in question. Not to do so seems exceptionally harsh in the case of those like Pilot Officer Bird who gave their lives – and, as we will see, he was not alone.

Pilot Officer Bird was a married man, his widow, Marjorie, taking him home to Yorkshire, where he was buried at Adel (St John the Baptist) churchyard. On his headstone was inscribed a poem he had found and adapted only five days before:

> *He has wings, for as the plane dived deep,*
> *His spirit, free within the realms of space,*
> *On newfound wings, flew with a swifter sweep,*
> *Fearless and laughing, to the Throne of Grace*

FRIDAY, 26 JULY 1940

In complete contrast to the previous day, low cloud and torrential rain dictated a lull in air operations. However, III/JG27's Me 109s flew a *Freie Hunt* at 09.45 hrs, encountering Hurricanes of 601 Squadron, up from Tangmere and patrolling fifteen miles South of St Catherine's Point.

Flight Sergeant Arthur Pond:

> I was Red 3 in the leading section of 'A' Flight, after taking off at 0925 hrs. The enemy was sighted going in the opposite direction, approximately 2,000ft above us. Red 1 ordered us into line astern. I went in behind him as Red 2 was a bit behind, being in a two-pitch Hurricane I was gradually falling behind Red 1 in the climbing turn. Red 2 was on my right. Two aircraft which I later identified as Me 109s came round onto our tails from the left, in echelon.

> I immediately went into a left-hand turn but noticed that Red 2 turned to the right and diving slightly with an Me 109 on his tail. I turned and got into position on the tail of this 109. My sight was extremely weak so could not use it properly. Red 2 began to go down emitting black smoke. I gave the 109 a long burst at about 100 yards range, he then broke off his attack on Red 2 and did a half roll.
>
> I followed him down, firing all the time until my ammunition was finished. The other 109 had meanwhile been firing at me without doing a lot of damage. I broke off the attack and dived to 2,000ft and returned to base, landing at 1005 hrs. The 109 on my tail did not follow me down.

Pond made no claim. Flying Officer Carl Davis, Red 1, leading 'A' Flight, hit a 109,

> and smoke appeared at once. He went down to sea-level and flattened out, and I chased him for about fifteen miles. He was unable to get away from me but I could not catch up, and I fired my remaining ammunition at about 600 yards. He was still smoking when I broke off the engagement.

Davis was credited with a 'damaged'. According to the ORB, an Me 110 was claimed as a 'probable', but no evidence exists to support this, or to support certain secondary sources accrediting Flying Officer Gordon Cleaver with a 109 destroyed.

No enemy fighters were lost in this engagement, although clearly the 109 attacked by Davis was badly hit. That combat perfectly evidences the 109's speed advantage over the Hurricane, something regarding which Sergeant Tony Pickering of 501 Squadron once remarked:

> I came across a lone Ju 88 somewhere over Kent, heading back to sea. I thought it would be no problem to catch up the Hun, press the button and that would be it. I slotted in behind and ran flat out to catch him. Suddenly he just pulled away from me, left me standing, had at least an extra 50 mph on me, and that was the last I saw of him. The Hurricane just wasn't fast enough, we even used to bend the throttle levers in flight trying to squeeze a bit more boost out of the Merlin. A Spitfire would have caught that Ju 88.

During 601 Squadron's sharp combat off St Catherine's Point, *Oberleutnant* Dobislav of 9/JG27, shot down and killed Pilot Officer Patrick Chaloner Lindsey, whose Hurricane crashed into the Channel two miles off St Catherine's Point.

At 11.42 hrs, 238 Squadron was ordered up from Exeter to patrol Swanage at 10,000ft. At 12.00 hrs, the Sector Controller alerted the Hurricane pilots to the presence of bandits at 12,000ft, South-west of Portland. Flight Lieutenant Stuart Walch, Blue Leader, reported the following:

> I saw three Me 109s about twenty-five – thirty miles South of Portland at about 14,000ft. I put Blue Section into line astern and climbed behind. Two Me 109s in vic formation and one loose on right. I took loose one and fired one short burst from a shallow quarter deflection. Me half-rolled then dived vertically down, then went into spin and broke up, the wings dropping off and fuselage going into the sea.

It was incredibly accurate and lucky shooting – Walch's burst of fire was of just one second. The victory was confirmed by both Blue 2, Pilot Officer Brian Considine, and Yellow 1, Sergeant Henry 'Taxi' Marsh, who also 'had a few cartridges at three Me 109s'. Walch had shot down *Feldwebel* Günther Böer of 2/JG27, who was reported missing. In response, Sergeant Ron Little 'had his hood partly shot away and two bullets in his parachute. He had attacked an Me 109 head-on.' Given that the pilot sat on his parachute, it was a lucky escape.

After the previous day's exertions, *Luftflotte* 2 no doubt welcomed the bad weather, restricting operations, and a much-reduced volume of shipping traversing the Channel. Nonetheless, nuisance raiders and reconnaissance bombers were active over England, seventeen bombs being dropped on Hastings, causing six fatal casualties; at 16.30 hrs twelve Spitfires of 65 Squadron, operating from Manston, were scrambled to intercept raiders off Folkestone:

> These raiders were not sighted but a Do 17 was observed and Red Section was detached to engage it, but owing to clouds it made its escape. Almost at the same moment, however, Blue Section sighted a Ju 88 and Blue 2, Flight Sergeant Franklin, chased it towards France. When climbing and closing in on the E/A, Blue 2 saw an Me 109 diving on his port side; he left the Ju 88 and manoeuvred into position and attacked the Me 109 from astern.
>
> Delivering a short burst from about 200–250 yards he saw the E/A crash into the sea about four miles off Folkestone. The Squadron returned to Manston without incident and later in the evening flew back to Rochford. We seem to be getting more action nowadays and Flight Sergeant Franklin is enjoying himself thoroughly, we hope he keeps up the good work. [ORB]

There is no German loss recorded attributable to this combat, although the claim was confirmed as destroyed.

The only other combat fought during daylight concerned Spitfires of Pembrey's 92 Squadron, at 17.17 hrs, as Pilot Officer Dennis Williams reported:

KANALKAMPF DIARY, 10 JULY – 31 JULY 1940

> I was Green 1, my Section was ordered to patrol between Skomers Head and St David's Head at Angels 10. About half an hour after we were informed that there was a bandit in the vicinity of Pembroke. I turned and almost immediately saw a Ju 88 about 5,000ft above us. I gave the Tally Ho and climbed towards him, Green 2 being on my right, Green 3 was below cloud.
>
> When about 500 yards behind and 300 yards below the E/A went into a dive, reading ultimately about 450 mph. I had everything open including the emergency boost control. Eventually I closed to about 250 yards and opened fire, doing quarter attacks allowing about ½ ring deflection.
>
> I also did a beam attack closing to 100 yards, two astern attacks range 250, closing in to 200 yards. All the while the E/A was going in and out of cloud. The last I saw of the E/A was disappearing into cloud with columns of thick black smoke coming out of the engine. I used all my ammunition before losing the E/A.

The Ju 88 escaped.

On this day, the weather also substantially reduced the number of sorties flown by both Coastal Command and Bomber Command, although a Dutch Fokker T-VIIIW in service with Coastal Command's 320 Squadron inexplicably crashed into the Irish Sea while patrolling a convoy, killing the four-man crew. Bomber Command's 2 Group efforts were considerably hampered by the weather, only three of fourteen Blenheims despatched to airfields in the Netherlands and the Dortmund power station managing to locate and bomb their targets. By night, a formation of Hampdens was more fortunate, locating oil refineries at St Nazaire and Nantes owing to bright moonlight, but otherwise nocturnal operations were a damp squib.

Similarly, *Luftwaffe* operations over England after dark were also on a reduced scale. *Unteroffizier* Georg Strickstrock piloted a I/KG4 He 111 engaged on minelaying in the Bristol Channel, dropping two near Barry Docks before turning for home when suddenly the bomber was engaged by a Hurricane.

During the afternoon, 'B' Flight of 87 Squadron had moved to Hullavington, near Bath, a training aerodrome, from where it was to carry out 'Cat's Eye' night-fighter patrols, and at 23.30 hrs, at 16,000ft a mile East of Portishead, the Australian Pilot Officer John Cock struck lucky:

> I was on patrol from Hullavington on Milk 'B' Line ... when I saw a E/A caught in searchlights, approaching my line, about 6 or 7,000ft above me. I climbed after it and opened fire from 250 yards ... on the third burst the rear-gunner stopped firing and the starboard engine stopped completely. The E/A turned left and I last saw it spiral to the left and disappear out of the beams, heading in a SSW direction.

The bomber was accredited as 'unconfirmed', but in fact crashed, out of control, at Longfield Farm, Smeathorpe, near Honiton. Only Strickstrock managed to bale out safely to be captured, his three crew-mates were killed in the crash.

According to Home Intelligence, 'Morale is still high and people are cheerful' – and Cirencester reported that 'few people took cover during a recent dogfight', doubtless referring to the previous day's action over Stroud, when Pilot Officer Bird brought down the Ju 88 at Oakridge. From Bethnal Green, however, came 'complaints of people smoking in air raid shelters; suggest atmosphere would be unbearable in a long raid and especially bad for children.'

SATURDAY, 27 JULY 1940

According to the 238 Squadron adjutant, Flying Officer A.L. David, at Middle Wallop, the weather remained 'dull, wind fresh and steady from NW. Clouds 10/10ths in several layers, lowest about 1,500ft' – arguably good conditions for shipping attacks. Indeed, *Stukas* of I/StG 77 soon took off from Caen, escorted by Me 109s of JG27, and headed towards Convoy *Bacon*, which had been observed chugging past Portland.

Surprisingly, the Middle Wallop Sector Controller only had one section of three 238 Squadron Hurricanes patrolling overhead, as Pilot Officer Charles Davis reported:

> Time up 0833 hrs for convoy patrol in Weymouth Bay where we picked up convoy. I was Red 2 but took over leadership for CO (Squadron Leader Fenton) at 0930 hrs as his R/T was U/S, and saw about twelve Ju 87s escorted by Me 109s flying at about 13,000ft. We were at about 9,000ft. I climbed behind as they turned towards France (position approx. ten miles South of Swanage) and ordered Section to pick E/A. I came astern of extreme left-hand Ju 87.
>
> They were in no formation. I fired one short burst from 250 yards, closing rapidly from astern and saw E/A start to burn (black smoke) from starboard wing. E/A then dropped its bombs at random into sea. I fired another, long, burst at 10 yards from astern and saw bits fly off machine, and it turned on its back and dived vertically into the sea. Both Squadron Leader Fenton (Red 1) and Sergeant Bann (Red 3) saw this and confirm it.

Squadron Leader Fenton chased an Me 109 which was attacking a Hurricane, presumably Sergeant Eric Bann, Red 3, until just two miles off the French coast, but was forced to break off and return home owing to being short of both fuel and ammunition.

As this raid retired, another wave was incoming, attacking Convoy *Bacon* off Swanage at 09.45 hrs. By this time, another section of 238 Squadron's Hurricanes were patrolling over the ships, and joined by the six Spitfires of 609 Squadron's 'B' Flight. The escorting Me 109s, however, successfully protected the dive-bombers, *Oberleutnant* Gerhard Framm of 2/JG27 shooting down Pilot Officer James 'Buck' Buchanan, whose Spitfire crashed into the sea.

The 25-year-old pilot remains missing, his loss another blow to 609 Squadron, which had already lost two pilots killed in action. Pilot Officer David Crook was flying that day and later wrote in his diary:

> All through July and early August we used to get regularly, the unpopular task, of escorting convoys up and down the Channel. The Germans at that time were concentrating mainly on attacking shipping rather than land objectives, and some very fierce fights used to occur when they bombed the ships.
>
> We loathed this work – the weather was brilliant and the Huns invariably used to attack out of the sun, and sometimes took the escorting fighters completely by surprise. Also, we were always outnumbered, sometimes by ridiculous odds and a lot of pilots were lost. Many of these were drowned without doubt, when their machine was hit and they descended into the water 10 or 15 miles from land, and were not found despite all the searching that took place afterwards.
>
> Two days after Gordon's funeral [Pilot Officer Gordon Mitchell, killed in action 11 July 1940], on July 27th, a convoy was in Weymouth Bay and a German force approached, and with a Hurricane squadron and we went to intercept it. A very confused action followed, in which most of us never saw or engaged the enemy, but we lost one pilot, Buchanan, who was almost certainly shot down by Me. 109s.
>
> We went out to search for him afterwards, and saw something in the water and directed the patrol boat to it as it looked like a parachute, but actually it was a stray barrage balloon in the water. All this occurred very uncomfortably close to the French Coast – we were forty or fifty miles out from England – and I was exceedingly glad to get back again.
>
> I think 'Buck's' death also was very largely due to inexperience and faulty tactics. We had not yet learnt that it did not pay to go out to sea to meet the enemy but to let them come to us. Also, we did not realise the importance that height meant. Afterwards we used to get as high as possible before going into action. This is the whole secret of success in air fighting.
>
> But 'Buck's' death was another in the series of unnecessary losses against which we had very little to show in the way of success

and I think that we all felt very depressed and discouraged. He was a jolly good chap and a very sound pilot.

However, we learned a lesson from these deaths, though it seems so terrible that in a war, experience is almost always gained at the expense of other men's lives.

'Buck' Buchanan had been only the second VR pilot to join this close-knit auxiliary unit, and while the squadron was still based in Scotland shared its first aerial victory of the Second World War. According to his friend, Flight Lieutenant Stephen Beaumont, 'Buck' was 'potentially ... one of the best pilots we had.'

Up from Westhampnett, Blue Section of 145 Squadron had seen the air battle in progress, some twenty miles South of The Needles, and hastened to join the fray:

Pilot Officer Storrar shot down an Me 109 into the sea and this combat was witnessed by a pilot from a Spitfire squadron. Flight Lieutenant Boyd was not so lucky; he engaged one Me 109 and soon found three others on his tail. Failing to shake them off he was forced to take violent evasive action for about fifteen minutes, at the end of which time he was down to sea-level and rapidly nearing the French coast.

Eventually the Me 109s broke off their attack (possibly owing to a shortage of ammunition) and Flight Lieutenant Boyd succeeded in reaching base, after exactly two hours flying, with only five gallons of petrol remaining. [ORB]

Thunder storms then brought further attacks on Convoy *Bacon* to halt.

Further West, at 15.09 hrs, Blue Section of the St Eval-based 234 Squadron, comprising Flight Lieutenant Pat Hughes (an Australian), Pilot Officer Francis Connor and Sergeant George Bailey, intercepted a Ju 88 reconnaissance bomber, damaging it – this probably being the Ju 88 of 3(F)/121 which crash-landed, having been damaged by fighters, back at its Chateaudun base, killing a crewman.

By that time, Convoy *Bacon* had steamed eastwards, passing into the 11 Group area. Wisely, Air Vice-Marshal Park moved three whole fighter squadrons to the Biggin Hill Sector's forward bases at Manston and Hawkinge. With the weather in that region fine and sunny, it was obvious that *Bacon* would come under further attack.

The enemy's next target, though, was Dover harbour, 3/*Erprobungsgruppe* 210 damaging the destroyer HMS *Walpole* at 14.30 hrs, returning at teatime to sink another destroyer, HMS *Codrington*, and damaging the depot ship HMS *Sandhurst*, these two ships being moored alongside each other in the Submarine Basin.

The previous day, 501 Squadron had moved from Middle Wallop in 10 Group to Gravesend in 11 Group, and at 17.45 hrs 'B' Flight was on patrol one and a half miles North-east of Dover, as Pilot Officer Kenneth Lee (Blue 1) describes:

Sighted E/A diving onto Dover docks and immediately led the squadron towards them when the Dover Defence Barrage opened up. I engaged one Me 109 pulling up from machine-gunning or bombing the docks, attacked with full deflection and then followed it round to take a further shot from full astern.

My tracer ammunition passed through the E/A, which dived steeply towards the sea, followed by Blue 3, who himself could not get within effective range and quickly lost sight of it. There were our Spitfires and other Me 109s engaged in the vicinity.

Having relieved 54 Squadron at Hornchurch the previous day, 41 Squadron had been brought forward from there to operate at Manston, and at '1800 hrs approx', according to Flight Lieutenant Terry Webster, he was,

leading Green Section ... on patrol over Dover, I saw bursts of AA fire from the shore batteries, and aircraft diving down on the harbour. I called Green and Blue Sections to follow me down. I then followed the aircraft in a steep dive but did not get in range until the enemy aircraft flattened out about 50ft above sea-level. I then fired two short bursts at about 150 yards. The E/A flew straight into the sea.

I then saw a further He 113 being attacked by a Hurricane. This aircraft, He 113, came down in the sea. I was then about eight miles from the French coast. On way home at about 20ft I was attacked by a further He 113. The combat consisted of a series of very tight turns at 50ft. I fired three short bursts with no apparent effect, then broke off the combat as I was approaching the French coast.

Webster claimed a 'He 113 unconfirmed destroyed', which was, of course, an Me 109, as was the second German fighter he had seen crash into the sea, which was that shot down by 501 Squadron's Pilot Officer Lee. There can be little or no doubt regarding these victories, particularly Lee's, which Webster witnessed, and yet there are no Me 109s recorded as being lost on this day by the *Luftwaffe* – raising the question as to just how accurate and comprehensive these German records really are.

Flight Lieutenant P.A.N. Cox, however, failed to return from this action, and remains missing. At the time, it was believed that Philip Cox had been hit by the Dover barrage, but more recently it has become clear that this popular flight commander was shot down by the Me 109 pilot *Leutnant* Horst Marx, of 3/ *Erprobungsgruppe* 210:

After a bombing attack on a relief cruiser in Dover harbour, the *Staffel* was returning in the direction of Calais. The last machine was engaged in combat and the whole *Staffel* turned. The English machine veered away, but was caught up by us. After two other aircraft had already fired at it, I managed to get within 40m and my first burst, from behind and below, set it on fire. It immediately dived blazing into the Channel.

That day, *Oberleutnant* Otto Hintze, 3/*Erprobungsgruppe* 210's *Staffelkapitän*, was flying no less than his 100th combat mission, and confirmed Hintze's report:

The English fighter, a Hurricane, attempted to escape in the direction of Dover. After a short burst I had to pull away to my left due to my greater speed. After completing the left turn, I saw that the Hurricane was hit by the third machine and shortly afterwards fell burning into the sea.

Feldwebel Büttner, flying No.2 to Hintze, added that:

After being told over the W/T to turn back for combat, we saw an enemy aircraft (Hurricane) which, as we drew close, sought to escape in low flight. The *Staffelkapitän*, behind whom I flew closely, reached the enemy aircraft, which tried to avoid the bursts of fire by turning, whereupon I was able to give two short bursts at the enemy. With the enemy aircraft suddenly pulling upwards, No 1 and 2 passed by it, due to greater speed. I then saw one of the following machines fire a heavy burst into the opponent, which crashed into the water.

These reports provide a perfect example of the rigorous process *Luftwaffe* victory claims went through before conformation, requiring witnesses.

Although *Erprobungsgruppe* 210 suffered no losses in this combat over Dover, a 2 *Staffel* Me 110 exploded after being hit by AA fire while attacking a flak ship North-east of Harwich. Nonetheless, it had been a most successful day for the unit, which, somewhat optimistically, claimed to have sunk four warships for a total of 80,000 tons. It was, though, undoubtedly a bad day for the RN, which was forced to abandon Dover as a base for its anti-invasion destroyers, which were moved to Harwich and Sheerness on the East Coast, causing Alexander McKee to observe hat 'the "flying artillery" of the *Luftwaffe* had virtually cleared the way across for their army – in daylight'.

There is no doubt that this development was in no small part down to the increased presence of Me 109s, being used in numbers, the German fighter proving itself to be a lethal opponent.

Alexander McKee continues:

A breathless silence settled down on the invasion coast. In front, the beaches were hedged with scaffolding, concrete blocks, barbed wire and mines; behind, it was sealed off by check-points on the roads, through which no one was allowed to pass unless he lived on the coast. It was a genuine frontline feeling – of silence and desertion and barbed tension, broken suddenly by violent action, which stopped as suddenly as it began, leaving only the frightened screaming of sea-gulls to die away gradually.

Indeed, since mid-July 1940, a curfew had been imposed under the auspices of the Defence Regulations affecting the boroughs of Gillingham, Queenborough, Margate, Ramsgate, Sandwich, Deal, Dover, Folkestone, Hythe, New Romney and Lydd, in addition to the urban areas of Sheerness, Whitstable, Herne Bay and Broadstairs, and rural districts of Strood, Swale, Sheppey, Eastry, Dover and Romney Marsh. People living in those places were prevented from being outside between half an hour after sunset and the same before sunrise, unless they had permission from the local police.

At 18.00 hrs, Squadron Leader Joe Kayll led 'A' Flight of 615 Squadron up from Kenley, bound for Hawkinge. Just before reaching the coastal aerodrome he was, notes the ORB, 'informed that an enemy seaplane was ten miles NE of Dover. Five of our aircraft attacked it and eventually it was seen to burst into flames and crash into the sea.' This was another Red Cross rescue machine of the *Seenotdienst*. There was no further action off the South Coast on this particular evening.

This skirmishing over convoys was wearing for both sides, and while unescorted bombers were easily dealt with, the strong fighter sweeps by Me 109s were a different matter – especially when sector controllers persisted in deploying individual sections of three or single flights, meaning that the RAF pilots were heavily outnumbered. As previously explained, pre-war tactical thinking and training in Britain revolved around these small formations, and the squadron was the underpinning tenet of the RAF's structure. One of the reasons for this, again as previously explained (see *The Gathering Storm*), was the limitations of the TR9D in-aircraft radio, which only provided for airborne pilots to speak with those in their own squadron and sector controller, but not pilots in other squadrons or other sectors' controllers.

Controlling large formations was, therefore, virtually impossible. Another readily identifiable issue for the defenders is that while RDF provided early warning of the enemy's approach, the limitations of the technology involved was unable to ascertain or predict height. Consequently, as far as sector controllers were concerned, much still relied upon guesswork when correctly predicting the enemy's intended targets and height.

Studying the combats to date, almost always the Germans commanded the height advantage – so it is difficult to understand why sector controllers deployed their fighters at much lower altitudes. Repeatedly, the record shows, leaders in the air wisely climbed higher than instructed, and rightly so. The lack of an efficient British air sea rescue service was also now showing up as a major deficiency, with many pilots baling out into the Channel, never to be seen alive again – and the loss of pilots was a vexing concern.

In the *Luftwaffe*, a fighter pilot was not rested, which is to say that he flew operationally until such time as he was either wounded, killed, or hopefully survived the war. This meant that combat and operational experience was constantly being accumulated. In the RAF, conversely, pilots flew tours, sometimes lasting weeks, usually months, and were removed from operations for periods of time, usually serving as flying instructors. While this arguably might have reduced combat fatigue, equally the interruption in operational flying could be considered a mistake, because when returning to the frontline, rested pilots needed to re-familiarise themselves with the tempo of battle – a sometimes traumatic process not all survived.

When to rest frontline pilots was a difficult question, because their place would be taken by novices with little or no combat experience. Inexperience and fatigue were demonstrable problems, causing many flying accidents. Between 10 July and 11 August 1940, for example, of the 107 RAF fighter pilots killed, eighteen lost their lives in flying accidents, causing Air Chief Marshal Dowding to observe that 'At this rate … Fighter Command would cease to exist by the end of 1940 through its own efforts, without any help from the *Luftwaffe*'.

On this day, 27 July 1940, Dowding ordered that from now on his pilots would have eight off-duty hours in every twenty-four, and a continuous twenty-four hours off every week; it was the best he could do.

Dowding's overall strategy was essentially based on maintaining a strong and effective reserve, enabling the rotation of depleted squadrons to refit and rest in quieter sectors, their places in the frontline being taken by squadrons from the North, which were duly rested and back to full strength. While pilots throughout Fighter Command flew endless convoy patrols, some seeing action against unescorted enemy reconnaissance bombers or nuisance raiders, it was clear that an exhausting battle was already being fought by 10 and 11 groups, over the Channel, while 12 Group's squadrons, covering the industrial Midlands and the North, much to their frustration, stood comparatively idly by.

Pilot Officer Denis Crowley-Milling, 242 Squadron:

> It was interminably boring. Very frustrating for all of us in 12 Group, lounging about and seeing little or no action while 11 Group's squadrons were in action daily over the Channel and elsewhere. By now, Douglas Bader, who was a man of action, was commanding our 242 Squadron at Coltishall in 12 Group and found this inactivity intolerable.
>
> Naturally Douglas wanted to get 242 Squadron into the action. He used to say 'Why don't they get us airborne when the Germans

are building up over the Pas-de-Calais?' He felt that we could then proceed south and meet the enemy formation on the way in.

To do so, however, would have potentially weakened 12 Group and failed to protect 11 Group airfields. And, frustrating though it was for 12 Group, 11 Group was doing well. Furthermore, the number of operational squadrons had risen from fifty-two to fifty-five during August, with six more under training. Moreover, in spite of Fighter Command losing seventy-four pilots killed, missing or captured, and forty-eight wounded in July 1940, overall pilot strength would rise from 1,259 on 6 July 1940 to 1,434 on 3 August 1940.

Sergeant David Cox, 19 Squadron:

> In June 1940, Air Vice-Marshal Leigh-Mallory visited 19 Squadron at dispersal at Duxford, just before the move to Fowlmere. The object of the visit was to inform 19 that now the Germans were at the Channel coast large attacks were expected from the *Luftwaffe*. I remember him saying that he had no doubt that his squadrons would intercept the enemy. His actual words were 'My squadrons will be there, there and there!', waving his right hand. I think this was an obvious reference to wanting to use large numbers of fighters together.

The uneconomic use of so many fighters, however, was contrary not only to the System but equally to Fighter Command's strategy and the 'Dowding System'. This represents an early indication of what would become a developing problem with 12 Group, and which, as we will see, eventually became a crisis.

By this time, 19 Squadron, was experimenting with cannon-armed Spitfires. In certain respects the Me 109E was technically superior to the RAF's fighters at this time, benefiting, for example, from a CS propeller and fuel-injection; the 'Emil' also packed a powerful punch with two 7.92mm nose-mounted machine-guns and a pair of wing-mounted 20mm Oerlikon cannons.

Attempts to address the lack of cannon-armed British fighters had been ongoing behind the scenes for some time, the fighting over France having made crystal clear the great destructive power of 20mm guns. Lacking cannon, therefore, put the RAF fighters at a disadvantage – requiring urgent redress. Consequently, a number of Spitfires were urgently fitted with the de Havilland CS propeller and a pair of wing-mounted 20mm Hispano-Suiza cannon, designated Mk IB – and allocated to 19 Squadron for evaluation.

On 1 July 1940, the squadron's CO, Squadron Leader Phillip Pinkham AFC, was notified of this change in aircraft and briefed his pilots accordingly:

> Squadron Leader Pinkham gave a lecture on merits and demerits of cannon Spitfires. It was evident that new attacks would have to be

developed to cope with the disadvantages and make full use of the advantages of the new armament. 19 Squadron are to be completely re-equipped with cannon Spitfires, though so far, we have but three.

Disadvantages (At the moment)
1. Stoppages too frequent. Stoppage of the one cannon makes it very difficult to keep a steady sight with the other.
2. Fire period restricted to six seconds, making defence against other fighter aircraft very difficult.
3. Lack of 'spread'.

Advantages
1. Terrific destructive power.
2. High muzzle velocity, decreasing amount of deflection necessary in deflection shooting.
3. Increased range and accuracy.

AC1 Fred Roberts, armourer, 19 Squadron:

We first became operational with the cannon Spitfires on 22 July 1940, this despite the recurring stoppages, which seemed irresolvable. Most of the trouble stemmed from the cannons being mounted on their sides, due to the Spitfire's thin wing section, which was not intended by the manufacturer. Side-mounting meant that empty shell cases were ejected sideways from the breech and deflected back into it.

Another stoppage was caused by the shell's nose dropping slightly and striking the breech-end of the barrel, causing the shell case to buckle at the neck. We fitted various kinds of deflector plates. We altered the angle of the plates. We fitted rubber pads to reduce the force of the spent shell case, but nothing worked. We also had magazine feed trouble. This was caused by the magazine lying on its side while mounted on the cannon. To counter this, we tried varying the tension applied to the spring, but that didn't work either.

We took a lot of stick from the pilots over the stoppages. For a while they wanted to blame the armourers. Then, when a full magazine of 20mm ammunition was expended, the pilots complained that they had only six seconds' firing time against eighteen with Browning .303 machine-guns.

In trying desperately to resolve all this we had little help and no encouragement from our armament staff at Duxford. In fact, Sergeant Thomas, who was supposed to guide us, we saw very little of. Even the 'experts' who came from AFDU at RAF Northolt to help us could only listen and learn.

Operational the cannon Spitfires may have been, but as far as Air Chief Marshal Dowding was concerned, 19 Squadron's Spitfires Mk IB were 'not yet fit to go into action', only 'the guns of about six Spitfires ... are working satisfactorily'. It would take 'a week to ten days', Dowding wrote to the Secretary-of-State for Air, for defects in the other aircraft 'to be rectified'. The C-in-C, however, recognised that,

> the cannon Spitfire is badly equipped to meet German fighters because it has only two guns, and even the Me 109 has two cannon and two machine-guns. Furthermore, it has fired off all its ammunition in five seconds ... the existing cannon Spitfire is not an attractive type, but has been necessary to produce as an insurance against the Germans armouring the backs of their engines. They have not done this yet, their engines are still vulnerable to rifle-calibre gun-fire and, therefore, the eight-gun fighter is a better fighting machine than one equipped with cannon only. If and when the Germans armour the backs of their engines the eight-gun fighter will be quite useless for the attack of bombers, except when employing deflection shooting, which is very difficult to apply accurately against high speed targets. We may, therefore, be driven to adopt the cannon fighter as the standard type. I cannot say that we shall have to, because the initiative rests with the enemy.

The importance of having effective cannon fighters was obvious – the solution, however, yet to be apparent.

For Bomber Command, owing to the weather on 27 July 1940, just three of fifteen 2 Group Blenheims despatched to attack German naval installations at Wilhelmshaven and invasion preparations at Ijmuiden managed to find and bomb their target. Flying unescorted over enemy territory in daylight was hazardous indeed, so the bravery of these crews must never be marginalised or overlooked. By night, Wellingtons and Hampdens attacked targets in Germany, starting fires at two oil refineries. Meanwhile, throughout the day, Coastal Command flew eighty-two patrols without loss.

SUNDAY, 28 JULY 1940

With the weather much improved, this was bound to be a day of action. At 05.25 hrs, for example, Blue Section of St Eval's 234 Squadron, up on the dawn patrol, was soon in action.

The Australian Flight Lieutenant Pat Hughes was leading Pilot Officer Kenneth Dewhurst (Blue 2) and the New Zealander Pilot Officer Patrick Horton (Blue 3) when a Ju 88 was sighted at 9,000ft, thirty miles South-east of Plymouth. Hughes and Horton were first to engage, followed by Dewhurst, who attacked 'from astern and slightly above, opening fire at 200 yards and closing to 50 yards. I delivered two bursts and was about to deliver final attack when E/A turned to starboard with starboard engine on fire and hit the water, disappearing in about ten seconds.'

One of this II/LG1 crew was rescued from the sea, wounded, while his two comrades remain missing. Fighter Command was certainly exacting quite a toll on these reconnaissance bombers, undoubtedly negatively impacting upon *Luftwaffe* air intelligence.

On 28 July 1940, so Battle of Britain folklore has it, Flight Lieutenant Adolph 'Sailor' Malan DFC, commanding 'A' Flight of 74 'Tiger' Squadron, and *Major* Werner Mölders – the 'Father of Modern Air Fighting' – met in combat over the Channel. In recent times, commentators have challenged this, accrediting Mölders' discomfort that day to Flight Lieutenant Terry Webster of 41 Squadron. Clearly, this requires further analysis...

In anticipation of heavy enemy air activity the Sector Controllers at Biggin Hill, Hornchurch and North Weald moved eight fighter squadrons to operate from forward coastal airfields at Hawkinge, Manston and Martlesham Heath. At 09.40 hrs, Flight Lieutenant Malan led 'A' Flight of 74 Squadron to Manston, 'B' Flight following an hour or so later. There the 'Tigers' awaited events. Two days previously, Squadron Leader Hilary 'Robin' Hood's 41 Squadron had arrived at Hornchurch from Catterick, and also spent the morning of 28 July 1940 at Manston. At lunchtime, Hood's Spitfires returned to Hornchurch, remaining at readiness.

The morning passed surprisingly quietly, then, at 13.30 hrs, Malan's 'A' Flight, comprising Pilot Officers John Freeborn, Bryan Draper, Douglas Hastings and Peter St John, was scrambled to intercept a large raid approaching Dover. At the same time, according to the 74 Squadron ORB, a section of three 257 Squadron Hurricanes, Pilot Officers The Hon. David Coke and David Hunt, led by Flight Lieutenant Hugh Beresford, was scrambled – although unrecorded is that Sergeant Ron Forward also flew on this sortie, again indicating how incomplete and inaccurate records often are.

Further confusion is caused by the 74 Squadron ORB, which states that at 13.50 hrs, also scrambled from Manston were Pilot Officers Hastings, Stevenson and Freeborn, and Sergeant Mould – somewhat remarkable considering that Freeborn and Hastings were already supposed to be in the air with Malan! This is clearly incorrect, as evidenced by the following combat reports ('significant statements' in italics); According to Malan's personal combat report, a total of 'thirty-six' Me 109s were engaged at 14.00 hrs – this being a fighter sweep in *Gruppe* strength:

> I was Dysoe Leader on interception patrol on reported enemy raid on Dover. Climbed to 18,000ft having been ordered to engage enemy fighters and leave bombers to the Hurricanes. Met up with six or nine Me 109s at 18,000ft, coming from sun towards Dover to attack some

Hurricanes. Turned onto their tails without being observed and led Red Section into attack. Gave one enemy aircraft about six 2-second bursts from 250 yards closing in to 100 yards. He attempted no evasive tactics except a gentle right turn, and decreasing speed, by which I concluded he had at least had his controls hit (shot away). I then turned onto another Me 109 which had turned past my nose and delivered three deflection bursts at 100 yards range. He went down in spiral. I then returned as my ammunition had run out.

The first 109 was credited as a 'probable', the second as damaged. 'Sailor' Malan's wingman was Pilot Officer Peter Stevenson:

I was Red 2 when 74 Squadron was ordered to patrol from Manston. At 18,000ft over Dover Red Leader engaged one of two Me 109s flying abreast, going east. I broke off and engaged the Me 109 on the port side. I gave him two 2-second bursts, closing from 250–200 yards. He dived and turned for the French coast. I saw smoke start coming from the port side of the engine.

I engaged another single 109 and gave a 3-second burst (deflection) at 300 yards range. I saw my De Wilde (tracer ammunition) enter his fuselage and he wobbled when I fired, as though he had been hit.

I saw a section of three Me 109s at 15,000ft, diving in line astern formation towards French coast. I dived after number three and gave him a 5-second burst from fully line astern. I saw he was hit hard. He slowed down and dropped below his formation as though he was out of control.

I saw a stream of lead pass below me. I immediately broke off and climbed. There were glycol and cordite fumes in the cockpit. My engine began to run roughly. I was at 20,000ft, half way across the Channel. I glided down towards Manston. At 2,000ft my engine was just about to seize up, so I lowered the retractable engine-driven undercarriage.

I force-landed at Manston with the wheels and flaps down, with the engine seized solid. There were two bullets in my oil tank. My elevator and rudder had been hit.

I noticed two formations of three Me 109s in line astern diving into the attack.

I noticed that the manœuvrability of the Me 109s was considerably better at height (20,000ft) than when they flew at 10,000ft and below.

Stevenson was credited with one Me 109 probably destroyed and two more damaged.

Pilot Officer Dillon Kelly of 'B' Flight, who is not even mentioned in the 74 Squadron ORB, also reported engaging thirty-six Me 109s at 14.00 hrs, 17,000ft over Dover:

> I was Blue 1 of 74 Squadron and flying about 300 yards astern and to port of Red Leader (Malan) when we saw some Me 109s a little below us (we were at 18,000ft).

This evidences the fact that, contrary to the ORB, 'Sailor' Malan was leading the whole of 74 Squadron, not just 'A' Flight. Kelly continues:

> Red Section turned and dived down to port. I likewise turned to port but found a formation in vic of three Me 109s pass across my nose. I took a snap shot at them but noticed no effect. Immediately after this I saw three Me 109s to port, diving down very fast.
>
> I found it necessary to use boost cut-out and dived down on the leading one, whom I managed to get on the tail of by diving steeply and turning left. I closed to 250 yards and opened fire with slight deflection and saw after a few seconds the machine turn left, dive, and a tongue of flame appeared on port side. It then dived down into the sea, burning.
>
> Blue 2 confirms that he saw smoke and glycol coming from enemy aircraft before he broke away to engage the second enemy aircraft.

There is no doubt that Kelly's 109 was destroyed, and he was credited with a 'confirmed'.

Pilot Officer Harborne 'Steve' Stephen:

> I was Blue 2 of 74 Squadron and on patrol over Dover at 1500 hrs approx. when we engaged several Me 109s. Three Me 109s started to dive towards the French coast when Blue Leader and myself dived after them. The Leader got in at least two long bursts and I saw smoke and glycol pouring out of enemy aircraft, which was diving very steeply towards the sea when I engaged the second one. The second enemy aircraft appeared to be hit in the tail and rudder. The burst of fire was about five seconds – range about 300 yards.

Having confirmed Kelly's 'kill', Stephen was awarded a 'damaged'.

Pilot Officer Harold Gunn:

> I was Green Leader of 74 Squadron and flying in the box behind Red Leader with sections line astern. On sighting six Me 109s at 18,000ft, Red Leader turned to port to engage. I began to turn my Section

to follow when I sighted another squadron of Me 109s, normal squadron formation, above, coming down sun. I immediately turned to starboard and climbed to engage – height 23,000ft to 25,000ft.

In the ensuing dogfight I found I was isolated. I engaged several Me 109s (about nine) and on several occasions was fired upon by enemy aircraft from the beam, quarter and head-on. One enemy aircraft I fired on for approximately seven seconds from dead astern, range 30 –150 yards – while he was diving on a straight course, he turned slowly on his back and was last seen going down steeply. This aircraft would probably crash five to ten miles north-east of Dover.

One enemy aircraft I attacked head-on, opened fire at 500 yards. I opened fire at approximately 400 yards. I observed smoke tracings from his guns passing overhead. He broke away straight down underneath me, missing my aircraft by only a few feet. No damage was observed as he passed from view beneath me, but I believe some damage must have been done to him while he broke as I was still firing.

Gunn, who would be shot down and killed a few days later, was credited with an 'unconfirmed'.

Pilot Officer John Freeborn:

I was flying as Yellow Leader when we intercepted approximately nine Me 109s at 18,000ft. Red Leader turned to attack enemy aircraft about 1,000ft below us. As Red Leader attacked, I observed approximately thirty Me 109s above and behind us. I climbed up and behind them.

I attacked one and did a slight deflection attack from above and behind. After a burst of about two to four seconds at a range of approximately 200 yards, enemy aircraft burst into flames. I was then attacked by enemy aircraft and returned to base.

Freeborn was credited with the Me 109 'destroyed, unconfirmed'.

Pilot Officer Peter St John:

I was Yellow 3 when I saw eight Me 109s. We climbed to the attack and I attacked an enemy aircraft which had broken away. I got onto his tail and he went into a very steep dive. I followed him and gave him a burst, firing 70 rounds per gun, at 250 yards range. I saw my shots going in and I looked behind me to see if there were any enemy aircraft on my tail. I saw four Me 109s diving onto my tail.

I increased my dive and went into cloud. I came out of cloud into the middle of a squadron of Hurricanes. After coming out of the dive I could see neither Hurricanes nor Me 109s. I climbed to 10,000ft and endeavoured to find my Squadron but was unable to. I heard over the R/T the order to land, so I then returned to Manston and landed.

St John was credited with a damaged Me 109.

During this engagement, the Spitfires of Freeborn and Stevenson were damaged but both pilots returned safely to base. Sergeant Tony Mould was shot down, baling out wounded, and Pilot Officer James Young was shot down over the Goodwin Sands and killed, both 'Tiger' losses recorded as 14.20 hrs.

The Hurricane pilots of 257 Squadron made no combat claims, but one of their number, Sergeant Forward, was shot-up and at 14.00 hrs crash-landed at Hawkinge. This combat, therefore, took place over Dover and the Channel between 14.00 hrs and 14.20 hrs.

According to the 41 Squadron ORB, Hood's Spitfires were not scrambled until 14.30 hrs, to carry out an 'interception patrol over Dover'. The following combat claims arose, timed at 15.00 hrs, 20,000–22,000ft, between Dover and Calais.

Flight Lieutenant Terry Webster, OC 'B' Flight:

> I was leading Green Section over to orbit Dover at 20,000ft. While the squadron was turning into the coast, I sighted two E/A about 2,000ft above me. I warned Blue Leader (Squadron Leader Hood) but received no reply. The E/A then turned to attack Blue Section.
>
> I told Green 3 to come into a No 2 Attack position. I opened fire at the outside aircraft, which I then identified as an Me 109, just as he opened fire on Blue 2. I fired a 5-second burst from the quarter, closing to dead-astern, opening at 200 yards and closing to 100 yards. I saw the E/A pull up and fall into a spin. It spun away very flat, out of sight.
>
> I then dived down after another E/A (He 113). On the way down I was passed by another E/A (He 113). I chased this down to sea level and out to sea. I fired short bursts, closing from 100 to 50 yards. I then saw thick black smoke coming from the cowling over the windscreen. I broke off the engagement as I saw five or six further enemy fighters about 2,000ft above me.

Webster was credited with an 'He 113' damaged and an Me 109 'probable'. The He 113, however, was a prototype German fighter which never saw operational service – although the German propaganda machine made believe it did.

Pilot Officer George 'Ben' Bennions:

> Yellow Section of 41 Squadron were detailed to act as rear-guard for the squadron, which was climbing to engage the enemy at 20,000ft,

when I sighted two E/A diving onto the leading Section from above. At that moment, Red 3 sighted the enemy and called a warning to the leading Section over the R/T.

The leading Section then took avoiding action by turning to port. One of the enemy aircraft turned to port and closed with Mitor Leader. While this was happening I ordered Yellow Section to carry out a Number One Attack on this aircraft. Using the emergency boost I closed right in using full deflection and firing at the enemy from 200 yards to 100 yards. The enemy turned over on its side and went almost vertically downwards. I followed using full boost and gave two more bursts of about four seconds each from a position slightly left of astern, and after the second burst the whole of the enemy fuselage was enveloped in thick black smoke.

I pulled out at 3,000ft to see what was happening, and looking in the mirror found two aircraft on my tail. I called to ascertain if they were Yellow Section but received no reply. Since practically all my ammunition was exhausted, I evaded these aircraft and returned to base at sea level, from a position about fifteen miles south of Dover.

Bennions was credited with an Me 109 'unconfirmed'.

Pilot Officer R.W. 'Wally' Wallens:

I was No 2 aircraft in Green Section, 41 Squadron, ordered to orbit Dover at 20,000ft. I saw two E/A 2,000ft above as Green Leader warned Blue Leader. I was left behind by Green Leader and Green 3, and was unable to catch up. While still 1,000ft below I saw one E/A attack Blue Leader. One aircraft of Yellow Section then attacked this E/A (Pilot Officer Bennions).

The E/A turned over and dived vertically for several thousand feet, giving off a trail of thick blue smoke. The E/A then levelled off for a few seconds and then dived again, giving off black smoke. I did not see this E/A crash but saw it last at approx. 5,000ft, diving steeply.

During this combat, Flying Officer Tony Lovell of 41 Squadron was shot-up and wounded, crash-landing at Manston.

Major Mölders had been appointed *Kommodore* of JG51 only the previous day, and wrote an account of this action:

My first flight against England will remain in my memory forever. I was flying with my Adjutant, *Oberleutnant* Kirchless. North of Dover we saw three Spitfires below us and more machines appeared out of the mist. We attacked the first three and I shot down one of them. However, by this time I was flying in the middle of eight or ten Englishmen and they seemed to be mad at me. They all dived towards me and was that my lucky break. Endeavouring to gain laurels at the expense of the solitary German, each hindered the other. I flew about furiously and confused them even more.

By then it was only a matter of time before I was hit. My machine rattled wildly. The radiator and fuel tank were damaged and all I could do was dive away to the Channel at 700kmh. The whole gang followed me like a waterfall. *Oberleutnant* Leppl had seen what was happening and succeeded in shooting down the Spitfire that was nearest to me. The pressure was off.

Luckily the engine kept going until I reached the French coast. Then it began spluttering. When I wanted to land, the undercarriage would not lower; I had to land with it retracted – which I managed successfully. When I wanted to clamber out of my machine my legs felt singularly weak. Examining them I saw large bloodstains. My visit to hospital proved that I had three splinters in my upper thigh, one in my knee joint and one in my left foot. In the heat of battle I had not felt a thing – the splinter in my kneecap is still there.

On this occasion I experienced the fatherly solicitude of our *Reichsmarschall* once more; he had me flown to the *Luftwaffen-Lazaret* [air force hospital] in Berlin. The eleven days in the *Lazaret* were a wonderful convalescence. I believe I was something of the 'showpiece' of the hospital and the sisters looked after me in a way that my own mother could not have bettered. Later on I sent the good people a sack of coffee.

What else is known of the German side? As usual, comparatively little – that is reliable, anyway – because so many *Luftwaffe* records were destroyed in 1945. The most reliable source is Caldwell (see Bibliography), owing to painstaking day-by-day reconstructions of combats involving JG26 from various primary sources, Allied and German.

According to Caldwell, 74 Squadron met I and II/JG51 (this was *Major* Mölders' 129th combat mission and his first as *Geschwaderkommodore*). No.41 Squadron, arriving on the scene after the 'Tigers', were attacked by *Major* Adolf Galland's III/JG26, which suffered no loss in the exchange. JG51 lost one Me 109 shot down into the sea, the pilot killed; another killed when crash-landing at Wissant; Mölders himself was shot-up, wounded, and made an emergency landing on the French coast. Nos. 74 and 41 squadrons claimed four Me 109s destroyed, three probably destroyed, and six more damaged. In total, the RAF lost two Spitfires destroyed, one pilot killed, and three more aircraft damaged, in addition to a single Hurricane which force-landed. The German combat claims are, in fact, remarkably accurate (Continental time, so an hour ahead of GMT):

KANALKAMPF DIARY, 10 JULY – 31 JULY 1940

> *Major* Adolf Galland, *Stab* III/JG26: Hurricane, 10 km NNE Dover, 6,000 metres, 15.14 hrs.
>
> *Oberleutnant* Joachim Müncheberg, *Stab* III/JG26: Hurricane, 15 km NE Dover, 15.15 hrs. Müncheberg shot up Sergeant Forward and was credited with having destroyed his Hurricane, which was seen to crash-land at Hawkinge.
>
> *Feldwebel* Konrad Carl, 9/JG26: Spitfire, NE Dover, 15.25 hrs.
>
> *Major* Werner Mölders: *Stab*/JG51, Spitfire, Dover, 15.30 hrs.
>
> *Oberfeldwebel* Karl Schmid, 1/JG51, Spitfire, Dover 15.15 hrs.
>
> *Oberleutnant* Richard Leppl, 1/JG51, Spitfire, Dover, 15.30 hrs.

Having read the RAF combat reports, the reader will appreciate the difficulty of confirming who shot down whom. That said, while two great aces meeting in combat makes for a great story, it is impossible to conclude from 'Sailor' Malan's combat report that it was he who shot-up Mölders.

Likewise, it cannot be said with any certainty whatsoever that Webster of 41 Squadron was responsible, taking aside any ambiguity over timings, and in fact I would suggest he was not. The most likely scenario, I would argue, is that it was 'Sailor' Malan's Red 2, Pilot Officer Peter Stevenson, who actually pursued the enemy across the Channel, hitting a 109 'hard' before getting shot-up himself – quite possibly by *Oberleutnant* Leppl. Whatever the truth, 'Vati' Mölders certainly had a lucky escape that day – as did several others on both sides.

After this fierce fighter action the *Seenotdienst* was active, searching the Channel for downed pilots. At 14.40 hrs, twelve Hurricanes of 111 Squadron scrambled from Croydon with orders to patrol Maidstone at Angels 20, but were diverted to the Channel, in view of the ongoing action. Off Dover, a He 59 seaplane was engaged and destroyed by Flying Officer Henry Ferris and Pilot Officer Basil Fisher, and another, ten miles West of Boulogne, by Sergeant James Robinson and Pilot Officer Robert Wilson.

Thereafter things quietened down over the Channel for the rest of the day.

At 17.05 hrs, Flight Lieutenant Brian Lane was up from Fowlmere in 12 Group with Sub-Lieutenant Arthur Blake and Pilot Officer Wallace 'Jock' Cunningham, the three pilots making up Red Section of 19 Squadron's 'A' Flight:

> Sub-Lieutenant Blake sighted a Ju 88 flying in opposite direction. Section gave chase, lost the E/A in cloud and found it again, whereupon the Ju 88 pilot, executed violent turns, doubtless to verify the rear-gunner's excited shouts, put his nose down and escaped into cloud at full boost, pouring smoke from his engine all the while. [ORB]

The Squadron's Yellow Section, however, had an uneventful day of patrolling – until returning to Fowlmere in high winds, Yellow 3, Sergeant Adrian Roden, overturned Spitfire R6627 at the end of his landing run; the pilot was fortunately uninjured.

For 2 Group Bomber Command it was a quieter day. That evening, nine Blenheims of Watton's 82 Squadron were despatched to attack Leeuwarden airfield, but owing to a lack of cloud cover all but one turned back. Wing Commander Lart, however, pressed home his attack, dropping bombs on Me 109s parked outside a hangar. On the return flight, however, the Blenheim was engaged by 4/JG27 over Den Helder and shot-up by *Leutnant* Herbert Kargel, although Lart managed to make it safely home to crash-land back at base. By night, eighty-nine British bombers were sent to various targets, and also laid mines; two battles and a Hampden failed to return.

On this day, Coastal Command suffered no loss, contributing photographic reconnaissance sorties from Norway to Cap-Gris-Nez, in addition to attacking oil tanks at Amsterdam and Cherbourg.

MONDAY, 29 JULY 1940

Following a misty dawn, a cloudless sky heralded another day of heavy fighting, with RDF soon reporting the assembly of a large enemy formation over the Pas-de-Calais. Although there were two large convoys off 11 Group's coast, following the attack on Dover harbour of two days previously, the Group Controller could not assume that these ships would be the raid's target. Consequently, fighters were not scrambled in numbers, but by 07.20 hrs it was clear that Dover was once more the enemy's focus.

At 07.10 hrs, Squadron Leader Don MacDonell scrambled from Kenley, leading four other of his 64 Squadron Spitfire pilots towards the trouble, while at 07.25 hrs, 501 Squadron's twelve Hurricanes likewise scrambled from Hawkinge, and eleven 41 Squadron Spitfires from Manston simultaneously took-off, vectored first to patrol base, then Dover.

The incoming raid comprised over forty Ju 87s drawn from II/StG1, II/StG4 and IV/LG1, escorted by up to fifty or more Me 109s from JG27, JG51 and JG52 – a huge raid indeed – and as the Hawkinge Hurricanes and Manston Spitfires scrambled, the five Spitfires of 64 Squadron, which were first on the scene, went into action. After the ensuing fight, MacDonell's pilots would claim the destruction of three Ju 87s and another damaged, in addition to two Me 109s destroyed and one damaged.

No.501 Squadron was first ordered up to 15,000ft, then changed to 8,000ft. Pilot Officer Kenneth Lee, Blue 1, was leading the squadron North-east over Sandwich before turning South-west towards Hawkinge.

According to Lee, at 07.45 hrs and with the mêlée in progress, the Hurricanes sighted,

> forty Ju 87s coming out of the sun. As we had been warned not to cross over the Dover AA barrage, I led the formation round to the West of it and then turned to intercept the Ju 87s which by this time had finished their bombing and had climbed to 2,000ft. The Squadron dived to attack and a general dog-fight developed.
> I chose a Ju 87 and got onto its tail, firing at it for ten seconds at 300 yards, seeing my tracer enter it. It dived down pouring out white smoke and owing to the general confusion I lost sight of it. As the E/A took evasive action in the form of steep dives and climbs there is nothing to suggest it was more than damaged. I returned to Hawkinge at 0801 hrs.

Pilot Officer John Gibson, 501 Squadron:

> I was leading Red Section when I sighted E/A approaching Dover Harbour. I followed Blue Leader (Pilot Officer Kenneth Lee) into attack and engaged a Ju 87, as E/A broke away from attack on harbour. I carried out a quarter attack and saw E/A diving steeply with black smoke pouring out.
> I broke off the attack and saw a Spitfire emitting white smoke with a Ju 87 on its tail. I carried out a No 1 Attack on the Ju 87, which burst into flame and plunged into the sea. This was also seen by Pilot Officer Bland. I then followed the damaged Spitfire back to the coast where it forced-landed in a field South of Deal. I saw the pilot get out, apparently uninjured. I then returned to base.

The Spitfire concerned was R6643, flown by Sergeant Arthur Binham of 64 Squadron, who came safely down near St Margaret's Bay.

For no loss, in this 'major engagement', as the ORB called it, 501 Squadron's pilots claimed 'Six aircraft ... destroyed (confirmed or probably destroyed) and four damaged'.

At 07.40 hrs, 41 Squadron arrived over Dover, as Flight Lieutenant Terry Webster reported:

> I was leading Green Section ... to engage enemy fighters over Dover. I was acting as look-out section when I saw several Me 109s approaching. I warned Mitor Leader (Squadron Leader Hood) and attacked a 109, opening fire at 200 yards and closing to fifty yards. I saw the aircraft catch fire and spin down. I then looked around for further aircraft attacking the squadron. I saw

the Me 109 spin down very flat, on fire, and hit the sea near the South Goodwin Lightship.

I then saw a squadron of Ju 87s dive-bombing. I joined on the end of the line diving on Dover and attacked the end aircraft, giving a 5-second burst from 250 yards to 50 yards. The aircraft was hit and smoke started to emerge, but during the attack I was engaged by three or four further 109s. I turned to attack these but on getting into position for a full deflection shot I pressed the 'tit' but nothing happened [no more ammunition].

I continued to make attacks at the 109s while losing height to sea-level. On reaching sea-level I used 12lbs boost and made for the coast. Seeing that my aircraft was damaged I landed at Hawkinge.

In addition to the Me 109 destroyed and the Ju 87 damaged by Webster, Squadron Leader Hood claimed a 109 and a Ju 87 destroyed, while Pilot Officer George Bennions chalked up a 109 damaged, and Sergeant Robert Carr-Lewty a 109 destroyed.

In this visceral action, however, 41 Squadron itself was hit hard by the German fighters: Flying Officer Douglas Gamblen was shot down and crashed into the sea; he remains missing. Moreover, the undercarriage of Flying Officer William Scott collapsed on landing back at base, his Spitfire having been damaged during the combat; Pilot Officer Bennions also crashed on landing back at base, with damaged flaps, and the fighters of both Webster and Pilot Officer John MacKenzie were also damaged.

No.56 Squadron's Hurricanes, up from Rochford, had been scrambled to patrol Whitstable at 5,000ft, arriving over Dover five minutes after 41 Squadron, at 07.45 hrs.

Flying Officer Steve 'Squeak' Weaver:

The Squadron was sent from Rochford to patrol Whitstable at 5,000ft. I was flying as leader of Blue Section. R/T communication was bad between the formation leader and base (North Weald). I was receiving well from base but they were not receiving me well. Base informed us of fifty E/A approaching at 2,000ft a place whose name I could not catch. When at 10,000ft over Deal we were told to orbit. Blue 3 gave warning of aircraft near Dover and Red 4 broke away to investigate. I then saw what appeared to be a dogfight over the sea east of Dover. I told the formation leader and went to the scene.

I saw an Me 109 on the tail of a Hurricane, the latter being on the tail of a 109. I got on the tail of the Me 109 and when he was 600 yards behind he opened fire on the Hurricane in from of him, which emitted white smoke. This may have been Red 3 (Flight Sergeant Cooney).

I fired a short burst at 400 yards which caused E/A to turn away from the Hurricane. I closed and fired at point blank range with intermittent bursts as he turned from side to side. Glycol streamed out from E/A after about eight seconds' firing, and after another four seconds' firing E/A burst into flames. I did not see him crash as another E/A was on my tail. I tried to turn behind him but lost him and returned alone.

Sergeant Hillwood (Blue 2) and Sergeant Smyth (Blue 3) both saw this E/A burst into flames. I was hit once in the tailplane.

Flight Sergeant Cecil Cooney, a pre-war airman who had made the quantum leap from metal rigger to fighter pilot, failed to return and was reported 'Missing'. Weaver's was 56 Squadron's only success in the engagement, in which Pilot Officer Maurice Mounsdon's Hurricane was also damaged, although he returned safely to base.

As the enemy withdrew, the 10,000-ton fleet depot ship HMS *Sandhurst* blazed away in the Camber, Eastern Dockyard. HMS *Codrington* had been tied up alongside when sunk two days previously, and now *Sandhurst* was also hit – which, being full of torpedoes, ammunition, fuel and oil was a great concern.

Four fire appliances of Dover's Auxiliary Fire Service raced to the scene, the firemen finding the ship wreathed in burning oil from a severed pipeline – and on the adjacent wharf was 200,000 tons of inflammable coal. Chief Fire Officer Ernie Harmer, Deputy Chief Fire Officer Cyril Brown and Section Leader Alec Campbell immediately set to with their colleagues helping sailors unload ammunition from the blazing ship, and fought to bring the inferno under control – a battle which took until 15.00 hrs to win.

For their incredible bravery that day, Harmer, Brown and Campbell were each awarded the George Medal, while The King's Commendation for Brave Conduct was given to Station Officer Harold Thomas Bookings and Fire Officers Ernest Alfred Foord, Edward Jesse Gore and Arthur Thomas Cunnington, in addition to Auxiliary Fireman, Lionel Rupert Hudsmith and John McDermott, the citation for which read:

> In a recent large-scale attack by enemy bombers on Dover Harbour, fires were started in ships and oil stores. Air raids continued throughout the day. During the attacks, all members of the Dover Fire Brigade and Auxiliary Fire Service engaged at the fires did excellent work in difficult and dangerous circumstances and the fires were eventually extinguished. The individuals named above volunteered to return to a blazing ship containing explosives, in which they fought fires while enemy aircraft were still in the neighbourhood.

This was the heaviest raid so far. Having already denied Dover to the RN as a destroyer base, it is arguable that *Oberst* Johannes Fink, the *KanalkampfFührer*, had achieved much of his objective. Thirty thousand tons of British shipping had been sunk, forcing the Admiralty to close the Channel to convoys by day.

Emboldened by this success, Fink's attacks on Dover Harbour represent a clear escalation in the fighting, as it was no longer just shipping in *Luftwaffe* bombsights. At 12.45 hrs, 'A' Flight of 610 Squadron was scrambled from Hawkinge,

> to intercept Raid 49 off Dungeness sighted a Do 215 at point indicated by R/T. E/A immediately dropped large number of bombs into sea, and turned for French coast. Spitfires attacked in succession, four using all their ammunition, and one about 800 rounds. E/A was considerably damaged, pieces falling off, and smoke pouring from port engine. Pilots comment on speed of E/A, necessitating opening the gate [emergency boost] wide to engage. Tactics adopted were evasive turns when – action broke off, E/A was last seen in mid-Channel, flying steadily at 50ft. [ORB]

The Dornier was claimed as damaged, which indeed this machine of *Stab*/KG2, engaged on reconnaissance, certainly was; it crash-landed back at St Inglevert with a wounded officer aboard. The reconnaissance, however, was successful, because Convoy *Cat* had been sighted; soon, preparations were underway for an attack by *Erprobungsgruppe* 210.

To the West, at 14.00 hrs, Red and Yellow Sections of 145 Squadron, aloft from Tangmere, sighted a Ju 88 twenty miles South of Worthing. Red Section climbed as a precaution against possible escorting fighters, while Yellow Section, comprising Squadron Leader John Peel, Pilot Officer Lord Kay-Shuttleworth and Pilot Officer Ernest Wakeham, attacked in turn. Before the combat concluded, Green Section's Pilot Officer Jas Storrar also got in an attack. 'The result of this attack by these four pilots was the complete destruction of the Ju 88, which crashed into the sea twenty miles off Worthing,' states the ORB. There were no survivors from this bomber, of 4/KG76.

There was also action off the East Coast.

At 14.45 hrs, Blue Section of 66 Squadron, Pilot Officers Bob 'Oxo' Oxspring, John Pickering and John Studd, 'intercepted He 111 off Lowestoft at 1445 hrs. E/A was shot down and destroyed.' This bomber, of I/KG53, crashed into the North Sea, killing the crew.

At 15.05 hrs, Blue Section of 85 Squadron, was patrolling a convoy, up from Martlesham Heath, when Flying Officer Patrick Woods-Scawen sighted a Do 17 ten miles East of Felixstowe, which he broke off to engage.

There followed a pursuit 'to within a few miles of the Belgian/Dutch coast', during which the Hurricane pilot 'badly maimed' the enemy bomber, which was 'last seen flying under difficulties. Flying Officer Woods-Scawen only broke off the fight when he had no ammunition left.' This was actually the aircraft of *Oberstleutnant* Genth, the *Kommandeur* of III/KG76, who was killed in the engagement, although the damaged aircraft returned to base.

That afternoon, Flight Lieutenant Howard 'Billy' Burton, the 1936 Cranwell Sword of Honour winner and an exceptional young officer, was also up from Coltishall, leading a section of 66 Squadron Spitfires, comprising Flying Officer Ernest Campbell-Colquhoun and Pilot Officer Leon 'Duke' Collingridge. At 9,000ft, fourteen miles East of Hammond's Knoll:

> Enemy (He 111) sighted at 1512 hrs about ten miles due East of us ... we approached head-on ... E/A flew below us at 9,000ft and saw crosses on upper wings. Section formed line astern and turned around and pursued E/A, which commenced turning to port. Section closed in and gave a burst about 350 yards with quarter deflection and then closed into range 300 yards, closing to 80 yards. Broke away to starboard and waited for numbers 2 and 3 to carry out attacks. Repeated attack from astern and closed into 150 yards with one long burst, finishing ammunition.
>
> Enemy appeared then to be slowing down and heading towards land. Waited on port side while numbers 2 and 3 finished their ammunition. Large plume of white vapour poured back from port engine. Little return fire experienced and not accurate. Enemy fired at about 1,000 yards. Enemy gradually lost height and made for cloud at Yarmouth, his port engine was stopped and he could not make height. After approaching Yarmouth he turned slowly to port and made off ESE at about 130–140 mph, losing height slowly.
>
> Enemy jettisoned about six bombs when ten miles off Yarmouth. I left enemy gradually losing height. Whenever I approached within about 1,000 yards, he kept shooting, but most inaccurately.

Pilot Officer Collingridge's Spitfire, however was hit in the exchange, forcing the pilot to crash-land on the beach at Orfordness; 'Duke' was injured and admitted to Ipswich Hospital.

The Spitfires' attacks were inconclusive, but the He 111 was clearly damaged – and subsequently intercepted by Blue Section of Debden's 17 Squadron, which was on patrol and vectored to intercept Raid X17:

> An He 111 was sighted at 4,000ft below cloud and the Section gave chase in line-astern. Flight Lieutenant Bayne, Blue Leader, delivered a frontal attack out of the sun, followed by a No 1 Attack, firing all his ammunition. The E/A dropped its undercarriage and jettisoned its bombs, pieces being seen to fall away from it and smoke pouring from both engines. Flying Officer Bird-Wilson (Blue 2) and Pilot Officer Wissler (Blue 3) followed Blue Leader with frontal and No 1 attacks, Blue 3 experiencing some fire from the rear-gunner but

sustaining no hits. After further attack the E/A crashed into the sea and three of the crew were seen to climb out into a rubber boat.

The enemy crew, however, would not be rescued from the cruel sea.

At 16.35 hrs, eleven Me 110s of *Stab*, 1 and 2/*Erprobungsgruppe* 210 took off from St Omer, escorted by thirty Me 110s of ZG26 – all bound for Convoy *Cat*, which was off Harwich. Flying Officer Kenneth Blair DFC was leading 151 Squadron, up from Rochford and patrolling the convoy, later reporting that at 17.15 hrs:

> We were ordered to intercept E/A fifteen miles East of Harwich, which were in the vicinity of a convoy. Convoy consisted of one damaged cargo boat and five naval ships. As we approached the convoy the E/A came down through the clouds in line astern and attacked the damaged cargo ship. I only saw the first one drop any bombs, which missed the target. I put the squadron into line astern and climbed up to their level (5,000ft) and attacked with the squadron from the rear of enemy formation.
>
> The first few E/A had not seen us but when we attacked fled into the clouds. I was able to contact one E/A and gave it two busts of fire lasting four seconds, 300/150 yards and using deflection for the first and astern for the second. The rear-gunner stopped firing after first few seconds.
>
> On the second burst the starboard engine caught fire and I was diverted to another E/A which was trying to attack me. When last seen E/A was well alight and appeared to be disabled.
>
> After I had moved into a better position I attacked the second E/A, which on seeing himself at a disadvantage climbed into the clouds and was not seen again.

Blair had hit the Me 110 of *Leutnant* Erich Beudel, whose gunner, *Obergefreiter* Heinrich Diemer, was wounded in the attack, which also damaged the fighter-bomber's radio electrical system, flaps, wings, tyres – and even hit an ammunition drum, which exploded. Beudel, however, managed to nurse his damaged aircraft back to St Omer, crash-landing at 18.05 hrs.

Flight Sergeant George Atkinson also hit a 110, reporting a 'thin trail of black smoke coming from the E/A's port engine'. This was claimed as damaged, as was another by Pilot Officer David Blomeley.

The Hurricane of Flying Officer Charles Whittingham was hit by an Me 110, however, causing him to forced-land at Martlesham Heath, and similarly Flying Officer Richard 'Dickie' Milne was also shot-up, crash-landing at Rochford. Hurricanes were claimed destroyed by *Oberleutnant* Karl-Heinz Meyer, *Oberleutnant* Sophus Baagoe, and *Unteroffizier* Walter Scherer, all of 8/ZG26.

The action was close to the 12 Group area and was too much for Air Vice-Marshal Leigh-Mallory, who, although 11 Group had not requested assistance, scrambled all of Coltishall's fighter squadrons at 17.15 hrs.

The following is from 19 Squadron ORB:

> Whole of "B" Flight in three sections of two aircraft (Blue, Green, Black) sent off in big alarm at Coltishall, when all available squadrons left the ground. "B" Flight ordered to attack approaching enemy bombers.

The outcome was frustrating for 12 Group, the enemy not being sighted and the action all over. The wisdom of scrambling so many fighters in response to this threat, however, was questionable, and early evidence of Leigh-Mallory's parochial perspective which looked only to the interests of 12 Group, and also further indicates a leaning towards the deployment of large formations of fighters – which was contrary to how the battle was being fought by 11 Group.

Interestingly, on this day the Deputy Chief of the Air Staff (DCAS), Air Vice-Marshal Sholto Douglas, ordered Fighter Command, Bomber Command and Coastal Command to carry out sharp attacks against enemy E-boat bases, coastal airfields and gun batteries. These attacks, Douglas stated, should be timed to hit enemy airfields immediately after German aircraft had landed following raids on Britain. Although E-boats could be attacked when their presence was known, airfields were notoriously difficult targets, due to being heavily defended, and therefore these attacks were unlikely to be successful. Moreover, the constant enemy air activity over the Pas-de-Calais made it impossible to identify when a raid was in progress until it started moving out across the Channel; due to the speeds of the aircraft involved, the enemy were only five minutes flying time from Dover when thus identified (an observation putting the problem of early interception by 11 Group into sharp focus).

In fact, the time from a raid being identified to it re-crossing the French coast was usually no more than thirty minutes. To strike when the German bombers had just landed, therefore, RAF bombers would have to be brought to readiness whenever such a *Luftwaffe* raid appeared possible. Furthermore, in the wake of having engaged an incoming threat, 11 Group would clearly have difficulty in supplying enough fighters to escort such a counter-attack.

Fortunately, Air Chief Marshal Dowding's SASO, Air Vice-Marshal Douglas Evill (previously Bomber Command's SASO) recognised these difficulties and felt that such an operation would be most unwise. Having liaised with his opposite number at Bomber Command, and, of course 11 Group's Air Vice-Marshal Park, Evill argued that it would be far better to make such an attack in strength, following extensive reconnaissance and target study. Fortunately, Douglas heeded this advice, and the DCAS's potentially suicidal scheme came to nought.

Nonetheless, Dutch airfields, and Bremen, were the targets for fourteen 2 Group Blenheims on this day, although owing to the lack of cloud cover only six found and bombed their objectives. One Blenheim, of 82 Squadron, was lost, shot down over Texel by *Leutnant* Hans Bosch of *Stab* II/JG27. Unfavourable weather also hampered nocturnal raids on Germany, but there were no losses. Similarly, although two Hudsons were hit by flak attacking oil installations at Amsterdam, Coastal Command suffered no casualties.

The Daily Home Intelligence Report:

> A most reliable observer, at the end of a tour through many parts of England, says 'People don't want exhortation to be cheerful: they are cheerful. They don't want to be told to be good: they are as cooperative as they can be. What they want is information and explanation with lots of jam by way of music, processions, flags, songs and all the rest.' This sums up many other reports.

The report concluded that 'Priestley's *Postscript* [was] warmly appreciated', referring to the previous evening's weekly BBC radio broadcast by the popular playwright, broadcaster, novelist, social observer and socialist J.B. Priestley.

These 'fireside chats' began on Wednesday, 5 June 1940, immediately after Dunkirk – and became the most popular series of talks in the history of British broadcasting to date. Countless people tuned in their wireless sets to listen to Priestley, whose show was shifted to Sunday evenings and in which he commented on the war, society and much else besides. Indeed, by the time of his final *Postscript*, on Sunday, 20 October 1940, Priestley had become massively influential owing to the great reach radio gave his views, which were sometimes openly critical of the War Cabinet. In time, Priestley became second only to Churchill in terms of listeners but was ultimately taken off air for his overtly left-wing views.

On the evening of Sunday, 28 July 1940, Priestley's 'warmly appreciated' *Postscript* concerned a family party to which he had recently been invited by friends, celebrating the safe return of their son, an RAF bomber pilot who had been rescued with his crew from the North Sea, having been shot down. Priestley had fought in the First World War but had subsequently become incensed at the world to which veterans had returned, one that failed to live up to the expectations and ideals they fought for. Indeed, in his celebrated *English Journey* (1934), he wrote bitterly of certain of his friends having been unable to attend a regimental reunion on account of being unable to afford appropriate clothing. In the broadcast in question, Priestley asked 'what are we civilians prepared to do?' in return for the 'skill, devotion, endurance and self-sacrifice' by the 'young men of the RAF':

> And surely the answer is that the least we can do is to give our minds honestly, sincerely and without immediate self-interest, to the task of preparing a world really fit for them and their kind – to arrange for them a final 'happy landing'.

Don't insult them by thinking they don't care what sort of world they're fighting for. All the evidence contradicts that.

After Priestley was taken off air, his *Postscripts* were published in book form, which he never anticipated, so we have a verbatim record of his broadcasts (see Bibliography). These passages provide a colourful glimpse of Britain in 1940, including this reference to visiting Margate in the summer of 1940 (*Postscript*, Sunday, 14 July 1940):

> Along the road there were things that weren't quite what they first appeared to be .... The Bren guns seemed to be getting mixed up with the agricultural life of North Kent. The most flourishing crop seemed to be barbed wire. Soldiers would pop up from nowhere and then vanish again – unless they wanted to see our permits ... A field would have a hole in it, made at considerable time, trouble and outlay of capital, by the German Air Force. An RAF lorry went past, taking with it the remains of a *Heinkel* bomber ... But there we were at last – on the front at Margate ... But no people! – not a soul ... an air raid warning didn't seem to matter much . . I say to all of you who are listening ... This Margate I saw was saddening and hateful; but its new silence and desolation should be thought of as a bridge leading us to a better England, in a nobler world. We're not fighting to restore the past; it was the past that brought us to this heavy hour; but we *are* fighting to rid ourselves and the world of the evil encumbrance of these Nazis so that we can plan and create a noble future for all our species.

Lieutenant Arthur Hague was an RN reserve officer previously serving on the Blue Funnel passenger line, and had reported for duty at Southampton's Naval Office on 29 July 1940:

> Our senior officer was Commander 'Mutt' Owles. He explained that owing to the German occupation of the French coastline, convoys had become heavily exposed to air attack by the *Luftwaffe*. Of the twenty-one ships of Convoy CW8, travelling westward through the Straits of Dover on 25 July 1940, only eleven ships had succeeded in passing Dungeness and convoys in both directions had been temporarily suspended. It had therefore been decided that each future convoy would be a combined naval and air operation.

Commander Owles was forming the Channel Convoy Mobile Balloon Barrage Flotilla, according to the official HMSO history of *The War at Sea 1939–45*, 'an extemporised and possibly unique force, manned by men of at least a dozen nationalities intended to protect the Channel convoys from the depredations of enemy dive-bombers'.

According to Lieutenant Hague, the unit's ships were,

> a miscellaneous collection of tugs and tenders [which] included two Antwerp cutters which had escaped the German invasion and had assisted in Operation *Dynamo* under their own crews. On reaching the UK they had been commissioned under the White Ensign as HM ships *Astral* and *Borealis*. Owles had chosen the former, and, as next senior officer, I took the latter .... Dockyard mateys were busy fitting the winch and towing wire cage for the RAF barrage balloon we would tow. An RN Patrol Service crew of sixteen, mostly fishermen, arrived next day from HMS *Europa*, their Lowestoft base, closely followed by three aircraftmen who were to handle the balloon ... The total armament of each ship in the Flotilla comprised two Hotchkiss machine-guns mounted above the bridge.

Lieutenant Hague provisioned HMS *Borealis* over the next few days – and would soon see action.

Squadron Leader Don MacDonell, 64 Squadron:

> I shot down a *Stuka* and an Me 109 on 29 July 1940. It was also our best Squadron record to date. In all we accounted for ten enemy aircraft and the total broadcast by the BBC for the whole of Fighter Command was around eighty, for the loss of thirty-odd of our own. I was in London that evening with Diana. We were walking down Park Lane when a group came up to us and cried 'Eighty of the bastards shot down!'
>
> Diana said, 'Yes, and he was one of the Spitfire pilots in the battle!'
>
> They hoisted me onto their shoulders and carried me to the RAF Club. I couldn't invite them in as they were fairly drunk – but it was quite an occasion.

TUESDAY, 30 JULY 1940

Low cloud and drizzle restricted operations, making for a much quieter day. At 12.05 hrs, Flight Lieutenant Fred 'Rusty' Rushmer was up from Montrose and leading Green Section of 603 Squadron's 'B' Flight, patrolling Stonehaven, when alerted by the Sector Controller to a bandit fifty miles East of Montrose.

Vectored South-east, Green 2, Pilot Officer 'Raz' Berry, and Green 3, Pilot Officer Peter Pease, spotted a He 111 of 4/KG26, which the Spitfires lost no time in attacking – leaving the bomber smoking from both engines and diving towards the sea. Rushmer reported that the *Heinkel* 'pancaked on sea, bursting into flames on impact. Circled wreckage in company with an Anson, no survivors seen.' The bomber, however, had returned fire before its demise, hitting the Spitfires of Rushmer and Pease, both of whom nonetheless returned safely to base; it was Pease's first experience of aerial combat.

Pease, an Old Etonian and an historian of Trinity College, Cambridge, was the son of Sir Richard and Lady Pease, had flown with the University Air Squadron (UAS) before being commissioned into the RAFVR in 1938. Called to full-time service in October 1939, the 22-year-old Pease had only recently completed his service flying training and after converting to Spitfires at Aston Down reported to 603 Squadron on 6 July 1940, along with his friend, Pilot Officer Richard Hillary – who would, in due course, write his classic memoir *The Last Enemy*. Hillary had previously read Modern Greats and History at Oxford, where he too learned to fly with his UAS and was commissioned into the RAFVR. When war broke out, it had been welcomed by Hillary:

> I was glad for purely selfish reasons. The war solved all problems of a career, and promised a chance of self-realisation that would normally take years to achieve. As a fighter pilot I hoped for a concentration of amusement, fear and exaltation which it would be impossible to experience in any form of existence. I was not disappointed.

Of Pease, Hillary wrote:

> Here was a man better orientated than I ... a product of the old-school-tie system ... more than comfortably off ... brought up in the orthodox Tory tradition ... I often attacked him and accused him of living in an ivory tower, but he refused to be drawn; indeed, there was little reason why he should be, for it was only too obvious that that he was liked and respected by everyone in the squadron. It was, in fact, almost impossible to draw him into an argument on any subject ... I tried everything ... I particularly wanted to make him talk about the war.

Finally, Pease relented, when Hillary cornered his friend while the pair travelled by train to collect two new Spitfires, and gave forthright reasons for volunteering to fight:

> I would say that I was fighting the war to rid the world of fear – of the fear of fear ... If the Germans win this war, nobody except little Hitlers will dare do anything. England will be run as if it were a concentration camp, or at best a factory. All courage will die out of the world – the courage to love, to create, to take risks, whether

physical or intellectual or moral. Men will hesitate to carry out the promptings of the heart or the brain because, having acted, they will live in fear that their action may be discovered and themselves cruelly punished. Thus all love, all spontaneity, will die out of the world. Emotion will have atrophied. Thought will have petrified. The oxygen breathed by the soul, so to speak, will vanish, and mankind will wither.

The argument continued until the journey's end, Hillary arguing more selfish reasons for fighting, until Pease concluded that:

> I am sure you will change your tune. It won't be long, either. Something bigger than you is coming out of this, and as it grows you will grow with it. Your preconceived notions won't last long ... I'm sure it needs only some psychological shock, some affront to your sensibility, to arouse your pity or your anger sufficiently for you to forget yourself.

As we will in due course discover, these were prophetic words indeed.

Across the Channel, on the afternoon of 30 July 1940, the *Kommodore* of *Erprobugsgruppe* 210, *Hauptmann* Walter Rubensdörffer and *Leutnant* Hans Herold, of 1 *Staffel*, took off from St Omer in their Me 110s, heading for the Thames Estuary on an armed reconnaissance, seeking shipping.

Heading in the same direction, at 15.00 hrs, Flight Lieutenant Harry Hamilton was leading Red Section of the Martlesham Heath-based 85 Squadron's 'A' Flight to patrol Convoy *Pilot*, off Harwich:

> I sighted two Me 110s about ten miles off Aldeburgh, flying North, about 5ft above sea-level, at about 280 mph. E/A put on speed and turned East and endeavoured to escape. We gave chase in line-astern for thirty-five miles. I got abreast of the E/A to identify it, and then delivered a stern attack, firing a 5-second burst, following with another stern attack, firing another long burst. E/A opened fire at 1,500 yards and continued firing during attacks. I then broke away in order to gain height and speed for another attack, and saw E/A lurch to the left and his nose drop towards the sea. I saw Red 2 (Flight Sergeant Sammy Allard) close in and open fire, and E/A hit the sea and broke up. I saw one man in the sea and a pulled parachute about ten yards away from him. I then chased the second E/A with Red 2, but he escaped into cloud.

Flight Sergeant Allard also 'chased the second Me 110' before rejoining Red 1 and returning to base.

The combat had taken place just 5ft above the waves, the unlucky 110 crew being *Leutnant* Herold and *Obergefreiter* Lothar Lilienthal. *Hauptmann* Rubensdörffer, according to the 85 Squadron ORB, 'thought discretion the better part of valour and made off home'. The *Kommodore* had had a lucky escape on this occasion.

Throughout the day, in spite of the poor weather, Coastal Command continued patrolling, while twenty-four 2 Group Blenheims attacked airfields in the Netherlands, Belgium and France, in addition to targets at Paderborn and Gelsenkirchen. From the Paderborn raid, a Blenheim of 15 Squadron was lost, probably shot down off the Dutch coast by *Unteroffizier* Joachim Schreckenberg of 8/JG54, who recorded his second victory at 14.20 hrs. That night, the weather prevented a maximum effort, but a handful of Wellingtons attacked oil plants and marshalling yards in Germany.

The Daily Home Intelligence Report confirmed that 'Morale remains steady'. Meanwhile, the South-Eastern Region reported that:

> News of Dover air battle has had heartening effect, especially in other coastal towns. Opinion widely held that Hitler has changed his plans. Rye and Winchelsea beach dwellers, who have had to evacuate at short notice for military reasons, were outside special areas scheme and there is no central authority to ensure their welfare.

WEDNESDAY, 31 JULY 1940

On this day, Hitler held an important conference at the Berghof, the *Führer*'s mountain retreat on the *Obersalzberg*, with von Brauchitsch and Raeder. Certain things had become clearer since the previous conference, on 21 July 1940, not least the fact that Britain was determined to fight on, causing Hitler to observe that 'her spirits have revived again'. Raeder reported that from the naval perspective preparations were well advanced: the fleet required to transport men across the Channel would be ready by mid-September and accommodated at the Channel ports.

Providing the *Luftwaffe* had achieved aerial supremacy, mine clearance in the Channel would take three weeks, and German minefields would begin being sowed at the end of August. The *Kriegsmarine* chief predicted that his navy would be ready to execute *Seelöwe* by 15 September 1940 – but favoured a postponement, just to be sure, until May 1941.

Hitler remained sceptical regarding the feasibility of the proposed operation, but was satisfied with Rader's report and progress. Raeder had argued, however, for a landing on a reduced front – but Hitler backed Halder's broad front plan and ordered that air attacks aligned to achieving *Seelöwe* should begin immediately – making this, arguably, another contender for the day on which the Battle of Britain could be considered to have begun.

Hitler knew, though, that this was a high-risk operation, not least because of the unpredictable weather and his *Kriegsmarine*'s inferiority to the RN – and was clearly uncertain regarding the *Luftwaffe*'s ability to wrest aerial supremacy from the RAF: 'If results of air warfare are unsatisfactory, invasion preparations will be stopped. If we have the impression that the English are crushed and that effects will soon begin to tell, we shall proceed to the attack' – meaning a seaborne invasion.

As ever, Hitler saw Russia as the main prize and key to his strategy. In the event of *Seelöwe* being impossible, Hitler decreed that 'we must eliminate all factors which allow England to hope for a change in the situation'. Those 'factors' were support from America and Russia – and Hitler saw the destruction and control of Russia as all. If Germany conquered Russia, he argued, the result would be an increase in Japan's influence in the Far East, which would preoccupy the United States: 'If Russia is smashed, Britain's last hope will be shattered. Germany will then be master of Europe and the Balkans.'

According to Halder's diary, Hitler announced his intention to invade Russia in the spring of 1941, which, to some degree, was an exit strategy should *Seelöwe* fail and Britain still be fighting on – but, ideally, a two-front war was to be avoided and therefore Britain's rapid defeat was of enormous importance. Hitler's main objective in the autumn ahead was a decisive attack on Britain – which he would not be diverted from.

If his previous attitude towards the prospect of war with, and an invasion of, England had been 'half-hearted', with his strategy now clear, the *Führer* was resolved. There would be no negotiated peace while Churchill remained Prime Minister, and so the only way forward was to unleash the *Luftwaffe* against Britain as never before. From this point onwards and for the coming weeks, *Seelöwe*, underpinned everything – and the invasion was entirely reliant upon the outcome of the *Luftwaffe* assault.

On the Channel coast, however, a thick haze on this significant day made operations difficult for both sides.

At 04.00 hrs, Squadron Leader John Thompson led his 111 Squadron Hurricanes from Croydon to operate from Hawkinge. At 07.10 hrs Red Section was scrambled and ordered to patrol mid-Channel, above cloud. Ten minutes later Green Section, led by Flight Lieutenant Stanley Connors DFC, was scrambled to patrol the same area, below the band of cloud, and at 3,000ft intercepted and engaged a Ju 88 reconnaissance bomber. The enemy aircraft was engaged by all three Hurricane pilots involved (the other two being Pilot Officer Jack Copeman, Green 2 and Sergeant Ralph Carnal, Green 3) and last seen at 1,000ft diving vertically, noted the ORB, 'into the mist covering the sea and disappeared. All RDF tracks ceased.' It would seem, though, that the Ju 88 escaped, possibly by flying home very low, beneath the radar beams.

Similarly, at 08.00 hrs, Red Section of Tangmere's 145 Squadron caught a Do 215 'about fifteen miles south-east of Bembridge and Red Section No.2, Flying

Officer Ostowicz was able to get in three short bursts before the bandit disappeared in cloud. The extent of damage to the Dornier was unknown.'

Antoni Ostowicz was Polish and among the first of his countrymen to become operational in an RAF fighter squadron, having reached England in late 1939. Commissioned into the RAFVR and converted to Hurricanes at 6 OTU, Ostowicz had joined 145 Squadron on 16 July 1940. These trained pilots from the occupied lands were, of course, welcome and essential reinforcements – but there were difficulties.

Firstly, the obvious language barrier; secondly the adjustment to service in the RAF and operating modern fighter types. The process had, however, started to form squadrons comprising personnel from the occupied lands: on 10 July 1940, the first of these, 310 (Czech) Squadron had been formed (operational 17 August 1940), then the two Polish squadrons, namely 302 on 13 July 1940 (operational 11 September 1940), and 303 (operational 30 August 1940).

The next reconnaissance bomber intercepted was by Red Section of Northolt's 1 Squadron, when, at 11.25 hrs, Flying Officer Peter Matthews, Pilot Officer John Davey and Sergeant Henry Merchant attacked a lone Do 17 at 8,000ft, eight miles South of St Catherine's Point:

> It dived to sea-level and made for the coast of France. No 1 attacked in line astern and the attack was pressed home several times. Although about 5,000 rounds of ammunition were fired, the Do 17 got away with one engine damaged. [ORB]

This, surely, indicates how difficult German bombers could be to destroy with rifle-calibre ammunition.

On this last day of July 1940, 74 Squadron's Spitfires were in action again. Flight Lieutenant 'Sailor' Malan and 'A' Flight were up from Manston but unable to catch the Me 109s sighted over the Channel.

At 16.00 hrs however, 'B' Flight became embroiled with 109s of II/JG51 over 'Hellfire Corner'. *Hauptmann* Horst Tietzen, *Staffelkapitän* of 5/JG51, shot down Sergeant Fred Eley, who crashed into Folkestone harbour and was killed, while *Oberleutnant* 'Joschko' Fözö, *Staffelkapitän* of 4/JG51, killed Pilot Officer Harold Gunn.

More fortunate was Flight Lieutenant Piers Kelly, who survived being badly shot-up by another 4/JG51 *experte*, *Leutnant* Erich Hohagen. In response, Sergeant Bill Skinner claimed a 109 destroyed, but with two pilots missing on return to Manston, the 'Tigers' needed a morale-boosting lift – and got one: 'Sailor' Malan was awarded a Bar to his DFC, and Pilot Officer John Freeborn – now an ace with five confirmed victories – was awarded a well-deserved DFC.

According to an anonymous 74 Squadron fitter:

> Having spent many hours patching up his (Sailor's) Spitfire ready for the next trip I could well realise the marvellous escapes he

must have had. Although his Spitfire came back battered each time he would not part with it in exchange for a new and more modern one. His instructions to his crew were 'My machine has got to be serviceable. There is no excuse.' His engine had to go first time, the radio-telephone just had to function even if his junior pilots' radios failed at times. And his guns weren't allowed to have stoppages.

On one occasion it was my job to work out in the open all night with a hand torch to renew his battered tailplane. I don't quite know how I managed it: but I knew it just had to be done by 0400 hrs. Flight Lieutenant Malan got in his cockpit and said 'Contact', without asking if I had finished. In fact I was struggling with the last stubborn split pin.

The day came when we were shown films of his combats which was a tonic to us all after eight months of terrible waiting, but always ready. The greatest thrill of all was the night of the first raids when Flight Lieutenant Malan went up alone through intense gunfire and shot down two German machines in what seemed like less than ten minutes. In my heart, I knew that this was another award for my Flight Commander.

He was right. The citation for 'Sailor' Malan's Bar, gazetted on 13 August 1940, read as follows:

Since the end of May 1940, this officer has continued to lead his flight and on many occasions the squadron, in numerous successful engagements against the enemy. During the Dunkirk operations he shot down three enemy aircraft and assisted in destroying a further three. In June 1940, during a night attack by enemy aircraft, he shot down two *Heinkel* 111s. His magnificent leadership, skill and courage have been largely responsible for the many successes obtained by his Squadron.

It was far from one-sided however. There were now seven 'Tigers' who had failed to return, although two were known to be prisoners, and Sergeant Mould remained in Dover Military Hospital after baling out three days previously. Even the increasingly legendary 'Sailor' Malan had narrow escapes:

The sky's very small when you want to hide ... I did everything but fall into the sea to dodge them. I was partly shot up. I had glass from a broken windscreen in my eyes. Each time I could see one coming down I swung round to face it. They only left me when I reached our coast. I still don't know how I got down on the deck safely. When I went into interrogation, the Station Commander said: 'This looks like a man who could use a tot of brandy, Doctor.'

I said 'I'd like two of those. I always thought it was coloured water you kept in those bottles anyway!'

At 17.45 hrs, Pilot Officer Kenneth Lee of 501 Squadron led four Hurricanes up from Hawkinge, being joined five minutes later by the CO, Squadron Leader Harry Hogan, patrolling over Ashford. At 12,000ft, Flight Lieutenant John Gibson sighted two Do 17s over Saltwood, one of which he engaged and damaged before both escaped into cloud.

While returning to Hawkinge, however, the engine of Pilot Officer Ralph Don's Hurricane burst into flame, forcing the pilot to take to his parachute. The aircraft crashed at Lydden Marsh, inland of Folkestone, and Don was admitted to Canterbury Hospital – his injuries would keep him out of the battle until 10 October 1940.

At Coltishall in No.12 Group, 19 Squadron was celebrating the award of a DFC to Flight Lieutenant Brian Lane, the commander of 'A' Flight. On the squadron's first full-formation combat over the French coast on 26 May 1940, the CO, Squadron Leader Geoffrey Stephenson, had been shot down and captured. Thereafter, it had fallen to Lane to lead the squadron throughout the *Dynamo* fighting and until Squadron Leader Phillip Pinkham was appointed to command five days later. Pinkham, a Leigh-Mallory favourite, had no combat experience, however, and was preoccupied with getting the troublesome cannon-armed Spitfire issue resolved. Consequently, leadership of the squadron in the air continued to largely test on the 23-year-old Lane's shoulders as the senior flight commander; his well-earned DFC citation reads:

> This officer has displayed great gallantry and coolness in the face of the enemy during operations in Belgium and France. When his Squadron Commander was missing he led the squadron and on eight occasions led a wing of four squadrons over enemy territory. His resourceful leadership and courage have contributed largely to success of Squadron, which is credited with having destroyed thirty enemy aircraft and possibly another eleven.

Pilot Officer Wallace 'Jock' Cunningham:

> We of 19 Squadron were lying in the sun at Coltishall along with Douglas Bader and other 242 Squadron pilots. There was some banter going on and Douglas asked Brian 'What's that?', in his usual cocky fashion, thrusting his pipe at Brian's new DFC ribbon. '*I* must get one of those', said Bader, and, as we all know, he did just that!

During the day, a Coastal Command Hudson of 500 Squadron had a lucky escape when hit by a Royal Navy anti-aircraft ship East of Harwich, wounding the observer, although the aircraft returned safely to base.

The lack of cloud over France, however, once more frustrated Bomber Command's 2 Group, only eleven Blenheims of twenty-eight hitting their targets, a variety of airfields and industrial facilities. One of these aircraft, of 114 Squadron based at Horsham St Faith, was shot down West of Ijmuiden by *Leutnant* Helmut Henstedt of 8/JG54, the crew of which were captured. By night, Le Bourget airfield, invasion ports and industrial targets were all attacked, in addition to mines being sown, two Hampdens engaged on the latter activity failing to return.

As far as the day battle was concerned, Fink had undoubtedly achieved a victory in denying Dover as a base for the RN's anti-invasion destroyer fleet, but more ships had been sunk through nocturnal minelaying than actual bombing attacks. Moreover, the *Luftwaffe* was becoming more acquainted with the Spitfire, which was no obsolete fighter-type like those previously encountered.

The more numerous Hurricane pilots, although at a technical disadvantage against the Me 109, were fighting with great courage, 11 Group's penny-packet formations of sections or flights frequently meeting far greater odds and not hesitating to engage. Indeed, Fighter Command Intelligence Summary No.182 records this remark by a captured ZG76 Me 110 pilot who stated that the RAF pilots were fighting with 'Kolossalen Virbissenheit' – or with tremendous stubbornness.

Part II
KANALKAMPF DIARY
1 August – 12 August 1940

THURSDAY, 1 AUGUST 1940

It was on this date that, following the previous day's high-level conference, Hitler formalised the result of those deliberations by issuing Directive No.17:

The *Führer* and Supreme Commander of the Armed Forces	*Führer* Headquarters, 1st August 1940. 10 copies

DIRECTIVE No. 17 FOR THE CONDUCT OF AIR AND SEA WARFARE AGAINST ENGLAND

In order to establish the necessary conditions for the final conquest of England I intend to intensify air and sea warfare against the English homeland. I therefore order as follows:

1. The German Air Force is to overpower the English Air Force with all the forces at its command, in the shortest possible time. The attacks are to be directed primarily against flying units, their ground installations, and their supply organisations, but also against the aircraft industry, including that manufacturing antiaircraft equipment.
2. After achieving temporary or local air superiority the air war is to be continued against ports, in particular against stores of food, and also against stores of provisions in the interior of the country.
3. Attacks on south coast ports will be made on the smallest possible scale, in view of our own forthcoming operations.
4. On the other hand, air attacks on enemy warships and merchant ships may be reduced except where some particularly favourable target happens to present itself, where such attacks would lend additional effectiveness to those mentioned in paragraph 2, or where such attacks are necessary for the training of air crews for further operations.
5. The intensified air warfare will be carried out in such a way that the Air Force can at any time be called upon to give adequate support to naval operations against suitable targets. It must also be ready to take part in full force in Operation *Seelöwe*.
6. I reserve to myself the right to decide on terror attacks as measures of reprisal.

7. The intensification of the air war may begin on or after 5th August. The exact time is to be decided by the Air Force after the completion of preparations and in the light of the weather.

The Navy is authorised to begin the proposed intensified naval war at the same time.

[signed] Adolf Hitler

These written orders by Hitler provide clarity: the intention was now for the *Luftwaffe* to neutralise Fighter Command, seizing aerial supremacy so that the invasion could proceed. Furthermore, this assault would be intense, so as to achieve the objective quickly – very important given that in a few weeks the weather would deteriorate and in itself prevent a sea crossing. Moreover, the *Luftwaffe* was additionally ordered to lay siege to island Britain, focusing on food-stores and other essential provisions, although attacks on southern ports were to be reduced, owing to Germany's need to use them in the event of the invasion succeeding. 5 August 1940 was set for the day this new aerial offensive would begin, providing the *Luftwaffe* time to prepare, although this start-date was weather-dependent.

The German air assault was no longer appended to either blockade or 'Air Fleet Diplomacy'; crucially, it was now at the very core of Hitler's strategy against Britain – the prospect of a successful and rapid strategic bombing campaign having now superseded the policy of a drawn out naval and aerial siege. According to the German historian Cajus Bekker, writing in the late 1960s, though, Directive No.17 was simply a 'masterpiece of vague expression', and *Oberst* Paul Deichmann, II *Fliegerkorps* Chief of Staff, remarked that his impression of these orders was 'that we would *not* be landing'. It is difficult to understand this perspective, however, given that it is unsupported by the evidence, and begs the question, given the campaign's ultimate outcome, did post-war German commentators deliberately down-play Operation *Seelöwe*? Indeed, this is something we will investigate further in due course.

Although not mentioned in Directive No.17, we now know that the invasion of Russia in spring 1941 was an integral part of Hitler's wider strategy against Britain. A year before, Hitler's generals had baulked at the prospect of a war against Britain – but had no such reservations regarding the Soviet Union, which they fully expected to roll up and defeat in another lightning-quick war lasting just a matter of weeks. In the meantime, Hitler's full-focus was now the air war against Britain, although fully aware that *Seelöwe* was an incredibly high-risk enterprise, and while experienced in river crossings, his *Wehrmacht* had none of such seaborne operations. Indeed, there was no facility within the command structure for the three services to cooperate and collaborate in a combined services approach.

Hitler was fully aware of this, of course, and while now focused on this new assault he knew that the stakes were high and the outcome far from certain. Consequently, there is no doubt that Hitler still hoped for a diplomatic solution –

but many of the 'Last Appeal to Reason' leaflets dropped over southern England on the night of 1 August 1940 were auctioned to raise money for the Red Cross and certainly not taken seriously.

The Daily Home Intelligence Report makes clear that,

> a feeling of complacency is beginning to grow in some quarters. There is shown a fairly widely held belief that invasion may be indefinitely delayed ... Though morale is good, many do not go to bed or else sleep fully clothed. Voluntary evacuation continues from Dover area, but a number who left some weeks ago have now returned. All large hotels in Eastbourne have closed down, and few boarding houses are doing any business.

On the morning of this first day of August 1940, inevitably German reconnaissance bombers were active. The first action of the day involved 13 Group's 616 Squadron, based at Leconfield. At 11.59 hrs, both Red and Yellow Sections were scrambled to patrol two convoys, *Agent* and *Arena*, twenty miles North-east of Flamborough Head; eight minutes later the Spitfires were over the North Sea, twenty miles North-east of Flamborough Head, when Red 1, Squadron Leader Marcus Robinson, sighted a Ju 88 bombing the ships.

The Spitfires gave chase as the raider made off at full boost, heading for cloud cover, both Robinson and his Red 3, Sergeant Marmaduke Ridley, managing two short bursts, one of which Red 2, Flight Lieutenant Richard Hellyer, confirmed caused black and white smoke to emit from the Ju 88's port engine. Attempting to catch the bomber before it disappeared into cloud, Squadron Leader Robinson's air speed in the dive was off the clock, and estimated at 520 mph. Nonetheless, the bomber escaped and Red Section returned to base at 13.35 hrs. Sergeant Ridley's Spitfire, however, had been hit by return fire in both his wireless set and an engine bearer, but the pilot was unhurt.

In the South there was action for Tangmere's 145 Squadron, the Hurricanes of which also engaged enemy reconnaissance bombers. At 14.20 hrs, Flight Lieutenant Roy Dutton led Red and Yellow Sections up on patrol, five minutes later the Sector Controller detaching Yellow Section, led by Pilot Officer Ernest Wakeham, to patrol Selsey Bill before vectoring the fighters towards Brighton, searching for a bandit.

At 14.50 hrs, fifteen miles South of Hastings, Wakeham found a layer of 8/10ths cloud between 2,000–2,500ft, so ordered Yellow 3, Pilot Officer Lord Kay-Shuttleworth, to provide top cover above the clouds, while the remainder of the Section dropped below. Wakeham then sighted the enemy aircraft, a Henschel 126, at 1,500ft, in the exact position given by the Controller. Yellow Section then attacked the Henschel, a single-engine aircraft with a crew of two and armed with just a single fixed forward-firing MG 17, and a rearwards firing MG 15, on a flexible mount, operated by the observer.

KANALKAMPF DIARY, 1 AUGUST – 12 AUGUST 1940

The enemy pilot immediately turned South, but when Yellow 2, Sub-Lieutenant Ian Kestin, attacked from astern his Hurricane was hit by return fire from the rear-gunner – the British fighter immediately diving straight into the sea from 400ft. The Henschel then dived to sea-level, jinking, while Wakeham pressed home further attacks, silencing the rear-gunner: 'I then closed to 100 yards, firing a long burst. The Henschel turned sharply left and dived into the sea, leaving only a patch of oil, about twenty miles South of Hastings.' Wakeham then orbited the oil patch marking the crash-site of his Yellow 2, but Sub-Lieutenant Kestin, another gallant FAA pilot seconded to Fighter Command was never seen again.

No.145 Squadron's Red Section also intercepted a reconnaissance bomber, a Ju 88, which Flight Lieutenant Roy Dutton, and Pilot Officers Robert Yule (a New Zealander) and Lionel Sears, damaged at 15.00 hrs, seven miles South of Beachy Head. All three pilots expended all of their ammunition, but the bomber, although 'damaged and smoking made good its escape'.

While further to the north-east the Coltishall Sector Controller was preoccupied with patrolling convoys *Agent* and *Arena*, now steaming South off the Norfolk coast; at 15.15 hrs, a lone Ju 88, having used cloud cover to approach its target undetected, dive-bombed the Boulton and Paul Riverside Works in Norwich, setting fire to the joinery department and office. Nine workers were killed and twenty more injured. The raider also strafed adjacent streets and Thorpe Station as it made off. There had been no warning that sudden and violent death was about to visit the city, causing the following day's Daily Home Intelligence Report to document that 'Need for declaration of a clear policy with regard to sirens regarded as urgent in Norwich; there is faith in shelters, but no opportunity for using them … The apparent absence of RAF and AA protection over Norwich is causing disquiet.'

To date, only Dover had been mentioned by name in the press as having suffered air attack, but details of this raid were now released for publication, 'causing mixed feelings'. It was a difficult balancing act for the Ministry of Information (MoI), between releasing war news potentially damaging to morale, or being as transparent as security allowed. On 17 June 1940, the RMS *Lancastria* had been sunk by a Ju 88 off St Nazaire during Operation *Aerial*, the urgent evacuation of British nationals and military personnel from France, a fortnight after the conclusion of *Dynamo* – resulting in the largest loss of life in British maritime history (the ship's capacity was 1,300 but more recent estimates consider between 4,000–7,000 passengers lost their lives).

Initially, news of the tragedy was suppressed but eventually released, and on 2 August 1940 the Daily Home Intelligence Report observed that, 'The withholding of news about the *Lancastria* is having a noticeable effect on people's belief in "official news". Comments show increasing scepticism.' This controversy doubtless explains the decision to begin releasing more details of air attacks to the press.

By evening, Convoy *Pilot* was also off the Norfolk coast and occupying Coltishall's squadrons.

Pilot Officer Wallace 'Jock' Cunningham, 19 Squadron:

> Flying from Coltishall we routinely flew up and down the North Sea. The graveyard of the Dogger Bank showed up the dangerous task of these underpaid, little appreciated merchant seamen. Hopefully our presence frightened off the odd raid. We sat at low level east of the convoys, looking into the setting sun. Any sign of an attacker and we made a great show, chasing off the poacher. Sometimes when it was judged too dark for the bombers we would be instructed to 'pancake'; once a mile or two west of the convoy and we would see AA flashes – the bomber had watched us against the setting sun and noted our departure.
>
> I recall one thick, misty day over the North Sea trying to find a convoy. I would be vectored onto the convoy's position but at a height of several thousand feet, which was necessary for contact with base. When I descended through the murk to try and find the convoy, trying to guess where fog stopped and sea started, no contact was made. This occupied me for a time but I guess that the Controller decided that if I had so much difficulty, having the benefit of his assistance, then the convoy was safe from attack!

At 17.45 hrs that evening, Flying Officer George Christie and Pilot Officer John Latta, both Canadians, and Sergeant Eric Richardson formed Green Section of 242 Squadron's 'B' Flight and took off from Coltishall to patrol *Pilot* – which had now attracted the attention of KG4's bombers.

At 18.10 hrs, at 200ft twenty-five miles East of Lowestoft, Christie sighted a Ju 88, climbing East at 200 mph, about half a mile away. Upon seeing the Hurricanes approaching, the German pilot climbed steeply, to 900ft, disappearing into cloud. Ordering Latta and Richardson to remain on patrol below cloud, Christie continued searching for the raider – which emerged from cloud three minutes later and two miles to the East. Christie attacked, inconclusively, before once more the Ju 88 entered cloud and made good its escape. Christie resumed his patrol, encountering another Ju 88 at 18.25 hrs, just below cloud, which likewise climbed into the clag.

Again, Christie pursued his quarry, catching sight of the bomber in the cloud and attacking from below in a vertical climb before his Hurricane stalled and the 'E/A disappeared'. Then, a He 111 suddenly appeared out of cloud, immediately in front of Christie, the rear-gunner of which opened fire, inaccurately, with tracer ammunition. After dropping two bombs on the convoy, both of which missed, this bomber also climbed into cloud.

Once more, Christie set off in pursuit and attacked, firing,

> continually at 100 yards ... and observed pieces of starboard wing by the motor break away. I followed him up through cloud and had

another good shot at him in a small gap in the clouds from a range of fifty yards ... his starboard wing and motor were damaged.

Owing to being short on fuel, however, Christie was forced to break off his attack and return to base landing at 19.20 hrs. Sergeant Richardson also engaged a Ju 88, the destruction of which he was accredited with, but no personal combat report appears to have survived.

Pilot Officer Michael Appleby:

> My Squadron, 609 'West Riding', was an auxiliary unit, although I was a Volunteer Reserve pilot. Towards the end of July 1940, Dowding ruled that all pilots should have at least eight hours stand down time in any 24, and at least 24 hours continuous time off once a week. To enable us to do this we had a further intake of newly qualified pilots.

Coastal Command was also busy, eighty-five aircraft being engaged on a variety of sorties, including anti-invasion patrols reconnaissance and searches. Two Coastal squadrons suffered losses.

No.236 Squadron, Thorney Island:

> Photographic reconnaissance aircraft reported a concentration of enemy aircraft at Cherbourg. Orders were issued that 59 Squadron (thirteen machines) should bomb and 236 should immediately afterwards 'shoot up' the aerodrome. Four of our ten aircraft were to wait outside at as great a height as possible under the prevailing conditions to deal with enemy aircraft. Just before the aircraft left a weather report was received from Met. Office saying that the weather conditions over Cherbourg would be fine and without cloud. This weather report turned out to be quite inaccurate.
>
> At 1500 hrs Squadron Leader P.E. Drew, Pilot Officer McDonough, Flight Lieutenant Power, Pilot Officer Innes and Pilot Officer Lumsden left the ground. At 1505 hrs Sergeant Smith flew to catch up Squadron Leader Drew's Section and at the same time Flying Officer Moore, Pilot Officer Moore, Pilot Officer Russell, Pilot Officer Peachment and Pilot Officer Riley – the Section that had to wait outside Cherbourg to look after the bombers and ground-strafing machines – left Thorney Island.
>
> Pilot Officer Peachment returned to base from about twenty miles out to sea owing to engine trouble and landed at 1545 hrs. Pilot Officer Moore took his Section to one – two miles off Cherbourg as he had orders not to go over the target. One E/A approached and took evasive action on seeing our aircraft. One burst of fire given

and received without result. The weather was fair with low cloud and haze over the target. They landed at Thorney Island at 1625 hrs.

Flight Lieutenant Power and his Section overshot Cherbourg and returned over the Channel Islands and landed at Thorney Island at 1715 hrs without any incidents. Fair weather but a lot of low cloud. Squadron Leader Drew, Pilot Officer McDonough and Sergeant Smith made a ground attack at between 50 and 70ft from the ground, in the wake of the bombers on machine-gun and coastal battery positions West of the aerodrome and along Dique-de-Querqueville. Machine-gun crews were scattered with possible casualties and a fire was seen on NE corner of aerodrome.

A number of bombs were seen exploding on the aerodrome. After the first attack Sergeant Smith lost sight of the other two machines and he eventually landed at base 1640 hrs with bullet and AA damage to tail. Squadron Leader Drew, with his air-gunner, Flying Officer Nokes-Cooper, and Pilot Officer McDonough with his air-gunner, Sergeant Head, failed to return, as did the CO of the bombing Squadron, Wing Commander Weld-Smith.

Squadron Leader Drew commanded the squadron from the time it was re-formed on 31 October 1939 and the loss of such a much-loved leader is a bitter blow to the entire Squadron. Pilot Officer McDonough, who is an Australian, was also another original member of the squadron, a pilot of great dependability and utmost determination.

The popular Squadron Leader Peter Drew, a married man, was buried by the Germans at Biville churchyard; his air-gunner 32-year-old Flying Officer Benjamin Nokes-Cooper, who also left behind a widow, was interred at Bayeux. The epitaph on the latter's headstone, chosen by his family, was the second of 'Four Epitaphs' composed by the poet John Maxwell Edmunds and published in *The Times* on 6 February 1918:

Went the day well?
We died and never knew,
But, well or ill,
England, we died for you.

The 23-year-old Australian Pilot Officer Bryan McDonough and Sergeant Frederick Head were reported missing. Both have no known grave.

No.59 Squadron also found itself rudder-less after this operation, having also lost its CO, Wing Commander Reginald Morgan-Weld-Smith, a 29-year-old married Scot who was buried at St Pierre-en-Port Communal Cemetery. Significantly, given the lack of recognition for Coastal Command crews in this epic struggle, his headstone's epitaph reads 'Of Seend Manor, Wiltshire, England. Killed in the Battle of Britain'. Killed with him were his observer Pilot Officer David Davis AFM, who was of Jewish heritage, buried at St Valery-en-Caux, and air-gunner Sergeant Peter Pryde, interred at Veules-les-Roses Communal Cemetery, the airmen's bodies having been washed up at various places on the French coast.

The Coastal Command Blenheims had been intercepted by Me 109s of 8/JG27 off Cherbourg, *Oberleutnants* Walter Adolph and Erwin Düllberg, and *Oberfeldwebel* Hans Richter all claiming victories – which, given Sergeant Smith's damaged aircraft, was 100 per cent accurate.

Blenheims of 2 Group Bomber Command were also tasked with attacking enemy airfields. Thirty-six aircraft sallied forth but only twenty-four hit their targets, mainly airfields in the Netherlands.

No.114 Squadron, Horsham St Faith:

> Pilot Officer Tasker, Sergeant Summers and Sergeant Levack took off at 1405 hrs on a bombing mission against the enemy occupied airfield at Haamstede on the island of Schouwen. The English coast was left at Orfordness at 1433 hrs. Over the North Sea cloud cover was 10/10ths at 1,000 to 2,500ft but commenced breaking up at the Dutch coast. Landfall was made at Haamstede and our aircraft altered course to the South and turned to approach from inland.
>
> A shallow dive attack was made down to 600ft and the stick fell across the hangars, the first bomb bursting on a newly constructed camouflaged hangar. The rear-gunner machine-gunned and damaged two Me 109s on the aerodromes and also a moving lorry which stopped abruptly when hit. The Observer, using his blister gun, fired at buildings. No flak fire was encountered. The pilot climbed into cloud and turned for base.
>
> The pilot reports that, near the English coast, he was followed by an unidentified aircraft to within two miles of Orfordness.

This first crew had achieved surprise – but the Germans were alert when a second Blenheim appeared. Although only one aircraft was lost, *Oberleutnant* Franz Eckerle of 6/JG54 claimed a Blenheim 5 km off Haamstede, and *Oberfeldwebel* Michael Hauer of 4/JG54 another 20 km off Haamstede. One of these pilots, therefore was responsible for the destruction of Blenheim R3898, the crew of which, Pilot Officer John Goode, and Sergeants Ernest Will and Victor St George Barrow were all buried in Bergen-Op-Zoom cemetery.

By night, Bomber Command Wellingtons and Hampdens attacked industrial targets and marshalling yards in Germany without loss.

Across the North Sea, *Reichsmarschall* Göring threw a garden party in The Hague, appearing in a newly designed white uniform, at which were gathered his senior commanders on the *Kanalfront*. *Oberst* Theo Osterkamp recalled that

'Everybody with a name or rank worth mentioning was there.' The purpose of the gathering was for Göring to share Hitler's new plans for prosecuting the war against Britain:

> The *Führer* has ordered me to crush Britain with my *Luftwaffe*. By delivering a series of very heavy blows I plan to have this enemy, whose morale is already at its lowest, down on his knees in the nearest future so that our troops can land on the island without any risk.

Oberst Theo 'Onkel' Osterkamp, *Kanalkampf JagdfliegerFührer*:

> According to information from the Intelligence Service, Britain disposed in its southern sector at the most 400–500 fighters. Their destruction in the air and on the ground was to be carried out in three phases: during the first five days, within a radius of 150–100 kilometres south and south-east of London; in the next three days within 50–100 kilometres, and during the last five days within a 50-kilometre circle around London. The whole operation, then, should be over in thirteen days. That would irrevocably win absolute aerial superiority over England and fulfil the *Führer*'s mission.
>
> I must have made a terribly stupid face, but in my case that should scarcely attract any attention. Göring looked up, saw me, and said 'Well, Osterkamp, have you got a question?'

Osterkamp explained that while his JG51 was the sole Me 109 unit on the Channel coast, he believed that Fighter Command had concentrated some '500–700' fighters around London, and believed that since then the force had increased further still. No.11 Group's actual strength was 204 Spitfires and Hurricanes, and Air Chief Marshal Dowding had not substantially reinforced Air Vice-Marshal Park, in order to both provide an effective defence to the country as a whole and disperse his fighters. On this occasion therefore, although *Luftwaffe* Intelligence had over-estimated 11 Group's strength, Osterkamp's estimation was way in excess of Park's actual strength – and this can only be because of his personal experience of the fierce RAF resistance while flying combat missions.

Osterkamp also opined that 11 Group's new units were all Spitfire-equipped, the type being comparable in performance to the Me 109 – which Göring angrily dismissed, arguing that the British were 'too cowardly' to meet Osterkamp's fighters in battle – which, of course, was complete nonsense. What Osterkamp had actually reported was that it was clear the RAF fighters had been ordered to avoid fighter-to-fighter combat, in order to preserve resources – a very different thing.

Osterkamp asked his chief how many fighters would be at his disposal for this new assault, hoping for '1,200–1,500' fighters. He was 'bitterly disappointed' to learn that the reality was around 700 Me 109s and 229 Me 110s.

Of the *Luftwaffe* bomber force, Osterkamp remembered greater concerns: 'I was completely staggered when the two *Luftflotten* reported that they had not even 700 bombers operational' each. Göring was shocked. This was not the available force reflected by figures provided to him by the *Luftwaffe* Quartermaster General: a total of 1,191 twin-engine bombers and single-engine dive-bombers in Kesselring and Sperrle's commands, and a further 123 bombers and 34 Me 110s in Stumpff's *Luftflotte* 5.

Nonetheless, to the 'Iron One', the prospect of his *Luftwaffe* failing to achieve what was possibly the greatest prize of all was simply inconceivable – that just thirteen days were considered necessary to do so was delusional.

FRIDAY, 2 AUGUST 1940

On this day, the OKL circulated a directive based upon the previous day's Hague conference, outlining the thirteen-day aerial campaign against Britain. The objective of this so-called *Adlerangriff* (Eagle Attack) was clear: the destruction of the RAF. The plan called for *Luftflotten* 2 and 3 to launch the attack with three successive raids on a scale hitherto unseen. Then, the following day, *Luftflotte* 5 would attack from Norway. It was anticipated that to reduce Fighter Command to less than 300 aircraft would take just four days.

In 1921, the Italian General Giulio Douhet had published *The Command of the Air*, in which he theorised that in future 'The disintegration of nations ... will be accomplished directly ... by aerial forces.' Many dismissed his writings as absurd – but Göring and other German air force officers took note. During the Spanish Civil War, at Guernica the *Luftwaffe* had provided a terrifying and early example of the destruction air power was capable of, following this up with similarly violent aerial bombardments of Warsaw and Rotterdam in 1940.

Douhet had advanced the strategy of aerial bombing delivering a 'knockout blow', neutralising the enemy's war industry and relentlessly attacking civilian populations in order to cause panic, destroy morale and even cause uprisings against their own governments which had failed to protect them. Future events would prove Douhet wrong, because civilian populations under fire would prove stoic, but his theories found a disciple in Göring, who, *Oberst* Werner Kriepe, a former bomber commander, now a staff officer, recalled was 'entranced' by the Italian's theories. Consequently, Göring now believed that his *Luftwaffe* alone could defeat Britain – and was eager to set about the task. Setting aside the inescapable fact that Douhet's was a flawed doctrine, the problem was that the *Luftwaffe* had been created not as a strategic air force equipped with heavy bombers (ironically Göring had cancelled the four-engine bomber programme in 1937), but essentially as flying artillery intended to support the army with light and medium bombers. Göring was now, therefore, preparing for a campaign his *Luftwaffe* was actually ill-equipped to effect.

Supporting the army in assault river crossings was one thing, but a seaborne invasion, taking aside the *Luftwaffe*'s inadequacy to mount a strategic bombing campaign, was quite another: the Channel was too wide, meaning that the Me 109, like the Hurricane and Spitfire designed and intended as a short-range defensive interceptor, would continue to operate at the extremity of its range, providing little fuel for combat over south-east England, and the twin-engine Me 110 – in which Göring put great store – although enjoying greater range had already proved no match for the RAF's single-engine fighters.

Going forward, the *Luftwaffe* Chief of Staff, *Generalmajor* Hans Jeschonnek, approved a plan by *Oberst* Paul Deichmann, Chief of Staff to General Bruno Loerzer's *Fliegerkorps* II to destroy Fighter Command in the air. To date, in spite of *Oberst* Fink's success in denying the RN Dover as a base, defence of the Channel convoys had not enticed Fighter Command to battle en masse. Deichmann, who had served in the RLM as a staff officer since 1934 and had never flown in combat, firmly believed that only one target would force the RAF fighters off the ground in great numbers: London. Hitler, however, still cautious of Britain, refused to permit this, repeating: 'I reserve the decision on terror attacks to myself'. So far, not even Bomber Command's nightly raids on Germany had made Hitler unleash 'annihilating reprisals'. So attacks on London were forbidden, and instead other means had to be found with which to bring Fighter Command to battle.

Consequently, it was decided that the primary focus of the *Adlerangriff*, scheduled to begin on 10 August 1940, was airfields known or believed to be used by Fighter Command – and here again is revealed another *Luftwaffe* deficiency: the failure of air intelligence. It was clear that *Oberst* 'Beppo' Schmid failed to appreciate how Fighter Command was organised, deployed and controlled, this leading to his inaccurate *Studie Blau*, which informed the OKL, erroneously, as to these crucial subjects. As a result, target selection in the *Adlerangriff* would frequently be way offline, failing to prioritise what were actually targets crucial to Fighter Command's operation.

For what the *Luftwaffe* was about to do, and in respect of the proposed sea-crossing, there was no precedent. When William of Normandy successfully crossed the Channel in 1066 and landed at Hastings, air power was unheard of and therefore not a consideration for the 'Conqueror'. All that, of course, had changed; the sky now a battlefield every bit the same as both land and sea. For Operation *Seelöwe* to succeed, great inter-service cooperation was required – and yet all three services had different ideas, the army and navy in dispute over whether the landing should be on a broad or narrow front, and, significantly, *Grand-Admiral* Raeder and *Reichsmarschall* Göring did not get on.

Both Raeder and *Generaloberst* Halder, the OKH chief looked to the *Luftwaffe* to achieve aerial supremacy as a prelude to a landing. Göring saw things differently: the *Reichsmarschall* believed that his *Luftwaffe* alone (given Douhet) could bring Britain down without the need for an invasion. Indeed, Deichmann personally viewed '*Seelöwe* and the air offensive as two quite independent projects', and

KANALKAMPF DIARY, 1 AUGUST – 12 AUGUST 1940

Kreipe remembered that at Sperrle's *Luftflotte* 3 HQ, 'We did believe that a strong air force could strike a decisive blow against the United Kingdom, provided the Army and Navy were fully committed to an invasion' – but not that the *Luftwaffe* could subdue Britain alone. Kreipe also stated that Göring 'never had much faith' in the prospect of an invasion, mainly owing to his personal contempt for Raeder and poor opinion of the *Kriegsmarine*.

Kesselring, whose *Luftflotte* 2 was closest to south-east England, 'recommended the invasion very strongly' to Göring, and admitted that he personally 'believed in it too'. Either way, Kreipe, who had been present at the Hague conference, was sure that 'For the first time in modern history, the people of England were now to feel the full and direct impact of war on their own soil: their morale was expected to deteriorate in consequence.'

At this time, Fighter Command comprised fifty-eight squadrons, of which twenty-nine were Hurricane-equipped, but only seventeen had the superior Spitfire. Of these, three Hurricane and four Spitfire squadrons were based in 10 Group, and twelve Hurricane squadrons and just five with Spitfires in 11 Group – and it would be in the skies over southern England that this battle would be decided. Additionally, there were seven squadrons of Blenheims, two of Defiants, and even one Fleet Air Arm Fulmar squadron and another flying obsolete Gladiator biplanes.

In truth, and without in any way marginalising the courage and contribution of aircrew operating these other types, it was the single-engine Hurricanes and Spitfires that really mattered – and there were, excluding reserves, just 288 of both types in 10 Group and 11 Group – facing the 2,000 fighters and bombers of *Luftflotten* 2 and 3. Although at the Hague conference *Oberst* Osterkamp had been 'bitterly disappointed' with having been allocated some 700 Me 109s and 229 Me 110s, his single-engine fighter force alone outnumbered 10 Group's and 11 Group's Hurricanes and Spitfires by over 3:1. No.12 Group, which could be called upon to both defend 11 Group's airfields while Air Vice-Marshal Park's fighters were engaged further forward and reinforce the south-east if necessary, comprised of three Hurricane squadrons and four of Spitfires, another eighty-four fighters, but essentially the brunt of this coming battle would be borne by 11 Group. It was not just numbers that were important, however: performance was too.

The Germans had tested and compared captured Allied aircraft at E-Stelle Reclin, where *Major* Werner 'Vati' Mölders flew and evaluated three of the enemy aircraft types he had been shooting down:

> It was very interesting to carry out the flight trials at Rechlin with the Spitfire and Hurricane. Both types are very simple to fly compared to our aircraft, and childishly easy to take-off and land. The Hurricane is good natured and turns well, but its performance is decidedly inferior to that of the Me 109. It has strong stick forces and is 'lazy' on the ailerons.

> The Spitfire is one class better. It handles well, is light on the controls, faultless in the turn and has a performance approaching that of the Me 109. As a fighting aircraft, however, it is miserable. A sudden push on the stick will cause the engine to cut, and because the propeller has only two pitch settings (take-off and cruise), in a rapidly changing air combat situation the engine is either over-speeding or else is not being used to the full.

Over Dunkirk it had rapidly become obvious that the Spitfire's performance was compromised by its two-pitch propeller, providing just coarse and fine pitch, while the Me 109's VDM constant-speed airscrew rotated nearly through 360°, enabling the pilot to select the optimum pitch for any given situation, perfectly matching engine revs. At the RAF's request, de Havilland modified a Spitfire by adding a small Constant Speed Unit, which controlled pitch through oil pressure, thereby converting its two-pitch propeller to constant speed. The modified Spitfire had a shorter take-off run, climbed faster and maximum service ceiling was increased by 7,000ft to 34,400ft.

On 22 June 1940, Lord Beaverbrook instructed de Havilland to urgently upgrade all existing Spitfire, Hurricane and Defiant propellers in the field, the company despatching engineers two days later to begin this process on Fighter Command's airfields. The work would be completed by 16 August 1940, by which time as we will see, the fighting was heavy and that extra performance was vital. The Rolls-Royce Merlin's lack of fuel injection, however, could not be addressed and was something the RAF pilots had to cope with.

The fighting thus far had also led to certain improvements being absorbed into the 109 programme, leading to the Me 109E-4. This variant had seat and head armour to protect the pilot, and the fuel tank, upon which the pilot effectively sat, and which had been found vulnerable from an astern attack, was also armoured. The canopy was redesigned, offering better visibility, and armament was finally standardised at two wing-mounted Oerlikon cannons and twin-engine cowl-mounted machine-guns. A certain amount of aircraft, designated Me 109E-4B, were modified to carry a single *Sprengbombe Cylindrisch* (SC) 50 kilo bomb, enabling the 109 to be used in a *jadgbomber* role. The Me 109E-7, produced in August 1940, had a 300-litre auxiliary fuel tank in an attempt to improve range, or alternatively could carry an SC 250 kilo bomb.

At the start of the war, the British aircraft factories were all 20 per cent below their target output, and by the time of Dunkirk had fallen behind so much that manufacturers were collectively 1,000 aircraft behind contract. On 14 May 1940, however, the Ministry of Aircraft Production (MAP) was established under the highly motivated, resourceful and energetic Lord Beaverbrook (see *The Gathering Storm*).

By June, Beaverbrook had cracked the whip: 446 fighters were produced that month; 496 more in July, 476 in August, 467 in September and 469 in October. This meant that as fighters were lost in battle they were replaced. Of crucial importance is that the production of British fighters massively outstripped German production: between June and October 1940, Germany's factories churned out a total of 1,870 fighters – Britain's response was 3,958. But there were still not enough of the superior Spitfire. Between 6 July and 1 November 1940, 991 Hurricanes were produced but only 608 Spitfires.

Popular myth has it that the Spitfire was such an advanced design that each aircraft took two-and-a-half times as long to produce than the simpler Hurricane. While this is true, the fact of the matter is that Supermarine's small workforce and premises at Woolston was too small to mass produce anything. This was formerly a comparatively small factory producing, in the main, biplane flying boats, which suddenly found itself swamped by large orders for Spitfires. The solution was to apply the principals of mass-producing automobiles to Spitfires and so a new factory was erected for this purpose at Castle Bromwich in Birmingham, equipped by Morris Motors and run by Lord Nuffield. Unfortunately, it proved much more difficult to adapt the automotive industry to the production of aircraft, leading to Beaverbrook taking control of the operation shortly after being appointed Minister – by which time not one Spitfire had emerged from Nuffield's factory.

'The Beaver' gave control of the Castle Bromwich Aeroplane Factory (CBAF) to the aircraft manufacturer Vickers, and things began moving immediately. Experienced workers were brought to Birmingham from Supermarine at Southampton, and the more complex components were produced at Southampton. In June 1940, Beaverbrook's target of just ten Spitfires was miraculously achieved; twenty-three followed in July, thirty-seven in August and fifty-six during September.

The important thing is that all of these Spitfires now being produced by the CBAF were new Mk IIs. This enjoyed several benefits over the Mk IA currently in operational service and it was naturally important to expedite production and delivery to the squadrons. The Spitfire Mk II was powered by the Merlin XII, which produced 1,175 hp, as opposed to the Mk IA's Merlin III's 1,030 hp. The Mk II's top speed was 370–15 mph faster than the Mk IA. The new Spitfire's rate of climb was 2,600ft a minute, 473ft a minute more than the Mk IA. The new engine was fitted with a Coffman automatic starter, which reduced starting time, and, most importantly, all of the new Spitfires were fitted with the Rotol CS propeller as standard. The first Mk IIA was delivered to 611 Squadron at Digby on 22 July 1940, and as the battle progressed, numbers would increase.

On 2 August 1940, Squadron Leader Ronald 'Boozy' Kellett, at Northolt, formed and was in command of 303 (Polish) Squadron – which at first existed in name only. That Kellett spoke French fluently, had experience of forming squadrons and converting pilots to the new monoplane fighters, doubtless explained his selection for this role.

Squadron Leader Kellett:

> The day in August came when a body of men wearing dark blue battledress and berets arrived, with strange words of command

and an unusual facial appearance. They were soon sorted out into flights 'A' and 'B', and 'C' for maintenance, and bit by bit order appeared out of chaos. We officers met in the Mess and we learnt something of the battle of and their escape from Poland to France, and arrival in England. They mostly spoke French, which enabled me to communicate reasonably freely with them.

To overcome the language difficulty and procedural differences, a system of 'double-banking' was adopted in these squadrons; RAF officers were in charge, but their roles were duplicated by Polish officers, who shadowed their English-speaking counterparts. No.303 Squadron – named after Kosciusko, a Polish national hero who had been General Washington's adjutant in the American War of Independence, and later a national leader – was formed from two Warsaw-based PAF squadrons, which were smaller than RAF squadrons. Consequently, the Polish 111 became 'A' Flight, and 112 'B'. The Polish officer duplicating Kellett's role was Squadron Leader Zdzislaw Krasnodebski, while the Canadian John Kent, commanding 'A' Flight, was shadowed first by Flight Lieutenant Henneberg, then Flight Lieutenant Urbanowicz, and in 'B' Flight, Flight Lieutenant Athol Forbes' Polish counterpart was Flight Lieutenant Lapkowski. Like Kellett, Forbes also had good French, while Kent's was poor, so the 'A' Flight commander took to learning Polish, which was much appreciated by his Polish subordinates.

In August 1940, certain of 303 Squadron's pilots were sent to RAF Uxbridge on an R/T course, and for others English lessons began. Today, it is difficult to imagine how primitive some things were just over eighty years ago.

Sergeant Reg Nutter, a Hurricane pilot of 257 Squadron, also attended that R/T course and recalled that:

> This proved to be quite interesting as it had a two-fold purpose – to train pilots in R/T procedures and to train the controllers who would later control us from Operations Rooms. Marked out on the playing fields was a large map of the British Isles and a part of Western Europe. We pilots were given tricycles, which had formerly been used to sell ice cream! In the box at the front was a TR9 radio, which, at the time, was standard aircraft equipment.
>
> We wore headphones and were surrounded by a set of blinker-like boards, which restricted our vision. The driving chain and sprockets were arranged in such a way that when we pedalled twenty-five times the wheel moved round just once! Thus our speed across the maps matched the speed of fighter aircraft across the ground at normal throttle settings.
>
> Down in the stadium a complete Operations Room had been built. This was fully manned by trainee Controllers, WAAF Plotters etc. On top of the stadium was a spotter who passed our position,

and the position of the person designated as the 'enemy', down to the Operations Room. The 'Controllers' could then vector us by radio to make interceptions. We both learned a lot from the course but found it somewhat difficult to sit down on our final return to the squadron. Pedalling around in the hot sun in a serge uniform made one quite sore in a certain part of one's anatomy!

At Northolt, work was ongoing to convert the Poles to the Hurricane. Many of the Poles were experienced pilots, and had even seen combat – but although some had flown obsolete French monoplanes, none had flown modern RAF fighters. That said, both of Squadron Leader Kellett's English-speaking flight commanders had only just converted themselves to the Spitfire and Hurricane, and, along with their CO, experienced a pilot though he was, neither had yet been in combat.

So, as with other many other squadrons at the time, everyone was learning. In addition to the language barrier, the Polish pilots faced another difficulty, in that the controls of British aircraft were contrary to Polish machines. For example, in Polish aircraft the throttle was pulled back to accelerate, whereas in British designs power was increased by pushing the throttle forward. All of this took time to overcome, but did nothing to mollify the Poles' frustration at being unable, as yet, to fight Germans. Nonetheless, after the Poles were first checked out in the Link Trainer simulator, training continued apace, on the ground and in the air.

Squadron Leader Kellett commented that 'Converting the Poles to Hurricanes was going well, apart from one or two landings with the undercarriage up.' This, however, was far from uncommon when pilots were changing over from flying biplanes with fixed undercarriage; the 303 Squadron British CO continues:

> We had all learned certain Polish words: 'Klapy' = flaps [which biplanes did not have), and 'potwozie' = undercarriage, so in the air we could remind the pilots of these needs. The rumour circulated that the Poles were so keen to land that they failed to put the undercarriage down – typical schoolboy humour imparted to high places. I would have none of this, as they were very quickly being converted to Hurricanes and had retractable undercarriage for the first time.
>
> There was an incident that illustrated the problem of language and non-communication. A principal of the dispersal of aircraft was no aircraft should be nearer than, say, twenty yards from the next, and on seeing two aircraft wing tip to wing tip, I ordered a Polish airman to start one so that it could be taxied to another place. There was a certain amount of gesticulating which I ignored.
>
> I should have noticed that the air pressure for the brakes was nil, but once the aircraft was started I taxied onto the slope of the taxi-track. I tried the brakes to turn the aircraft but they didn't work – and within seconds the eight-ton aircraft had crashed into one of the

dispersal huts, destroying its propeller and not improving the hut either! As chance would have it, the Command Accident Officer was just walking to dispersal and witnessed the event. He told me not to report the accident, saying there were too many to deal with and that he quite understood the reason.

During the training period I had, with the agreement of General Ujesjski, recruited more pilots from the Polish collecting depot at Blackpool and think we had about thirty-two operational pilots in the squadron. It was therefore possible for each pilot to be on duty twenty-four hours on and twenty-four off. We changed over at one o'clock. No pilot on duty was allowed to leave the Mess, early bed and early rising, the squadron being on readiness from half an hour before sunrise until half an hour after sunset. We suggested to the ground crews that they should do the same but British and Polish NCOs replied that while our pilots were in the air they wanted to remain on duty, and so it was. I don't believe any Squadron had better NCOs or aircraft maintenance than 303.

The Poles represented the largest group of foreign nationals serving with the RAF at this time, although for some reason – which he never explained – Air Chief Marshal Dowding was initially mistrustful of both the Poles and Czechoslovaks. While the time required to overcome the language barrier delayed the creation of Polish and Czech squadrons, Dowding's curious attitude was undoubtedly another. There were now two Polish (302 and 303) and one Czech (310) squadrons – all would soon prove themselves in battle and be more than welcome reinforcements for Fighter Command.

Friday, 2 August 1940 was a day of rain and cloud over southern England, making for reduced enemy air activity. No.19 Squadron's Flight Lieutenant Clouston, up from Duxford's satellite airfield at Fowlmere, to which the squadron had been dispersed, with Pilot Officer Burgoyne and Pilot Officer Aeberhardt, intercepted a He 111 off Cromer Knoll, at 11.15 hrs, while patrolling a convoy.

Each member of Blue Section fired at the bomber. The ORB states:

> Flight Lieutenant Clouston, who was in an eight-gun aircraft, disabled the starboard engine and possibly killed the rear-gunner. The machine carried out evasive tactics, making full-use of 9/10ths stratus cloud at 1,500ft, escaped eastwards.

The other two Spitfire pilots were flying the still troublesome cannon-armed Mk IB, which were already notorious for jamming at the worst possible moment and would cause 19 Squadron considerable angst in the coming weeks. This He 111 was claimed as damaged and represented 19 Squadron's first action of the Battle of Britain.

KANALKAMPF DIARY, 1 AUGUST – 12 AUGUST 1940

On this day, the Ellerman Line-owned and Liverpool-registered British merchantman SS *City of Brisbane* was bound for London from Port Pirie, Australia, carrying lead, flour, tinned fruit and other foodstuffs, when the ship was attacked and badly damaged by German bombers. Beached on the southern end of Long Sand in the Thames Estuary, the battered hulk burned for three days before breaking in half and sinking.

Eight Indian sailors were killed, all of whom remain missing and are remembered on the Chittagong Memorial, commemorating the 400 sailors of the Indian Navy and 6,000 of the Indian Merchant Navy lost at sea during the Second World War. One man, fatally wounded, was brought ashore, but died on 11 August 1940. Indeed, between 2 July and 8 August 1940 inclusive, at least 227 merchant seamen lost their lives in the English Channel, the youngest being several 16-year-olds; the oldest was aged 66.

What is surprising, however, is that many were not British. For example, ten sailors lost with the SS *Aeneas* on 2 July 1940 were from Hong Kong. Indians, like those lost on SS *City of Brisbane*, however, made up the largest number of non-British personnel, either serving with seagoing lines or the Indian Merchant Navy. On 29 July 1940, for example, of the thirteen men killed when the SS *Clan Monroe* went down, twelve were Indians. Interestingly, all of these Indian sailors who lost their lives aboard these two ships appear to have been Muslims from pre-partitioned India, the jewel in Britain's Empire.

Although no figures are available for 1940, in his article 'Merchant Seamen During the War', which was published in 1946, Sir William Elderton stated that in 1938 there were 192,375 men employed on British merchant ships, of whom only 131,885 were British; the others were foreigners, 9,790 mainly Europeans, and 50,700 Indians and Chinese. By 1938, 27 per cent of seamen engaged on foreign-voyages were Chinese or Indian, with a further 5 per cent including Arabs, West Africans and West Indians domiciled in British ports. It was these men who crewed the 'Coal Scuttle Brigade' and merchant ships bringing essential supplies to the besieged island in summer 1940 – a rarely acknowledged fact.

On this day, Coastal Command escorted seventeen convoys, and further, routine, patrols were carried out by eighty-one aircraft in addition to eighteen providing air cover for RN operations off the East Coast. Hudsons attacked three U-Boats, two inconclusively, while 224 Squadron claimed one as damaged, and successful reconnaissance flights over enemy territory were also completed. No.59 Squadron, however, suffered another loss when *Oberleutnant* Paul Temme of *Stab* I/JG2 intercepted and shot down a Blenheim reconnoitring Cherbourg; Pilot Officer Peter Drew and Sergeants Arthur Herbert and James Close were all killed.

It was also a busy day for Bomber Command's 2 Group Blenheims, thirty-six of which were sent to attack enemy airfields; twenty-four of these aircraft bombed their targets, while the rest turned back owing either to unsuitable weather conditions or technical issues. Damage was caused to Soesterberg, Schiphol Merville and Evere aerodromes, and aircraft were strafed on the ground at Waalhaven.

Squadron Leader Young of 110 Squadron was forced to abandon his attack owing to intense flak, and having successfully bombed his target, Sergeant Maurice Hards' aircraft was also hit by flak; wounded, Hards managed to return to Wattisham, where he crashed on landing, although fortunately his crew were unhurt. 18 Squadron's Flying Officer John Douch bombed Leeuwarden but Me 109s were already scrambling from the airfield to intercept the Blenheim. Attacked by three 109s, Douch's air-gunner, Sergeant Bassett, returned fire, hitting the fighter of 5/JG27's *Staffelkapitän*, *Hauptmann* Albrecht von Ankum-Frank, which immediately crashed, killing the pilot.

Sergeant John Davies of the same Squadron was en route to attack Haamstede when his aircraft was intercepted and shot down before making its bombing run – the Blenheim crashed near New Haamstede and exploded, killing the crew. Two Me 109 pilots claimed Blenheims destroyed that lunchtime, *Unteroffizier* Hans Schätzel one at Ijmuiden, and *Feldwebel* Fritz Oeltjen another over the Zuidersee.

By night, Bomber Command Wellingtons, Whitleys and Hampdens attacked a variety of targets in Germany. Wellingtons started fires at an oil refinery in Hamburg and at the *Kriegsmarine*'s Emden base, while Whitleys hit oil installations at Salzbergen and Emerich, and Hampdens lit fires at oil facilities at Hannover and Emmerich. Airfields were also bombed and mines sown. On the return flight from Hamburg, a 115 Squadron Wellington, up from Marham, crashed into the sea, killing the crew, but a 99 Squadron Wellington was more fortunate and claimed the destruction of an Me 110 night-fighter.

SATURDAY, 3 AUGUST 1940

Although the impending *Adlerangriff* was being planned, Germany had continued to seek a diplomatic solution – this time through the Swedish king, who addressed the British Government on this day. Churchill remained unmoved, making clear that before Britain would ever consider terms with *Herr* Hitler there would first need to be 'effective guarantees, by deeds, not words ... forthcoming from Germany which would ensure ... free and independent life of Czechoslovakia, Poland, Norway, Denmark, Holland, Belgium and above all France'.

Flying Officer Frank Brinsden, 19 Squadron:

> At squadron level I don't think we were fully aware of what was going on. We were just keen to have a crack at the Germans, and the prevalent attitude was that we couldn't wait for them to come. Given that the Belgians and French had proved of little use during the defence of their homelands, we were glad to be on our own. We were absolutely confident that we were better than the enemy and wanted an opportunity to bloody Hitler's nose.

There would little opportunity on this day, however 'to bloody Hitler's nose', because poor weather once more significantly reduced the scale of air operations, there being no contest between Fighter Command and the *Luftwaffe* over either the Channel or Britain – a welcome respite indeed, although the monotonous convoy protection patrols were still flown.

Coastal Command continued flying its usual sorties and three 235 Squadron Blenheims attacked a He 115 seaplane over the North Sea at 16.30 hrs, claiming it as damaged; a Blenheim was hit by return fire in the engagement but returned safely to base. Detling's 59 Squadron lost another Blenheim, which failed to return from a nocturnal raid on Emden, and a 206 Squadron Hudson disappeared while on a routine patrol over the North Sea.

No.2 Group's Blenheims continued attacking enemy airfields, damaging hangars at Schiphol and Haamstede, stores at Abbeville, and a troop convoy was strafed from low-level. One 139 Squadron aircraft failed to return, the crew of which were killed, and a Fairey Swordfish of 812 Squadron FAA, attacking Rotterdam, was also lost. At night, industrial and naval targets were hit in Germany, a 49 Squadron Hampden ending up in the North Sea having run out of fuel on the return flight from Kiel, and a 75 Squadron Wellington, having attacked Horst crashed at Barton Mills Suffolk, killing Squadron Leader Wilfred Collett.

This day marked the start of the bank holiday weekend, Home Intelligence remarking on the 'large holiday crowds' – but the Kentish coast remained deserted of all but the military, stoic residents and those with essential business there. Life, however, went on: the RAF fielded an eleven against the London Fire Service at Lords; the actors Laurence Olivier and Jill Esmond received their *decree nisi*, and the American film director Daryl Zannuck sent a cheque for £2,000 to buy an ambulance.

Significantly, on this day, Captain J.C. Kelly Rogers of British Overseas Airways made the first passenger flight from Britain to America in the flying boat *Clare*. When the flying boat returned five days later, her passengers included the first Americans engaged by the MAP to ferry aircraft from factories and repair depots to the squadrons and other units.

SUNDAY, 4 AUGUST 1940

Again bad weather, sea fog and low cloud, and doubtless preparations for the *Adlerangriff*, prevented the *Luftwaffe* from any major operations. There was no combat for Fighter Command, and no losses.

Lieutenant Arthur Hague, HMS *Borealis*:

> On Sunday, 4 August 1940, our motley cavalcade of the Mobile Barrage Balloon Unit, with balloons close-hauled, followed *Astral*

down Southampton Water to pick up the East bound convoy, which had left Falmouth the previous day. I do not recall receiving any technical information or appreciation of enemy intentions but it was generally known that the Germans were already mounting heavy guns near Cap Gris Nez with which to shell Allied shipping attempting the Channel passage, and that German radar on the cliffs at Wissant, opposite Folkestone, would give them ample warning of approach.

Our orders were to position ourselves around the convoy to deter *Stuka* dive-bombers from pressing home their attacks for fear of the 3,000ft of wire by which the balloons were secured. On joining the convoy I moved to take station ahead of a large ungainly vessel, HMS *Borde*, leading the port column, only to be warned by signal to keep clear as she was a 'mine bumper'. The large structure mounted on her foc'stle was a powerful electric coil designed to detonate any magnetic mines coming into its field ahead of her. As darkness fell we ran into thick fog but no untoward incidents occurred.

As the convoy steamed East, elsewhere a Coastal Command Hudson attacked a U-Boat seventy-two miles off Cape Wrath, hitting the conning tower and bows, sinking it, and a patrolling Blenheim attacked a squadron of E-boats near Le Havre, recording near misses.

Thorney Island's 236 Squadron reported that:

Flying Officer Moore, Pilot Officer Peachment and Sergeant Sharp left to escort reconnaissance aircraft to Le Havre. On return journey, while in a very tight vic formation, they were attacked by four Me 109s, two from each side. Our aircraft kept in extremely tight formation and by controlled fire from the rear gunners quickly shot down one E/A in flames and the other made off.

The two remaining E/A followed our machines to within fifteen miles of Brighton but were kept at a distance by the tight formation and accurate rear gunners. Pilot Officer Peachment's machine was damaged and the three machines landed at Ford at 1735 hrs where the machine was left. [ORB]

Peachment had been shot-up near Le Havre by *Feldwebel* Rudolf Täschner of 1/JG2, who was credited with the bomber's destruction.

Owing to the weather, 2 Group flew no operations, and for the same reason only eleven Whitleys of 4 Group Bomber Command were detailed to attack oil refineries at Sterkrade-Halter and Emmerich. Fires were started at the former target and a hangar was also hit at Krefeld aerodrome. All of the Whitleys returned safely.

Squadron Leader Don MacDonell, 64 Squadron:

> As a Sector Station, Kenley had its own Sector Operations Room under the control of Squadron Leader Norman. I made it a custom to visit the Ops Room as often as possible, especially following a particularly heavy engagement. Though the plotters might well have been wholly preoccupied with further incoming raids, there was always one very attractive WAAF who brought me a cup of coffee and said 'Glad it went all right, sir' – even if it hadn't.

MONDAY, 5 AUGUST 1940

Although this was bank holiday Monday, most factories and offices worked a normal day. The Daily Home Intelligence Report stated: 'There is little change in morale which continues to be high'… There were large holiday crowds over the weekend but there is still a good deal of confusion about the official attitude to holidays.'

Clear skies and sunshine, a direct contrast to the last few days, suggested that there would be action this day. The first incursion was a sweep of the Dover Strait by I/JG54, which was first met by the Spitfires of 65 Squadron, up from Manston and patrolling a convoy off Dover, at 09.00 hrs.

Sergeant Harold Orchard, 65 Squadron (Red 3):

> We were at 19,000ft when we sighted approximately – six to eight Me 109s between us and the French coast at about 9,000ft. My Section dived to attack them and I attacked one which was attempting to evade by diving; he turned and I overshot him, only getting a short burst at him from 300 to 250 yards range.
>
> I had lost considerable height and now saw two others in front of me, also diving towards the French coast, and I followed, getting in two 1-second bursts from 300–100 yards on the first one, when white smoke came from it. I overshot this one owing to initial speed but saw it lurching from side to side as it got nearer the water.
>
> I then attacked the third one but only got a short burst from 350 yards at him before I lost him in haze at about 100ft above the water, one mile off the French coast.

The second Me 109 attacked by Orchard was credited as a 'probable'.

Meanwhile, Blue Section of 65 Squadron was en route from Rochford for Manston when vectored to Dover where the Spitfires were attacked by Me 109s. In the ensuing combat, Sergeant Joseph Kilner attacked a 109 over the mid-Channel, claiming it as a probable, while Sergeant William Franklin claimed one damaged. Kilner reported having seen a Spitfire going down trailing smoke – Blue 1, Sergeant Wilford Walker, had been hit by *Oberleutnant* Reinhard Seiler and the aircraft set on fire; fortunately, Sergeant Walker made a safe forced-landing at Manston, but was wounded in the shoulder.

At 08.15 hrs, Squadron Leader Don MacDonell had led two sections of 64 Squadron up from Kenley on an 'interception patrol' over the Channel, being joined five minutes later by the Spitfires of Yellow Section. Having joined the squadron on 27 July 1940 and making his first operational flight two days later, Yellow 3 was Sergeant Jack Mann, who reported that at 09.10 hrs,

> I heard warning of E/A over R/T. Squadron turned to starboard and leading formation broke up formation of E/A. I attacked one Me 109 without apparent result and from ensuing dive saw another Me 109 climbing away. I followed this aircraft until it stall-turned when I got in a long burst. E/A dived with smoke trail behind. At 5,000ft it turned onto its back and was observed by Squadron Leader MacDonell to crash into the sea.

This was Mann's first combat and aerial victory, which occurred for miles of Calais and was most likely *Oberfeldwebel* Karl Schmid of 5/JG51, who was killed. Leading the charge against the 109s, Squadron Leader MacDonell claimed one of the German fighters destroyed – in what he later described as 'a life and death joust' – and damaged another, and Flying Officer Herbert Woodward claimed one 'unconfirmed', although Schmid was the only 109 lost and another returned to base damaged.

This was not, however, without loss to 64 Squadron: Sergeant Lewis Isaac, a 24-year-old who had joined the unit with Sergeant Mann and also flying his first sortie, was picked off while weaving behind the squadron as 'Tail End Charlie'. The Welshman crashed into the sea and remains missing. Also, Pilot Officer Arthur 'Art' Donahue was shot-up and crash-landed, uninjured, at Hawkinge. One pilot of 5/JG51 claimed a Spitfire off Cap Gris Nez, and three of 7/JG51 all claimed Spitfires South-west of Dover, so on this occasion the German combat claims were equally optimistic.

'Art' Donahue, in fact, occupies a special place in this narrative, being the first American volunteer to appear in our chronicle – requiring explanation, because the United States remained neutral at this time. To understand this, we need to travel back to the First World War, and even before.

When the First World War began in 1914, most Americans viewed the distant conflict as a purely European affair and American President, Woodrow Wilson, was committed to maintaining the United States' neutrality. Whereas the First World War, fought between the Central Powers of Germany, Austria-Hungary and the Ottoman Empire against the Allies, led by Britain, France and

Russia, was Europe's first head-on collision with industrial warfare, America had already experienced such a tragedy in its still fairly recent Civil War of 1861–1865.

During that internal conflict, industrial technology and science had devised new means of killing: steam-powered, 'ironclad' warships replaced fighting sail; repeating firearms superseded muzzle-loaded weapons, and the lethal machine-gun made its debut; aviation had played a part for the first time, with balloons being used for reconnaissance; trains conveyed troops infinitely faster than the horse, and the telegraph accelerated communications. All of these things, and more, combined to cause over 200,000 fatal casualties, a shocking death-roll, which, for the first time, saw casualties buried in individual, named, graves in battlefield cemeteries, as opposed to the anonymous mass graves of the past.

This recognition, therefore, made the loss of an individual significant, worthwhile, a never-to-be forgotten and 'supreme sacrifice' for a just cause. Still feeling the effects of these losses only half a century before, and with vast 'gardens of stone' on home soil, little wonder, then, that in 1914 Americans had no desire to send their young men into the latest European meat grinder.

America's neutrality ended in 1917, however, following Germany's resumption of unrestricted submarine warfare, and an attempt to draw Mexico into the war against the Allies. Four million Americans volunteered for service; 116,000 would not return from the Western Front. By the Armistice of 11 November 1918, there had been some 20 million military and civilian deaths, and even more wounded. Then came the Spanish influenza pandemic of 1918–20, striking down at least another 17 million, and by some estimates even up to 100 million worldwide. It was against this backdrop of loss and suffering that the Versailles Peace Conference was held in 1919; tragically, the resulting settlement – heavily influenced by Woodrow Wilson – completely failed to secure a lasting peace, serving only to plant the seeds of a whirlwind which germinated into the even greater humanitarian disaster that was the Second World War.

Ten years after Versailles came the Wall Street Crash followed by the Great Depression, all of which pushed America towards 'Isolationism' – essentially, non-involvement in European and Asian wars and foreign politics. The 'Isolationists' argued that the marginal advantages achieved for American interests during the First World War did not justify the casualties sustained, and that consequently, every effort should in future be made to avoid getting drawn into another war on far-off shores.

The Isolationists also advanced the argument that American involvement in the so-called 'Great War' had been driven by bankers and businessmen waxing fat on the war in Europe, and so in future America should steer clear of financial agreements with countries at war. Indeed, America had not even joined the League of Nations for fear that membership, owing to the Collective Security clause, could trigger involvement in another European war. And so, between the wars, distanced from Europe and Asia by the Atlantic and Pacific oceans respectively, America concentrated on internal affairs.

By the mid-1930s, however, it was clear that another war in Europe was likely. With this in mind, on 31 August 1935, Congress passed the first Neutrality Act, prohibiting Americans exporting arms, ammunition and 'implements of war' from the United States to belligerent foreign powers. The following year, the legislation was bolstered further still through the prohibition of American loans to foreign countries at war. That year, the Spanish Civil War began, and many young men from the Western democracies volunteered to fight there against fascism. This led to American citizens being banned from travelling on belligerent ships, and, among other things, civil wars were specifically included within the Act's parameters.

American President Franklin D. Roosevelt, however, was not in complete accord with American Isolationism and ongoing neutrality, and as a concession to him, the 1937 Act provided for a 'cash and carry' like arrangement whereby, at the President's discretion, belligerent nations could buy supplies, excluding actual arms, from America, and transport these items in non-American vessels. The President had deliberately engineered this as a means of helping Britain and France in the event of a war with Nazi Germany, but the Act only provided this arrangement for two years.

In November 1939 though, after the commencement of the Second World War in Europe, the last Neutrality Act was passed, which lifted the arms embargo while retaining other restrictions. In practical terms, these Acts enabled the US Government to accommodate the American public's popular desire for isolationism while still interacting, to a degree, on the wider world stage.

For some young Americans, regardless of the Neutrality Act, there was a strong desire to join the fight against fascism. The problem, however, was that the Act made it a criminal offence for an American citizen to join the armed forces of a belligerent nation – punishment being up to a decade behind bars, loss of US citizenship and a maximum fine of $20,000 – a veritable fortune in those days.

That, and the widely held view, articulated by the American Ambassador in London, Joseph P. Kennedy, that Britain had no hope of winning the war, might have been considered sufficient to dissuade any American volunteers keen to emulate Ernest Hemmingway's Spanish Civil War adventures in this new European war. But it did not. The first American volunteer was an impressive individual: the Olympian, wealthy banker and civilian pilot Billy Fiske – who circumvented the Neutrality Act by pretending to be Canadian.

Others followed, including experienced civilian pilots Andy Mamedorf, Eugene Tobin and Vernon 'Shorty' Keough – all keen for adventure and a chance to fly the RAF's new, modern, monoplane fighters, especially the Spitfire. Men like these, who were already civilian pilots of some experience, were welcome recruits for the RAF – especially because, unlike the Poles and Czechs, there was no language barrier. 'Art' Donahue, from St Charles, Minnesota, had learned to fly privately, receiving both his private and commercial pilot's licenses before his nineteenth birthday, and was also among the first Americans to travel to Canada, enlist in the RCAF and travel to England.

Arriving in Britain on 30 June 1940, the 27-year-old American was commissioned into the RAFVR, and on 7 July 1940 began conversion to Spitfires at 5 OTU, Aston Down. On 3 August 1940, Pilot Officer Donahue reported for flying duties with 64 Squadron at Kenley, and on this day, 5 August 1940, along with Sergeants Mann and Isaacs, made his first operational flight, resulting in his crash-landing at Hawkinge.

One of nine American volunteers serving with Fighter Command during the Battle of Britain, of him Squadron Leader Don MacDonell wrote that:

> While at Aston Down I had met and become friends with Art Donahue ... After I left to command 64 Squadron, Art asked if he could be posted to serve with me. He served me with great loyalty and gallantry. He became the 'pet' of the squadron. He was a little over 5ft tall with close-cropped blond hair and bright blue eyes. He was killed in 1942.

Returning to the events of 5 August 1940, during the afternoon another convoy attracted the *Luftwaffe*'s attention off Dover, a single 'He 111' approaching. At 15.00 hrs, Flight Lieutenant Terry Webster was leading 'B' Flight of 41 Squadron, patrolling the convoy:

> I was Green Leader ... we were flying at 20,000ft below a cloud layer (21,500ft) when a single aircraft was seen to emerge from the cloud. Blue Section did not investigate in case it was a decoy, and especially since we had been warned of a fifteen plus raid approaching us. I climbed towards the aircraft which I identified as a He 111, leaving my No 2 and 3 to join up with Blue Section and form a rear-guard for me. E/A made for cloud and I followed.
>
> As he entered I got in a medium burst using a quarter attack. I opened at 250 yards and closed to 100 yards. I could see my bullets entering the E/A but without apparent effect, suggesting E/A was heavily armoured. E/A continued dodging in and out of cloud and I swung round to attack from astern. I used the remainder of my ammunition and managed to put one engine out of action. I last saw E/A making a shallow dive towards the French coast. About forty Me 109s, which appeared from above the cloud, closed in and escorted the damaged He 111 home.

Three sections of 151 Squadron, up from Rochford, were also patrolling mid-Channel at 15.00 hrs, at 20,000ft. Red Section engaged a single 'Ju 88', Red 2, Sub-Lieutenant Henry Beggs, a Fleet Air Arm pilot, fired a long burst from 'dead astern' and saw 'volumes of smoke issuing from both sides of E/A's fuselage and from the engine ... I last saw E/A over French coast with clouds of black smoke pouring from both wings'.

Flight Lieutenant Kenneth Blair DFC was leading Yellow Section and reported seeing the 'Ju 88' and 'thirty Me 109s'. While Red Section tackled the bomber, Blair led Yellow to engage the Me 109s. Two cannon rounds passed in front him, followed by two Me 109s, which overshot, providing an opportunity for the Hurricane pilot to counter-attack: 'My first burst of three seconds hit the first Me 109, which half-rolled into the sea.' Blair then came under further attack and forced to break away; back at base, Pilot Officer John Alexander confirmed having seen the 109 go down, and 'splash marks in the sea', and Sergeant George Atkinson witnessed 'an aircraft fall into the sea in mid-Channel'.

No apparent casualty in German records corresponds to this claim, which was undoubtedly confirmed. There can be little or no doubt, though, that 151 Squadron had encountered the same raider intercepted by 41 Squadron, after it had been damaged by Flight Lieutenant Webster and picked up by the Me 109s of JG51. It seems that both squadrons misidentified the bomber, however, as no He 111s were lost in such circumstances this date – but a Do 17 of 3/KG3 crash-landed at Le Culot aerodrome upon return from an operational sortie, and another of 7/KG3 failed to return from a combat flight.

This was the final fighter combat of the day – perhaps surprisingly given the weather, although clearly there was much activity across the Channel as both *Luftflotten* prepared for the imminent *Adlerangriff*. The convoy over which the combats had been fought was that being escorted eastbound by the Mobile Barrage Balloon Flotilla, as Lieutenant Arthur Hague recalled:

> That evening we entered the Thames ... Except for my breakfast I had not left the bridge of HMS *Borealis* since sailing from Southampton some thirty-six hours earlier and I was dog-tired. But I managed a few lines home, 'Of course it will be better later on' – how wrong I was!

Sixty-seven Coastal Command aircraft flew the usual round of convoy, anti-invasion and anti-submarine patrols in addition to various reconnaissance sorties, the only loss being a 206 Squadron Hudson which crashed upon return to Bircham Newton, killing the crew. All nine 2 Group Blenheims tasked with either reconnaissance or attacking enemy airfields in the Netherlands were forced to abandon their sorties owing to the lack of cloud cover.

By night, eighty-five Wellingtons, Hampdens and Whitleys again visited industrial and naval, targets in Germany; all returned safely.

TUESDAY, 6 AUGUST 1940

At Carinhall, Göring conferred with his *Kanalfront Luftflotten* chiefs, Kesselring and Sperrle, to decide the finer points of the *Adlerangriff*. The new assault was to be launched against the RAF and Britain's aircraft industry on *Adler Tag* (Eagle Day) – provisionally scheduled for 10 August 1940. Assuming that the destruction of 11 Group would take just four days, and annihilation of the wider RAF in four weeks, it was anticipated that Operation *Seelöwe* could then go ahead in mid-September 1940.

Since the air battles of 29 July 1940, owing to both the weather and preparing for the *Adlerangriff*, German air operations against Britain had been on a reduced scale – which had not gone unnoticed by Germany's Italian allies; not being privy to Hitler and Göring's plans, however, the reason was unclear to Dino Alfieri, Mussolini's ambassador to Berlin, as Count Ciano recorded: 'Alfieri now says that German activity is slowed down and this time fails to explain the reason. Could there be anything in the rumours about a separate peace through the King of Sweden?'

Two days previously, Ciano had written that 'From Berlin, Alfieri reports that the sudden return of Hitler and of the highest Nazi officials leads him to suspect imminent operations, about which, as usual, we have been told nothing.' This was frustrating for Mussolini, who, according to Ciano, 'definitely wants to participate in an attack on Great Britain, if it occurs', although on 16 July 1940 Hitler had written to the Duce declining,

> in a definite and courteous way the offer to send an Italian expeditionary force. He explains his refusal by saying that logistic difficulties would arise in supplying two armies. Göring too, in a conversation with Alfieri, said that Italian aviation has too important a task in the Mediterranean to scatter its forces in other sectors. The Duce was very much annoyed by the refusal.

For now, there would be no opportunity for the Italian air force, the *Regia Aeronautica* to play a part in the aerial campaign about to be unleashed against Britain.

Given the recent lack of activity by the German bomber force, however, eight convoys in total left British ports during this twenty-four-hour period, while two were incoming, all heavily protected by fighters.

At 05.45 hrs, Flight Sergeant Geoffrey 'Sammy' Allard DFM led Yellow Section of 85 Squadron, comprising Sergeants John Ellis and Walter Evans, up from Martlesham Heath to patrol a convoy off the East Coast. While over Lowestoft, Flight Sergeant Allard,

> was warned that E/A were in the vicinity; after orbiting once at 10,000ft, Yellow Leader sighted a Do 17 to his left and 1,000ft below; he promptly delivered a quarter beam attack, closing from 300 yards

to 50 yards with a 5-second burst and put the port engine out of action. Yellow 2 and 3, Sergeants Evans and Ellis, delivered their attacks and the Do 17 went into a low left-hand dive through the clouds. It was next seen a few moments after a few ft above the drink and out of control; a second or two later the tail broke off and the E/A nosed into the sea and disappeared almost immediately. A destroyer and one identified ship proceeded to area where E/A disappeared. [ORB]

The Do 17, of 7/KG3 was confirmed destroyed and shared equally by the three Hurricane pilots of Yellow Section; the four-man crew remain missing.

At 16.15 hrs, Squadron Leader Marcus Robinson, Flight Lieutenant Richard Hellyer and Sergeant Marmaduke Ridley, Red Section of Leconfield's 616 Squadron, scrambled to investigate an 'X-Raid'. At 17.07 hrs, a Ju 88 was sighted twenty miles East of Flamborough Head and attacked by Robinson and Ridley before the raider disappeared in cloud. 'All of our aircraft were hit by pieces off E/A, but returned safely,' concluded the ORB.

These were Fighter Command's only combats on this day, one of low cloud and high winds across the Channel and whole of Britain.

Coastal Command flew a number of routine patrols and reconnaissance fights, but thirty-nine of the forty-two 2 Group Blenheims undertaking attacks on enemy airfields and carrying out reconnaissance were forced to abandon their sorties due to the adverse weather.

The bad weather persisted into the night, but nonetheless twenty-five Wellingtons of 3 Group attacked oil installations and communication targets in Germany, while sixteen 'Wimpys' were sent to bomb various enemy airfields in Germany and the Netherlands. Twelve Hampdens of 49 Squadron carried out a mining operation off the Scandinavian coast, but Sergeant Robert Jennings DFM and crew simply disappeared and are commemorated on the Runnymede Memorial to missing British and Commonwealth aircrew.

Daily Home Intelligence Report:

> Morale is high ... There are many in authority who feel that the present lull should have been used (and might still be used) for a clear statement of a constructive peace policy on our part. Some of our reports show that there are members of the public who would like to be given the opportunity of reading for themselves the German leaflet giving Hitler's speech in full, and thus assuring themselves that nothing had been hidden from them. They are under the impression that definite 'peace terms' have been put forward by Hitler.

In Tunbridge Wells, there was apparently 'Dissatisfaction in villages in Defence Areas that police permission was not always granted for relatives to visit them while Londoners enter areas by cycle on by-roads and are not stopped.'

WEDNESDAY, 7 AUGUST 1940

So far, *Luftwaffe* losses were sustainable but the fighting to date indicated certain difficulties. Fighter Command clearly remained an effective force and was not suffering a death-blow of casualties in the coastal fighting. It was decided, therefore, that bomber formations must penetrate further inland, providing escorting fighters a greater opportunity for combat with the RAF – but this would actually give the defenders more time to reach high altitudes, as opposed to the short time available to do so during the Channel interceptions.

The German fighter leaders on the *Kanalfront* were also realising that their 980 fighters were unlikely to be sufficient in order to defeat 11 Group, because the numbers of escorting fighters needed to be three times that of the bombers, and some fighters had to be held back because the RAF fighter pilots were doggedly pursuing German aircraft all the way to the French coast. Moreover, the Me 110 was proving a failure as an escort fighter, thus reducing the number of efficient fighters available for the job in hand.

By now, the Germans also realised that RAF fighters were controlled from the ground, having listened to R/T orders directing the defending aircraft to accurate interceptions. On this day, *Luftwaffe* Intelligence circulated a report to all operational commands regarding its appreciation and understanding of how RAF fighters were controlled, believing this to be territorially inflexible and inferring that deeper penetrations by mass formations would overwhelm Fighter Command's system:

> As the British fighters are controlled from the ground by R/T their forces are tied to their respective ground stations and are thereby restricted in mobility, even taking into consideration the probability that the ground stations are partly mobile. Consequently, the assembly of strong fighter forces at determined points and at short notice is not to be expected. A massed German attack on a target area can therefore count on the same conditions of light fighter opposition as in attacks on widely scattered targets. It can, indeed, be assumed that considerable confusion in the defensive networks will be unavoidable during mass attacks, and that the effectiveness of the defences may thereby be reduced.

To some extent the Germans were right. The limitations of the in-aircraft R/T used by the RAF at the time was explained in *The Gathering Storm*, but suffice it here to say that, at this time, pilots could only speak to other members of their own squadron in the air, but not other units, and their own Sector Controller. This made controlling large numbers of fighters in the air by an airborne leader almost impossible once battle was joined, and a squadron passing from, say, the Duxford Sector of 12 Group into the 11 Group area could not communicate with that group's sector controllers, only its Duxford host (as we will see in due course).

Nonetheless, as the bulk of fighting would be borne by 11 Group fighters and sectors, this was not really any great consideration. In the main, though, the German report was inaccurate, providing another firm indication as to how faulty intelligence was informing *Luftwaffe* strategy and tactics.

In the enemy camp, the differences of opinion between the *Heer* and *Kriegsmarine* regarding a landing on a broad or narrow front came to a head on this day. Raeder had planned for a crossing of the Dover Strait and landing on a narrow front, regardless of Halder's preference for a broader landing – but had failed to communicate this to Halder, who exploded upon reading Raeder's report on 4 August 1940 and complained to Jodl. This led to a heated meeting on the Channel coast on 7 August 1940 between the *Heer* and *Kriegsmarine* chiefs of staff, the *Kriegsmarine* Chief of Operations, *Admiral* Schniewind, arguing that a landing on a front 230 miles wide, from the Nore to Lyme Bay, was simply impossible, being far beyond the ability of the limited naval resources available.

Further, Schniewind tried to make Halder understand that the only hope of success lay in a Dover crossing and landing, supported by coastal artillery and the *Luftwaffe*. Halder responded that such a landing would be suicidal, while Schniewind retorted that the broad front would be similarly so, given the close proximity of both Portsmouth and Portland RN bases to the proposed landing areas. Unable to resolve the matter, the issue had to be referred to Hitler.

By day, although the weather had improved somewhat, there was still cloud and rain to the East, and no raids were mounted against Britain. There was, however, a little excitement for 607 'County of Durham' Squadron, an auxiliary Hurricane squadron based at Acklington, in Northumberland, as Pilot Officer Harry Welford recalled:

> Although we continually practiced formation flying, aerial combat and No 1 and 3 attacks, we also flew patrol duties along the north-east coast, providing aerial cover to the merchant and fishing convoys. On 7 August 1940, we spotted a Ju 88 weather plane in the distance and flew 100 miles out to sea after it, but didn't intercept because he made it into cloud just as we came within firing distance. In fact it was stupid of us to go so far out, but in the excitement of the moment one gets carried away, even though strict instructions had been dished out not to stray too far from the coast.
>
> These convoy patrols covered from Acklington to Scarborough but only five–ten miles out to sea. About this time I had my first flight in a Spitfire, which was a lovely aircraft to fly, not that different to the Hurricane except that in taxying the nose seemed to rear right up in your line of vision, and you had to swing from left to right, this being rather heavy on the brakes and in danger of burning out the brake shoes.

Twenty-five merchant ships, mostly colliers, heavy with coal from northern England and all requisitioned by the Admiralty, had assembled off Southend. This

KANALKAMPF DIARY, 1 AUGUST – 12 AUGUST 1940

was Convoy CW9 (Coal-West 9), codenamed *Peewit*. Having forced the RN out of Dover, Göring had boasted that the *Luftwaffe* had control of the Channel, and the traitor William Joyce – better known as the infamous 'Lord Haw-Haw' – lost no time in referencing this on his Hamburg-based Nazi propaganda radio show, goading the British that it was no longer the 'English Channel' but part of the 'German Ocean'.

Churchill was incensed. The intention now was to prove the Göring and Lord Haw-Haw wrong – by forcing a passage through the Dover Strait for *Peewit*. The convoy was to weigh anchor at 14.00 hrs on 7 August 1940, heading for the wharves of Portsmouth or Southampton.

Lieutenant Hague, HMS *Borealis*:

> We picked up the West bound convoy CW9 passing the Nore Light Vessel. It consisted of twenty-five coasters escorted by nine RN escorts including two destroyers and our Mobile Balloon Barrage Flotilla. On leaving the Thames the convoy formed into two columns with *Astral* and *Borealis* ahead of the port and starboard columns respectively. Night fell as we passed Dover and in a calm sea under a moonless sky we crept past Beachy Head.

There was, however, great danger ahead, by both night and day – and thus the scene was set for intense fighting over *Peewit* in the hours of day and night ahead.

On this day, twenty-eight Blenheims of 2 Group were despatched to attack oil facilities and factories in Germany and airfields in the Netherlands and France. Owing to the weather all but two turned back. One of these successfully attacked Haamstede airfield, catching 4/JG54 on the ground: two Me 109s were destroyed, five more damaged and two pilots killed – effectively removing this unit from the battle for over two weeks.

That night, the weather affected operations, preventing most aircraft finding their targets, but fires were started at Homburg and Emmerich, and at a nearby aerodrome, and Kiel dockyard was also attacked. Hampdens laid mines in the Langelands Belt, a strait between the Danish islands of Zealand and Funen; there were no losses. A Coastal Command Hudson, however, failed to return from a reconnaissance sortie to the Norwegian coast.

The Daily Home Intelligence Report noted, 'Good weather and holiday spirit have made a valuable contribution to continued cheerfulness'. In London, 'People everywhere reported to be in good spirits and quite cheerful. At the moment the war is somewhat in the background … One London factory with 400 men in Home Guard still without uniforms and rifles.'

In the South-Western Region, 'Prospect of invasion of Britain faced calmly. Surprise and little anxiety in Dorset that there have been no raids for a week. Stronger hatred of Germans in Dorset than elsewhere in Region attributed to low machine-gunning attacks in this county.'

THURSDAY, 8 AUGUST 1940

Although *Peewit* had safely passed through the Dover Strait under cover of darkness, the convoy's presence had not gone unnoticed by the Germans – owing to the recently installed Freya radar on the French coast. And therein lay a tale.

In 1936, Professor R.V. Jones had worked for the Air Ministry to develop the early warning system that became RDF and in 1939 this brilliant mind was appointed Assistant Director of Intelligence (Science) at the Air Ministry. On 5 July 1940, the British Code and Cypher School at Bletchley Park decoded a German Enigma message referring to 'Freya-*Meldung*' (Freya reporting), which piqued Jones's interest given that he had already heard of 'Freya *Gerät*' ('Freya' apparatus). But what, exactly, was 'Freya'?

Since 27 June 1940, when an Enigma message was deciphered referring to setting up '*Knickebein* and *Wotan* installations near Cherbourg and Brest', Jones suspected that the German signal referred to some kind of radar apparatus. Was this also the case regarding 'Freya'?

Referring to a book on Nordic mythology, Jones found a clue: 'Freya was the Nordic Venus who had not merely sacrificed but massacred her honour to gain possession of a magic necklace, "Brisinga-men". The necklace was guarded by Heimdall, the Watchman of the Gods, who could see a hundred miles by day or night.'

From this, Jones suspected that 'Freya' referred to 'a coastal chain and detecting system with a range of 100 miles'. Arguably '*Heimdall*' was more appropriate – but 'Freya' less obvious. Jones was right. Freya's 1.2 metre wavelength provided for a small, rotating, aerial and mobility – whereas the huge Chain Home pylons were deeply rooted in concrete. Freya's range was ninety-nine miles, while Chain Home's was 180 miles, but, unlike the British RDF, the German system was unable to determine altitude.

The *Kriegsmarine*, in fact, had been working on Freya since 1937, but no effort was made to incorporate the radar into Germany's aerial defence system before the war. That changed on 18 December 1939, when two Freya stations detected RAF Wellingtons approaching Wilhelmshaven and successfully guided *Luftwaffe* fighters to intercept them – albeit after ships in the port had been attacked – destroying fourteen British bombers. The advantage and potential of Freya was immediately obvious, leading to a chain of Freya stations monitoring Germany's western border by spring 1940, and, after the Fall of France, a further seven sites were installed along the north-west French coast.

On 29 July 1940, contrary to orders, the destroyer HMS *Delight* had departed Portland naval base in broad daylight – leading to detection by the Cherbourg-based Freya. *Luftflotte* 3 then launched an attack on the ship by *Stukas* of II/StG2, sending it to the bottom of the Channel, twenty miles South of Portland. Bletchley Park intercepted and decoded a German signal stating that *Delight* had been 'sunk with the aid of Freya reports'. The destroyer, however, was not flying a balloon, and nor were RAF fighters patrolling overhead – leading Jones to conclude:

> The apparatus must have been able to detect her directly ... It appeared to be sited near the village of Audeville on the Hague-peninsula north-west of Cherbourg, but it had to be very different to our own coastal chain stations, since it was completely undetectable on the best air photographs we possessed ... This confirmed the idea that Freya was a fairly small apparatus, which had already been suggested by the fact that it had been set up so quickly after the Germans had occupied the Channel coast.

Active though German reconnaissance bombers were, the realisation had now dawned that *Oberst* 'Papa' Fink had undoubtedly been assisted by Freya in his efforts to date. And now, Freya had detected *Peewit*, which, in the early and dark hours of 8 August 1940, was now steaming westward towards the Isle of Wight.

Lieutenant Arthur Hague, HMS *Borealis*:

> Some time in the middle watch I became aware of the powerful throb of engines and assumed this to come from enemy bombers crossing the Channel on a night raid. Suddenly, a loud explosion lit the sky and I saw that the coaster immediately astern of *Borealis* had fallen out of line and was listing. Instantly I realised that the throb came from enemy E-boats, which must have been lying in wait to launch a torpedo attack from the inshore side of the convoy. I immediately ordered 'hard a port', to minimise our silhouette to our invisible attackers.
>
> As the ship's head slowly swung to port the phosphorescent wake of a torpedo sped out of the darkness under our starboard counter and emerged to port. Had we remained on our original course it would have registered a direct hit. By this time another ship had been torpedoed and all hell broke loose in the convoy.
>
> Tracer fire lit up the sky and some of the coasters appeared to be firing at each other. When dawn broke most of the ships were sailing close inshore under the cliffs when escorts harried them back into some semblance of formation. Meanwhile, I snatched a few hours' sleep.

The convoy had been hit by the German 1st *Schnellboot* Flotilla, comprising four E-boats, commanded by *Kapitänleutnant* Heinz Birnbacher, who had already been decorated with the *Ritterkruez* for his successes during the Norwegian campaign and Channel fighting. In this ambush, off Beachy Head and Newhaven, the enemy had lain in wait, having correctly anticipated the convoy's course via the mine-free shipping lanes.

During the resulting attack, *Holme Force* and *Fife Coast* had been sunk; *Ouse* had collided with *Rye* while taking evasive action and also sank. The damaged

Rye remained afloat, however, as did *Polly M*, but only just. The destroyer HMS *Bulldog* returned fire and claimed destruction of an E-boat but the convoy had been broken up, now snaking over ten miles, and would never properly resume formation. The worst, though, was yet to come – from the air.

At 06.20 hrs, a Do 17 reconnaissance bomber reported the position and progress of *Peewit*, on which *Generalfeldmarschall* Hugo Sperrle, commander of *Luftlotte 3*, now planned massive daylight attacks by the *Stukas* of *Fliegerkorps* VIII. Very shortly, it would prove a busy day indeed for 10 and 11 groups, Fighter Command.

At 08.30 hrs, 145 Squadron was scrambled to patrol the battered convoy, now about five miles East of St Catherine's Point, Squadron Leader John Peel taking-off from Westhampnett, leading 'A' Flight's Hurricanes towards *Peewit*. Ten minutes later RDF detected thirty plus bandits off Cherbourg, and at 08.45 hrs, the Tangmere Sector Controller scrambled 'B' Flight of 145 Squadron, led by Flight Lieutenant Adrian Boyd.

Then, at 08.55 hrs another of equal size between the Seine's mouth and Selsey Bill: both waves of enemy aircraft were heading straight for *Peewit*. At 09.00 hrs, battle was joined, ten miles South of the Isle of Wight, the twelve Hurricanes of 145 Squadron engaging, according to Squadron Leader Peel, 'very large' numbers of 'Ju 87, Me 109 and Me 110'. Me 109s of JG27 were escorting twice the number of *Stukas*, and 145 Squadron hurtled into action, engaging the escorting fighters.

Squadron Leader John Peel,

> saw E/A dive-bombing convoy ... There appeared to be Me 110s and Me 109s. Dived onto Me 109 at 1,000ft, gave a 5-second burst from astern and E/A became enveloped in smoke and dived into sea. Pilot of this aircraft baled out before his aircraft hit the sea. I saw Red 3 attack another Me 109 fifty yards on my port beam and shoot it down into the sea. Both these aircraft were confirmed. I then attacked several Ju 87s which were flying South.
>
> During these attacks E/A invariably went into a steep turn either before or after first burst. One 87 succeeded in getting on my tail and did some accurate shooting, a bullet passing through my cockpit fairing ... I attacked one Me 109 with a long-range deflection shot but could not close to decisive range as he was travelling too fast. I then returned to base to refuel and rearm.

Pilot Officer Peter Parrott was up, flying as Yellow 2 in Squadron Leader Peel's Flight:

> I saw about seventy enemy aircraft approaching The Needles from the South. Yellow 1 led the Section into the sun and I delivered an astern attack in company with Yellow 1 on two Ju 87s. After two

short bursts I broke away, as I saw there were enemy fighters in the vicinity. I climbed up. As I was climbing, an Me 109 passed in front of me, about 100 yards away.

I followed him round and gave him a full deflection burst of about two seconds. He then pulled up in a steep climb and fell away in a spin, with a little smoke coming out of his engine. My windscreen was then oiled up by oil from my airscrew, and I saw three Me 109s coming down on my tail. I therefore broke away and dived into cloud, as I could not see anything through my windscreen.

Flight Lieutenant Adrian Boyd:

I got onto the tail of one Me 109, put a short burst into him, and he went straight into sea ... I then went in to attack two more Me 109s, one of which half-rolled onto his back and dived straight into the sea without my having opened fire. It seemed his control was locked and he thus failed to pull out of his dive. I attacked the second Me 109 and hit him but he did not come down.

No.145 Squadron's 'bag was six Ju 87s, three Me 109s destroyed and others damaged'. It was a brilliant result: the dive-bombers were kept away from the convoy, many jettisoning their deadly cargoes randomly into the sea as they attempted to escape the Hurricanes' wrath, and no ships were lost. Indeed, having taken place seaward of the convoy, the ships' crews were apparently largely unaware of the violent combat occurring overhead.

Lieutenant Commander Owles of HMS *Astral* recorded in his log: 'Clouds of smoke and spray apparently on our course. Machines have been circling overhead but so high that we can't say definitely whose they are. Presumably ours.'

As T.C.G. James wrote in the official Air Historical Branch narrative (see Bibliography), 'This was an unwitting tribute to the work of 145 Squadron.' This successful action was not without loss to 145 Squadron though: 'A' Flight lost Pilot Officer Lionel Sears, while 'B' Flight's Sergeant Eric Baker likewise failed to return; both pilots remain missing.

At 09.00 hrs, 609 Squadron's Spitfires had scrambled from Warmwell to reinforce 145, but arrived too late to intercept. According to the ORB, as far as 609 Squadron was concerned, however, the fighting over *Peewit* on this day represented the start of the 'Nazi Blitz ... with a series of intensive attacks on a convoy attempting to progress from the needles to Weymouth Bay ... The convoy advertised its presence by flying silver barrage balloons and made it difficult to bring up prompt aid by sailing fifteen miles out to sea.'

That may have been so – but the Germans' awareness of *Peewit* had nothing to do with balloons: the enemy had Freya and their side.

Having suffered casualties early on in the Battle of Britain, 609 Squadron, like many others, had rejected the Fighter Command vic of three formation and was experimenting with its own ideas:

> At this time the squadron used a formation which had many theoretical advantages but which proved in practice extremely difficult to hold together. The leading flight flew together in Flight line-astern with a section on either flank and staggered about 1,500ft up. In a turn, or flying into the sun, it was very easy for the flanking sections to lose sight of their leader. Later this difficulty was overcome by bringing the flanking sections down to nearly the same height as the latter. [ORB]

Next, the action temporarily shifted eastwards, to the 11 Group and *Luftflotten* 2 sectors. A small enemy force crossed the Kentish coast over Dover at 10.38 hrs, but could not be visually tracked by the Observer Corps owing to cloud cover. These intruders were Me 109s of *Hauptmann* Adolf Galland's III/JG26, which had joined with II and III/JG51 on a sweep of the Channel and south-east Kent, which headed North-east after crossing the coast.

At 10.15 hrs, the flight of Hornchurch's 65 Squadron operating from Manston was scrambled to patrol base – but was bounced over Manston by III/JG26: Flight Sergeant Norman Phillips and Sergeant David Kirton were both killed, their Spitfires 'bursting into flames on impact'.

Ten minutes before 65 Squadron had scrambled, Squadron Leader Don MacDonell had led up a flight of 64 Squadron Spitfires from Kenley to patrol south-east Kent. Although according to the ORB, 'No contact was made'. Sergeant John Squires, very likely the 'Tail-end Charlie', weaving back and to at the squadron's rear, was picked off unseen by *Hauptmann* Johannes Trautloft of *Stab* III/JG51. At 11.10 hrs, Sergeant Squires crash-landed at Great Cauldham, Capel-le-Ferne, and was subsequently admitted to Canterbury Hospital suffering a broken arm and jaw, and from shock.

As the Me 109s withdrew, off Ramsgate, at 11.35 hrs, *Oberleutnant* Gerhard Schöpfel, *Staffelkapitän* of 9/JG26, claimed a 'Handley' destroyed South of Ramsgate, although this was actually a 2 Group Blenheim of West Raynham's 18 Squadron, sent to attack airfields at Schiphol and Valkenburg. The bomber crashed into the Channel, killing the crew. This was Schöpfel's fifth aerial victory – making him an ace.

At 11.25 hrs, thirteen Spitfires of 41 Squadron had scrambled to reinforce 65. At midday, Green Section was despatched to investigate a small enemy formation over Manston – Me 109s of *Stab* III and III/JG51 hoping to bring further RAF fighters to battle. The German pilots would not be disappointed.

Pilot Officer Ronald 'Wally' Wallens, Green 3:

> We dived from 25,000ft down to 12,000ft and identified the aircraft as Me 109s, in straggling formations of three or four in wide vics.

I attacked the rear aircraft of the latter formation from astern and broke away to see my leader attack and the E/A went straight into down into the sea. I then found another single Me 109 and attacked from astern, using only a very short burst. Blue and white smoke immediately poured from this machine, which went straight into the sea (mid-Channel).

I returned to Manston and landed, but took off immediately (without rearming or refuelling) as I realised the fight might still be in progress. I climbed to about 12,000ft and came across a lone Me 109 returning home I again attacked from astern and a short burst was sufficient to send this aircraft into the sea in the middle of the Channel.

Flight Lieutenant Webster, returning from the engagement (he had apparently been across to Calais) saw this machine crash.

All my attacks (I find I only used 389 rounds) were from astern and just a question of pressing the 'tit' for a one-second burst: each time I must have hit the petrol tank or pilot since E/A went straight in.

Flight Lieutenant Terry Webster also claimed Me 109s destroyed in the action, a running battle between Manston and Calais during which 41 Squadron suffered no loss.

At 11.20 hrs, Squadron Leader Don MacDonell had again led a flight 64 Squadron up from Kenley to patrol the south-east Kentish coast and Channel. Between 12.15 and 12.30 hrs, at 8,000ft over the Channel, two miles South-east of Dover, the Spitfires were bounced by some twenty Me 109s, breaking the Flight up into sections, which engaged individually.

Sergeant Jack Mann:

I turned through 180° and was attacked head-on by E/A without result. Still turning I got onto the tail of a further E/A and got in a 3-second burst on ¼ deflection. E/A straightened out for a few seconds, smoke began to pour out astern and E/A turned onto its back and dived. A certain loss but unconfirmed as cloud obscured sea and ground (CO confirms E/A out of control).

I gave chase to further E/A which headed back towards France. I got several bursts of fire at short range until I had to break off to prevent ramming. A black smoke trail appeared and two larger fragments came adrift. I was attacked by four Me 109s and turned into local cloud. This occurred four–six miles North of French coast. It is possible that the E/A was able to glide this distance. This aircraft was camouflaged in two shades of grey and green and bore figure 8. Just aft of the cockpit.

Sergeant Mann was credited with one Me 109 confirmed, the other damaged. Squadron Leader MacDonell also claimed a 109 destroyed, while Sergeant Peter Hawke claimed one damaged. Pilot Officer Peter Kennard-Davis, having just converted to Spitfires at Aston Down and joined 64 Squadron only five days previously, was shot down in flames at 12.05 hrs. The 20-year-old-pilot baled out but was wounded in the head, chest, buttocks and legs, in addition to suffering a broken pelvis. Admitted to Royal Victoria Hospital, Dover, he sadly died there two days later.

On this day, instead of sweeping in strong formations the German fighters had operated in many smaller formations, making it difficult for Sector Controllers to second-guess their intentions. Various RAF squadrons were scrambled and vectored to intercept, only to find the Germans either retiring or not present at all. The cloud cover, impeding the Observer Corps, was also a great help to the enemy. Now, the action reverted westwards; the enemy had regrouped and was unleashing another attack on the beleaguered Convoy *Peewit*.

That morning, at 09.10 hrs, 257 Squadron had left Northolt for Tangmere, to remain at readiness there. At exactly midday, Flight Lieutenant Noel Hall led Blue, Yellow and Green Sections up to patrol *Peewit*.

Then, at 12.10 hrs, more than 100 bandits were detected by RDF twenty miles North of Cherbourg, approaching *Peewit*, which was now straggling between St Catherine's Point and The Needles. Hall's Hurricanes were the first RAF fighters to intercept this massive raid, engaging the Me 109 escorts at 12.10 hrs, mid-Channel.

In the resulting clash, Pilot Officers Arthur Cochrane and Kenneth Gundry both claimed Me 109s destroyed, while Gundry also damaged another, and Sergeant Ronald Forward damaged a Do 17. It was a black day, however, for the still comparatively inexperienced 257 Squadron: Flight Lieutenant Noel Hall, Flying Officer Brian D'Arcy-Irvine and Sergeant Kenneth Smith were all lost.

Sergeant Reg Nutter, 257 Squadron, recalled that, 'In this, our first major action, we lost three pilots. This, loss, coupled with the recent change in command, caused our morale to drop very sharply.'

Lieutenant Arthur Hague, HMS *Borealis*:

> CW9 plodded on until 1219 hrs when, about four miles South of St Catherine's Point, a formation of German fighters fell upon the balloons which, under a hail of incendiary bullets, rapidly disintegrated in flames. Then, out of the sun, roared a flight of Ju 87 dive-bombers. The distinctive 'W' shaped profile getting larger and larger held a horrible fascination until the pilot released his bomb and zoomed up again. Our pair of Hotchkiss guns proved no deterrent and a second later there was a violent explosion from the foredeck. The foremast jack-knifed and everything moveable on the bridge crashed about us. Fortunately there were only three serious casualties.

Within minutes, RAF fighters were overhead, dogfights developed and the bombers fled. A survey of the damage to *Borealis* showed that the collision bulkhead was holding but that the electrical steering gear had failed. While we struggled to master the hand steering, Chief Engineman Taylor managed to caulk the leaking gravity fuel tank sufficiently to keep the main engines supplied.

By this time I had transferred my three casualties to the escort trawler HMS *Green Fly* and those hands not essential to the working of the ship to HMS *Astral*. The sub, midshipman, chief engineer and I stayed in an attempt to save the ship. HMS *Elan II*, another of our flotilla, then took us in tow, stern first, to minimise pressure on the collision bulkhead, while HMS *Renee* secured alongside to steer the tow.

RAF fighters were constantly in the air, by sections or flights, but not all made contact. No.213 Squadron's Yellow Section, for example, comprising two experienced Belgian pilots, namely Pilot Officers Maurice Buchin and Jacques Philippart, with the recently arrived Pilot Officer Alexander Osmand, took off from Exeter at 12.15 hrs, but missed the Germans. In his flying logbook, Osmand wrote: 'Yellow patrol. St Catherine's Point – 15,000ft above a convoy. Too late – ships on fire but enemy gone.'

At 11.55 hrs, Flight Lieutenant Sir Archibald Hope, the 17th Baronet of Craighall, led his 'A' Flight of the socially elite auxiliary 601 Squadron up from Tangmere, also heading for *Peewit*. At 12.30 hrs, 18,000ft over the sea some ten miles South of St Catherine's Point, the six Hurricanes went into action against Me 109s of JG27.

Pilot Officer John McGrath, 601 Squadron:

> When slightly East of Needles E/A and other aircraft seen in supposed dogfight. Yellow Section went into line astern and orbited before attacking. I broke away and did a stall-turn onto an Me 109 which was on the tail of a Hurricane, and did a practically head-on attack. He made no noticeable manoeuvre until he passed underneath my aircraft. I again stall-turned onto the same aircraft only to see it roll over onto its back and spin into the sea, smoking violently from port side of engine and wing. This is confirmed by Yellow 1, Flying Officer Davis.
>
> Shortly afterwards an Me 109 got on my tail so I dived at full throttle and then zoomed in order to roll off the top of the loop. On flattening out I did a stall turn to the left, to find that E/A had not followed me but had done a medium right-hand turn.
>
> As I came down on him he dived to the left, giving me a perfect full deflection shot. I fired a 2-second burst and followed him down,

no smoke could be seen but aircraft seemed to spin out of control. I didn't fire again but continued to follow him down till he hit the sea. Presumably the pilot was killed immediately.

By now, no other 601 Squadron aircraft were in sight and so I returned to base, landing at 1308 hrs.

Pilot Officer Howard Mayers, an Australian who had only been with 601 Squadron for five days, was also successful, claiming an Me 109 'probable'. In total, 601 Squadron's operational sorties totalled fifty-eight hours and eleven minutes – more than double that of the previous day, indicating how busy 8 August 1940 proved to be.

No.238 Squadron's Hurricanes were next in action, although before relating their contribution to the defence of *Peewit*, we hear from the CO, Squadron Leader Harold Fenton:

> Our routine was to rise before first light, about 0330 hrs, have a coffee and go to dispersal. We then spent the day there, being scrambled at intervals, either the whole Squadron or a section of three, depending upon enemy activity. 609 Squadron, flying Spitfires, was also at Middle Wallop and we took it in turns to spend every third day at Warmwell, near Weymouth ... I have never been a keen early riser!
>
> Arriving at dispersal at 0400 hrs, most of the boys were able to curl up and get to sleep again, but once up, I had had it. Every time the telephone rang I gave a jump! ... We were often released for meals but, quite often, the Tannoy would announce '38 to readiness', so we would drop everything and dash back to dispersal.
>
> On 8 August 1940, we were, as usual, at readiness at first light. After breakfast, my Adjutant, Noel David, fetched me back to the office for a rare spell of administration. As soon as I left dispersal the squadron was scrambled – led by Flight Lieutenant Stuart Walch, and intercepted a big raid on a convoy South of the Isle of Wight.

Twelve of 238 Squadron's Hurricanes scrambled from Middle Wallop at 12.09 hrs. They were tasked to defend *Peewit*:

> A confused dogfight occurred, in which nine E/A fell to our guns. The scoring being: two Me 109s confirmed (PO Davis and FO Hughes), two Me 109 confirmed Sergeants Seabourne and Domagala (Polish), two Me 110 unconfirmed FO Stebrowski (Polish) and Sergeant Domagala (Polish); two Me 109s unconfirmed (PO Cawse and Sergeant Batt) and one Do 215 unconfirmed (Sergeant Little). This fight took place about six miles South of the Needles at about 12,000ft, above cloud. The E/A first attacked the convoy by shooting

down its balloon barrage. Number of E/A said to be 40+. When our aircraft arrived the E/A were dive-bombing the convoy. [ORB]

It was a hectic combat – but not without loss for 238 Squadron:

> Flight Lieutenant Turner and Flying Officer MacCaw have been missing since this engagement, although at least one of them is believed to have baled out, and landed by parachute.
>
> Flying Officer MacCaw came to the RAF through the University of Cambridge and had been with an Army co-op squadron before coming to 238, of which he was an original pilot … his slightly dreamy, dignified, personality is greatly missed. He was clearly material from which the best type of officer is made.
>
> Flight Lieutenant Turner's keenness, energy and good humour made him very popular with everyone, and his strong, reliable, character made him an excellent second-in-command. He has been greatly missed. [ORB]

Squadron Leader Fenton:

> During the scrap, Eric Turner, the 'A' Flight Commander, was shot down. There was no rescue launch in the area so I went out to look for him – on my own, as the others were all being refuelled and rearmed. I found no trace, but while searching I spotted a German seaplane at sea-level.
>
> I went down to attack, gave him a long burst but, being much faster, I overshot and his gunner must have got in a lucky one which cut an oil pipe. My windscreen was covered in black oil. I turned North but shortly my engine seized. Having so little height, I had to ditch rather than bale out.
>
> The propeller had stopped. I undid everything, harness and parachute straps, and to this day I can remember holding off above the waves. I had a Mae West on, of course, but this was in pre-dinghy days. I was thrown clear but banged my head on the way out – probably on the reflector sight on the windscreen. My un-pulled parachute was close-by and as buoyant as a lifebuoy, so I bobbed about for half an hour, somewhat dazed by the bang on the head.
>
> Fortunately, I had been seen by HMS *Basset*, an Admiralty Armed Trawler … a couple of the crew went over the side and hauled me out. They took me to the cabin, offered me Navy rum, put my uniform to dry and bandaged my head wound … They had had a rough time en route from Dover, torpedo attack, air bombed, the lot.

Not long after I was picked up the convoy was bombed again. Lying in the cabin with loud bangs going off, this did little for my morale. This time the ship fished out another pilot and he turned out to be German. We shared the cabin for the rest of the day. He had a little English so we managed to converse to some extent. I remember he hailed from Leipzig and flew an Me 110. Like me he had to strip for his clothes to dry and his few possessions comprised a large pack of condoms – I do not know that he thought he was coming for, with the next five years as a POW!

Flight Lieutenant Eric Turner, a Falkland Islander, was never seen again, and remains missing. Flying Officer Derek MacCaw's remains were later washed up on the enemy coast and interred at Sennerville-sur-Fécamp churchyard.

Five minutes after 238 Squadron had gone into action over *Peewit*, so too did its sister squadron, 609, at 12.40 hrs. Following what had been a run of bad luck caused by inexperience and poor sector controlling, this was 609's first day operating under 10 Group control, and according to the ORB, 'As far as 609 Squadron was concerned,' the first day on which 'the Nazi Blitz began.'

That morning, the Spitfires had scrambled at 09.00 hrs but arrived over *Peewit* too late to intercept.

Pilot Officer David Crook, 609 Squadron:

On 8 August 1940, we were down at Warmwell, and soon after dawn ordered to patrol a convoy off The Needles. It was a very clear day with a brilliant sun – just the sort of day that the Germans love, because they come over at a very big height and dive down to attack out of the sun. By doing this cleverly, they used to render themselves almost invisible until the attack was delivered. We hate these clear days and always pray for some high cloud to cover the sun.

This convoy was a very big one and escorted by several destroyers and balloons towed from barges in order to stop low dive bombing. I remember thinking at the time that there was obviously going to be a lot of trouble that day, because this convoy was far too large a prize for the Hun to miss. How right I was!

About 1130 hrs, six of us were ordered off again, but one turned back almost immediately with oxygen trouble, so there were only five of us. We steered out towards the convoy, which was now about twelve miles South of Bournemouth. There was a small layer of cloud and while dodging in and out of this, Mac [Flight Lieutenant James McArthur] and I got separated from the other three, and a moment later we also lost each other.

While looking around to try and find them, I glanced out towards the convoy and saw three of the balloons falling in flames. Obviously, an attack was starting and I climbed above the cloud layer and went towards the convoy at full throttle, climbing all the time towards the sun so that I could deliver my attack with the sun behind me.

I was now about five miles from the convoy and could see a big number of enemy fighters circling above, looking exactly like a swarm of flies buzzing round pot of jam. Below them the dive bombers were diving down on the ships and great fountains of white foam were springing up where their bombs struck the water. I could see that one or two ships had already been hit and were on fire.

I was now at 16,000ft above the whole battle and turned around to look for a victim. At that moment a Hurricane squadron appeared on the scene, and attacked right into the middle of the enemy fighters, which were split up immediately, and a whole series of individual combats started covering a very big area of the sky.

I saw several machines diving down with smoke and flames pouring from them, and then I perceived an Me 109 flying about 4,000ft below me. I immediately turned and dived down on him – he was a sitting target, but before I got to him a Hurricane appeared and shot him down in flames. I was very annoyed! I looked round but the attack was finished and the enemy were streaming back towards the French Coast, where it was very unwise to follow them.

Three ships in the convoy were blazing away fiercely and destroyers were taking off the crews. All the balloons had been shot down. I turned back for the English Coast and landed at Warmwell, to find everybody back safely and that the CO, Squadron Leader Darley, Michael Appleby and John Curchin had each destroyed an Me 110, while Mac had shot down two Junkers 87 dive bombers. He would have gotten an Me 110 also and had got his sights on it but nothing happened when he pressed his trigger. His ammunition was finished! So, a very lucky Me 110 lived to fight another day.

Pilot Officer Michael Appleby:

On 8 August 1940, I flew four times. On one of those sorties I was number two to Squadron Leader Darley, who put me in such a position over some Me 110s attacking a convoy that I had nothing to do but press the firing button – and both the engine cowlings and cockpit canopy came off as the aircraft was seen to dive into the sea. Much to the delight, we subsequently heard, of the Royal Navy!

The next RAF fighters on the scene were the three Hurricanes of 145 Squadron's Blue Section, led by Flight Lieutenant Adrian Boyd and scrambled from Tangmere at 12.40 hrs. Five minutes later, as the ORB points out, Boyd's heavily outnumbered formation engaged 'some twenty-five enemy aircraft twenty-five miles South of the Isle of Wight; in this action, three Me 110s and one Me 109 was shot down. Blue Section suffered no losses.'

At 16.00 hrs, Squadron Leader Peel scrambled from Tangmere, leading two further sections of 145 Squadron into action over *Peewit* ten minutes later, intercepting over 100 enemy aircraft which were attacking the battered convoy.

Pilot Officer Peter Parrott:

> We were ordered to patrol Swanage at 15,000ft, at 1600 hrs. I was flying No 2 in Yellow Section. When over The Needles a large number of E/A were seen dive-bombing the convoy. Yellow 1 led the Section to attack two Me 109s. I broke away and found a Ju 87 pulling out of its dive, after bombing. I attacked E/A from beam and he immediately turned-tail and headed north.
>
> I continued to attack from astern, and E/A finally crash-landed in a field on the edge of the sea, about two miles west of St Catherine's Point. The pilot appeared to be alright, and the aircraft, which struck a tree at the end of its landing run, did not appear badly damaged.

This was a *Stuka* of 4/St 77, which the pilot, *Unteroffizier* F. Pittrof, forced-landed at St Lawrence, on the Isle of Wight. His gunner, *Unteroffizier* R. Schubert, was killed.

In this action, 145 Squadron claimed the destruction of six Ju 87s and two Me 110s – but not without loss: three Hurricane pilots were reported missing.

Pilot Officer Parrott continues:

> On that day, in total, 145 Squadron claimed twenty-one enemy aircraft destroyed, and more possibly destroyed or damaged (although German records confirm that only seventeen were destroyed in total). We lost five pilots, among whom was Flying Officer Dickie Shuttleworth, who had been with us for some days. When I went over to Tangmere to collect our mail, one of the letters for him was marked from the House of Lords – and that was the first time any of us realised that he was a peer of the realm.

Lord Richard Ughtred Kay-Shuttleworth had, in fact, chosen to serve without his baronial title, hence his comrades' surprise. Now, the gallant former JP and Lancashire County Councillor was at the bottom of the Channel, never to be seen again. Similarly, Pilot Officer Ernest Wakeham and Sub-Lieutenant Francis Smith (of the Fleet Air Arm) were also reported missing.

Bestwood was a small collier in *Peewit*, just 200ft long, armed with a just single Lewis machine-gun. Fortunately the ship survived *Peewit* unscathed, although as his vessel passed the Nab Tower, her Master Captain J.H. Potts, said of the air attack that 'The scene changed in an instant from a perfectly flat sea to a typhoon.' This great air battle would now develop between the Nab and Dunnose, that great cliff on the Isle of Wight's southern shore.

At 16.00 hrs, 152 Squadron's 'B' Flight was also scrambled, rapidly lifting off from Warmwell and heading out to sea and *Peewit*. On reaching the convoy, according to Pilot Officer Douglas Shepley, the Spitfires were 'attacked by numerous Me 109s'.

At 16.07 hrs, Shepley opened fire on ten Me 109s at 16,000ft, ten miles South of Swanage, when a previously unseen enemy fighter that had been on his tail overshot, providing the RAF pilot a perfect target. Opening fire at fifty yards, the 109 was soon pouring black smoke and Shepley broke away with 'bits coming from it, his tail unit being apparently very seriously damaged'.

Pilot Officer Timothy Wildblood joined three Hurricanes chasing a 109 to the French Coast, at which he fired an ineffective burst from long-range. Pilot Officer Edward Hogg attacked two 109s successively, leaving one trailing black smoke. The engagement would prove memorable, however, for Sergeant Denis Robinson – his experience proving the folly of the tight 'vic' formation of three fighters:

> By this time I had destroyed an Me 109 on 25 July 1940 and another on 5 August 1940, but now it was my turn to be shot down by Me 109s of II/JG53, the 'Ace of Spades' *JagdGeschwader*, off Swanage, in Spitfire K9894. The facts are not particularly gratifying for either myself or Pilot Officer Walter Beaumont, who was also shot down with me that day. We were returning from a patrol in which we had intercepted the enemy and had used all our ammunition. Our eight Browning machine guns used ammo fast due to the limited storage space in the Spitfire's wings, and there was never more than fifteen seconds total fire power available.
>
> So we were returning to our base at Warmwell to refuel and rearm. There were three of us flying in vic formation with Beaumont on the left of the Flight Leader and myself on the right. We were flying in very tight formation probably about a foot from the leader's wingtips. Therefore, Beaumont and I had our eyes and concentration firmly fixed on the leader's aircraft. This was the way we flew in close formation early in the Battle until we learnt better later. Unfortunately, a group of Me109s spotted us and carried out an attack on our unprotected rear, which we had offered them on a plate.
>
> We ought to have known better, and actually did. We knew that it was vital to keep a good lookout at all times, but were lulled into a false sense of security and had relaxed our vigilance briefly. After all, we had had our scrap, were nearly safely home and, anyway, we had no ammo.
>
> The first thing I felt was the thud of bullets hitting my aircraft and a long line of tracer bullets streaming out ahead of my Spitfire.

In a reflex action I slammed the stick forward as far as it would go. For a brief second my Spitfire stood on its nose and I was looking straight down at Mother Earth, thousands of feet below. Thank God my Sutton harness was good and tight. I could feel the straps biting into my flesh as I entered the vertical with airspeed building up alarmingly. I felt fear mounting. Sweating, mouth dry and near panic. No ammo and an attacker right on my tail.

All this happened in seconds, but now the airspeed was nearly off the clock. I simply had to pull out and start looking for the enemy. That's what I did, turning and climbing at the same time. As I opened the throttle fully, with emergency boost selected to assist the climb, I noticed wisps of white smoke coming from the nose of my fighter. God, no! Fire! Suddenly the engine stopped. Apparently, a bullet in the glycol tank had dispersed all the coolant and even the faithful Merlin could not stand that for long at full power.

So that explained the white smoke. Blessed relief. The fuel tanks of high-octane fuel are situated very close to the pilot in a Spitfire. The dread of being burnt to death was one of the worst fears. It drew heavily on any reserves of courage one had. You can imagine by now, my eyes searching ... wildly, frantically looking for my adversary – but, as often happens in air combat, not a single plane was to be seen in the sky around me. The release of tension as I realised my good fortune is something that cannot be described.

You only know what it is like to be given back your life if you have been through that experience. The problems that still confronted me, sitting in the cockpit of a battle-damaged Spitfire, seemed almost trivial in comparison with my situation of a few seconds before. I experienced this feeling several times during the Battle and it had a profound effect on me, which remains with me to this day. It somehow changed my value system, so that things that had seemed important before never had the same degree of importance again. Maybe this is what generated the anti-authority behaviour among us. It was no good telling us not to do a victory roll because our aircraft may be damaged, for example, because this seemed a trivial risk compared with our experiences of combat.

The end of the episode was something of an anti-climax. I still had plenty of altitude and time to think. I prepared to bale out and began going through the procedure in my mind. Release the Sutton harness, make sure all connections to flying helmet are free, slide the canopy back, roll the aircraft until inverted, push the stick forward and out you go. Then start counting before pulling the D-ring. How many? My memory went blank. Was it three or ten? God! There is a vast difference between the two, I thought. Well, as long as the interval is sufficient to get clear of the aircraft before pulling the D-ring it should be OK.

During this soliloquy I'd got the Spit into a steady glide. It was gliding rather like a brick, but handling reasonably well and responding to the controls almost normally. I surveyed what I could see of the damage from the cockpit. Not much, apart from a few bullet holes here and there – particularly in the starboard wing. It worried me to abandon the old bus to certain destruction on to heaven knows what, perhaps a school full of children. Besides, I was by no means convinced that the bale-out procedure I had rehearsed was not without considerable risk. I could get caught up in the cockpit paraphernalia ... I might be struck by the tailplane ... or what if the parachute didn't open? No. I decided to stay with her and force-land in a suitable field.

By now most of the fields looked pretty small, so I decided it would be with the wheels-up. I picked a field near Wareham that looked suitable, slid back the canopy and commenced an approach. At about 200ft the boundary loomed up. Full flap and a flare out near the ground achieved a creditable touch-down. So far so good. I was quite pleased with myself as the Spit slithered across the grass. Then, suddenly, I felt her going up onto her nose and, I thought, onto her back. With an almighty crash the canopy slammed shut over my head and the cockpit filled with dirt, completely blinding me.

The aircraft seemed to me to be upside-down and I was trapped. That awful fear of burning returned at full strength. I grabbed the canopy with all my might and threw it backwards. To my utter amazement it shot back easily, and the excessive adrenaline-boosted force I had used nearly tore my arms from their sockets. Now I could see that the aircraft had finished up vertically on its nose, in a ditch I hadn't seen from the air.

My actions now became somewhat comic. It was obvious that I could easily jump clear and I commenced to do so without much hesitation. To my utter horror I couldn't move. Suddenly, I realised I was struggling against the Sutton harness, still buckled firmly in place. An instant pull released the pin. I was free. As I stood up to jump my head was jerked violently backwards. This time it was my flying helmet still attached to the radio and oxygen sockets in the cockpit.

Removing this final impediment I jumped to the ground, leaving my helmet in the cockpit. To my surprise the Spitfire didn't burn. I stood back and took in the scene as locals arrived to convey me to a pub near Wareham and fill me with whisky. I had a slight bullet graze on my leg, but was otherwise unhurt and felt strangely elated. Next day I was back on ops again.

Later my thoughts turned to my actions at the time and to my survival. Firstly, I must have sensed without fully realising it that the tracer from the enemy fire was coming from left to right direction. Since I was on the right of the Section Leader I could not turn left and collide with him. The only a way to go was a right-turn, which would enable the attacker to tighten his turn and would have made me an easy target.

The instant reaction of stick hard forward, causing the Merlin engine to belch smoke from the exhausts may have convinced the Me 109 pilot that he had been successful in his attack, or perhaps the sudden change in attitude of my aircraft caused the attacker to overshoot his target. Also, the Me 109s operating over the Dorset coast were far from their French bases and being short of fuel couldn't hang around too long in a dogfight or pursuit. It would have been nice for us if we had known this fuel problem at the time, but we did not. I only found this out years later, after the war. To this day I still do not know what gave me that sixth sense and instant reaction to jam the stick hard forward.

Telling this story helps me to deal with my survival syndrome. In a difficult-to-describe way, it is though I am speaking for the other chaps who did not make it. Their final story would have been infinitely more readable than mine. One constantly asks: 'Why did I survive ... why did others not?'

Sergeant Robinson had come down near Langton Matravers. Pilot Officer Beaumont was shot-up by a 109 while attacking another, his cockpit filling with smoke as his Spitfire span away out of control. Recovering, he made a safe forced-landing near Sergeant Robinson; neither pilot was hurt.

At 16.05 hrs, the whole of 213 Squadron was scrambled from Exeter with orders to patrol the Portland area at 12,000ft. At 17.35 hrs, Red Section engaged Me 109s just 100ft above the waves, fifteen miles North of Guernsey.

Flight Lieutenant John 'Jackie' Sing reported that:

> No 2 of Red Section sighted two Me 109s. Having identified then Red 2 attacked one while I was trying to find the second, which had climbed into the sun. I saw Sergeant Norris (Red 2) open fire and hit auxiliary tank on Me 109. He then broke away. The machine had apparently suffered no other damage so I attacked and shot it down in flames. I then saw the second Me 109. This I caught up and gave it a short burst before running out of ammunition. No apparent damage done to second Me 109.

Sing was credited with the enemy fighter destroyed. It was an exciting sortie for Pilot Officer Alexander Osmand, flying in Yellow Section, being his first sight of the enemy, recording in his logbook 'Portland to St Catherine's Point to ten miles South of Bridport. Saw Red Section chase two Me 109s!'

At 16.43 hrs, all four sections of 43 Squadron, up from Tangmere, had also joined the fray over *Peewit* – losing Pilot Officers Johannes Oelofse, a South African, and John Cruttenden, both of whom crashed into the Channel and were killed. More fortunate, however, were Pilot Officers Frank Carey and Charles Woods-Scawen, both of whom returned to base safely having been shot-up and wounded.

Lieutenant Arthur Hague, HMS *Borealis*:

> We made good progress towards Portsmouth until about 1700 hrs when a further wave of dive-bombers appeared overhead. Vulnerable and defenceless as we were there was little alternative but to take to the only remaining boat and lie off from where we had an uninterrupted view of the action, as RAF fighters swept down on the enemy. Clusters of jettisoned bombs detonated around us and several bombers fell blazing into the sea.
>
> Afterwards, pulling back to our ship we found her listing heavily to port, having sustained a direct hit or near miss which must have damaged the bulkhead. So HMS *Renee* picked us up. About twenty minutes later *Borealis* slid, stern first, beneath the waters of the English Channel. I remember *Renee*'s captain shouting to one of his crew to remove his cap as a mark of respect!

As the enemy retired, the scene was positively Wagnerian: burning balloons and ships provided a dramatic backdrop for the thirty or so airmen of both sides bobbing around in the sea, shot down and hoping for rescue. The convoy itself was decimated: seven ships had been sunk, fourteen damaged with a total of twenty-four sailors killed; only four ships remained intact. Also among the dead, sadly, was AC1 Raymond Wheeler, killed aboard RAF High Speed Launch (HSL) 116, whose loss was covered by the *Western Mail* five days later:

> Although not a 'good sailor', Raymond Wheeler, a 17-year-old RAF wireless operator, of Southampton, volunteered to serve in a launch sent to rescue Nazi airmen shot down in the Channel. The launch was machine-gunned by nine German warplanes and Wheeler was killed.
>
> While the launch cruised in rough sea Wheeler had been so seasick that another member of the crew had to support him, but the boy would not give in and continued to send messages until the enemy planes attacked.
>
> He carried out his duties very gallantly and stayed at his post to the end, Wheeler's mother was told by the young wireless operator's commanding officer.

The gallant teenager's grave can be found today at All Saints' churchyard, Fawley, Hampshire.

Squadron Leader Fenton, 238 Squadron:

> The convoy was thoroughly disorganised by late afternoon: some ships had been sunk and those remaining were ordered into port. I was put ashore at Gosport late that evening and taken to Haslar RN hospital to have my head sewn up ... The place was full of casualties from the Convoy.

Lieutenant Hague once again:

> It was later officially stated that some 300 enemy planes took part in these attacks. Those ships of CW9 *Peewit* which survived the bombing continued westwards with their trawler escorts. The remaining ships of our flotilla, minus their balloons, made for Portsmouth. Renee anchored in St Helen's Roads overnight and the following day landing we *Borealis* survivors to the Royal Navy Barracks.

On this day, which had seen the heaviest fighting to date, Fighter Command lost fourteen Hurricane and Spitfire pilots, missing or killed in action, while another later died of wounds. Of these, twelve were lost in the defence of *Peewit* – the most losses in a single day thus far.

No.145 Squadron, in fact, had suffered the highest number of casualties defending the convoy, five of its pilots being either reported missing or known to have been killed in action. In response, 145 had claimed twenty-one enemy aircraft destroyed, prompting the following congratulatory signals:

Secretary of State for Air	'Congratulations on your splendid achievements today.'
CAS	'Well done 145 Squadron on your hard-fighting today. Good work by all.'
AOC 11 Group	Group Commander sends warm congratulations to 145 Squadron on their outstanding success during three heavy engagements against superior numbers today and sincerely hopes that some of the missing pilots will turn up as frequently happened in the past. Today's fighting demonstrates fine offensive spirit, good leadership and straight shooting which reflects great credit to the whole Squadron.'

KANALKAMPF DIARY, 1 AUGUST – 12 AUGUST 1940

The squadron responded to Air Vice-Marshal Park, AOC 11 Group, with the following acknowledgement:

> Your message greatly appreciated by all ranks of the squadron. We consider ourselves lucky for the opportunities we were given today.

Perhaps the simplest but most moving tribute was received fifty years later by Wing Commander Peter Parrott, as he later became, in a letter from Lieutenant Commander Arthur Hague, as the former captain of HMS *Borealis* was all those years later, 'Thanks for all that you and your colleagues in 145 Squadron did for my shipmates and myself on that day.'

In total, the RAF pilots had claimed thirty-one enemy aircraft confirmed destroyed and twenty-eight more unconfirmed in the defence of *Peewit*, and a further seventeen damaged. The Air Ministry claimed that 400 German aircraft had been involved, sixty of which were destroyed for the loss of sixteen RAF fighters.

These figures were inevitably exaggerated, given the ferocity and extent of the fighting, but even so, the *Luftwaffe* had suffered the loss of eight Me 109s, a 110 and seven *Stukas* destroyed, plus eighteen more fighters and dive-bombers damaged – some terminally. *Peewit* had undeniably suffered – but Convoy CW9 had got through, despite the enemy's best efforts, and the determination of the defenders was now crystal clear.

On the wider front, there was little action for Fighter Command's squadrons not engaged in the defence of *Peewit*, although at 14.40 hrs, Red Section of 234 Squadron, based at St Eval in Cornwall, intercepted and damaged a Ju 88 reconnaissance bomber over Falmouth, this being shared by Pilot Officer Edward Mortimer-Rose and Sergeant Alan Harker.

On this day, Fighter Command's disposition and strength was:

10 Group	3 Hurricane, 4 Spitfire, 1 Blenheim and 1 Gladiator squadrons.
11 Group	13 Hurricane, 6 Spitfire and 2 Blenheim squadrons.
12 Group	5 Hurricane, 6 Spitfire, 2 Defiant and 2 Blenheim squadrons.
13 Group	8 Hurricane (plus one flight of 232 Squadron), 3 Spitfire, 1 Defiant and 1 Blenheim squadrons.

Air Chief Marshal Dowding now had twenty-nine squadrons of Hurricanes and nineteen of Spitfires – and, when all is said and done, it really was these two types that mattered in the daylight battle. It can also be seen that although the greater strength was deployed in 11 Group, there remained a fair spread of Hurricane and Spitfire squadrons throughout the Command – the strategy of which would soon pay dividends.

On 8 August 1940, while Nos. 10 and 11 groups of Fighter Command defended *Peewit*, seventy-seven aircraft of Coastal Command flew various anti-invasion, anti-submarine and reconnaissance sorties, although the lack of cloud cover over the Continent hampered these operations.

Flight Lieutenant Fletcher, commanding 'B' Flight of 235 Squadron, led three Blenheims escorting a 59 Squadron aircraft on a reconnaissance of Le Havre and Trouville but were attacked by fifteen Me 110s of II/ZG2. In the running battle that followed, two of the Blenheim gunners claimed to have destroyed one of their assailants in flames, the Blenheims returning to base without loss. Meanwhile, the majority of 2 Group's Blenheims were forced to abandon their various sorties owing to unfavourable weather, only the airfields at Valkenburg and Schiphol being bombed by two aircraft.

That night, Bomber Command sent Wellingtons to attack the battleship *Bismarck* at Hamburg, and various military and industrial targets in Germany, including airfields. One Hampden failed to return from a raid of Ludwigshaven. The *Luftwaffe* was also active by night, some forty raiders crossing the English coast, mostly from *Luftflotte* 3, concentrating on the western half of England, with Birmingham being hit for the first time. There was minor enemy air activity around Norwich and Dover to the East and South-east, although the purpose of these incursions appears mainly to disrupt and harass the civilian population.

Daily Home Intelligence Report:

> Morale is high and people are cheerful ... The effect of the Prime Minister's warning about invasion is wearing off and many people are now more apprehensive of a long and dreary winter than of immediate invasion.

FRIDAY, 9 AUGUST 1940

Pilot Officer Peter Parrott, 145 Squadron: 'Following *Peewit*, we were given a day off.' It was a well-earned respite.

After the previous day's exertions, and because preparations were underway for *Adler Tag*, the *Luftwaffe* much reduced its air operations on this day. At 05.40 hrs, however, Blue Section of 213 Squadron, Pilot Officer Wilfred Sizer, Flight Sergeant Charles Grayson and Sergeant Sydney Stuckey, was aloft from Exeter and patrolling the area between base and Yeovil – home to the Westland aircraft factory. Over Yeovil, the Hurricanes intercepted a Ju 88, the rear-gunner of which Sizer silenced before the bomber escaped.

In the north-east, a He 111 of 7/KG26 bombed Sunderland, causing widespread (but not serious) damage, and was intercepted over Newcastle at 11.50 hrs by Yellow Section of 79 Squadron, scrambled from Acklington to intercept. Flight Lieutenant Rupert Clerke, Pilot Officer George Nelson-Edwards and Sergeant John Wright attacked, but the bomber escaped into cloud with white smoke pouring from both engines. Green Section, led by Pilot Officer Thomas Parker, was also vectored to intercept, catching the *Heinkel* gliding through cloud. The raider crashed into the sea off Sunderland, the enemy crew fortunately being rescued and captured by the RN.

At 14.15 hrs, 234 Squadron's Red Section, comprising Pilot Officer Edward Mortimer-Rose, Pilot Officer Richard Hardy and the Polish Sergeant Joseph Szlagowski, was up on patrol from St Eval over Falmouth when, as Hardy reported:

> At 7,000ft sighted E/A (Do 215) at 3,000ft above cloud. Quarter attack carried out on port side, diving slightly and overtaking. Broke away to port in cloud and that was the last I saw of E/A.

The other two pilots' attacks were similarly inconclusive, although the section was credited with a 'damaged'.

In spite of the reduced air activity, the day was not without loss, sadly, for Fighter Command, as the Drem-based 605 Squadron reported on events occurring at 16.45 hrs:

> Sergeant (Robert) Ritchie, while returning from a patrol with CO (Squadron Leader Walter Churchill) and Pilot Officer (Cyril) Passey suspected glycol leak developed while aircraft was six miles out to sea, East of Dunbar, height 15,000ft. It is assumed fumes asphyxiated pilot and aircraft dived into sea one mile offshore. Pilot picked up by motor patrol vessel *Eunmara* but Sergeant Ritchie was dead, due to a broken neck. [ORB]

At 15.55 hrs, ten Spitfires of 64 Squadron were scrambled from Kenley and vectored towards Dover, where Me 109s of JG51 were strafing the balloons of 961 Balloon Squadron. In the ensuing action, Sergeant Jack Mann's Spitfire was hit by a 20mm Oerlikon round, although the pilot was unhurt and he returned safely to base. No losses were suffered by the enemy.

During the day, Coastal Command flew the usual round of routine sorties, although 59 Squadron attacked and damaged the German airfield now established on Guernsey, as did a 2 Group crew, the majority of which had again been forced to abort owing to unsuitable weather conditions. No.59 Squadron ended the day with an aircraft and crew missing from a reconnaissance of Cherbourg, and 500 Squadron lost an Anson, coned in searchlights, while patrolling the Dutch and Belgian coasts.

By night, Wellingtons attacked a factory in Köln, various other industrial targets in Germany and airfields in the Netherlands, in addition to dropping propaganda leaflets. Whitleys successfully attacked an aluminium factory at Ludwigshaven and two airfields; all night-raiders returned safely.

Daily Home Intelligence Report:

> The news of the RAF successes yesterday has produced general satisfaction in south-western and Midland Regions. Scotland records

cheerful comment, but some people are wondering whether our losses in ships and planes do not outweigh the German losses. There is general satisfaction that the Germans state have lost only two planes. Belfast records great admiration and enthusiasm at the result of the air battle.

Edward Bishop, journalist:

> Congratulations flowed ... Civilians were heartened by the figures. Eagerly, they bought newspapers, as avid as punters for the 'results', and the newspaper sellers rose to the occasion. Their chalked-up headlines caused much amusement and delight: 'Only another 39 down but extra time being played – 61 after extra time.'
> Every fighter pilot on both sides was anxious to notch-up victories, and the exaggerated figures exhilarated the people of both nations. Communiques from the Channel coast brought joy into the hearts of the German people in the Fatherland. Germans found a fascination in discussing what were, as they now thought, the last days of England ... The delight at the *Luftwaffe* figures was enhanced by 'ball-by-ball' commentaries which the radio relayed as air attacks increased ... Less than a year earlier, Britain had declared war, an action which seemed inexplicable to Germans who believed they were tidying up their eastern frontiers for the security of Western Europe. Now, Britain must pay for her foolish interference with the *Führer*'s programme.

SATURDAY, 10 AUGUST 1940

Right up until the previous day, the OKL intended to unleash the *Adlerangriff* and make 10 August 1940 the much-vaunted *Adler Tag* – the launch of an unparalleled aerial assault on the RAF. For all the Wagnerian rhetoric, the day would be a damp squib: thunder storms swept across northern France, the English Channel and the British Isles. There was nothing for it, the meteorological people advised: *Adler Tag* had to be postponed until 13 August 1940.

At 05.20 hrs, three sections of 501 Squadron's Hurricanes left Gravesend and flew down to operate from Hawkinge. Patrolling over the coastal airfield at 07.25 hrs, Red Section encountered and attacked what was believed to be either a snooping Do 17 or Do 215, but the German pilot easily slipped away safely into the clag.

Just after 18.00 hrs, three bombs fell on Norwich, causing little damage, although one hit a timber shed at the Carrow Works. Similarly, owing to the weather, this raider also escaped unscathed.

As ever, Coastal Command was active throughout the day, patrolling and maintaining reconnaissance of the enemy ports along the Dutch and north-west

French coasts. During the afternoon, the Thornaby-based 220 Squadron Hudson flown by a Sergeant Knowles encountered a Blohm & Voss Ha 140 seaplane some fifty miles off Cromer, which was initially misidentified as an easy-prey He 115. Having manoeuvred into an attacking position the Blenheim crew realised its mistake as the faster German aircraft turned the tables.

Nonetheless, several hits were recorded against the Ha 140, which broke off the action and Sergeant Knowles returned safely to base. Spitfires of both 'A' and 'B' Flights of 541 Squadron, 1 PRU, were also active photographing the enemy coastline, although low 10/10ths clouds around Le Havre hampered photography in that area. No.2 Group's Blenheims were again similarly impeded by the weather, only eight managing to find and bomb airfields in the Netherlands and France. A Blenheim of Wattisham's 110 Squadron inexplicably failed to return from one of these sorties, and Watton's 82 Squadron lost an aircraft to the guns of 8/JG2's *Oberleutnant* Karl-Heinz Metz off Le Havre; both crews were killed.

That night, Bomber Command attacked naval and oil installations in addition to German airfields, one Hampden of 144 Squadron failing to return from a raid on Homburg.

Daily Home Intelligence Report:

> Morale [in London] on the whole quite good but in some of the poorer districts people rather unhappy and worried about making ends meet, especially where husband on service and evacuated children always needing new clothes.

The Eastern (Cambridge) Region noted that:

> There is still a tendency for people to express perplexity at the big difference between our planes and those of the German Command. When German communiques claim equally overwhelming successes many people suspect that our own communiques are drawn up on a similar principle There is a general desire for a convincing explanation as to why our own air craft are so strikingly superior.

SUNDAY, 11 AUGUST 1940

Although the actual *Adler Tag* had been postponed until 13 August 1940, the *Luftwaffe* in France was now well organised, ready and eager for the assault to begin.

The heavy fighting over *Peewit*, however, had perhaps caused the OKL and OKW to ponder the unpalatable fact that Fighter Command was not going to be a pushover – possibly explaining why Count Ciano recorded in his diary that,

> The German air force has asked that our planes be sent to collaborate in the action against England. When we offered them a month ago they were promptly refused. Now Germany asks for them. Why? I am not very much in favour of this for technical and political reasons.

On what would be a viscous day of fighting, the enemy's opening salvo was aimed at Dover. At 07.30 hrs, four 64 Squadron Spitfires were scrambled from Kenley and vectored towards Dover – but before the RAF fighters arrived on the scene, at 07.37 hrs, Me 109s of 3/*Erprobungsgruppe* 210 attacked, destroying more of 961 Balloon Squadron's barrage balloons. The air raid warning siren wailed over Dover just before the first balloon burst into flame above the Crabble Athletic Ground, and seconds later another was set alight flying from Cherry Tree Avenue. Also, the Dover gasworks in Union Road received a burst of 20mm cannon fire, setting sheds afire, while houses were damaged in Randolph Road.

Just as quickly as the violence arrived, it disappeared, the 109s withdrew from their lightning-quick raid before being intercepted. Seconds later, Me 110s of *Erprobugsgruppe* 210 bombed Dover Harbour, again escaping interception, although without causing serious damage.

At 05.05 hrs, 32 Squadron had once more flown from Biggin Hill to operate from Hawkinge. From there, at 07.40 hrs, Flight Lieutenant Mike Crossley DFC led 'A' Flight up to patrol Hawkinge at 15,000ft, followed by Flight Lieutenant Peter Brothers and 'B' Flight five minutes later.

Too late to intercept *Erprobungsgruppe* 210, German fighters remained active and between Dover and Deal, Crossley observed,

> nine Me 109s coming towards him at same level. He fired a burst but observed no damage; at same time three Me 109s dived from behind. Pilot Officer [Anthony] Barton, who was No 3, fired at the last one and saw large pieces falling off it. The destruction of this aircraft was confirmed by searchlights. [ORB]

At 07.50 hrs, 74 'Tiger' Squadron – with the newly promoted Squadron Leader 'Sailor' Malan DFC leading – was scrambled from Manston.

Squadron Leader Malan:

> I was Dysoe Leader when Squadron was sent off to intercept bandits approaching Dover at a reported height of 13,000ft. I climbed on a ENE course to 20,000ft into the sun, and then turned down-sun towards Dover, and surprised eight Me 109s at 20,000ft, flying in pairs, staggered in line astern, towards Dover.
>
> I ordered the squadron to attack. Some of them adopted the usual German fighter evasive tactics – i.e. quick half-roll and dive. On

KANALKAMPF DIARY, 1 AUGUST – 12 AUGUST 1940

this occasion, as the air seemed clear of German aircraft above us, I followed one down and overtook him after he had dived 2,000ft – opening fire during the dive at 200 yards range with deflection. He levelled out at about 12,000ft when I gave him two 2-second bursts at 200 yards range. He was in a quick half-roll and dived towards the French coast.

I closed again to 100 yards range and gave him another two or three 2-second bursts, when he suddenly burst into flames and was obscured by heavy smoke. This was at 4,000ft, one-mile NW of Cap Gris Nez. I did not watch him go in but flew back as fast as I could. I did not see the engagement of the rest of the squadron.

Normally I have strongly advised all pilots in the squadron not to follow 109s on the half-roll and dive because in most cases we are outnumbered, and generally at least one layer of enemy fighters is some thousands of feet above. It was found that even at high altitudes there was no difficulty in overtaking E/A on diving, apart from the physical strain imposed on the body when pulling out.

Malan was credited with an 'unconfirmed destroyed'.

It was a hectic and confused combat, once more fought against elements of JG51, with various *Staffel*-strength formations sweeping over the Channel. The 'Tigers', having attacked out of the sun and achieved complete surprise, also claimed seven other Me 109s destroyed, a probable and three damaged.

Only one of these destroyed claims was confirmed however, and just one Me 109, in fact, is known not to have returned to France, that being *Feldwebel* Walz of 5/JG51, who remains missing and was very likely 'Sailor' Malan's victim. No.74 Squadron also suffered a loss, although Pilot Officer Stevenson baled out of his Spitfire over the Channel and, having drifted eleven miles out to sea, was luckily rescued by a Motor Torpedo Boat.

This was the only Spitfire down in this engagement, although between 08.03 and 08.10 hrs, three JG51 pilots each claimed a Spitfire destroyed over Dover. It is also likely that the 'Me 109' confirmed by 'searchlights' as having been destroyed by 32 Squadron's Pilot Officer Barton was, in fact, Stevenson's crashing Spitfire.

After the initial combats off Dover, however, a lull then followed, until 09.00 hrs when nine enemy aircraft stooged around the Dover Strait for thirty minutes before being reinforced. Ten minutes later, thirty more 'bandits' approached Dover.

At 09.32 hrs, 64 Squadron's Spitfires were scrambled from Kenley, Dover-bound, followed at 09.50 hrs by those of 74 Squadron from Manston, and at 11.00 hrs 32 Squadron's Hurricanes from Biggin Hill. At 09.51 hrs, 64 Squadron sighted twenty Me 109s over Dover, but being 9,000ft below the Germans it was another ten minutes before the Kenley Spitfires engaged. Indeed, by the time both 64 Squadron and 74 Squadron came into action, the Germans were already retiring.

No.64 Squadron engaged Me 109s at 10.15 hrs, as Pilot Officer Leonard King, Yellow 1 of 'A' Flight, reported:

> I was flying eastwards just North of Dover when I observed AA fire bursting at 13,000ft. I headed towards the bursts and observed from the last burst the direction of E/A. I intercepted approximately six but these were diving so fast I was unable to engage. The second occasion I was flying East at 18,000ft over mid-Channel when I saw a flicker of sunlight on aircraft cabin roof about 6,000ft higher and to the North of me.
>
> I climbed to 24,000ft and observed approximately twelve Me 109s going SE. I engaged the last one and delivered an astern attack at 150 yards, closing to 90 yards. I gave E/A one burst 2 seconds and one 3 seconds. The E/A dropped port wing, turned over and dived seawards. I then saw tracer passing my cabin and I broke away to the right to shake off the Me 109 on my tail.

King was credited with a 109 destroyed, as was Squadron Leader MacDonell, while Pilot Officer James O'Meara claimed one 'unconfirmed'.

Simultaneously with 64 Squadron, Squadron Leader Malan led 74 into action:

> I was Dysoe Leader ordered to intercept enemy fighters approaching Dover. I climbed on a north-easterly course to 24,000ft and did a sweep to the right, approaching Dover from the sea. I saw a number of small groups of Me 109s in mid-Channel at about 24,000ft and we approached most of them, diving towards the French coast.
>
> I intercepted two Me 109s, dived onto their tails with Red Section. I delivered two 2-second bursts at 150 yards, but as I was overshooting I went off and the remainder of the Section continued the attack. I immediately climbed back towards where Blue and Green Sections were waiting above and tried to attract their attention, but owing to R/T difficulties did not manage to get them to form up on me.
>
> I proceeded towards Dover by myself. I attacked two Me 109s at 25,000ft about mid-Channel, delivered two 2-second bursts with deflection at the rearmost one, and saw my bullets entering the fuselage with about 15° deflection. He immediately flicked off to the left and I delivered two long bursts at the leading one. He poured out quite a quantity of white vapour. Eight 109s, who had previously escaped my attention, dived towards me and I climbed in right-hand spiral, and they made no attempt to follow.
>
> I proceeded towards Dover on the climb and saw ten Me 109s at 27,000ft in line astern with one straggler, which I tried to pick off but

was unable to close the range without being turned on by the leader of the formation. I circled on a wide sweep with them for about ten minutes while I attempted to notify the remainder of the squadron by R/T. This proved to be impossible, owing to heavy atmospherics, and in the end I gave up and returned to Manston.

The Me 109 was claimed as damaged. Warrant Officer Ernest Mayne also damaged a 109 and claimed another destroyed (unconfirmed), as did Pilot Officer Freeborn. The enemy fighters belonged to III/JG26, which had been balloon-busting at Dover harbour; *Leutnant* Bürschgens' Me 109E-1 was damaged and force-landed near his base at Caffiers.

Some of 74 Squadron's combats had occurred at 27,000ft, 'Sailor' Malan adding to his report that, 'it seemed to me that at 27,000ft I had no superior speed or manoeuvrability over the 109'. In previous combats 74 Squadron's pilots had reported their Spitfires outfighting the 109 at heights of up to 20,000ft – but the German fighter was found to excel at high altitude, 25,000ft and above, being slightly superior to the Spitfire and considerably better than the Hurricane. In fighter combat, height is everything – so this performance advantage was a very definite plus for the enemy.

At 07.30 hrs a hostile plot had appeared on the radar screen approaching a northbound convoy off Southend, *Booty*, *Agent* and *Arena*, comprising over fifty merchant ships. A section of 56 Squadron's Hurricanes were up from North Weald and patrolling over the convoy but saw no trace of the enemy owing to thick cloud – but the Germans spotted and reported the convoy's position.

Erprobungsgruppe 210 took-off at 11.20 hrs, rendezvousing with its Me 110 fighter escort, provided by ZG26, at 1,500ft over Gravelines – heading for the merchantmen, now off Harwich-Clacton. Flying a mixture of Me 110s armed with a hefty 30mm cannon and others fitted out for the fighter-bomber role with external bomb-racks, 1/*Erprobungsgruppe* 210 attacked the convoy, without interference from RAF fighters, in concert with Do 17s from 9/KG2, which now specialised in anti-shipping raids. Soon over their target, cloud was problematic, but *Hauptmann* Rubensdörffer's men claimed the destruction of an 8,000-ton ship, probably the 5,500-ton tanker *Oiltrader*, which was badly damaged. The SS *Kirkwood* was also hit but remained afloat, and HM Trawler *Edwardian*, a trawler converted to minesweeping configuration, was so badly hit that the skipper, James Ramshaw, could only save his ship, with three dead crew aboard, by running aground.

No.610 Squadron's Spitfires had been brought forward from Biggin Hill to Hawkinge, Squadron Leader John Ellis leading Red, Green, Blue and Yellow Sections off at 10.46 hrs to patrol the Channel:

> Red Section ordered to investigate E/A on water in mid-Channel, remainder of Squadron acting as above guard. Flight Lieutenant Brian Smith (Red Leader) attacked a He 59 flying low over the water

off Calais, giving it two or three short bursts and seeing his tracer appear to hit it – E/A used gentle evasive turns. He then fired at another E/A without result. Flying Officer [Douglas] Wilson saw three motor boats off Cap Gris Nez pointing towards Dover. Flying Officer Bernard Gardner saw a large splash which he attributes to an aircraft crashing in the Channel but was unable to identify it.

Flight Lieutenant Smith was credited with having damaged the enemy Red Cross seaplane at 11.15 hrs – but two 610 pilots were missing: Flight Sergeant John Tanner and Sergeant William Neville, the former's remains later washing ashore on the French coast; the latter was never seen again. It is likely that these two pilots were ambushed and picked off by *Hauptmann* Dietrich Hrabak and *Oberfeldwebel* Karl Hier of 4/JG54, who both claimed Spitfires over the Channel at this time.

At 11.45 hrs, while the *Erprobungsgruppe* and KG2 attack was in progress, Flight Lieutenant William Harper was leading 'A' Flight of 17 Squadron, operating from Debden's forward base at Martlesham Heath, patrolling near the northbound ships, when he sighted,

a number of E/A and with Pilot Officer (Leonard) Stevens attacked an Me 109 but lost it in cloud. Pilot Officer Stevens then attacked an Me 109 but lost it in cloud. Pilot Officer Stevens then attacked and destroyed an Me 110 Jaguar and gave a short burst at a Do 215 but did not observe result.

Flying Officer (David) Hanson attacked an Me 110 Jaguar and put starboard engine out of action. Enemy return fire started a fire in his cockpit which he put out by side-slipping, and damaged his undercarriage. Pilot Officer (Kenneth) Manger DFC, leading Yellow Section, chased an Me 110 eastwards and is missing. Pilot Officer (Geoffrey) Pittman and Sergeant (Glyn) Griffiths attacked and destroyed an Me 110 Jaguar.

After return from the patrol, Pilot Officer Stevens took off to search for Manger. Flight Lieutenant Harper, Pilot Officer Pitman and Sergeant Griffiths also searched extensively on their way back to Debden.

Flight Lieutenant Manger remains missing.

Squadron Leader Peter Townsend had led Yellow Section of his 85 Squadron, also operating from Martlesham, up to patrol the convoy at 11.30 hrs, arriving ten minutes later, sighting an unidentified aircraft at 4,000ft, a couple of miles away but which disappeared into cloud when the Hurricanes turned to investigate.

Three miles East of the convoy, at 11.50 hrs, Townsend again encountered the aircraft, now identified as a Do 17, at which he fired a short burst from 300 yards astern, causing black smoke to emit from the starboard engine before the raider once more slipped away into cloud. Townsend's Yellow 2 had fallen behind owing to engine problems, so the CO of 85 Squadron continued patrolling eastwards when, some thirty miles East of the convoy, the Hurricane pilot saw 'twenty plus Me 110s circling at about 4,000ft', which he reported to 'Hornpipe' (Debden Sector Control).

Upon sighting the British fighter, the Me 110s turned East:

> I followed, intermittently losing sight of them, and finally decided to return to convoy. Unfortunately I sighted land some twenty miles South of convoy, when twenty miles off coast. Turned North and saw large splash in sea, fifteen miles NE at approx. 1210 hrs. Proceeded towards it. Passed two Spitfires proceeding South. In vicinity of splash (approx. thirty–forty miles East of Harwich) came upon twenty plus ME 110 again. Waited above in cloud cover and picking what seemed to be an isolated one some 200ft below, dived steeply head-on and took snapshot, bullets appeared to enter right wing of Me but no result observed.
>
> Immediately on breaking upwards saw I was being attacked head-on by ME 110; we passed each other pretty close, and I withdraw at high speed towards nearest cloud. (Me's were circling and it was a matter of extreme difficulty to select an outsider without getting involved in circle). Emerged from cloud again and selected another prospective victim. Dived from above and behind but was immediately attacked by another from behind.
>
> After a short burst – inaccurate – hurried into cloud again pursued by my attacker. Spitfire only other British aircraft seen, attacked him and he immediately turned down towards 'circle' again, turned on him to attack as he went down, but he rejoined 'circle' before I could get a good lead on him. Spitfire seen deploying into cloud. As petrol was low and my efforts to isolate a single Me 110 were not being very profitable, I withdrew to the West and landed at Martlesham Heath.

Squadron Leader Townsend was credited with a Do 17 damaged, while Sergeant Harold Allgood and Sergeant Cyril Hampshire were both awarded Me 110s destroyed but 'unconfirmed'. Pilot Officer David Hanson and Flying Officer Leonard Stevens both returned to base in shot-up Hurricanes.

The Spitfires Squadron Leader Townsend had seen were those of 74 Squadron; Pilot Officer John Freeborn:

> I was leading 74 Squadron when it took off from Manston at 1145 hrs to patrol a convoy off Clacton. While on patrol I sighted a formation of forty Me 110s in vics of three and four approaching the convoy

below the clouds (8/10 heavy cumulus at 4,000ft). I led the squadron in a diving attack into the defensive circle which the E/A formed. In the dive and climb which followed I fired at three E/A, and in each case saw my de Wilde ammunition registering hits.

The combat then developed into a dog-fight, in the course of which I was able to get on the tails of two E/A, in each case firing 2-second bursts from 200 yards closing to 100 yards. In one case the E/A dived straight into the sea and in the other case he E/A pancaked on the sea and then sunk.

In the resulting combat, the 'Tigers' claimed ten Me 110s destroyed in total, all 'unconfirmed', one probable and five damaged, although there appears no doubt regarding the fate of those Freeborn attacked. In this hectic action, 1/*Erprobungsgruppe* 210 lost two of the 30mm cannon-armed Me 110C-6s.

One of these was flown by *Leutnant* Kurt Bertram, the 20-year-old brother of the unit's *Staffelkapitän, Oberleutnant* Otto Bertram, who was last seen pursuing a Hurricane over the Thames Estuary – but with two Spitfires on his tail; it would be Kurt Bertram's first and last engagement, as neither he nor his *Bordfunker, Obergefreiter* Gerhard Mertins, were ever seen again.

The Me 110 flown by *Gefreiter* Christian Weiss, whose *Bordfunker* was *Obergefreiter* Richard Keilhaupt, was seen by comrades to alight on the sea – and was very likely that which Freeborn described having 'pancaked' upon the waves. Although a dinghy was thrown to the downed crew by *Feldwebel* Lutz, both enemy airmen also remain missing.

The combat had not gone entirely 74 Squadron's way, however. Pilot Officers Denis Smith (unusually a veteran of the Spanish Civil War, having flown against Franco in the Republican Air Force) and Donald Cobden (a New Zealander) were both killed – undoubtedly by *Oberleutnant* Heinz Schoenfeldt and *Feldwebel* Otto Rückert, both of 3/*Erprobungsgruppe* 210, who each claimed a Spitfire destroyed.

Another sweep by *Luftflotte* 2's Me 109s was met by 'A' Flight of 64 Squadron, between 11.55 and 12.15 hrs, mid-Channel.

Sergeant Jack Mann:

> Patrolling as Yellow 3 with seven other aircraft of 64 Squadron we encountered a number of Me 109s south-east of Dover. My Section climbed away and prepared to attack from above but owing to a slightly dud motor I was left astern. I turned and attacked a straggling aircraft of a section of six Me 109s. I positioned myself on its tail and followed it round as it turned, getting in a 6-second burst on slight deflection. A smoke-trail appeared and E/A dived. I broke off as the remaining E/A prepared to attack.
>
> Later while patrolling over Dover an Me 109 appeared below me over our coast and heading for France. I dived and positioned myself

on its tail and opened fire with a 5-second burst at 250, then dived and came up beneath E/A and gave a long burst, finally coming up onto its tail again at 50 end still firing. E/A lost speed and I climbed to watch effect of fire.

A thick trail of black smoke appeared together with flashes of flame. E/A dived in a spiral turn and disappeared through cloud, heading for English coast. I did not see it crash but assume it must have hit the sea about eight–ten miles N. of Cap Griz Nez.

In this action Mann was credited with one probable and another 109 damaged, while Squadron Leader Don MacDonell, Pilot Officer James O'Meara and Flight Sergeant Adrian Laws all damaged enemy fighters. Flying Officer Christopher Andreae's Spitfire was hit by a cannon shell, however, although he returned safely to Kenley.

On this day, another RAF fighter squadron brought forward was 56, Flying Officer Steve 'Squeak' Weaver leading 'A' Flight from North Weald to Rochford at 05.15 hrs. At 11.45 hrs, the Hurricanes took-off on their second convoy patrol of the day off the Thames Estuary and, declares the ORB, 'returning for lunch Sergeant (Ronald) Baker ... was seen to go down and bale out, having apparently been attacked by a lone Spitfire. He was picked up by a destroyer but was already dead.'

In the confusion and tension of battle, and given the speed of combat, the human eye was easily deceived; both misidentification of aircraft and so-called 'friendly fire' were far from uncommon.

At 13.40 hrs, Flight Lieutenant Stanley Connors DFC was leading 'B' Flight of Croydon's 111 Squadron, which was also operating from Hawkinge, on patrol off Margate when another raid was mounted against *Booty*, *Agent* and *Arena*:

> At 17,000ft I noticed fifteen Me 109s pass over our formation 3,000ft above; they disappeared into the sun and a few moments later I noticed one Me 109 climbing up behind Green 3. I turned towards the E/A which immediately dived for cloud cover. I followed him down through gap in clouds and found a destroyer being attacked by a Ju 87. I noticed a number of Me 109s below cloud and attacked the nearest to me with a 2-second burst, dead astern, and followed him down until he crashed into the sea and caught fire. I then attacked another Me 109 with a 1-second burst, and short burst at a Ju 87, but as my windscreen was completely obscured by oil from E/A I had brought down, I landed at Manston without observing result.

During the action, Connors had watched Pilot Officer Jack Copeman 'spin slowly into the sea'; the pilot was killed, his body later washed ashore on the Belgian coast.

It would prove a most costly engagement for 'Treble One':

> Remainder of Squadron maintained height of 15,000ft on instruction from Controller and intercepted three formations of seven Do 215s each, flying in five sections of three aircraft ... Blue Section leading Squadron. Squadron Leader (John) Thompson turned line-astern and when within 400 yards, echelon formation.
>
> The attack was made from below and astern, and in spite of intense fire from enemy, formation was pressed home to within 100 yards. Squadron Leader Thompson observed a bright glow of fire in the fuselage of the E/A he attacked. A further attack was prevented by an Me 109 which is presumed to have shot down Blue 2, Pilot Officer (John) McKenzie, and Blue Leader, after chasing this 109 away, landed Hawkinge 1441 hrs.
>
> In the meantime, 'A' Flight, led by Flying Officer Henry Ferriss DFC made an attempt to pass the Dorniers and deliver a head-on attack – the enemy formation changed course in a NE direction and shortage of fuel prevented the manoeuvre being carried out. Beam attacks were delivered by Red Section, but results could not be observed. Each pilot fired about 800 rounds and encountered heavy return fire. They refuelled at Manston before returning to Hawkinge at 1511 hrs. Blue 3, Sergeant (Harry) Newton, crash-landed near Martlesham with empty petrol tanks.
>
> Remainder of Yellow Section, Pilot Officer (Robert) Wilson and Sergeant (Robert) Sim were seen to go into the attack on the Dorniers from astern. One aircraft was seen by Sergeant Newton with its engine smoking badly after the attack. Both are missing and must be presumed to have been shot down into the sea.

The Me 109 destroyed by Flight Lieutenant Connors, and the Do 17 damaged by Squadron Leader Thompson, was a poor return: four Hurricanes had been lost with their pilots, although Sergeant Newton survived his crash-landing unscathed.

At 14.10 hrs, the same enemy formation was also intercepted by 74 Squadron, once more led in the air by Squadron Leader Malan:

> I was Dysoe Leader and told to patrol Manston at 10,000ft. I climbed through 10/10 cloud with the eight machines in two sections of four. On emerging through cloud, I spotted about thirty Ju 87s in a long line of small vic formations, about fifteen Me 109s about 2,000ft above and half a mile astern. On sighting us, the bombers dived towards a gap in the cloud while the 109s closed their range with the bombers.
>
> I ordered Blue Leader to attack the bombers while I attacked the fighters with Red Section. I closed the range with the fighters and

attacked an Me 109 as he dived through a gap. I opened up with 30° deflection at 200 yards and closed to 100 yards dead astern. After the third 2-second burst he burst into flames and went into the sea approximately off Margate.

I immediately climbed towards the cloud and then dived towards another group of four Me 109s and delivered 30° deflection bursts of about three seconds at about 20 yards. I saw no results. As my ammunition was now expended I returned to Manston.

This 109 was credited as destroyed but unconfirmed, although there can be no doubting that the enemy fighter was destroyed. In this action, 3/JG3 lost two Me 109E-1s, with both pilots killed. Pilot Officer John Freeborn claimed a 109 destroyed and another damaged, and both Flying Officer John Mungo-Park and Pilot Officer Stephen Harborne a 'destroyed' each.

It was the fourth time the 'Tigers' had seen action that day – and an indication of what lay ahead.

Throughout the morning and until early afternoon, *Luftflotte* 2 had maintained the pressure by sending successive waves of fighters across the Channel, in addition to targeting the northbound convoy. It had already become standard practice for certain 11 Group squadrons to move to operate from forward airfields at first light, concentrate the fighters close to the coast on account of the limited warning owing to the enemy's short Channel-crossing.

Air Vice-Marshal Park, however, refused to commit all those forward fighters to battle en masse and largely continued patrolling and intercepts using sections and flights. The action fought by 74 Squadron off Margate was the last daylight combat of the day over the south-east – and in any case, the enemy's main effort was a massive attack by *Luftflotte* 3 on Portland naval base. The increased *Luftflotte* 2 activity over the Dover Strait was intended to divert attention from the forces assembling to attack Portland, and so prevent 11 Group squadrons reinforcing the defence of Portland, some 200 miles West of Dover. This was not apparent to Fighter Command until after the event; in real time, all controllers could do was second-guess the enemy's intentions and react accordingly.

At 09.35 hrs, Squadron Leader John Peel led six 145 Squadron Hurricanes up from Westhampnett (Goodwood), the Tangmere satellite airfield, to patrol the Swanage area. Five minutes later, Flight Lieutenant Mark 'Hilly' Brown DFC, a Canadian, took-off from Northolt with 'A' Flight of 1 Squadron, followed at 09.45 hrs by three more Hurricanes of 'B' Flight, along with Flight Lieutenant Willie Rhodes-Moorhouse and four Hurricanes of 601 Squadron's 'B' Flight, which were joined by six of 'A' Flight at 10.00 hrs. At around the same time, Squadron Leader Darley led the Spitfires of 609 Squadron's 'B' Flight up from Warmwell to patrol Weymouth Bay (official records are incomplete and fail to record the exact time).

At 09.45 hrs, the radar station at Ventnor on the Isle of Wight had reported an enemy force of thirty-plus assembling over the Baie de la Seine, and as there were no convoys in the Channel at the time, RAF controllers rightly predicted that the enemy would make for a coastal target. Given the distance from Cherbourg, unlike the raids on the Dover Strait, Sector Controllers had more time to scramble and position their squadrons.

Four Spitfires of 152 Squadron, led by Squadron Leader Peter Devitt, had already taken off from Middle Wallop at 10.00 hrs, heading for Warmwell, when given orders in the air to head for 'a point between Portland and Swanage'. By 10.05 hrs, the enemy were thirty miles South of St Catherine's Point – their target clearly being the Portland naval base (which, being outside the proposed invasion area, the Germans considered a primary target because anti-invasion sorties could be launched from there by the RN).

At the same time, fifty-plus bandits were reported fifteen miles North of Cherbourg, heading towards Portland, and at 10.09 hrs nine-plus were detected twenty-six miles North-west of Cherbourg. Consequently, at 10.09 hrs, twelve Hurricanes of 213 Squadron were scrambled from Exeter, twelve more of 238 Squadron from Middle Wallop at 10.14 hrs, and seven of 87 Squadron, also from Exeter, at 10.15 hrs.

For once, the Germans were to be met by a comparatively strong force of – albeit still outnumbered – RAF fighters: sixteen Spitfires and fifty-eight Hurricanes. The enemy was soon mid-Channel, this 'Valhalla' advancing on a five-mile front and the largest yet unleashed against Britain: fifty-four Ju 88s of I and II/KG54, and twenty He 111s of KG27, escorted by sixty-one Me 110s of I and II/ZG2, along with thirty Me 109s of III/JG2. Moreover, the selection of a mainland target represented a shift away from attacking convoys.

The first of the defenders to engage was 609 Squadron, which met '100+' fifteen miles 'SSE of Swanage' at 10.15 hrs, according to Flying Officer John Dundas, leading Yellow Section as top cover at 24,000ft, ten miles West of the Isle of Wight:

> I lost sight of Squadron Leader ... I headed South hoping to catch him up, but only found nine Hurricanes about half way across the Channel. I then turned back and noticed white smoke trails above on the port beam. I put Yellow Section into line astern and circled round in a wide climbing turn. There was a great number of Me 110s circling around and above each other in a fairly tight left-hand circuit, with what I imagined were a number of 109s well above them.

On cue, five miles South-east of Portland, the sixty Me 110s of I and II/ZG2 had formed a huge defensive circle, an *Abwehrkreis*, aiming to attract the defending fighters, thus diverting their attention from the bombers. From that point onwards, the sky over Weymouth Bay, stretching from Rufus Castle on the Isle of Portland eastwards to Lulworth Cove, was full of a mass of orbiting aircraft.

As Pilot Officer David Crook, also of 609 Squadron, later wrote, 'Several other squadrons soon joined us and altogether it looked as though it was going to be a big show ... our first really big action of the war'.

KANALKAMPF DIARY, 1 AUGUST – 12 AUGUST 1940

Flying Officer John Dundas:

> I attacked a 110 from above at about 20° deflection. The Me turned sharply to left in a climbing turn. I closed into point blank range and fired a burst of about 2 seconds, nearly colliding with him as I broke away. I could see my shots striking his fuselage but could not see any definite results. During this attack I suffered rear gunfire.
>
> The 110s were giving each other excellent protection and it was some time before I could get my sights on another Me without exposing myself unduly. My second attack was also made in a left-hand climbing turn allowing full deflection. I fired from 250 to 100 yards for about 4 seconds and saw both his motors smoking and the machine staggered and fell over to the left.
>
> As I broke away I felt and saw shots going through my starboard wing and rudder, so I pulled the plug and disappeared as fast as possible. The Me's were able to gain height in climbing turns and I had the impression that the pilots manoeuvred them pretty adroitly.
>
> We were obviously and hopelessly outnumbered, and I lost my Section before going into the attack, though I did not know this at the time. On returning via Portland at 2,000ft I was shot at – rather unnecessarily and inaccurately – by AA batteries.

Dundas returned to Warmwell with Spitfire R6769 streaming glycol, but was himself unhurt.

Squadron Leader Darley led 'B' Flight into attack the Me 110s and Me 109s milling about over Weymouth Bay, flying straight across the circle 'and taking full deflection shots'. Pilot Officer David Crook was with his CO:

> We saw a big enemy fighter formation out to sea and went out to attack it, climbing the whole time as they were flying at about 24,000ft. Some Hurricanes (very probably 601 Squadron) were already attacking the *Messerschmitts* and the latter had formed their usual defensive circle, going round and round on each other's tails thus making an attack rather difficult, as if you attack an enemy there is always another enemy behind you. We were now about a thousand feet above the Me's at about 25,000ft and the CO turned around and the whole of 609 went down to attack.
>
> We came down right on top of the enemy formation, going at terrific speed, and as we approached them, we split up slightly, each pilot selecting his own target. I saw an Me 110 ahead of me going across in front. I fired at him but did not allow enough deflection and my bullets passed behind him. I then closed in on him from behind and fired a good burst at practically point-blank range. Some black

smoke poured from his port engine and he turned up to the right and stalled.

I could not see what happened after this as I narrowly missed hitting his port wing. There were many more enemy fighters round me and a terrific fight was going on. I couldn't see another target in a good position for me to attack, and it was rather an unhealthy spot in which to linger so I turned and dived back to the coast and landed at Warmwell to refuel and rearm.

Although not involved personally, having taken command of 601 Squadron the previous day, Squadron Leader The Hon. Edward Ward's report provides a point of reference:

When airborne, orders were received to proceed to Portland. When approximately twenty miles south of St Catherine's Point, enemy aircraft were sighted about twenty miles south of Swanage, in numbers estimated by various pilots as being from fifty to 200, in layers from 15,000 – 25,000ft. 601 Squadron were ordered to attack the upper layers of fighters, which were identified as Me 109s and Me 110s at 22,000ft.

Flight Lieutenant Willie Rhodes-Moorhouse:

I was Blue 1, with Blue Section leading the squadron. Red Section and Green Section were on my left and right respectively with Yellow Section in the box. We were ordered to patrol St Catherine's Point at 20,000ft, then told to go to Portland.

When just south of Swanage at 19,000ft, I saw a very large number of E/A milling around some miles to the south, so I turned towards them. At this moment my engine stopped, so I ordered the squadron to continue without me. By this time, I had found out that I had been running on reserve. I had lost height and the rest of the squadron.

While climbing up to the E/A already mentioned, three Me 109s attacked from my left, so I turned towards them and approached head-on, with E/A and myself both firing. After passing underneath E/A, made very violent right-hand turn and spun down to 14,000ft. I then climbed again 25,000ft and circled round, above the main body of aircraft, trying to identify them – and found them to be all Me 109s circling round in sections of three to five, in line astern at various heights. I then dived across this mass of E/A, firing as and when a target presented itself and climbed up the other side (in this attack one E/A was hit but cannot confirm it crashing).

I then turned and made a similar dive in the opposite direction. This time I approached a section of three Me 109s from the stern right-hand quarter, firing in front of the leader but not allowing enough deflection. Nevertheless, I hit the two machines directly behind, one going down in flames, the other went down in a steep dive, both of which I saw crash into the sea.

Until this point E/A had been so intent on watching each other that I had been unnoticed. But I was then attacked by four Me 109s and thinking I was out of ammunition took cover in cloud and returned to base, just below cloud, to find I had fired 300 rounds in seven guns and 100 in the eighth, which had a broken Pawl spring. I landed at 1110 hrs. I saw a lot of bright green sea-markers in the sea where E/A must have crashed.

Rhodes-Moorhouse, son of the first ever air VC, claimed two Me 109s 'unconfirmed destroyed' in this combat, occurring twenty miles South of Swanage.

Back at Tangmere, in total, 601 Squadron's pilots claimed the destruction of twelve enemy aircraft with four more damaged. It had been a colossal scrap, a real aerial spectacle, the greatest so far during this crucial summer of 1940.

But four of 601 Squadron's pilots were missing. Pilot Officer Julian Smithers, an Old Etonian, former stockbroker and pre-war Legionnaire, had been shot down and killed, his body later washing up on the French coast. Flying Officer James Gillan, an SSC officer, and Pilot Officer William Dickie of the RAFVR were never seen again. The fourth pilot missing was Flying Officer Richard Demetriadi, in Hurricane R4092, UF-U. The youngest pre-war 'Legionnaire', as the socially elite auxiliaries of the 'Millionaire's Mob' called themselves, Demetriadi was the brother-in-law of Rhodes-Moorhouse, again illustrating the close personal bonds in such units. Squadron Leader Ward's report explained that the missing pilot,

> was engaged in the general dogfight which followed the attack. It was observed by another pilot that petrol was leaking badly from Flying Officer Demetriadi's aircraft, but the aircraft was still under control at the time. Nothing further has since been seen or heard of the pilot or aircraft [on 15 September 1940, however, Richard Demetriadi's body would be washed ashore near Cayeux-sur-Mer, in which cemetery the 21-year-old was buried, the news eventually filtering back to England via the town's Mayor and French International Red Cross].

At 10.30 hrs, the Hurricanes of 145 Squadron also engaged over Weymouth Bay, claiming three Me 110s and two Me 109s destroyed, and two 110s and a 109 damaged. Squadron Leader Peel's Hurricane was shot-up and the pilot safely forced-landing on the Isle of Wight, and Pilot Officer Nigel Weir's aircraft was also damaged, necessitating a crash-landing near Christchurch.

Two pilots, however, had been shot down over the sea, never to be seen again: Flying Officer Guy Branch and the Polish Flying Officer Antoni Ostowicz – the latter at 10.35 hrs, being the first of his countrymen to die in the Battle of Britain.

Over the Channel, at 10.45 hrs, the three sections of 1 Squadron Hurricanes were pounced upon and broken up by Me 109s:

> Pilot Officers Charles Chatham and George Goodman sighted an E/A which they identified as an Me 110. The two pilots raced each other to get to the target first. Chatham won by a short head and gave a preliminary burst which silenced the rear-gunner. Two members of the crew were seen trying to open the cockpit and a drogue was thrown out, attached to 200 yards of wire, without, however, inconveniencing the pilots.
>
> When Chatham broke away after setting fire to the starboard engine Goodman closed to within fifty yards. After a steady burst of about five seconds, the 110 hit the water and broke up. Goodman took a clear film of the wreckage. Meanwhile, Flight Lieutenant Mark Brown encountered another Me 110 mid-Channel. He attacked and after three bursts at close range the port engine was obscured by smoke and the 110 dived steeply in flames.
>
> Pilot Officer Harold Mann saw the port engine explode with a burst of flame. The day's score was two Me 110s destroyed. [ORB]

Again, however, this was not without loss: Pilot Officer John Davey was killed when attempting to crash-land his crippled Hurricane on the Isle of Wight's Sandown gold course.

No.152 Squadron's four Spitfires also engaged the enemy fighters over Weymouth Bay:

> Eighteen 109s were sighted in a dogfight with either Spitfires or Hurricanes. They broke up and started back to France. Squadron Leader Devitt and Pilot Officer Dudley Williams chased them but were unable to get within effective range. Squadron Leader Devitt fired a few rounds at about 500 yards but without apparent result.
>
> Pilot Officer Timothy Wildblood attacked a 109 and closed to fifty yards, and this E/A was seen to dive vertically into the sea, he then turned to attack another 109 together with Pilot Officer Douglas Shepley; he fired remainder of ammunition and then broke away, leaving Pilot Officer Shepley to continue attack.
>
> Black smoke was seen coming from this machine, which dived fast and steadily downwards. Flight Lieutenant Derek Boitel-Gill

KANALKAMPF DIARY, 1 AUGUST – 12 AUGUST 1940

> saw Pilot Officer John Jones bale out and parachute open, but unfortunately no more was heard of Pilot Officer Jones who was therefore reported missing.

A Cranwellian, Pilot Officer Jones's remains later came ashore in France, the 21-year-old being interred at Sainte Marie Cemetery, Le Havre.

The Hurricanes of 213 Squadron 'Tally Ho'd' at 10.30 hrs. So far, the German tactic of drawing the RAF fighters away from the bombers had worked – but now Squadron Leader Hector McGregor led his Hurricanes against the enemy raiders over Portland Bill:

> Attacked Ju 88 in leading section from beam and gave 2-second burst and rear gunner stopped firing. Put a second burst into starboard engine, which caught fire and air raft crashed in flames on West side of Portland Bill. Attacked No 2 of 'A' Section of five Ju 88s, and saw petrol streaming from aircraft, but as No 3 of Section was about to drop his bombs, diverted my attack on to that aircraft, but ammunition ran out before any result observed.

McGregor was credited with one Ju 88 'conclusive', the other 'inconclusive'. Certainly, *Stab* II/KG54 *Totenkopf* lost two Ju 88s off Portland, one of which being the aircraft of *Major* Leonardi, the *GruppenKommandeur*, whose crew were all killed.

No.213 Squadron's claims were remarkably accurate overall, given that McGregor's pilots claimed seven Ju 88s destroyed and another shared between two Hurricanes, and two damaged; six were actually lost by I and II/KG54. One not in doubt was that shot down by Flying Officer Claud Strickland:

> Portland Bill at 10,000ft. I sighted about seventy E/A in waves, approaching Portland from the East. I called my Section together and climbed to seaward side of the enemy. We attacked the leading section of Ju 88s, which immediately started to dive and break formation, dropping their bombs wide of Portland. I picked out one 88 and gave him two short bursts on the way down, his port engine started to smoke quite a bit. He went down to about 2,000ft and I gave him two more bursts, coming in on a quarter attack.
>
> The rear-gunner ceased firing and the starboard engine looked as though it was u/s. Aircraft was then losing height rapidly and I gave him two more short bursts and then followed him right down. He forced-landed on Portland Bill with undercarriage up.
>
> I saw three airmen get out and were captured by the Army. I then flew away and tried to find some more E/A but by that time they had all gone. I saw several E/A falling in flames. The only evasive action

by E/A was to throttle right back and use diving breaks and turning towards me. It was quite effective and caused me a certain amount of trouble because I was apt to overshoot. All my Section returned to base separately.

This Ju 88, of *Stab* II/KG54, flown by *Oberleutnant* Wette, hit the telephone cables of the Blacknore Battery, collapsing its undercarriage, during a force-landing on Portland Head, the central flat-top of the 275ft high cliffs at Portland Bill known locally as 'The Castles'. The enemy pilot was severely wounded, some say by a burst of fire from a nearby machine-gun post as he exited the aircraft, and the whole crew was captured.

No.213 Squadron's success was not without casualties. Pilot Officer Alexander Osmand recorded in his logbook:

> Patrol over Plymouth, on to Portland at 15,000ft. Action! Ran into Ju 88s supported by Me 109s and 110s – about 120 altogether. No luck! Got shot-up by Me 109, and crash-landed at base.

Similarly, the Belgian Pilot Officer Jacques Phillipart returned to Exeter having sustained damage while attacking a Ju 88, and Sergeant Ernest Snowden's Hurricane was damaged in combat with an Me 110, forcing him to put down on the Lulworth Ranges. Not so lucky, sadly, were Flight Lieutenant Ronald Wight DFC and Sergeant Sam Butterfield DFM, both of whom were shot down and killed.

Having claimed a 109 'unconfirmed' over Weymouth Bay, Pilot Officer Douglas Shepley of 152 Squadron appears to have been the only Spitfire pilot to have attacked one of the bombers: 'I then saw a Ju 88 flying about 5,000ft below me to the East and followed it. I fired all my rounds without any apparent effect.' Shipley then returned to Warmwell.

With 238 Squadron's CO, Squadron Leader Fenton, in hospital following being shot down and ditching in the Channel on 8 August 1940, it fell to the senior flight commander, the Australian Flight Lieutenant Stuart Walch, to lead the squadron into action over Weymouth Bay.

At 10.14 hrs, Walch led seven Hurricanes of 'A' Flight up from Middle Wallop, followed two minutes later by four 'B' Flight aircraft. Ordered to patrol Portland, 238 Squadron met the enemy, 'A' Flight engaging the German fighters two miles East of Weymouth while 'B' Flight likewise became embroiled with the Me 109s and Me 110s five miles South of Swanage.

Pilot Officer Jack Urwin-Mann:

> I was Green Leader ... On crossing coast East of Portland at 16,000ft I saw about 100 E/A directly in front and about 5,000ft above. 'B' Flight immediately climbed into the sun to get behind and above. Green Section was to left and above Blue Section. Before I could

give the order we were attacked. I saw Green 2 shot down by an Me 109 which was diving and overtaking. Immediately I broke downwards and chased E/A.

At about 10,000ft I was within range and gave a very short burst at 250 yards and from above and astern. The E/A went into a vertical dive with thin stream of blue smoke trailing. I then went back to the approximate position where Green 2 was shot down and tried to locate the spot but was unable to see anything ... I saw what looked like a Spitfire dive straight into the sea. I then heard order to patrol Portland and proceeded there.

'Green 2' was Sergeant Fred Cawse, who was killed. Flying Officer David Hughes destroyed a 109 'confirmed'; Sergeant Leslie Pidd, one 'unconfirmed'; while Sergeant Eric Bann and Sergeant Henry 'Taxi' Marsh claimed a He 111. The Polish Sergeant Marian Domagala, however, was attacking a 109 when a Hurricane dived between him and the target, resulting in the unidentified Hurricane pilot being shot down. Urwin-Mann was mistaken in thinking he had seen a Spitfire crash into the sea though, as none were lost in this huge air battle.

Tragically, all of 238 Squadron's Blue Section – the gallant Flight Lieutenant Walch, the Polish Flying Officer Michal Stebrowski and Sergeant Geoffrey Gledhill – were all shot down and killed. Sergeant Pidd's aircraft was also shot-up, although he landed safely at Warmwell with just a cut hand. The loss of four pilots was a great blow to the squadron, and of these the squadron diary tells us:

Flight Lieutenant Walch, who is missing, was an officer of very great promise. He was dauntless in the face of danger, careless of his own personal safety and comfort, thoughtful for all who came in contact with him, and had an innate gift for administrative duty which should have taken him high in his country's service. A Tasmanian, he had been in the Royal Australian Air Force and had come to this country about three years ago to join the RAF and was one of the original flight commanders of this Squadron, the other having been Flight Lieutenant Kennedy, another recruit from the Royal Australian Air Force, of about the same length of service, and of equal promise, though of a different personality. It will be remembered that Flight Lieutenant Kennedy crashed fatally after combat in the same neighbourhood on the 13 July 1940.

Flying Officer Stebrowski was a Polish officer pilot of great experience who had been with the Squadron but a short time. He had flown in Poland and was of a very cheerful nature – his rugged face and gentle smile are greatly missed. He is the first Pole to be lost by this Squadron.

Pilot Officer Cawse had also been but a short time in the Squadron. A man of quiet manner and a happy disposition, he should have been most useful. He had graduated to Officer Pilot through Sergeant Pilot, and had only been commissioned a short time.

Sergeant Gledhill had been in the squadron barely a week and had hardly time to get to know his comrades or they to know him. A gentle boy, ruddy of countenance – he is the second NCO pilot to be lost. He went down in his first engagement with the enemy ... The only reflection of good there is in a gloomy day is that these gentlemen of England have exacted a toll which will go far to wear down the German Beast. [ORB]

Flying Officer David Hughes was promoted to Acting Flight Lieutenant and given temporary command of 238 Squadron, which had now lost two flight commanders killed and its CO wounded. The following day, the Adjutant flew to Colerne for an interview with the 10 Group AOC, Air Vice-Marshal Sir Quinton Brand, a South African, who agreed to withdraw the battered unit to rest and refit at St Eval for a month.

The Hurricanes of Exeter's 87 Squadron's 'B' Flight had scrambled at 10.15 hrs, the six Hurricanes led by the Malayan-born Flight Lieutenant Robert Voase Jeff DFC, intercepting the enemy ten miles South of Portland Bill. Pilot Officer Dennis David later recalled that, 'There didn't seem much we could do against the force, but we made to attack the Ju 88s as they turned away from Portland'.

Owing to the escorting enemy fighters, only two of the Hurricane pilots, however, managed to engage the bombers, Pilot Officer John Cock, another Australian, and Pilot Officer David, both claiming Ju 88s destroyed. Cock also claimed an Me 109 destroyed, as did David. Pilot Officer Andrew McLure claimed an Me 109 destroyed and (mistakenly) a 'He 112', and Flight Sergeant Ivor Badger one Me 109 destroyed and a second damaged. Almost inevitably, these successes were not without loss:

> Our casualties consisted of Flight Lieutenant Jeff DFC who was seen diving to the attack but not seen again. Flight Lieutenant Jeff was a most popular and efficient Flight Commander and his loss was a sad one for the squadron. Pilot Officer Cock, after his second combat, suddenly found his cockpit breaking in pieces as the result of an unseen attack. With difficulty he baled out, landing in the sea about 200 yards from the shore and managed to swim ashore, where he arrived dressed in a tunic and blue underpants – a somewhat fearsome spectacle. Fortunately Pilot Officer Cock was not injured badly: he escaped with a few splinters in his arm. [ORB]

Pilot Officer McLure was also shot-up by Me 109s but made it back to base. The loss of Flight Lieutenant Jeff, an experienced fighter pilot already decorated with the DFC and Bar, was keenly felt.

KANALKAMPF DIARY, 1 AUGUST – 12 AUGUST 1940

By now, the raid was retiring back to France and the RAF fighters were returning to their bases to rearm and refuel.

Pilot Officer David Crook, 609 Squadron:

> Everybody came streaming back in ones and twos, and to my surprise nobody was missing. It seemed too good to be true that we should all be safe after such a fierce scrap. We had shot down about five Me 110s and several more (like mine) were probably destroyed, but it is almost impossible (and very unwise) to stay and see definite results in the middle of such a mix up. All that you can do is to fire a good burst at some enemy and then, hit or miss, get away quickly.
>
> Some bombers had got through to Weymouth and Portland and there was a great column of smoke rising from a blazing oil tank, but no very serious damage had been done.

No.238 Squadron's ORB notes that, 'The Me 109s were dive-bombing from 10,000ft and their aim was pretty accurate as several fires (including an oil storage tank) were apparent at Portland Bill'.

The He 111s had started their bombing run at 15,000ft, and it was the Ju 88s that dive-bombed an oil storage depot from 10,000ft. Thirty-two bombs, in fact, were dropped on Admiralty property at Portland and three more on the RN Torpedo Dept at Bincleaves, Weymouth; fifty-eight bombs in total fell in the borough with more in the Channel, Portland Harbour and Balaclava Bay. The Verne Citadel and the naval base's oil storage tanks appeared to be the primary targets, two of the tanks being set on fire while the flames beside No.3 oil-tank at Portland were contained. The long, winding, road leading uphill to the Citadel was cratered, but fortunately the fire started in the naval hospital was rapidly brought under control; the blaze rendering the beach road impassable was due to burning grass.

The main oil pipeline had been fractured in three places, resulting in the loss of 200-tons of oil. The railway track near the shore-based anti-submarine training base HMS *Osprey* was destroyed, and the signalman at Portland Station was killed when his box was hit, and two destroyers were damaged in Portland Harbour. Twenty houses and a brewery were either demolished or virtually so, while a further 100 domestic dwellings were damaged by shrapnel.

The only other serious damage was to the shipwright's shop at Bincleaves, which suffered a direct hit. Considering the effort involved, this was not necessarily the serious damage to the naval installations hoped for by the enemy, whose aim had been mainly disrupted by 213 Squadron.

Although *Adler Tag* had been postponed until 13 August 1940, the events of 8 and 11 August 1940 nonetheless indicated a significant increase in the tempo and weight of enemy air attacks. On this hard-fought day of 11 August, which had seen the heaviest raid so far, Fighter Command lost twenty-five pilots who were killed – the highest number of fatalities since the Fall of France (and throughout the entire sixteen-week long Battle of Britain).

Worryingly, the number of pilots lost exceeded that of the daily provision of replacements – and, of course, these new pilots lacked combat experience. Fighter Command had flown over 400 interception sorties, nearly 200 more protecting convoys and a further 150 routine patrols. Nonetheless, Fighter Command could increase this effort without being overstretched – but so too could the Germans, who had only committed some 400 aircraft to battle on this significant day.

Generalfeldmarschall Hugo Sperrle, commanding *Luftflotte* 3, was delighted with the day's result, signalling his fighter units and congratulating them on their 'excellent' performance 'near Portland'. *Oberleutnant* Paul Temme, the adjutant of I/JG2, remembered that orders for the day were to 'tie down the British fighters, come what may, for thirty-five minutes. No quitting before time' – and that the German fighters had indeed done an 'excellent' job of committing the defending fighters was indisputable. In future, the RAF pilots would need to find a way to get through to the bombers, come what may.

After this great air battle, *Seenotdienst* He 59s were naturally most active, one of which was destroyed at midday in mid-Channel by Squadron Leader Michael Anderson and Pilot Officer Edward Crew in their 604 Squadron Blenheim, up from Middle Wallop and searching for that sector's six missing pilots. Nonetheless, the German ASR system was efficient, as an anonymous *Oberleutnant* from ZG26 recalled:

> The coast was some way off and the water was cold. The current was carrying us away from land. My wireless operator had a good idea – he fired a flare. That saved us. German fighters saw us in the water and four *Messerschmitts* circled overhead. Despite the cold we two smiled at each other, even if we were exhausted and injured. The fighters fortunately signalled a He 59 *Seenotmaschine,* which came and took us aboard a short time later.

At 19.10 hrs, Green Section of 41 Squadron, comprising Flying Officer John Boyle, Pilot Officer 'Wally' Wallens and Sergeant Edward Darling, which had been withdrawn from Hornchurch to rest at Catterick two days previously, shared the destruction of a 1(F)/121 Ju 88 reconnaissance bomber. The enemy aircraft crash-landed at Newton Moor, near Whitby, with one dead crewman; the other three German airmen were captured. This was the last combat of the day.

Elsewhere, Coastal Command carried out its usual operations, a Blenheim destroying an Me 109 over the Channel during a reconnaissance of Le Havre. An Anson of St Eval's 217 Squadron, however, was shot down by a reconnaissance Ju 88 of *Küstenflieger Gruppe* 806 some forty miles North-west of Land's End, and a Detling-based 53 Squadron Blenheim patrolling Dunkirk and Dieppe was destroyed by *Oberfeldwebel* Willi Grosse of 3/JG52.

By night, Cherbourg's oil tanks were set alight by 59 Squadron, and Swordfish laid mines. No.2 Group's Blenheims attacked enemy airfields and contributed to ASR sweeps over the Channel, while after dark Bomber Command's Wellingtons, Whitleys and Hampdens again visited a variety of industrial targets in Germany.

J.B. Priestley, extract from *Postscript*, Sunday, 11 August 1940:

> It may be possible yet, even while we struggle and endure, and at last batter our way through to victory, to achieve what's long been overdue in this island, and that is, not only to retain what is best out of an old tradition, but to increase that heritage by raising at last the quality of our life. No burden, it seems, is too great for the people. Then there can't be too rich and great a reward for the people.

MONDAY, 12 AUGUST 1940

On this day the *Luftwaffe* liaison officer at OKW, *Major* Freiherr Sigmund von Falkenstein, at last reported to *General der Flieger* Hans Jeschonnek, the *Luftwaffe* Chief of Staff, that the weather was set fair for 13 August 1940. Jeschonnek conferred with *Generaloberst* Alfred Jodl, the OKW's head of Operations Staff, confirming that in view of the favourable weather conditions, he expected *Reichsmarschall* Göring to order the *Adlerangriff* imminently.

It was obvious by now, however, that Fighter Command was greatly assisted by RDF, and the previous week Jeschonnek had signalled *Luftflotten* 2 and 3 ordering that when the new offensive came, 'known British radar stations' were 'to be attacked in the first wave … in order to eliminate them as early as possible'.

If that could be achieved, then the *Luftwaffe* would benefit from the RDF blackout arising, so destruction of the radar sites was a priority. With the *Adler Tag* scheduled for the following day, with the weather also favourable on 12 August, now was clearly the time to neutralise Fighter Command's RDF. The stations at Dunkirk (near Faversham in Kent), Dover, Rye and Ventnor (on the Isle of Wight) were the selected targets, and *Luftflotte* 2 assigned the task to *Hauptmann* Rubensdörffer's *Erprobungsgruppe* 210.

With these sites destroyed, blinding the RAF early warning system from Portland to the Thames Estuary, the plan was then to attack the coastal aerodromes of Lympne, Manston and Hawkinge. What lay ahead, therefore, was even heavier fighting than the previous day – and as the sun rose both sides prepared for battle.

From the outset, RDF recorded enemy air activity over the French coast by single aircraft coming and going between 05.00 and 07.00 hrs, and at 07.20 hrs the escort destroyer HMS *Withrington* was unsuccessfully attacked by a solo raider off the Scillies.

Simultaneously, two small formations, one of '6+' behind Cap Gris Nez, which soon struck out towards Dungeness, the other of just three over the central Dover Strait, were detected, as a result of which twelve Spitfires of 610 Squadron, led by Squadron Leader John Ellis, were scrambled from Hawkinge with orders to intercept, and as a precaution six Spitfires of 54 Squadron's 'B' Flight hurriedly took-off from Manston to patrol base.

At first, neither enemy formation crossed the English coast, it soon becoming apparent that they were awaiting the assembly of more forces. At 07.44 hrs, '20+' were indicated over Guînes and a few minutes later another of similar size over Cap Gris-Nez. Consequently, the Hurricanes of 111 Squadron, which had flown from Croydon down to Hawkinge at dawn, were also scrambled to patrol base at 10,000ft. The first enemy formation to cross the Kentish coast did so at 08.12 hrs: nine Do 17s of KG3, escorted by Me 109s of *Hauptmann* Kurt Fischer's I/JG26, incoming over Romney Marsh at 16,000ft and heading to attack the coastal airfield at Lympne.

No.610 Squadron engaged immediately:

> Nine E/A were sighted over New Romney in very tight vic formation in sections of three ... Squadron climbed to attack from 10,000ft. Twelve escorting Me 109s came down to attack and a general engagement took place. Flight Lieutenant (Brian) Smith was hit by two cannon shells in the cockpit and baled out over the Channel, burnt about the face and neck. He was picked up by a motor boat and landed at Dover. Flying Officer (Frederick) Gardiner was wounded slightly in his left leg by a cannon shell, his left aileron, wing and petrol tank being also damaged.

In response, two Me 109s were claimed confirmed destroyed, six more unconfirmed destroyed and two probables. Only two enemy fighters were actually destroyed though: *Leutnant* Regenauer, who was captured, and *Oberleutnant* Friedrich Butterweck, killed when his Me 109 exploded over Standard Hill Farm, Elham. Once more, though, the German fighters had performed well, keeping the Spitfires away from the bombers – which successfully hit Lympne, an advance coastal landing ground, leaving few buildings undamaged.

Meanwhile, 54 Squadron climbed to 27,000ft over Dover, sighting twenty-four Me 109s of JG54 2,000ft below. The Spitfires dived to attack at 08.30 hrs, as Pilot Officer Colin Gray, a New Zealander, reported:

> Fired 3-second burst at one Me 109 which smoked, caught fire, and then commenced to spin in flames. Fired short burst at a second Me 109 from fifty yards and observed glycol streaming from port radiator. I chased the enemy aircraft back to French coast in a dive, firing all the time until ammunition ran out. I pursued the E/A over

KANALKAMPF DIARY, 1 AUGUST – 12 AUGUST 1940

Cap Gris Nez and observed him forced-land on the beach with wheels up. E/A written-off.

In this sharp action over the sea, Pilot Officer Gray was credited with one Me 109 destroyed and a probable, while Pilot Officer Henry Matthews likewise claimed one destroyed and a probable. Pilot Officer John Kemp was shot-up and wounded, crash-landing at Lympne. Likewise, Pilot Officer Douglas Turley-George crash-landed at Denton, near Hawkinge, with shrapnel wounds; and Pilot Officer Eric Edsall made a safe forced-landing at Dartford.

Between 08.50 and 09.30 hrs, the enemy remained active over the Channel, in reduced numbers, so 43 Squadron, up from Tangmere, patrolled South of the airfield, while 501 Squadron was up over Hawkinge and 65 Squadron, scrambled from Hornchurch, stooged around over Chatham. It was now, however, that the all-important RDF stations were targeted.

Earlier that morning, around 07.30 hrs, *Erprobungsgruppe* 210 went forward from Denain to operate from Calais-Marck airfield – from where *Hauptmann* Walter Rubensdörffer's men were to hit the four selected Chain Home stations. The *Kommodore* himself was to attack the Dunkirk radar; *Oberleutnant* Otto Hintze's 3 *Staffel* Me 109s were to hit Dover, being the closest target; *Oberleutnant* Martin Lutz's 1 *Staffel* Me 110s' objective was Pevensey, and *Oberleutnant* Wilhelm-Richard Rössiger's 2 *Staffel* Me 110s were briefed to bomb Rye.

The whole formation took-off at 09.30 hrs, heading across the Channel.

Hintze attacked first, diving into wind at 45° and aiming for the base of the great masts. Those all-important, towering, 300ft high pylons survived unscathed, but buildings were hit. At Rye Chain Home Station, Rössiger's formation was detected over the French coast, climbing, then diving from 18,000ft – straight towards Rye: the target was obvious for those within. Leading Aircraftswoman Daphne Griffiths recalled being so frightened as the bombs rained down that she was unable to speak or move, paralysed by fear. Absurdly, the telephone rang as the building was hit: 'Air Raid Warning Red' – which the beleaguered radar personnel hardly needed telling. After what felt like hours but was actually minutes, it was all over. An AA soldier had been killed and six wounded, the roadway was cratered, the cookhouse destroyed and water mains severed.

Although, once more, the great masts were undamaged, Rye was temporarily out of action, as was Pevensey and Dover; only Dunkirk remained operational, despite huts being hit. As Daphne Griffiths recalled, though, 'Already the stand-by Diesel generator was providing us power and we were soon back on the air – and plotting.' After the attacks, *Erprobungsgruppe* 210 streaked back to France without being intercepted.

At 10.11 hrs, explosions suddenly occurred in Dover's St Radigund's Road, then in Minnis Lane, Prospect Place, Victoria Street and Noah's Ark Terrace, four houses being demolished at the latter; three civilians were seriously injured and two killed. The defending AA gunners were confused, however, as no enemy aircraft could be seen. This was not the *Luftwaffe*'s doing, though: these were the first 536lb shells fired by the three massive 283mm Krupp K5 railway guns located near Calais – a new menace for 'Hellfire Corner' to contend with.

With three Chain Home Stations now blind, *Luftflotte* 2 next launched dive-bombing attacks against the eighty ships of two convoys off the North Foreland and Thames Estuary, although this raid was detected by the Foreness RDF. At 11.00 hrs, a flight of 65 Squadron Spitfires was scrambled from Manston to patrol the Hawkinge area, from which airfield, at the same time, the whole of 501 Squadron was sent up with orders to patrol the North Foreland and Thames Estuary off Westgate. Already patrolling the convoy off the North Foreland were the Hurricanes of 151 Squadron – which sighted fifteen Ju 87s escorted by twenty Me 109s, attacking a ship some way from the convoys. Unable to penetrate the fighter screen and get to the dive-bombers, the Hurricanes were attacked by Me 109s of *Hauptmann* Adolf Galland's III/JG26.

In short order Flying Officer Aidan Tucker and Pilot Officer Robert Beley, a Canadian, were both shot down into the sea; the two pilots were rescued from the water but the latter later died of wounds at Manston; Pilot Officer Kenneth Debenham was 'badly shot-up' but managed to safely put down at Rochford. The squadron executed no damage to the enemy in this exchange.

At 11.30 hrs, 501 Squadron met the same raiders between Deal and Ramsgate, engaging the Ju 87s – claiming six destroyed, two probables and three damaged, and an Me 109 probable. No.65 Squadron's Spitfires also engaged at 11.30 hrs, off Deal, as Sergeant Joseph Kilner reported:

> I was flying as Blue 2 and the squadron sighted and attacked enemy fighters at 24,000ft. I attacked an Me 109 flying last in a formation of seven in line astern, circling about 2,000ft below myself. I attacked from astern, opening fire at 200 yards and closing to fifty yards, with three short bursts. The starboard undercarriage leg fell out and swung loose. The E/A, apparently out of control, lost height rapidly and was soon enveloped in smoke.

Kilner was credited with a 'probable', the 65 Squadron pilots collectively claiming three Me 109s destroyed, three probables and another damaged – all without loss to themselves. In this action, the Controller had used Spitfires, with their superior high-altitude performance to attack the high-flying Me 109s, while the Hurricanes were directed to the dive-bombers lower down. This would, in fact, soon become the way of RAF interceptions.

These skirmishes in the Dover Strait were soon followed by what would be the biggest German effort of the day: a mass attack by elements of *Luftflotte* 3 on the Ventnor Chain Home site and Portsmouth.

At 11.28 hrs, Poling RDF station detected two formations of thirty-plus over Cherbourg, with smaller formations, doubtless fighters, milling about. This was

KANALKAMPF DIARY, 1 AUGUST – 12 AUGUST 1940

actually almost 100 Ju 88s of *Oberst* Dr Fisser's KG51, who was also the overall formation commander, escorted by Me 110s of ZG2 and ZG76, and Me 109s of JG53.

By 11.40 hrs, the threat had begun moving out across the Channel, separating into two formations, the most westerly of which being plotted as '150+', heading for the Isle of Wight, the other on course for Selsey Bill, '30+'.

At 11.40 hrs, Squadron Leader Hill Harkness's 257 Squadron was sent from Northolt to Tangmere, but before landing was vectored to Portsmouth, and at 11.45 hrs the Spitfires of 266 Squadron (more of which in due course) took off from Tangmere to patrol base. No. 10 Group ordered 152 Squadron up at 11.58 hrs, the Spitfires hastening towards the Isle of Wight, and two minutes later 609 scrambled from Warmwell, while 213 was up from Exeter, joined at 12.10 hrs by 145 Squadron from Westhampnett.

As the enemy formation approached Portsmouth, the city's fifty 'blimp' strong balloon barrage was rapidly run up to 6,000ft, and the AA gunners opened up. While the Ju 88s approached Portsmouth and Ventnor, 609 Squadron reported, the ORB notes, that 'an enormous circle of Me 110s orbited East of the Isle of Wight ... at least eighty Me 110s in this one formation', as the Germans attempted to repeat their successful tactics of the previous day.

Among the first RAF squadrons to engage this massive raid on Portsmouth, at 12.15 hrs, was 145 Squadron, as Pilot Officer Peter Parrott reported:

> At 1210 hrs we were ordered to patrol Selsey Bill to Bembridge. I was flying Red 3. E/A were sighted, as soon as we took off, over Portsmouth, going south. We went into line astern, and I saw a Ju 88 break away from the main formation, being attacked by a Spitfire, which broke away and went home. The E/A appeared to be undamaged, but the rear-gunner was not firing.
>
> I delivered my attack after which E/A lost height and speed. E/A finally crashed into the sea about fifteen – twenty miles south of Selsey Bill. There were two survivors, but there was very little chance of them being picked up. As I was returning I saw a British pilot fall into the sea by parachute.
>
> I circled him and repeatedly dived on him. I led a minesweeper to him, and saw him picked up about a mile east of the Nab lighthouse. I then returned to base and landed at 1250 hours.

The Ju 88 destroyed was a machine of II/KG51, the crew of which remain missing. There were no RAF fighter pilots recovered from the sea in this area that day, so it is likely that the airman seen picked up was actually German.

Off Selsey Bill and South of St Catherine's Point 145 Squadron claimed the destruction of a Ju 88 by Flight Lieutenant Roy Dutton, while Parrott was credited with a 'probable', along with the Polish Flying Officer Witold Urbanowicz; Pilot

Officer Jas Storrar claimed an Me 110 'probable', and Flying Officer Michael Rowley a 'Do 17 probable'. One entire section of the squadron's Hurricanes, however, failed to return: the Polish Flight Lieutenant Wilhelm Pankratz and Sergeant Josef Kwiecinski, and Sergeant John Harrison; all three pilots remain missing.

The twelve Spitfires of 266 Squadron, patrolling from Tangmere at 20,000ft when diverted to Portsmouth, arriving 'after bombs had been dropped and enemy was making for home at 250 mph, between 7,000 and 12,000ft.' At 12.10 hrs, the Spitfires engaged the Ju 88s over Bembridge on the Isle of Wight, and South of the island, over the sea. Flight Lieutenant Dennis Armitage:

> I was flying Yellow 1 in 'A' Flight. Made two attacks, starting from the beam. (1) Smoke and flame coming from port engine at breakaway. (2) Smoke only from port engine, think not seriously damaged. E/A fire was observed when in astern position, attacks made from slightly below, and all went above our aircraft. No fire observed on this or another one. The E/A flew straight all the time on a southerly course. Weather was fine, no cloud, and sun almost directly overhead.

Armitage was credited with one Ju 88 'probably destroyed' and another damaged, in total 266 Squadron claiming four enemy aircraft destroyed, two probables and no less than nine damaged. The Spitfire of Pilot Officer Wycliff Williams, a New Zealander, was shot-up by *Oberleutnant* Gerhard Homuth of 2/JG27 and damaged in the oil system, forcing the RAF pilot to crash-land in flames at Bembridge; Williams had just enough time, in fact, to scramble out of the aircraft and achieve a safe distance from it before the petrol tank exploded. Pilot Officer Dennis Ashton, though, was shot down in flames, crashing into the Channel, from which his body was later recovered by HMS *Cedar* and buried at sea.

The Spitfires of 152 Squadron went into action at 12.15 hrs, also taking on the Ju 88s attacking Ventnor:

> In a patrol over St Catherine's Point, Pilot Officer Edward Hogg and Pilot Officer Walter Beaumont intercepted eighteen Ju 88s. Pilot Officer Beaumont attacked one of them and put his starboard engine out of action. Pilot Officer Hogg saw a machine go into the sea. Pilot Officer Hogg and Pilot Officer Beaumont attacked another machine and observed a large piece of metal fall off this E/A. Pilot Officer Hogg was convinced that this machine would be compelled to force-land on the Isle of Wight. Sergeant Edmund Shepperd encountered eighteen Ju 88s. He attacked one of them, and Pilot Officer Ian Bayles saw the port engine in flames. He then attacked another and

expended all his ammunition. He followed this machine down and saw it land in a field and burst into flames.

Pilot Officer Timothy Wildblood attacked an Me 109 and got in one burst of fire but with unknown result. He then attacked an Me 110 which went down in an inverted spiral dive but did not see it actually crash. Flight Lieutenant Derek Boitel-Gill attacked an E/A which burst into flames and crashed. He then fired at another which flew through his burst but did not catch fire. He then attacked another machine but did not see result of attack.

Pilot Officer Hogg attacked a Ju 88. He fired all his rounds and this machine was seen to crash into the sea. Unfortunately, Flight Lieutenant Carr Withall and Pilot Officer Douglas Shepley failed to return.

Flight Lieutenant Withall, an Australian, was a highly experienced pilot, having been among the first pilots to fly a Spitfire, as he was serving on 19 Squadron at Duxford when the first of the type were delivered in August 1938. In May 1939, he became commander of 'A' Flight, before a posting to command 152 Squadron's 'A' Flight five months later. Withall, who had damaged a Ju 88 on 13 July 1940, was exactly the kind of officer Fighter Command could so ill afford to lose. Similarly, Pilot Officer Shepley had recently recorded combat success; both men remain missing. In response, 152 Squadron four Ju 88s and one Me 110 destroyed, a Ju 8 'probable' and two damaged.

Squadron Leader Hector McGregor and 213 Squadron arrived over the combat area after the enemy bombers had done their deadly work, so he led the Hurricanes to mid-Channel, hoping to contact the retiring Germans. Off Bognor Regis, some twenty miles South-south-east of the Isle of Wight, at 12.35 hrs McGregor caught an Me 110 flying home – which he promptly shot down into the sea: 'no one got out'.

Pilot Officer Alexander Osmand was also up, on his second patrol of the day, later recording in his logbook 'Chased Me 109s and Me 110s to France, where they circled. Got chased out of it by 109s!' In total, 213 Squadron claimed eleven Me 110s and a 109 destroyed, but two pilots were lost: Sergeant Geoffrey Wilkes and Sydney Stuckey were both missing.

No.43 Squadron's 'A' Flight also entered the fray after the retiring Germans, at 12.30 hrs, South of Worthing, subsequently claiming a Ju 88 probably destroyed and a number of 'He 111s' damaged (which were actually also Ju 88s). Nine minutes later, 609 Squadron went into action off the East Coast of the Isle of Wight; Flying Officer John Dundas (Yellow 1):

Yellow Section were behind Red Section until Red 1 (Squadron Leader Darley) made his first attack. We went in in line-astern. I picked an Me 110 as it came around in an anti-clockwise circle and fired a burst of approximately two seconds, allowing double and upward deflection on the beam. Range approx. 300–100 yards. I saw results in that fragments flew off starboard side of wing and engine, and flames came from starboard engine. Height approx. 15,000ft.

Broke away vertically down and through layers of circling Me 110s; climbed up again to 18,000ft outside the circle. The second time I repeated a similar attack but soon found myself firing head-on at an oncoming Me 110 which fired back. Both parties fired inaccurately.

Broke away again through many Me's and while attempting to climb up near Portsmouth was attacked at 12,000ft by a 109 with a red spinner which fired wildly, diving down sun. I lost this E/A immediately. Climbing to attack the 110s about ten miles SE of Isle of Wight and waited for a gap in the circle. I found one and was able to come in astern of an Me 110 and fired a 5-second burst from dead astern at 450–250 yards. I had to break off then as other Me's were coming down at me, but I saw plenty of smoke coming from both engines. I then broke away and as Me's appeared to be going back I returned to base.

Dundas was credited with a 110 destroyed, as were Flying Officer Henry 'Mac' Goodwin, Pilot Officers Charles 'Teeny' Overton and Michael Staples; Sergeant Alan Feary claimed a 109 destroyed, and Pilot Officer David Crook two. As the squadron diary commented, 'The morning's fighting yielded a very satisfactory score for no loss.'

At 12.45 hrs, Squadron Leader Hill Harkness and 257 Squadron engaged the Portsmouth raiders, engaging over Portsmouth and Spithead. Harkness would claim a 'Do 17 probable', Flight Lieutenant Hugh Beresford an Me 110 'probable'. Pilot Officer Carl Capon a 'He 111 probable', and Pilot Officer Arthur Cochrane, a Canadian, a 'He 111 damaged'.

Sergeant Reg Nutter, 257 Squadron:

For me personally, the Battle of Britain remains a vivid kaleidoscope of memories. I recall trying to warn Pilot Officer Capon that he was about to be attacked by a 109, but my radio was unserviceable; I remember The Hon David Coke returning from a battle over Portsmouth during which a German bullet had nicked him in the little finger of the throttle hand. Once I chased a lone Do 17 reconnaissance bomber in and out of the clouds along the south coast, while listening to American jazz music coming over the squadron frequency. Vivid memories all.

It was in this combat, in fact, that Coke was wounded, crash-landing on the mainland and being admitted to the Royal Naval Hospital Haslar. One Hurricane, though, was missing: Pilot Officer John Chomley, a 20-year-old Rhodesian, who was never seen again.

Oberleutnant von Hofe of JG3 was among the escorting Me 109 pilots:

> Six Spitfires dived down from the left, turning towards us. We zoomed up very tightly and they flashed by behind us. We went into a diving turn to the right and the leading 109s of our *Staffel* got behind the Spitfires. All our guns were firing. Two Spitfires went down trailing smoke, one of them exploded after a 1,000 metre dive, the other one flew away trailing white smoke. The other Spitfires turned sharply to meet us and fired away at our *Staffel*'s rearmost machines.
>
> We then got behind the enemy fighters. The *Kommandeur* set one of them on fire and the English pilot baled out immediately. His parachute blossomed beneath us. The rest of the Tommies dived away, showing us their blue bellies and 'peacock's eyes'. Two of our aircraft reported that they were leaving the formation as both had been badly hit The *Kommandeur* ordered two others to cover and escort them home.
>
> Once again, we were flying near the bombers, from which we had been separated in combat. One of them fell back some 200 metres behind the formation. A long white smoke cloud trailed from the right engine. A hit!
>
> Some of our fighters covered the machine which lagged further and further behind. The bomber's right propeller was stationary but apparently the machine could maintain its altitude and was still protected by fighters. I certainly hope it reached the French coast.

As the retiring enemy was pursued across the sea, Portsmouth was left greatly damaged: the railway station and oil tanks, among other installations, and three small vessels were all destroyed; the loss of human life was also high: ninety-six navy personnel and civilians died during this raid.

The second, smaller, enemy formation dive-bombed the Chain Home station at Ventnor, fifteen 500kg bombs finding their mark, destroying every building on site and damaging the aerials – putting this RDF station out of action for three days.

It was not just the British, however, who were left counting the cost in the wake of this devastating raid: KG51 lost ten Ju 88s, including the *Geschwaderkommodore*, *Oberst* Dr Fisser, and virtually every bomber returned damaged by AA fire or RAF fighters. For some unknown reason, the German fighters only appeared to engage offensively when the Ventnor force was suffering heavy losses, so on this occasion the RAF fighters were more successful at destroying the enemy bombers than the day before.

British Air Intelligence reported on the methods and effectiveness of the enemy fighter escorts:

> Escorting fighters are dispersed in various positions relative to the bomber formations they are protecting. During the early phase of attacks on this country it was usual for the fighter escort to fly behind and several thousand feet above the bomber formation. If our fighters attacked the bombers, the escort would descend and attack them providing that they (the German fighters) were not outnumbered. If our fighters attacked the enemy fighter escort, the latter would usually form a self-defensive circle, thus ceasing to afford protection to the bombers which they were supposed to be escorting.
>
> Heavy casualties suffered by the bombers led to a change of tactics involving an increase in escorting fighters with new dispositions relative to the bomber formations. Fighters were encountered ahead and on both flanks as well as above and behind the bombers and usually flying in close proximity to the latter. On occasions the individual bomber units were found to be more spaced out with fighters weaving among them.
>
> Accompanying formations of fighters have also been observed acting as a remote escort of 'freelance' patrols, flying at a great height above and in the vicinity of the bomber formations, but they have rarely taken offensive action.

For 266 Squadron, the opportunity for action on 12 August 1940 was unexpected. This was a 12 Group squadron, based at Wittering – and 12 Group, defending the industrial Midlands and the North, had yet to play any part in the fighting over south-east England. Indeed, up there in 12 Group, Air Vice-Marshal Leigh-Mallory's pilots continued flying the monotonous round of convoy protection patrols of the East Coast and chasing reconnaissance bombers – while all the while hearing of the intensifying action over the South Coast.

As we have seen, on 29 July, the DCAS, Air Marshal Douglas, had ordered that enemy airfields should be attacked by Bomber Command immediately after the raiders had landed, the impracticality and danger of such a suggestion being recognised by the Fighter Command SASO, Air Vice-Marshal Evill, who prevented these operations going ahead. The scheme was supported by the AOC of 12 Group, Air Vice-Marshal Leigh-Mallory, however, who was desperate to get into the battle and wrest some glory from his rival, Air Vice-Marshal Park.

On 9 August 1940, 266 Squadron was sent from Wittering to Northolt, thence to Tangmere 'for operational duties under Coastal Command, arriving at 17.25 hrs'. The following day, the squadron remained at Tangmere, on readiness, receiving a 'Warning order ... for Squadron to be prepared for move to Eastchurch', the latter being a Coastal Command aerodrome on the Isle of Sheppey, situated on the southern shore of the mouth of the Thames Estuary in the 11 Group Fighter Command area.

On 10 August, 266 Squadron's ground personnel left Wittering for Eastchurch, the move completed by 13.30 hrs on 12 August. At 17.40 hrs, the squadron's Spitfires arrived at Eastchurch from Tangmere, there joining 'B' Flight of 12 Group's 19 Squadron. Squadron Leader Phillip Pinkham, 19's CO, wrote that his orders were to 'escort the Battle boys on a beat up of the other side' – meaning that the Spitfires were to escort obsolete Fairey Battle bombers – which had taken such a beating in France – to attack the enemy invasion ports and other targets.

The folly of such an enterprise is inconceivable, and it is questionable as to whether Air Chief Marshal Dowding, who delegated tactical control to his group commanders, even knew about this. Fortunately, however, the events of 13 August 1940 – as we will discover – prevented these operations from going ahead.

Let us now return to the air-fighting on 12 August, which had so far seen precision raids on the RDF stations at Dunkirk, Dover, Rye and Pevensey, and the heavy attack on Portsmouth and the Ventnor Chain Home Station. With Dover, Rye, Pevensey and Ventnor RDF temporarily blind, the action was about to increase further still.

As the Portsmouth and Ventnor raiders withdrew, at 12.20 hrs large enemy formations were detected in the Dover Strait while twenty-plus were off Cap Gris-Nez, forty-plus behind it, and various smaller formations. Clearly, more trouble was brewing. At 12.20 hrs, 501 Squadron's Hurricanes were scrambled to patrol Dover, and at the same time, 615 Squadron was ordered up from Kenley and vectored to Southampton – but en route were sent to intercept an incoming raid over Beachy Head.

At 12.45 hrs, 615 met Me 109s engaged on a *Freie Hunt*:

> Red Section attacked and Flight Lieutenant Gaunce shot one down confirmed. One burst into flames and the other blew up and dived into the sea. Flight Lieutenant Gaunce's aircraft was covered in oil when he returned here. Pilot Officer Hugo shot down one which fell into the sea, the pilot was waving. Pilot Officer Hugo landed to report this at Hawkinge and a boat was despatched to rescue the pilot. Pilot Officer McClintock in his first combat engaged an Me 109 and damaged it for certain. [ORB]

It was a good result for 615 Squadron, which suffered no losses in the engagement; in fact, it was a good day all-round for the squadron: Flight Lieutenant Lionel Gaunce (Canadian), Flying Officer Peter Collard and Pilot Officer Petrus 'Dutch' Hugo (South African) all received notification of their DFC awards.

The fighter sweep engaged by 615 Squadron, however, was a diversionary raid away from another attack by *Erprobungsgruppe* 210 – this time on Manston airfield.

Just after noon, fourteen Me 110s of *Stab*, 1 and 2 *Staffel* of *Erprobungsgruppe* 210 took off from Calais-Marck, closely escorted by seven 3 *Staffel* Me 109s; eighteen Do 17s of KG2 were then to hit the airfield, the raid's withdrawal being covered by JG26.

Flying Officer Al Deere, 54 Squadron:

> We had just settled down to the inevitable game of cards in our dispersal hut at Manston (pontoon was the normal relaxation between operations) when the telephone shrilled warningly. How we hated the dispersal telephone; its very note was abnormal and the unexpectedness with which it rang had the immediate effect of producing an awful sick feeling in the pit of one's tummy.
>
> A pin could have been heard to drop as, with cards poised and eyes turned expectantly towards the orderly as he reached for the receiver, we strained to hear the message from the now faintly urgent voice which came over the wire. 'Hornet Squadron scramble'. Table, cards and money shot into the air as the pilots dived headlong for the door.

No.54 Squadron managed to get away before the raid came in, but, clawing for height over Dover, did not engage.

At 12.45 hrs, 65 Squadron's Spitfires were scrambled from Manston, but during this process the Me 110s and 109s hit the airfield – hard and fast. Fortunately, because Manston was a grass airfield and not restricted to the width of a concrete runway, only one of the Spitfires failed to get airborne, the propeller of Pilot Officer Kenneth Hart's aircraft being damaged, but fortunately the pilot was unhurt.

Among 65 Squadron's pilots was the Supermarine test pilot Jeffrey Quill, who insisted upon flying operationally to gain more knowledge and experience of how the Spitfire performed in actual combat:

> We were just formed up on the ground and waiting Sam's [Squadron Leader Sawyer, the CO] signal to start rolling. I was therefore looking out to my left towards the leading section when I became aware of, rather than actually hearing, a sort of reverberating 'crump' behind and to my right. I looked quickly over my right shoulder to see one of the hangar roofs close behind us ascending heavenwards ... I caught a glimpse through smoke of what looked like a Bf110 pulling sharply out of a dive and immediately concluded that it was high time for Quill to be airborne!

RAF Manston's ORB states:

> At 1250 hrs the aerodrome was heavily attacked by approximately fifteen Me110s and some *Heinkels* [sic] and bombed at low altitude;

some 150 HE bombs were dropped; the aerodrome was pitted with approximate 100 craters and rendered temporarily unserviceable; two hangars were damaged, and workshops were destroyed; in the latter building a civilian clerk was killed, this being the only fatal casualty; the raid lasted approximately five minutes.

No.501 Squadron was airborne, however, and engaged the raiders, reported by Sergeant James 'Ginger' Lacey as '20 Me 110 and 20 Me 109, approx. between Manston and Ramsgate, 1240–1245 hrs', as the Germans headed home.

Lacey further reported that:

> I was No 3 in Red Section of 'A' Flight when 501 Squadron engaged a number of Me 110 Jaguars and Me 109 over Manston. I picked an Me 110 Jaguar which was proceeding eastwards at 5,000ft, approximately, over Ramsgate. I opened fire at 250 yards and continued firing until I was out of ammunition.
>
> Long streams of white smoke poured from both engines or wings, and as I finished firing the pilot jumped with his parachute. I immediately dived into the nearest cloud as I had no more ammunition and there were lots more E/A, so I did not see the Jaguar crash or where the pilot land. I then proceeded beck to base and landed.

As no *Erprobungsgruppe* 210 fighters were lost it is unclear which aircraft Lacey claimed to have destroyed. Over Manston, Flight Lieutenant George Stoney and the Polish Flying Officer Stefan Witorzenc both damaged Me 110s, but another of the squadron's Poles, Flying Officer Kazimierz Lukaszewicz, who had only joined the squadron five days before, was shot down over the sea and never seen again – probably by *Leutnant* Horst Marx of 3/*Erprobungsgruppe* 210.

Having taken off amid the shower of bombs, minutes later 65 Squadron engaged Me 109s over Margate. For no loss, the Irish Flying Officer Brendan 'Paddy' Finucane, Flying Officer Tommy Smart and Pilot Officer Felix Gregory all claimed Me 109s probably destroyed. From the air, 54 Squadron's Flying Officer Al Deere could see Manston aerodrome, 'half hidden in a mushroom cloud of smoke which drifted across its bomb-cratered surface'. Indeed, 54 Squadron was diverted to land at its home base of Hornchurch.

When 54 returned to Manston later that day, Deere described the scene:

> The airfield was a shambles of gutted hangars and smouldering dispersal buildings, all of which were immersed in a thin film of white chalk dust which drifted across the airfield and settled on men, buildings and parked aircraft in the manner, and with the appearance of, a light snow storm. The rows of yellow flags, marking the safety

lane for landing, and the chalk-coated men and materials were to become symbolic of Manston in the days that followed, and remain as a lasting impression with all those who worked and operated from there in August 1940.

Although much damage was caused to airfield buildings and facilities, only one Blenheim was destroyed and just one Spitfire had suffered minor damage. So, although the enemy believed that Manston had been completely destroyed, to the credit of all involved, within twenty-four hours this station was also back on 'top line'.

There was no further action in the afternoon, and by 16.00 hrs the Channel was virtually clear of enemy aircraft – but not for long.

The enemy's operations on this day clearly marked a change in strategy and significant escalation in the fighting, with RDF stations, airfields and the port of Portsmouth all coming under heavy aerial bombardment. Consequently, when four German formations were detected at 16.45 hrs, two of fifty-plus, one thirty-plus and another of twenty-plus, the 11 Group Controller, in anticipation of another airfield attack, scrambled 64 Squadron from Hawkinge at 16.45 hrs, and five minutes later the Hurricanes of 32 Squadron from the same airfield. At 17.20 hrs, 56 Squadron scrambled from Rochford, and at 17.25 hrs, all of 501 Squadron took-off from Hawkinge, while 54 Squadron was ordered up from Hornchurch.

The first defending squadron to engage was 32, combats occurring between Manston and Dover between 17.20 and 17.50 hrs, as running battles developed:

> Ordered patrol Hawkinge at 10,000ft. When over Dover sighted 30/40 Do 215s escorted by 30/40 Me 109s flying at 12,000'ft. After the initial engagement the squadron became split up and various combats took place ranging from Dover to North of Whitstable. Aircraft shot down by the following:
>
> Flight Lieutenant Crossley: one Me 109 confirmed, one Unconfirmed.
> Flying Officer Humpherson: one unconfirmed.
> Pilot Officer Grice: one Do 215 damaged.
> Pilot Officer Proctor one Me 109 unconfirmed.
> Sergeant Higgins, Pilot Officer Pniak, Pilot Officer Gardner: four unconfirmed.
> Pilot Officer Smythe: one Do 215 confirmed.
> Sergeant Bayley: one Do 215 confirmed.
> Squadron landed individually at various times. [ORB]

Pilot Officer Anthony Barton, however, was shot-up and crash-landed near Hawkinge, but was safe.

KANALKAMPF DIARY, 1 AUGUST – 12 AUGUST 1940

One enemy formation, comprising a *gruppe* of Do 17s escorted by Me 109s, also in *gruppe* strength, was incoming over the North Foreland at 17.33 hrs and engaged by Nos. 54 and 56 squadrons.

Flying Officer Al Deere of the former reported that his combat occurred ten miles off North Foreland, at 17.30 hrs, at between 17,000 and 20,000ft:

> I was leading 54 Squadron (eleven aircraft: two sections of four, one of three) on patrol inland of Dover at 21,000ft when a raid was reported approaching Manston aerodrome. I saw about fifty bombers over the North Foreland turning from West to East. At this moment Blue Leader gave a Tally Ho of aircraft over Dover. I instructed him to remain with me and we would attack the raid over Manston, which at a distance appeared unescorted. Blue Leader did not hear this order and together with Yellow Section engaged bombers over Dover.
>
> I did not realise Blue Leader had left me until I came within striking distance of bombers now flying East ten miles off the North Foreland, then he said he was engaged over Dover. Me 109s appeared from the left as I closed in on the bombers, so I gave the order for my sections to break and engage fighters.
>
> After a quick turn I saw an Me 109 shoot a Spitfire down in flames and I got on the Me 109's tail and dived from 17,000ft to 11,000ft, firing short bursts at 250 yards when enemy burst into flames and continued in a vertical dive towards the sea.
>
> On the return journey I ran into about twelve Me 110s in mid-Channel and was able to surprise them as I was approaching from direction of French coast. I fired a long burst at about 150 yards and the enemy turned towards France. I fired two more long bursts, using deflection, and enemy prepared to pancake on sea. I followed him down and saw the man climbing into a rubber dinghy. I had a front gun exercise at him, but, unfortunately, a 109 came from out of the blue and shot hell out of me. I retired with 12 Boost.

The Spitfire Deere had seen shot down was that of the American Pilot Officer 'Art' Donahue, of 64 Squadron, which was also engaged over the Dover area. Donahue baled out with leg wounds and burns, but was safe. Flight Lieutenant Lawrence Henstock was also shot-up, managing to land at Hawkinge, the 64 Squadron 'bag' being one Me 109 destroyed 'confirmed' another 'unconfirmed', with one damaged and a Do 17 'probable'.

The speed of the defenders' reaction, however, must have made the Germans realise that already the radar stations were largely functioning again.

Flight Lieutenant 'Squeak' Weaver of 56 Squadron, up from Rochford, reported that at 17.30 hrs, ten miles North of Margate:

When airborne, 'B' Flight joined us and led us to attack E/A reported approaching Manston. We saw then ten miles east of us, flying north. 'B' Flight leader ordered sections into echelon right and led us to attack. I selected the left-hand E/A of the extreme right-hand rear section of the E/A, who were flying in close formation in three lines of sections of three, in vic line astern. I attacked from dead astern, giving a four-second burst at 400 yards, experiencing intense return fire at that range.

This burst had no apparent effect. I then closed and gave him a continuous burst at 250/200 yards, using all my ammunition. E/A began to give out black smoke and I broke away. While at 250 yards' range, after about eight seconds firing my windscreen and leading edges began to get coated with oil. On landing, Pilot Officer Joubert and Flying Officer Westmacott confirmed that they had seen the E/A which I had attacked blow up in the air. E/A kept close formation throughout the attacks and adopted no evasive action.

This 'Do 215' was confirmed as destroyed. The bombers were escorted by a large number of enemy fighters, Sergeant Smythe destroying an Me 109 while Flight Sergeant Frederick 'Taffy' Higginson damaged another. Interestingly, Sergeant George Smythe, yet another former aircraft apprentice, and a successful fighter pilot, had fitted enlarged ammunition boxes to his aircraft, containing an extra 400 rounds.

Clearly, however, the 56 Squadron diarist was a master of the understatement, recording that 19-year-old Pilot Officer Geoffrey Page 'baled out but was rescued slightly burned'. Later, Pilot Officer Barry Sutton remembered that 'There was a tremendous explosion on my right, only a few feet away, probably ten yards away, which was Geoffrey. Such a sheet of flame came out of his aeroplane that I couldn't conceive he could have survived, I thought he must be dead already.'

Page, though, was still alive in his blazing Hurricane:

It was like a blast furnace coming straight up at my face and hands. One hand was still on the throttle and I remember looking at it rather fascinated, just watching the burning taking place. Layers of skin were burnt off and rolled up like parchment. I vividly remember screaming in terror when the aircraft was hit, a ball of fire, but as I was losing consciousness a tremendous calm came over me, nature's way of protecting one, and all the fear went. I accepted the fact that I was about to die. I half-rolled the aeroplane and fell out of it. Then there was a thump as the parachute opened.

My first instinct was to look up, to check if the parachute was on fire, fortunately it wasn't. I then took stock of my personal situation. First thing I noticed was this awful smell of my own burning flesh. Then I looked down and saw that my trousers had been blown completely off, plus one shoe. Then I splashed into the sea, feet first, so thought I'd just float around a bit until picked up. Then I discovered that this life-saving jacket, which for obvious outstanding reasons was known as a 'Mae West', had been burnt through, so I had to swim for it.

As I was swimming along I remembered that my dear mother had given me a brandy flask, which I had filled up at great expense as a young pilot officer and was in my breast pocket. I got the brandy flask out but couldn't get the cap off, so held it between my wrists and tried to use my teeth. At that point a wave came and washed the flask away before I had taken a sip. I have to say I was pretty angry then.

Fortunately, Page was rescued at 17.50 hrs by the Margate Lifeboat – his 'slight' burns actually requiring two years' hospitalisation as one of plastic surgeon Sir Archibald McIndoe's famous 'Guinea Pigs' at East Grinstead. Incredibly, Page recovered, returned to operational flying, became a decorated ace, and survived the war. He later founded the Battle of Britain Memorial Trust, the driving force behind creation of the National Battle of Britain Memorial on the cliffs above Folkestone.

At 17.35 hrs, 501 Squadron's Pilot Officer John Gibson was over Lympne, engaging what he identified as 'He 113s':

I was No 2 in Red Section when the squadron was ordered off to patrol Hawkinge. The enemy was sighted approaching Lympne from the SW. There were about eighty machines and I think that they were Do 17s. Behind and above was a very strong formation of fighters. Looking behind own Squadron I noticed that the rear sections and Red Section No 3 were not there. I afterwards learnt that they had pursued some E/A that were below us. This left only the Squadron Leader and myself and we carried on travelling West, climbing into the sun.

As we were turning to the right to deliver the attack I noticed in the rear vision mirror an aircraft diving. I called to Red 1 about it, pulled away to the right, and saw two *Heinkel* 113s on my tail. I dived into and got out of a cloud and found the two E/A behind me on the left.

From this time on I did not see Red 1. I began steep turning to the right and finally I managed to turn to the right inside and catch up one of the E/A: I gave him two bursts and suddenly saw him turn over on his back and go down over the vertical. The other E/A had been circling above and came down. I got on the tail of the first. As I dived down following the first E/A I saw white tracer coming from behind I immediately dived into another cloud but could not find the other E/A when I emerged again. I then returned to base.

Gibson was credited with an Me 109 destroyed, which was 501 Squadron's only combat claim in this interception.

The enemy formation bound for Manston was diverted from its objective by the strong fighter opposition, instead dropping bombs near the villages of Bekesbourne and Patrixbourne. Unfortunately, the same could not be said of the raids heading for the airfields at Hawkinge and Lympne.

At 17.30 hrs, *Erprobungsgruppe* 210 swept in to attack Hawkinge, as the Station ORB recorded:

> An enemy bombing attack by Ju 88s [*sic*] against the Station was carried out at 1730 hrs and lasted for approximately ten minutes. One hangar, No. 3, was almost completely wrecked while another, No 5, was partially wrecked. A number of bombs of heavy calibre, including incendiary, were dropped.
>
> The aerodrome and buildings were machine-gunned during the attack. The main stores were partly damaged by fire, the clothing store almost completely. The fire was quickly brought under control by RAF personnel aided by local Auxiliary Fire Service. The Station Workshops were wrecked. Two houses in the Airmen's Married Quarters, occupied by airmen, were destroyed. Twenty-eight craters were made on the aerodrome, the largest being 76' x 72' x 28' deep, and the smallest 10' x 10' x 8' deep, but the aerodrome was not rendered completely unserviceable. Repairs to the surface were immediately commenced by the Royal Engineers already attached for such work.
>
> Ground Defences were surprised and no guns, except two Hispano were fired. The altitude of the attacking aircraft was such that it was impractical for the PACU to be brought into action. Two civilians, Mr Brisley and Mr Caistor, employed by contractors of the Works Directorate, were killed and three airmen, Corporal McColl, attached from RAF Station Yeadon, AC2 Symes, attached from RAF Station, Kenley, and AC1 Langdon of RAF Station, Hawkinge, were killed. Six airmen received severe injuries and were admitted to the Kent and Canterbury Hospital, Canterbury. The casualties occurred to personnel employed in No 3 hangar. Two Spitfire aircraft, under repair, were seriously damaged, while one or two others were struck by splinters. The two non-operational aircraft on charge were damaged but repairable.

By the end of the day, Manston was unserviceable, and the runways of Hawkinge and Lympne were badly cratered. All three stations had been heavily damaged – but by the following morning both Manston and Hawkinge were once more fully operational. The attack on Lympne, which saw some 200 bombs dropped on the airfield, was yet another indication of poor *Luftwaffe* air intelligence leading to questionable target selection and effort being expended which could – and should – have been better employed elsewhere: Lympne was not a Fighter Command airfield, so its loss made no difference to 11 Group.

While Air Vice-Marshal Park's fighters flew nearly 500 sorties on this day, the Germans had made a huge effort, with nine *Kampfgeschwadern* engaged and *Erprobungsgruppe* 210 being especially hard worked. Given that the RDF stations and airfields were soon back on line, arguably the enemy's results were not commensurate with the great effort involved.

The Daily Home Intelligence Report, London Region, reported, 'Jubilation over air battles. RAF highly praised in all quarters – results having a heartening effect.'

Nonetheless, the events of this day in particular set the scene for the next few weeks of fighting which lay ahead – the hammer blows to come falling squarely on 11 Group's airfields.

At 17.00 hrs, the OKL signalled the *Luftflotten*: the *Adlerangriff* was to commence at 07.30 hrs the following day.

Reflections

The Breaking Storm began by discussing the validity of 10 July 1940 as the start-date of the Battle of Britain, suggesting that 2 July 1940 may have been more appropriate, given that on that date the OKW decided that if aerial superiority could be achieved by the *Luftwaffe*, a seaborne invasion of Britain may be a possibility. This volume, however, has looked deeper still at Germany's plans, which are worth reviewing here.

On 13 July 1940, Hitler approved the OKH's invasion plan, and on 16 July 1940 issued his oft-quoted *Führer* Directive No.16, outlining his intention to invade Britain 'if necessary', in the event of Britain refusing to come to terms.

A diplomatic solution and blockade, not invasion, however, were Hitler's preferred options. Indeed, he remained reluctant to aggressively prosecute the war against England, and, rightly, especially feared the RN. Indeed, while *Oberst* 'Papa' Fink, the *KanalkampfFührer*, began attacking Channel-bound convoys with increasing shows of strength, such operations were hardly going to decisively defeat Britain – and, emphasising his caution, Hitler refused to allow the battering of inland targets or an all-out aerial bombardment of the civilian population. No, his mind was focused on achieving a diplomatic solution, and arguably these operations over the Channel, and his 16 July 1940 Directive, were actually intended as shows of strength to frighten Britain into surrendering in order to avoid terror and destruction from the air.

This 'Air Fleet Diplomacy' was exactly the kind of brinkmanship, of course, that had been so successful for Hitler in the late 1930s – but Hitler was no longer dealing with the appeaser Neville Chamberlain. Winston Churchill was a very different prospect and, as an historian, knew that states which meekly surrender disappear, while those that go down fighting are resurrected, their spirit and flame never extinguished.

Consequently, there was never any chance of Britain complying with Hitler's 'last appeal to reason' on 19 July 1940. Indeed, that Lord Halifax, previously an appeaser and great ally of Chamberlain's, broadcast Britain's rejection, sent the *Führer* a strong message. With Britain refusing the back down, reluctant though he remained, Hitler had no choice but to order air operations aligned to achieving Operation *Seelöwe* should begin immediately – with the proviso that 'If results of air warfare are unsatisfactory, invasion preparations will be stopped.' Arguably, though, from 31 July 1940 there was no turning away from Britain – so that date too is a contender for the actual start of the Battle of Britain.

All these years later, of course, we know much more about Hitler's strategy and plans, much of which was unknown, I daresay, when Lord Dowding wrote his Despatch in 1946. Were the great man still with us, the question I would ask him is: given what we now know, would he still choose 10 July 1940 as the Battle of Britain's start-date? Reviewing the evidence, as we have, I think that unlikely, and would argue that 31 July 1940 would be more appropriate, because, as discussed, it was on that dates that air operations were harnessed to effecting the conditions necessary for Operation *Seelöwe*.

It is often said that the *Kanalkampf* represented a period of time during which the *Luftwaffe* probed Britain's defences – but this is unsupported by the evidence. Fink's intention, although hamstrung by being unable to attack inland targets, was clearly to bring Fighter Command to battle over the dangerous sea, and it is interesting how the day-fighting intensified along a broad front, from Portland to the Thames Estuary, from late July 1940 until the *Adlerangriff* began in earnest on 13 August 1940 – as we will explore in Volume 3, *Battle of Britain: Attack of the Eagles, 13 August 1940–18 August 1940*.

The *Kanalkampf* did, though, represent an important period of fighting because Fink effectively denied the Royal Navy of its Dover base and the advantage RDF gave the defenders was recognised – although, that said, it is hard to understand why more effort was not made to destroy the Chain Home Stations. That, very likely, comes down to the demonstrably poor air intelligence that the *Luftwaffe* suffered from throughout the entire Battle of Britain, with lacking or inaccurate information influencing questionable target selection.

Take, for example, the heavy fighting on 12 August 1940, which saw four RDF stations damaged but only temporarily taken off air, and only hit once that day, while other major raids focused on Portsmouth and three coastal airfields – one of which, Lympne, bracketed by 200 HE bombs, was not even a Fighter Command airfield. Going forward, this would be a common feature of the *Luftwaffe*'s operations.

It is also interesting that the Italians offer of supporting the air offensive against Britain was initially rejected by Hitler – but followed up with an invitation to participate on 11 August 1940. Three days before, the fighting had increased significantly, and the events of 11 August 1940 must have impressed upon the enemy that defeating Fighter Command was clearly not going to be a pushover.

From the defenders' perspective, we have seen how more often than not, particularly early on in the fighting, that sections of three fighters, or flights of six, were scrambled more commonly than an entire squadron of twelve. This was partially owing to the need to carefully shepherd limited resources but was also because pre-war training mainly revolved around the section or flight.

The limitations of airborne communications were also a factor, with pilots being able to talk to their own squadron and sector controller, but not pilots of other squadrons or other sector controllers – making control of large formations impossible for a leader in the air once battle was joined. Considering the size of many enemy formations being met by these 'penny packets' of RAF fighters, it is easy to see how the legend of The Few later arose – and the matter of formation sizes will become increasingly significant as our narrative progresses.

During this first phase, combats were mainly fought from low to medium altitudes at which the Hurricane performed well, even out-performing the Me 109, which it could out-turn on occasions. The superiority of the Spitfire in matching the Me 109, which was excellent above 25,000ft, whereas the Hurricane was not, had been recognised, and in August certain sector controllers had begun trying to despatch Hurricanes to attack enemy bombers, while Spitfires tackled the German fighters.

It was a wise tactic, and as the fighting wore on would become standard practice, when practically possible, and in the fighting ahead the Hurricane's rugged frame and numbers, coupled with the Spitfire's high-altitude performance would make the types perfectly compatible stable-mates. The same could not be said of the Defiant turret-fighter, however, which had suffered terribly on 19 July 1940, indications being that it lacked the necessary performance and armament for day-fighting.

From a *Luftwaffe* perspective, it was equally clear that the much-vaunted *Stuka* was vulnerable to attack by enemy fighters, for which it was no match, and could not, therefore, operate without fighter escort. In the fighting ahead, the Me 110's flaws would also be exposed, and so, really, in terms of fighters, the Battle of Britain was already becoming a contest between Hurricanes, Spitfires and Me 109s. In terms of replacement aircraft, so far this was not a problem for either side, and nor would it be for Fighter Command. Interestingly, on 30 June 1940 Fighter Command fielded 1,200 operational single-engine pilots, that figure, in spite of casualties, increasing to 1,377 on 27 July, and 1,796 by 2 November.

The *Luftwaffe*, however, had 906 on 1 June, this figure decreasing to 869 by 1 August, and just 673 on 1 November. In what was a war of attrition, the German fighter pilots were losing by the time *Adler Tag* was launched on 13 August. The great advantage enjoyed by the *Jagdwaffe*, however, was combat experience, which the replacement RAF pilots did not have, and so statistics do not tell the full story.

This narrative has also explored the operations of both Coastal Command and Bomber Command, and will continue to do so, emphasising that this great battle to defend Britain was not, in fact, exclusively fought by Fighter Command. As this first phase of the Battle of Britain concluded, for example, on the night of 12/13 August 1940, the eve of *Adler Tag*, Bomber Command mounted further raids on German airfields and industrial targets – including the heavily defended Dortmund-Ems Canal, which the Hampdens of Nos. 49 and 83 squadrons were tasked with attacking from low-level.

Flight Lieutenant Roderick Learoyd of the former unit pressed on with a determined attack from 150ft, even after the all of the aircraft preceding him being shot down. Coned and virtually blinded by searchlights, his own Hampden hit,

Learoyd successfully bombed his aqueduct target near Munster – and returned home safely. For this 'signal act of valour', Flight Lieutenant Learoyd was awarded the Victoria Cross, Britain's highest award for gallantry and supreme courage in the face of the enemy. It was, in fact, the third RAF VC of the Second World War, and the first of three more awarded during the Battle of Britain – only one of these, as we will see in due course, awarded to a fighter pilot.

While Fighter Command surely bore the brunt of the daylight battles in the direct defence of Britain, as we have seen Coastal Command and Bomber Command were also involved in both defending these shores and taking the war to the enemy across the sea. This, however, is often completely ignored or side-lined by commentators on the summer of 1940, so it is perhaps entirely appropriate that our narrative of the *Kanalkampf* concludes with a Bomber Command VC.

The last word on the *Kanalkampf* fighting goes to Pilot Officer Harbourne Mackay Stephen, a Spitfire pilot on 74 'Tiger' Squadron:

> Looking back, it was July, not August or September, that was the most intensive period of fighting. The Germans were bombing convoys and coastal targets, and waves of 109s kept coming over, day in, day out. We were on duty for long periods every day. It was exhausting.

Tuesday, 13 August 1940, would at last see *Adler Tag* unleashed …

Bibliography

The National Archives

The National Archives at Kew is the main repository for primary source documents; the following documents were consulted during the course of research for this book.

Operations Record Books
AIR 27/2018	'A' Flight, 1 Photographic Reconnaissance Unit
AIR 27/2015	'B' Flight, 1 Photographic Reconnaissance Unit
AIR 27/589	1 Squadron
AIR 27/32	3 Squadron
AIR 27/202	15 Squadron
AIR 27/252	19 Squadron
AIR 27/360	32 Squadron
AIR 27/441	43 Squadron
AIR 27/447	44 Squadron
AIR 27/460	46 Squadron
AIR 27/554	50 Squadron
AIR 27/503	53 Squadron
AIR 27/511	54 Squadron
AIR 27/528	56 Squadron
AIR 27/554	59 Squadron
AIR 27/598	66 Squadron
AIR 27/624	72 Squadron
AIR 27/640	74 Squadron
AIR 27/664	79 Squadron
AIR 27/681	82 Squadron
AIR 27/712	87 Squadron
AIR 27/776	97 Squadron
AIR 27/801	101 Squadron
AIR 27/813	103 Squadron
AIR 27/841	107 Squadron

BIBLIOGRAPHY

AIR 27/857	110 Squadron
AIR 27/866	111 Squadron
AIR 27/882	114 Squadron
AIR 27/969	141 Squadron
AIR 27/984	145 Squadron
AIR 27/1025	152 Squadron
AIR 27/1315	213 Squadron
AIR 27/1340	217 Squadron
AIR 27/1365	220 Squadron
AIR 27/1371	222 Squadron
AIR 27/1385	224 Squadron
AIR 27/1442	235 Squadron
AIR 27/1445	236 Squadron
AIR 27/1453	238 Squadron
AIR 27/1471	242 Squadron
AIR 27/1498	249 Squadron
AIR 27/1511	253 Squadron
AIR 27/1526	257 Squadron
AIR 27/1558	266 Squadron
AIR 27/1941	500 Squadron
AIR 27/1949	501 Squadron
AIR 27/1964	504 Squadron
AIR 27/2068	601 Squadron
AIR 27/2088	605 Squadron
AIR 27/2093	607 Squadron
AIR 27/2102	609 Squadron
AIR 27/2106	610 Squadron
AIR 27/2112	612 Squadron
AIR 27/2123	615 Squadron
AIR 27/2126	616 Squadron
AIR 27/2263	928 Squadron

Pilots' Combat Reports

AIR 50/1	1 Squadron
AIR 50/4	3 Squadron
AIR 50/9	17 Squadron
AIR 50/10	19 Squadron
AIR 50/16	32 Squadron
AIR 50/18	41 Squadron
AIR 50/19	43 Squadron
AIR 50/20	46 Squadron
AIR 50/21	54 Squadron

AIR 50/22	56 Squadron
AIR 50/24	64 Squadron
AIR 50/25	65 Squadron
AIR 50/26	66 Squadron
AIR 50/32	74 Squadron
AIR 50/33	79 Squadron
AIR 50/36	85 Squadron
AIR 50/37	87 Squadron
AIR 50/40	92 Squadron
AIR 50/43	111 Squadron
AIR 50/62	145 Squadron
AIR 50/63	151 Squadron
AIR 50/64	152 Squadron
AIR 50/83	213 Squadron
AIR 50/85	222 Squadron
AIR 50/89	234 Squadron
AIR 50/91	238 Squadron
AIR 50/92	242 Squadron
AIR 50/96	249 Squadron
AIR 50/100	257 Squadron
AIR 50/105	266 Squadron
AIR 50/165	601 Squadron
AIR 50/167	603 Squadron
AIR 50/171	609 Squadron
AIR 50/173	611 Squadron
AIR 50/172	610 Squadron
AIR 50/175	615 Squadron
AIR 50/176	616 Squadron

Casualty Files

AIR 81/2376	Sergeant I.C.C. Clenshaw
AIR 81/1140	Pilot Officer P. Litchfield
AIR 81/1158	Squadron Leader J.F. Stephens, Sergeants J.V. West and E.C. Parker
AIR 81/2452	Pilot Officer A. Bird
AIR 81/2721	Sergeant G.R. Collett
AIR 81/1320	Flying Officer R.S. Demetriadi
AIR 81/2446	Pilot Officer J.R. Hamar

Miscellaneous

AIR 22/296	Personnel: Casualties, Strength and Establishment of the RAF.

BIBLIOGRAPHY

Pilots' Flying Log Books (ranks as 1940)

Air Vice-Marshal Sir Keith Park (courtesy RNZAF Museum)
Squadron Leader D.R.S. Bader (courtesy RAF Museum)
Squadron Leader R.G. Kellett
Flying Officer M.T. Wainwright
Pilot Officer D.M.C. Crook (TNA)
Pilot Officer P.L. Parrott

German Documents

OKW Directives for Invasion of the UK, Operation *Seelöwe*, Summer and Autumn 1940, Bundesarchiv
Luftflotte 2 War Diary, available via Digital History Archive (see website detailed below)
German fighter combat claims can be found in the OKL records of the *Chef für Ausz. und Dizsiplin Luftwaffe-Personalamt LP(A)V* (available via various online sources)
German loss records can be found in the *Oberfehlsaber der Luftwaffe Genst. Gen. Qu/6 Abteilung/40.g. Kdos.I C*, records, preserved by the Imperial War Museum.

Unpublished Sources

Correspondence, papers and interviews, Dilip Sarkar Archive.
Original manuscript of *Spitfire Pilot*, Flight Lieutenant D.M. Crook DFC.
Memoir and papers, Group Captain R.G. Kellett DSO DFC VM RAF (Ret'd).
145 Squadron Association papers.
Memoirs, Lieutenant Commander A. Hague R.N.R.

Published Sources

Adams, P., *Hurricane Squadron: 87 Squadron at War 1939–1941*, Air Research Publications, New Malden, 1988
Aders, G. and Held, W., *Chronik: JagdGeschwader* 51 'Mölders', Motor Buch Verlag, Stuttgart, 2009
Addison, P. and Crang, J.A. (Eds), *The Burning Blue: A New History of the Battle of Britain*, Pimlico, London, 2000
Addison, P. and Crang, J.A. (Eds) *Listening to Britain: Home Intelligence Reports on Britain's Finest Hour – May to September 1940*, Vintage Books, London, 2011

Alexander, Kristen, *Australia's Few and the Battle of Britain*, Pen & Sword Books Ltd, Barnsley, 2015

Allen, Wing Commander H.R., *Fighter Squadron: A Memoir 1940–42*, Granada, London, 1982

Anon, *Air Intelligence: A Symposium*, RAFHS, London, 1997

Anon, *The Battle of Britain: August–October 1940*, Ministry of Information on behalf of the Air Ministry, London, 1941

Anon, *The Battle of Britain*, Air Ministry Pamphlet 156, Issued by the Department of the Air Member for Training, August 1943

Anon, *The Rise & Fall of the German Air Force 1939–45*, Air Ministry Pamphlet 248, Public Record Office, London, 2001

Anon, *The Second World War, RAF 1939–45, Flying Training: Volume One, Policy & Planning*, HMSO, London, 1941

Ashworth, C., *RAF Coastal Command: 1936–1969*, PSL, Sparkford, 1992

Bader, Group Captain Sir D.R.S., *Fight for the Sky: The Story of the Spitfire and Hurricane*, Sidgwick & Jackson, London, 1973

Bekker, C., *The Luftwaffe War Diaries*, Corgi Books, London, 1972

⎯⎯⎯⎯, *Hitler's Naval War*, Corgi, London, 1976

Birkenhead, Earl of, *Halifax: The Life of Lord Halifax*, Hamish Hamilton Ltd, London, 1965

Bishop, E., *The Battle of Britain*, George Allen & Unwin Ltd, London, 1960

Bowyer, M.J.F., *2 Group RAF: A Complete History, 1936–1945*, Faber & Faber, London, 1974

Calder, A., *The People's War: Britain 1939–45*, Pimlico, London, 2008

Caldwell, D., *JG26: Top Guns of the Luftwaffe*, Orion Books, New York, 1991

⎯⎯⎯⎯, *The JG26 War Diary: Volume One, 1939–42*, Grub Street, London, 1996

Campion, G., *The Good Fight: Battle of Britain Propaganda and The Few*, Palgrave-Macmillan, London, 2010

Cannandine, D. (Ed), *The Speeches of Winston Churchill*, Penguin, London, 1990

Churchill, W.S., *The Second World War, Vol II, Their Finest Hour*, Cassell & Co, London, 1949

Clapson, M., *Britain in the Twentieth Century*, Routledge, Abingdon, 2009

Collier, B., *The Defence of the United Kingdom*, HMSO, London, 1957

Cox, S. and Probert, H. (Eds), *The Battle Re-Thought: A Symposium on the Battle of Britain*, Airlife, Shrewsbury, 1991

Cox, S., 'RAF & *Luftwaffe* Intelligence Compared' in Handel, M.I. (Ed), *Intelligence & Military Operations*, Frank Cass, Abingdon, 1990

Dean, Sir Maurice, *The Royal Air Force in Two World Wars*, Cassell, London, 1979

Deere, Air Commodore A.C., *Nine Lives*, Hodder Paperback Ltd, London, 1959

Deighton, L., *Fighter: The True Story of the Battle of Britain*, Triad/Panther Books, St Albans, 1979

Dierich, W., *Kampfgeschwader* 'Edelweiss': *The History of a German Bomber Unit, 1939-45*, Purnell Book Services Ltd, London, 1975

_____, *Chronik: Kampfgeschwader 55 'Greif'*, Motorbuch Verlag, Stuttgart, 2012

Donnelly, M., *Britain in the Second World War*, Routledge, London, 1999

Donnelly, L., *The Other Few: The Contribution Made by Bomber and Coastal Aircrew to the Winning of the Battle of Britain*, Red Kite, Walton-on-Thames, 2004

Dowding, ACM Lord H.C.T., *Despatch: The Battle of Britain*, The London Gazette, London, 1946

Fenton, Air Commodore H.A., *Aquarius: The Man Who Holds the Watering Pott. A Flying Memoir 1928–1945*, privately published, Guernsey, 1990

Fleming, P., *Invasion 1940*, Rupert Hard-Davis, London, 1957

Foreman, J., *RAF Fighter Command Victory Claims of World War Two, Volume One*, Air Research Publications, Red Kite, Walton-on-Thames, 2003

Franks, N., *Air Battle for Dunkirk 26 May – 3 June 1940*, Grub Street, London, 2006

Galland, A., *The First and the Last: Germany's Fighter Force in the Second World War*, Fontana, London, 1954,

Gilbert, M., *The Second World War: A Complete History*, Weidenfeld & Nicolson, London, 1989

Gleed, Wing Commander I.R., *Arise to Conquer*, Victor Gollanz Ltd, London, 1942

Green, W., *Aircraft of the Battle of Britain*, MacDonald & Co Ltd and Pan Books Ltd, London, 1969

Handel, M.I. (Ed), *Intelligence and Military Operations*, Frank Cass, Abingdon, 1990

Hastings, M., *All Hell Let Loose. The World at War 1939–1945*, Harper Press, London, 2011

Hillary, R., *The Last Enemy*, MacMillan & Co Ltd, London, 1950

Hough, R., and Richards, D, *The Battle of Britain: The Jubilee History*, Hodder & Stoughton Ltd, London, 1990

James, T.C.G., *The Battle of Britain*, Frank Cass, London, 1990

Jones, Wing Commander I., *Tiger Squadron*, Award Books, New York, 1966

Jones, R.V., *Most Secret War: British Scientific Intelligence 1939–1945*, Hamish Hamilton Ltd, London, 1978

Kesselring, Field-Marshal A., *The Memoirs of Field-Marshal Kesselring*, Greenhill Books, London, 1997

Kershaw, I., *Hitler: 1936–1945, Nemesis*, Penguin, London, 2001

Lisiewicz, Squadron Leader M. (Ed), *Destiny Can Wait: The Polish Air Force in the Second World War*, William Heinemann Ltd, London, 1949

MacDonell, Air Commodore A.R.D. (MacDonell L. and MacKay A., Eds), *From Dogfight to Diplomacy: A Spitfire Pilot's Log 1932–1958*, Pen & Sword Books Ltd, Barnsley, 2005

Manvell, R. and Fraenkel, H., *Goering*, Greenhill Books, London, 2005

Mason, F.K., *Battle Over Britain*, Aston Publications, Bourne End, 1990

McKee, A., *The Coal-Scuttle Brigade*, Souvenir Press Ltd, London, 1957

Middlebrook, M. and Everitt, C., *The Bomber Command War Diaries: An Operational Reference Book 1939–1945*, Midland Counties Publications, Hinckley, 1996 and republished by Pen & Sword Books Limited as a paperback and e-book editions, 2014

Morgan, E. and Shacklady, E., *Spitfire: The History*, Key Publishing, Stamford, 1987

Muggeridge, M. (Ed), *Ciano's Diary 1939–1943*, William Heinemann Ltd, London, 1947

Murray, D. (Ed), *Vital Speeches of the Day, Volume VI*, Pro Rhetoric LLC, Chicago, USA, 1940

Orange, V., *Park: The biography of Air Chief Marshal Sir Keith Park*, Grub Street, London, 2001

_____, *Dowding of Fighter Command: Victor of the Battle of Britain*, Grubb Street, London, 2008

Overy, R., *The Air War 1939–1945*, first edition, Europa Publications Ltd, London, 1980

_____, *The Battle of Britain*, Penguin, London, 2004

_____, *Goering: The Iron Man*, Bloomsbury Revelations, London, 2021

Pope, R., *War & Society in Britain 1899–1948*, Longman, Harlow, 1991

Priestley, J.B., *Postscripts*, William Heinemann Ltd, London, 1940

Quill, J.K., *Spitfire*, Arrow Books, London 1985

Ramsay, W. (Ed), *The Battle of Britain: Then & Now, Mk.V Edition*, Battle of Britain Prints International Ltd, London, 1986

_____, *The Blitz Then & Now, Volume 1*, Battle of Britain Prints International Ltd, London, 1989

_____, *The Blitz Then & Now, Volume 2*, Battle of Britain Prints International Ltd, London, 1990

Richards, D., *RAF Bomber Command in the Second World War: The Hardest Victory*, Penguin, London, 2001

Rohwer, J. and G. Hunnelchen, *Chronology of the War at Sea*, Ian Allen Ltd, London, 1972

Rootes, A., *Front Line County: Kent at War, 1939–45*, Robert Hale Ltd, London, 1980

Roskill, Captain S.W., *The War at Sea 1939–45, Volume 1*, HMSO, London, 1954

Sarkar, D., *Battle of Britain 1940: The Finest Hour's Human Cost*, Pen & Sword Books Ltd, Barnsley, 2020

_____, *Douglas Bader*, Amberley Publishing, Stroud, 2013

_____, *How the Spitfire Won the Battle of Britain*, Amberley, Stroud, 2010

_____, *Letters from The Few: Unique Memories From the Battle of Britain*, Pen & Sword Books Ltd, Barnsley, 2020

_____, *'Sailor' Malan: Freedom Fighter*, Pen & Sword Books Ltd, Barnsley, 2021

BIBLIOGRAPHY

_____, *The Final Few*, Amberley Publishing, Stroud, 2015

Schenk, P., *Operation Sealion: The Invasion of England*, Greenhill Books, Barnsley, 2019

Shirer, W.L., *The Rise and Fall of the Third Reich*, Simon & Schuster, New York, 1960

Smith, M., Addison, J, and Crang, J.A. (Eds), *The Burning Blue: A New History of the Battle of Britain*, Pimlico, London, 2000

Townsend, Group Captain P., *Duel of Eagles: The Classic Account of the Battle of Britain*, Weidenfeld & Nicolson, London, 1990

Trevor-Roper, H.R. (Ed), *Hitler's War Directives 1939–45*, Pan Books, London, 1966

Vasco, J.J. and Cornwell, P.D., *Zerstörer: The Messerschmitt 110 and its Units in 1940*, JAC Publications, Norwich, 1995

Vasco, J., *Bombsights Over England: The History of Erprobungsgruppe 210 Luftwaffe Fighter-Bomber Unit in the Battle of Britain*, JAC Publications, Norwich, 1990

Williams, C., *The Battle of the Atlantic*, BBC Worldwide Ltd, London, 2002

Willis, J., *Churchill's Few: The Battle of Britain Remembered*, Guild Publishing, London, 1985

Wheatley, R., *Operation Sealion*, Oxford University Press, Oxford, 1958

Wood, D. and Dempster, D., *The Narrow Margin: The Battle of Britain*, Arrow Ltd, London, 1969

Wright, R., *Dowding and the Battle of Britain*, Corgi, London, 1970

Ziegler, F.H., *The Story of 609 Squadron: Under the White Rose*, MacDonald, London, 1971

Websites

The National Archives: www.nationalarchives.gov.uk
Commonwealth War Graves Commission: www.cwgc.org
Battle of Britain Memorial Trust: www.battleofbritainmemorial.org
Battle of Britain: The People's Project: www.battleofbritainthepeoplesproject.com
Dilip Sarkar: www.dilipsarkarauthor.com
Digital History Archive: www.digitalhistoryarchive.com
Kenley Revival Project: www.kenleyrevival.org
Battle of Britain London Monument: www.bbm.org.uk

YouTube

Charles Gardner's broadcast: https://youtu.be/nP0antMa_pA
Pathé News broadcast regarding bombing of Dover, 29 July 1940: https://youtu.be/DoJKk8q6NNs

Films

Although produced for either propaganda purposes or popular culture, the following films can provide an idea of the timeframe this book concerns:

The Lion Has Wings, directed by Michael Powell, Adrian Brunel and Brian Desmond Hurst (London Films, 1939).
Target for Tonight, directed by Harry Watt (Crown Film Unit, 1941).
A Yank in the RAF, directed by Henry King (Twentieth Century Fox, 1941).
Mrs Miniver, directed by William Wyle (Metro-Goldwyn-Mayer, 1942).
The First of the Few, directed by Leslie Howard (British Aviation Pictures, 1942).
Battle of Britain, directed by Guy Hamilton (Spitfire Productions, 1969).

Television

The World at War, directed by David Elstein (ITV, 1973).

Other Books by Dilip Sarkar MBE FRHistS

Spitfire Squadron: No 19 Squadron at War, 1939–41
The Invisible Thread: A Spitfire's Tale
Through Peril to the Stars: RAF Fighter Pilots Who Failed to Return, 1939–45
Angriff Westland: Three Battle of Britain Air Raids Through the Looking Glass
A Few of the Many: Air War 1939–45, A Kaleidoscope of Memories
Bader's Tangmere Spitfires: The Untold Story, 1941
Bader's Duxford Fighters: The Big Wing Controversy
Missing in Action: Resting in Peace?
Guards VC: Blitzkrieg 1940
Battle of Britain: The Photographic Kaleidoscope, Volumes I–IV
Fighter Pilot: The Photographic Kaleidoscope
Group Captain Sir Douglas Bader: An Inspiration in Photographs
Johnnie Johnson: Spitfire Top Gun, Part I
Johnnie Johnson: Spitfire Top Gun, Part II
Battle of Britain: Last Look Back
Spitfire! Courage & Sacrifice
Spitfire Voices: Heroes Remember
The Battle of Powick Bridge: Ambush a Fore-thought
Duxford 1940: A Battle of Britain Base at War
The Few: The Battle of Britain in the Words of the Pilots
Spitfire Manual 1940
The Sinking of HMS Royal Oak *In the Words of the Survivors (re-print of Hearts of Oak)*
The Last of the Few: Eighteen Battle of Britain Pilots Tell Their Extraordinary Stories
Hearts of Oak: The Human Tragedy of HMS Royal Oak
Spitfire Voices: Life as a Spitfire Pilot in the Words of the Veterans
How the Spitfire Won the Battle of Britain
Spitfire Ace of Aces: The True Wartime Story of Johnnie Johnson
Douglas Bader

Fighter Ace: The Extraordinary Life of Douglas Bader, Battle of Britain Hero (re-print of above)
Spitfire: The Photographic Biography
Hurricane Manual 1940
River Pike
The Final Few: The Last Surviving Pilots of the Battle of Britain Tell Their Stories
Arnhem 1944: The Human Tragedy of the Bridge Too Far
Spitfire! The Full Story of a Unique Battle of Britain Fighter Squadron
Battle of Britain 1940: The Finest Hour's Human Cost
Letters from The Few: Unique Memories of the Battle of Britain
Johnnie Johnson's 1942 Diary: The War Diary of the Spitfire Ace of Aces
Johnnie Johnson's Great Adventure: The Spitfire Ace of Ace's Last Look Back
'Sailor' Malan – Freedom Fighter: The Inspirational Story of a Spitfire Ace
Spitfire Ace of Aces – The Album: The Photographs of Johnnie Johnson
The Real Spitfire Pilot
The Real Hurricane Pilot
Bader's Big Wing Controversy: Duxford 1940.
Bader's Spitfire Wing: Tangmere 1941
Spitfire Down
Forgotten Heroes of The Battle of Britain
Faces of The Few
Spitfire Faces
Arise to Conquer: The Real Hurricane Pilot (introduction, commentary and photographs supplied to a new edition of Wing Commander I.R. Gleed DSO DFC's wartime memoir)
Free French Spitfire Hero: The Diaries of and Search for René Mouchotte (with Jan Leeming)
Battle of Britain: The Finest Hour in Cinema
Battle of Britain: The Movie (contributor to and publisher of the now late Robert Rudhall's original edition (2000), and editor and substantial contributor to 2022 revised edition)
Faces of HMS Royal Oak: The 'Mighty Oak' Disaster at Scapa Flow
Battle of Britain Volume 1: The Gathering Storm

Index

Aberdeen, 43, 81, 101, 107, 130, 133
Aeberhardt, Pilot Officer R.A.C., 214
Acklington, 228
Aircraft,
   Avro Anson, 37, 39, 83, 129, 189, 251, 274
   Bristol Blenheim, 18–19, 29, 37–8, 49, 56–7, 63, 67, 72–3, 76–7, 83–4, 86–7, 101, 113–14, 122, 129–31, 141, 152, 159, 169, 178, 185–6, 191, 196, 205, 215, 216–18, 226, 229, 234, 249–50, 253, 274, 288
   De Havilland Tiger Moth, 4
   Dornier Do 17, 2–4, 12–16, 21, 23, 30, 40–2, 44, 51–3, 66–7, 75, 81, 83, 88, 107, 110, 120–1, 128–30, 134, 143, 158, 182, 193, 195, 224–6, 232, 236, 252 257–8, 259, 262, 280, 282, 289
   Dornier Do 18, 130, 141
   Dornier Do 215, 4, 12, 14, 19, 29, 64, 82, 133, 138, 140, 182, 192, 238, 251–2, 258, 262, 288, 290
   Hawker Hurricane, 4, 7, 15, 17–18, 21–2, 31–2 *et. seq*
   Heinkel He 59, 37, 63, 109, 113, 177, 257, 274
   Heinkel He 111, 11, 29, 35–6, 40–6, 51, 65, 72, 81, 84, 100, 101, 133, 142, 159, 182, 183, 188, 202, 214, 223, 250, 271, 282
   Heinkel He 115, 110, 217, 253
   Junkers Ju 87, 23–4, 30–1, 55–6, 59, 62, 74, 98, 101, 110–11, 143, 145, 149, 151–2, 160, 178–80, 188, 218, 232–3, 236, 242, 261–2, 278, 296
   Junkers Ju 88, 13, 18, 31, 37, 45–6, 51–2, 66, 72–3, 77, 81, 84–6, 101, 107, 130, 132–3, 152–5, 157–60, 162, 169, 177, 182, 192, 200–202, 230, 224, 226, 228, 249, 250, 269–70, 274, 279–81
   Messerschmitt Me 109, 12–13, 25, 27, 38, 39, 54, 57, 75, 82, 89, 92–4, 97–8, 100, 108, 110–13, 118–19, 121–2, 136–8, 143, 145, 147–9, 151–2, 157–8, 160, 162–3, 169, 171, 173–6, 180, 186, 188, 206, 208–210, 216, 219–20, 224, 232–3, 236–8, 242–3, 246, 255–8, 260–3, 270–2, 274, 276–8, 281, 283, 285, 287–90, 292, 296
   Messerschmitt Me 110, 14–17, 30–6, 39, 46, 51–3, 56, 66–7, 72, 83, 89–90, 109, 111, 114, 118–22, 131, 133, 143–4, 149, 157, 164, 184, 190–1, 196, 206–209, 216 232, 238, 240, 242, 249–50, 253–4, 257–60, 264–5, 266–8, 270, 273, 277, 279–82, 286–7, 289, 296

Short Sunderland, 122, 129
Supermarine Spitfire, xii, 2–3, 5–6, 12–13, 16, 19, 22–4, *et. Seq*
Westland Whirlwind, 66
Airfields, Depots and RAF Stations in the United Kingdom,
Acklington, 37, 46, 47, 250
Aston Down, xii, 107, 153, 189, 223, 236
Bentley Priory, 96
Biggin Hill, 13–14, 29, 81, 88, 98, 110, 162, 170, 254–5, 257
Bircham Newton, 84, 224
Blackpool, 214
Catterick, 150, 170, 274
Church Fenton, 6
Coltishall, 2, 5–6, 8–9, 11, 21, 72, 128, 166, 183, 185, 195, 201–202
Coningsby, 57
Croydon, 15, 87–8, 147, 177, 192, 276
Debden, 22, 40–1, 258–9
Digby, 48, 77–8, 127, 211
Duxford, 5, 141, 167–8, 227, 281
Dyce, 43, 129
Eastchurch, 284–5
Exeter, 2, 30, 34, 66, 76, 101, 133, 143, 157, 237, 246, 250, 264, 270, 279
Fowlmere, 141, 167, 177–8, 214
Gravesend, 105, 162, 252
Halton, 41, 141
Hawkinge, 13, 15, 54, 58–9, 75, 87–91, 95–6, 98–9, 110–11, 144, 147–8, 151, 162, 165, 170, 174, 177–80, 182, 192, 195, 220, 223, 252, 254, 257, 261–2, 275–8, 285, 288–9, 291–2
Hendon, 10, 29, 99
Hornchurch, 46, 138, 149–50, 163, 170, 274, 277, 287–8
Horsham St. Faith, 196, 205
Kenley, 49, 53, 58, 87–8, 99, 110, 133, 144–7, 150, 165, 178, 219–20, 223, 234–5, 251, 254–5, 261, 285, 292
Kirton-in-Lindsey, 4
Leconfield, 200
Lossiemouth, 19
Lympne, 16–17, 29, 150, 275–7, 291–3, 295
Manston, 12–13, 15–16, 54–5, 64, 96, 106, 110, 119, 134, 136, 138, 140, 144–5, 152, 158, 162–3, 170–1, 174–5, 178, 193, 219–20, 234–5, 254–5, 257, 259, 261–3, 275–6, 278, 285–90, 292
Martlesham Heath, 40–1, 137, 170, 182, 184, 190, 225, 258–9, 262
Middle Wallop, 23–5, 29–30, 44, 47–8, 52, 84, 109, 119, 160, 162, 238, 264, 270, 274
Montrose, 81, 130, 188
North Weald, 41, 55, 106, 139–40, 151–2, 170, 180, 257, 261
Old Sarum, 119
Pembrey, 13, 18, 66, 132
Rochford, 55, 57, 106, 138, 152, 158, 180, 184, 219, 224, 261, 278, 288–9
Ruislip, 136
St. Eval, 37, 45, 162, 249, 251, 272
Stormy Down, 18
Sutton Bridge, 11, 75
Tangmere, 3, 28–30, 35–6, 44, 46, 49, 76, 84, 88, 99–101, 107, 110, 113, 120, 128, 140, 156, 182, 232, 237, 241–2, 247, 263, 267, 277, 279–80, 284–5
Thornaby, 253
Thorney Island, 49, 57, 63, 84, 113, 152, 203–204, 218
Turnhouse, 64, 88, 101
Uxbridge, 212

INDEX

Warmwell, 23, 25, 30, 31, 37, 44, 46–7, 51–2, 81, 84, 86, 110, 120, 143, 233, 238, 240–1, 243, 263–6, 270–1, 279
Wattisham, 19, 216
Westhampnett, 162, 232, 263, 279
West Malling, 17, 88–9
West Raynham, 234
Air Ministry, xiv, 19, 22, 27, 67, 73–4, 106, 117, 156, 230, 249
Air Raid Precautions, 44
Aitkin, Flight Lieutenant Max, 29
Alderney, 68
Alexander, Pilot Officer John, 224
Allard, Flight Sergeant Geoffrey 'Sammy', 190, 225
Allen, Flying Officer James, 42
Allen, Frazer, 44
Allen, Pilot Officer John, DFC, 134–6, 145
Allgood, Sergeant Harold, 259
Anderson, Squadron Leader Michael, 274
Andreae, Flying Officer Christopher, 261
Appleby, Pilot Officer Michael, 87, 203, 241
Armitage, Flight Lieutenant Dennis, 280
Ashton, Pilot Officer Dennis, 280
Assheton, Pilot Officer William, 142
Atkinson, Sergeant George, 184, 224
Atkins, Sergeant Fred, 96
Auxiliary Fire Service, 181, 292

Bader, Group Captain Sir Douglas, 5–11, 21–2, 166, 195
Badger, Flight Sergeant Ivor, 272
Badger, Squadron Leader John 'Tubby', 44, 120–1
Bailey, Sergeant George, 162
Baker, Sergeant Eric, 233
Baker, Sergeant Ronald, 56, 83, 261
Ball, Flying Officer Eric, 8
Bann, Sergeant Eric, 52, 160, 271

Barraclough, Sergeant Stanley, 13
Barran, Flight Lieutenant Phillip, 23–6
Barrage balloons, 81, 87, 187–8, 230, 239, 254, 257, 279
  928 (Balloon Barrage) Squadron, 81
  961 (Balloon Barrage) Squadron, 251, 254
  Channel Convoy Mobile Balloon Barrage Flotilla, 187, 217, 224, 229
Bartley, Pilot Officer Tony, 13
Battle of Britain, xii–xiv, *et seq*
  Dates, xii–xiv
  Dowding's Despatch, xii, 63, 295
Battle of Britain Clasp, xiv, 17, 99, 156
Battle of Britain Memorial Trust, vi, xi, 291
  National Memorial to The Few, vi, xi
Battle of France, xii, 6, 9, 106, 154
  Fall of France, xii, 5, 27, 29, 41, 74, 81, 106, 230, 274
Battle of the Barges, 57, 73, 77, 129–30
Bayles, Pilot Officer Ian, 82, 280–1
Bayne, Flight Lieutenant, 183
Bayne, Squadron Leader David, 99
Beachy Head, 3, 75, 128, 201, 229, 231, 285
Beamish, Wing Commander Victor, 41–2
Beamont, Pilot Officer Roland, 133
Beaumont, Flight Lieutenant Stephen, 162
Beaumont, Pilot Officer Walter, 243, 246, 280
Beaverbrook, Max Aitken, 1st Baron, 19, 29, 210–11
Beggs, Sub-Lieutenant Henry, 83, 224
Beley, Pilot Officer Robert, 278
Bennions, Pilot Officer George 'Ben', 174–5, 180

Benson, Pilot Officer Noel 'Broody', 130
Beresford, Flight Lieutenant Hugh, 170, 282
Berry, Pilot Officer 'Raz', 81, 130, 188
Besiegel, Wing Commander Walter 'Bike', 6
Binham, Sergeant Arthur, 54, 179
Bird, Pilot Officer Alec, 153–6, 160
Bird-Wilson, Flying Officer, 160
Bishop, Edward, 19, 39, 62, 252
Birmingham, 211, 250
Blake, Sub-Lieutenant Arthur, 177
Blair, Flight Lieutenant Kenneth Blair, 184, 224
Blayney, Pilot Officer Adolf, 23–4
Bletchley Park, 230
Bliss, Pilot Officer G., 39
Blomeley, Pilot Officer David, 184
Bloor, Sergeant Ernest, 127
Bognor Regis, 35, 281
Boitel-Gill, Flight Lieutenant Derek, 268, 281
Boulton and Paul Company, 201
Bovington, 47
Boyd, Flight Lieutenant Adrian, 36, 128, 224, 233, 241
Boyle, Flying Officer John, 274
Bramah, Sub-Lieutenant Henry, 66
Branch, Flying Officer Guy, 66–7, 268
Brand, Air Vice-Marshal Quintin, 272
Brighton, 88, 100–101, 105, 200, 218
Brimscombe, 155
British Army, 25, 33, 39, 47, 83, 86
  Royal Engineers, 292
British Broadcasting Corporation, 59, 62, 186, 188
British Expeditionary Force, 80
Brinsden, Flying Officer Frank, 216
Broker, Flight Lieutenant Richard, 152
Brooklands, 28
Brothers, Air Commodore Peter Malam, 98, 254

Brown, Deputy Chief Fire Officer Cyril, 181
Brown, Flight Lieutenant Mark 'Hilly' DFC, 263, 268
Brown, Sam, 45
Browne, Pilot Officer Dennis, 100
Buchanan, Pilot Officer James 'Buck', 161–2
Buchin, Pilot Officer Maurice, 237
Buck, Sergeant James, 100
Bulmer, Sub-Lieutenant Geoffrey, 15, 112
Burgoyne, Pilot Officer, 214
Burton, Flight Lieutenant Howard 'Billy', 183
Butterfield, Sergeant Sam, 270

Caister, Sergeant James, 101
Calshot, 67
Canterbury, 55, 112, 195, 234, 292
Capon, Pilot Officer Carl, 282
Carey, Pilot Officer Frank 'Chota', 100, 247
Carnal, Sergeant Ralph, 147, 192
Carr-Lewty, Sergeant Robert, 180
Cartwright, Sergeant H., xii
Castle Bromwich Aircraft Factory, 211
Cawse, Sergeant Fred, 238, 271
Chamberlain, Neville, 79–80, 131, 294
Chatham, 277
Chatham, Pilot Officer Charles, 268
Chomley, Pilot Officer John, 283
Christie, Flying Officer George, 202–203
Christie, Sergeant R.C., 19
Churchill, Winston, xii, 64, 79–80, 102–104, 114, 123, 131–2, 186, 192, 216, 229, 251, 294
Ciano, Count, 51, 79, 102–105, 126, 225, 253
Clacton, 119, 257, 259
Cleaver, Flying Officer Gordon, 35, 157

INDEX

Clenshaw, Sergeant Ian Charles Cooper, 4
Clerke, Flight Lieutenant Rupert, 250
Clouston, Flight Lieutenant, 214
Cochrane, Pilot Officer Arthur, 236, 282
Cock, Pilot Officer John, 159, 272
Coghlan, Flight Lieutenant John, 15, 55–6
Coke, Pilot Officer The Hon. David, 170, 282
Coleman, Pilot Officer Edward, 136
Collard, Flying Officer Peter, 59, 285
Collett, Sergeant George 'Dick', 134–7
Collett, Squadron Leader Wilfred, 237
Collingridge, Pilot Officer Leon 'Duke', 183
Connors, Flight Lieutenant Stanley, 94, 147, 192, 261–2
Considine, Pilot Officer Brian, 31, 53, 122, 158
Convoys, xii, xiii, 2, 9, 11–12, 14–17, 19, 23, 30, 36, 39–40, 42, 44, 51–3, 57, 59–60, 62–6, 72, 81–4, 86–7, 107–109, 111–12, 119–23, 127–9, 133–4, 138–9, 142, 144–5, 147–8, 150, 152, 159, 161–2, 165–6, 178, 181–2, 184, 187, 200–202, 208, 214–15, 217–19, 223–5, 228–33, 236–43, 247–9, 257–9, 261, 263–4, 274, 278, 284, 294, 297
  Agent, 200–201, 257, 261
  Arena, 200–201, 257, 261
  Bacon, 160–2
  Booty, 39–42, 57–9, 128, 257, 261
  Bosom, 108–11
  Bread (*CW3*), 12, 14–17
  Crumb, 53
  CW8, 144–5, 147–52, 187
  CW9 (*Peewit*), 229–33, 236–8, 240, 242–3, 247–50, 253
  HX56A, 129
  Jumbo, xii
  OA178, 120
  Pilot, 66, 190, 201
Cooke, Pilot Officer Charles, 2–3, 128
Cooney, Flight Sergeant Cecil, 180–1
Connor, Pilot Officer Francis, 162
Copeland, Pilot Officer Jack, 94–5
Copeman, Pilot Officer Jack, 192, 261
Cork, Sub-Lieutenant Dicky, 11
Coward, Noel, 29
Cowsill, Sergeant James, 56
Cox, Flight Lieutenant P.A.N, 110, 163
Cox, Flying Officer, 48
Cox, Sergeant David, 167
Cranwell, RAF College, 5, 7
  Sword of Honour, 183
Crew, Pilot Officer Edward, 274
Crombie, Sergeant Robert, 96
Cromer, 21, 253
Crook, Pilot Officer David, 25, 161, 240, 264–5, 273, 282
Crossley, Flight Lieutenant Mike, 109, 111, 144, 254, 288
Crowley-Milling, Pilot Officer Denis, 8, 166–7
Cruttenden, Pilot Officer John, 247
Curchin, Pilot Officer John, 42, 241
Cunningham, Flight Lieutenant John, 107
Cunningham, Pilot Officer Wallace 'Jock', 177, 195, 202
Curley, Sergeant Albert, 96
Cutts, Pilot Officer John, 142

D'Arcy-Irvine, Flying Officer Brian, 236
Darley, Squadron Leader Horace 'Uncle George', 26–8, 241, 263, 265, 281
Dalton-Morgan, Flight Lieutenant Thomas, 44, 51, 121
Darley, Squadron Leader Horace 'Uncle George', 26–8, 241, 263, 265, 281

Darling, Sergeant Edward, 274
Darwin, Pilot Officer Christopher, 101
Davey, Pilot Officer John, 193, 268
David, Flying Officer A.L., 160
David, Pilot Officer Dennis, 272
Davis, Flying Officer Carl, 157
Davis, Pilot Officer Charles, 35, 52, 108–109, 120, 160
Davis, Pilot Officer David, 205
Daw, Pilot Officer Victor, 144
Dawson-Paul, Sub Lieutenant Frank, 16–17, 54, 133, 147, 150–1
Deal, 12, 38, 54, 90, 96, 165, 179–80, 254, 278
Deansley, Flying Officer Christopher, 143
Debenham, Pilot Officer Kenneth, 278
Deere, Air Commodore Alan Christopher, xiv, 135–6, 286–7, 289
de Mancha, Pilot Officer Ricardo, 51, 121
Demetriadi, Flying Officer Richard, 267
Devitt, Squadron Leader Peter, 37, 46–7, 143, 264, 268
Dewar, Squadron Leader John Scatliff, 31, 33
Dewhurst, Pilot Officer Kenneth, 169–70
Dickie, Pilot Officer William, 35, 267
Dieppe, 141, 274
Dixon, Sergeant Frederick, 23
Dobislav, *Oberleutnant* Max, 24, 157
Don, Pilot Officer Ralph, 23
Donahue, Pilot Officer Arthur 'Art', 220, 223, 289
Donald, Flying Officer Ian Grahame, 96
Donaldson, Air Commodore Edward 'Teddy', 41, 58, 139–40
Doulton, Flying Officer Michael, 30, 107
Dover, 13, 15–16, 50, 53–5, 57, 59, 64, 68, 70, 89–90, 96, 98–9, 105, 107, 109, 111–14, 116, 130, 133–5, 140, 144–5, 147–51, 162–5, 170–1, 173–5, 177–82, 185, 191, 196, 200–201, 208, 219–20, 223, 228–9, 234–6, 239, 250–1, 254–8, 260, 263, 275–7, 285–6, 288–9, 295
Fire Brigade, 181
Dover Strait, 50, 70, 120, 134, 144, 152, 187, 219, 228–30, 255, 263–4, 276, 278, 285
Dowding, Air Chief Marshal Sir Hugh, xii, xiii, xiv, 9, 17, 27–8, 37, 63, 82, 123, 166–7, 169, 203, 206, 214, 249, 285
Dowding's Despatch, xii, 63, 295
Dowding System, 167
Draper, Pilot Officer Bryan, 13, 16, 170
Drummond-Hay, Flying Officer Peter, 24–5
Ducker, Flying Officer F.E.R., 87
Dundas, Flying Officer John, 53, 264–5, 281–2
Dundas, Group Captain Sir Hugh, 29
Dunkirk, xii, 5, 20, 27, 64, 80, 89, 136, 210, 274
Dungeness, 14–15, 182, 187, 276
Dungeness buoy, 15
Dunkirk Evacuation, *see Dynamo*, Operation
Dutton, Flight Lieutenant Roy, 3, 36, 76–7, 100–101, 200–201, 279
Dynamo, Operation, xii, xiii, 5, 20, 26, 64, 80, 88, 106, 122, 136, 148, 150, 186, 188, 194–5, 201, 210

Eastbourne, 200
Hospital, 75
Edge, Flying Officer A.R., 42, 84–6
Edsall, Pilot Officer Eric, 277
Edworthy, Sergeant Gerald, 127
Ellams, AC1 Bill, 77–9
Ellis, Flight Lieutenant John, 134, 148, 151
Ellis, Sergeant John, 225–6

INDEX

Ellis, Squadron Leader John, 257, 276
Eley, Sergeant Fred, 193
Engel, *General* Gerhard, 50
Enigma, 230
Evans, LAC David, 9
Evans, Sergeant Walter, 225–6
Evill, Air Vice-Marshal Douglas, 185
Exeter, 2, 30, 32, 34, 66, 75–6, 101, 133, 143, 157, 237, 246, 250, 264, 270, 272, 279
Eyre, Pilot Officer, 113

Falmouth, 17, 218, 249, 251
Feary, Sergeant Alan, 84–5, 282
Fenton, Squadron Leader Harold, 120, 160, 238–9, 248, 270
Ferriss, Flying Officer Henry, 16, 262
Fink, Oberst Johannes, 13–14, 39, 145, 181, 196, 231, 294–5
Finnie, Pilot Officer Archibald, 134–5, 150
Finucane, Flying Officer Brendan 'Paddy', 287
Filton, 17
Fiske, Pilot Officer Billy, 222
Fletcher, Flight Lieutenant, 250
Folkestone, 16, 90, 93, 111–12, 148, 150–1, 158, 165, 193, 195, 218, 291
Forbes, Squadron Leader Athol Stanhope, 212
Forward, Sergeant Ronald, 170, 174, 177, 236
Fözö, *Oberleutnant* Josef, 56, 193
Franklin, Pilot Officer William, 144, 158, 220
Franziket, *Oberleutnant* Ludwig, 23
Freeborn, Pilot Officer John, 12–13, 141, 170, 173, 193, 257, 259–60, 263

Galland, General Adolf, 135, 138, 145, 177
Gamblen, Flying Officer Douglas, 180

Gardner, Charles (BBC reporter), 59, 62, 76
Gardner, Flying Officer Bernard, 258, 288
Gard'ner, Pilot Officer John Rushton, 96
Gardner, Sub-Lieutenant Richard, 11
Gaunce, Flight Lieutenant L.M., 112, 144, 285
Gayner, Flying Officer John, 59
George Medal, 44, 181
Gibson, Flight Lieutenant John, 51, 179, 195, 291–2
Gillan, Flying Officer James, 267
Gillman, Pilot Officers Keith, 98, 144
Gilroy, Pilot Officer George, 43, 81, 133
Gledhill, Sergeant Geoffrey, 271–2
Gleed, Flight Lieutenant Ian 'Widge', 34
Gloster Aircraft, 153
Gloucester, 116
Glyde, Flying Officer Dickie, 34
Goebbels, Reichsleiter Joseph, 104
Goodman, Pilot Officer G.E., 147–8, 268
Goodwin, Flying Officer Henry 'Mac', 282
Göring, *Oberleutnant* Hans-Joachim, 32
Göring, Reichsmarschall Hermann, 32, 38–9, 71, 102, 105, 115–16, 118, 132, 205–209, 225, 229, 275
Gorrie, Pilot Officer, 51
Gracie, Flight Lieutenant Edward 'Jumbo', 15, 66, 106–107, 152
Gray, Pilot Officer Colin, 54, 136, 145, 276–7
Grayson, Sergeant Charles, 250
Great Yarmouth, 3, 72
Gregory, Pilot Officer Felix, 287
Gribble, Pilot Officer George, 134, 136
Grier, Flying Officer Thomas, 107
Grosvenor, Lord Edward Arthur 'Ned', 28–9

Gundy, Pilot Officer Kenneth Gundry, 236
Gunn, Pilot Officer Harold, 172–3, 193

Hague, Lieutenant Arthur, 187–8, 217, 224, 231, 236, 247–9
Haig, Flying Officer John, 133
Hailsham, 75
Halder, *General* Franz, 50, 150, 191–2, 208, 228
Halifax, Lord, 79–80, 123–6, 131–2, 294
Hall, Flight Lieutenant Noel, 236
Hall, Pilot Officer Roger, 47
Halliwell, Pilot Officer Antony, 93
Hamar, Pilot Officer Jack, 42, 57, 58, 139–40
Hamilton, Pilot Officer Arthur Charles, 96
Hamilton, Flight Lieutenant Harry, 190
Hampshire, Sergeant Cyril, 259
Hanks, Flight Lieutenant Peter Prosser, 153–6
Hanson, Pilot Officer David, 40, 258–9
Harborne, Pilot Officer Stephen, 172, 263
Hardy, Pilot Officer Richard, 251
Harker, Sergeant Alan, 249
Harkness, Squadron Leader Hill, 279, 282
Harper, Flight Lieutenant William, 258
Harwich, 3, 22, 65, 81, 133, 164, 184, 190, 195, 257, 259
Hastings, 158, 200–201, 208
Hastings, Pilot Officer Douglas, 97–8, 141, 170
Hawkings, Sergeant Redvers 'Reg', 35
Haworth, Flying Officer Joseph, 110
Hellyer, Flight Lieutenant Richard, 200, 226
Henneberg, Flight Lieutenant, 212
Henson, Sergeant Bernard, 98
Henstock, Flight Lieutenant Lawrence, 145, 150, 289

Hewitt, Pilot Officer Duncan, 44
Higginson, Sergeant Frederick 'Taffy', 15, 65–6, 290
Higgs, Flying Officer Thomas, 15–16
Hillary, Pilot Officer Richard, 189–90
Hillcoat, Flight Lieutenant H.B., 147
Hillwood, Sergeant Peter, 56, 181
Hipley, 45
Hispano-Suiza, 167, 292
Hitler, Adolf, xiii, xiv, 20, 38–9, 50–1, 64, 67, 71, 79–80, 102–104, 106, 114–19, 123–7, 132, 141, 189, 191–2, 198–9, 206, 208, 216–17, 225–6, 228, 294–5
   Directive No.16, 67–71, 294
   Directive No.17, 198–9
Holden, Flight Lieutenant Gus, 44
Holland, Pilot Officer Robert, 66, 149
Hogan, Squadron Leader Harry, 23, 109–10, 195
Hogg, Pilot Officer Edward, 143, 243, 280–1
Hogg, Pilot Officer Richard, 82, 143
Home Guard, 21, 154–5, 229
Hood, Squadron Leader Hilary 'Robin', 170, 174, 179–80
Hope, Flight Lieutenant Sir Archibald, 30, 237
Horton, Pilot Officer Patrick, 169–70
Howell, Flight Lieutenant Frank, 42, 84–5
Howley, Pilot Officer Dick, 96
Hubbard, Flight Lieutenant Thomas, 107
Hughes, Flight Lieutenant Pat, 162, 169, 238
Hughes, Flying Officer David, 271–2
Hugo, Pilot Officer Petrus 'Dutch', 59, 75, 112, 145, 285
Humpherson, Flying Officer John, 14, 111, 288
Hunt, Pilot Officer David, 170

INDEX

Jay, Pilot Officer Dudley, 34
Jeff, Flight Lieutenant Robert
   Voase, 272
Jeffrey, Flying Officer Alistair, 99, 147
Jennings, Sergeant Robert, 226
Jeschonnek, *Generalmajor* Hans, 118,
   208, 275
Jodl, *Generaloberst* Alfred, 49–50,
   116, 228, 275
Johnson, Ray, 47–9
Jones, Flying Officer Denys, 142
Jones, Pilot Officer John, 269
Jones, Pilot Officer Richard, 146
Jones, Professor R.V., 230
Jones, Wing Commander Ira, 18
Jowitt, Sergeant Leonard, 40–1

Kadow, *Oberleutnant* Gerhard, 33
Kayll, Squadron Leader Joe, 58–9, 165
Kay-Shuttleworth, Pilot Officer Lord,
   182, 200, 242
Keighley, Pilot Officer Geoffrey, 112
Kellett, Squadron Leader Ronald,
   211–13
Kellow, Flying Officer Raymond, 76
Kelly, Flight Lieutenant Piers, 193
Kelly, Pilot Officer Dillon, 172
Kemp, Pilot Officer John Richard, 96
Kennard-Davis, Pilot Officer Peter, 236
Kennedy, Flight Lieutenant John,
   52, 271
Kennedy, Joseph P., 222
Kesselring, *Feldmarschall* Albert, 102,
   118, 207, 209, 225
Kestin, Sub-Lieutenant, Ian, 201
Kidson, Pilot Officer Rudal, 96
Kilner, Sergeant Joseph, 219–20, 278
Kingcome, Flight Lieutenant Brian,
   13, 132
King, Pilot Officer Leonard, 256
Kirton, Sergeant David, 234
Knowles, Sergeant, 253
Knowles, Squadron Leader E.V., 106

Krasnodebski, Squadron Leader
   Zdzislaw, 212
Kwiecinski, Sergeant Josef, 280

Lacey, Sergeant James 'Ginger',
   110, 287
Lane, Flight Lieutenant Brian,
   177, 195
Lapkowski, Flight Lieutenant, 212
Latta, Pilot Officer John, 202
Lausch, *Feldwebel* Bernard, 13
Lawrence, Pilot Officer Keith, 45
Laws, Flight Sergeant Adrian, 261
Leathart, Squadron Leader James,
   107, 145
Lee, Pilot Officer Kenneth, 162–3, 178,
   179, 185
Leigh-Mallory, Air Chief Marshal
   Sir Trafford, 5–6, 40, 167, 185,
   195, 284
Leigh, Squadron Leader Rupert
   'Lucky', 6, 21, 128
Lindsey, Pilot Officer Patrick
   Chaloner, 157
Litchfield, Pilot Officer Peter, 59, 81
Little, Flying Officer Bernard, 23–24
Little, Sergeant Ron, 158
Local Defence Volunteers, *see* Home
   Guard
London, 25, 27, 43, 47, 62, 66, 105,
   116, 119, 122–3, 140, 155, 188,
   206, 208, 215, 222, 229, 253, 293
London Fire Service, 217
London Gazette, The, xii
Lonsdale, Pilot Officer John, 142
Lott, Squadron Leader George, 44
Loudon, Flight Lieutenant Malcolm, 95
Lovell, Flight Lieutenant Tony, 175
Lowestoft, 11, 83, 137, 182, 188, 202,
   225
Luftwaffe, xii, xiii, 3, 38–9, 50, 63, *et seq*
   Seenotdienst, 63, 64, 112, 165, 177,
   274

Lukaszewicz, Flying Officer Kazimierz, 287
Lulworth, 33
  Cove, 47, 264
  range, 270

MacCaw, Flying Officer Derek, 31, 239–40
MacDonald, Flight Lieutenant Peter, 5, 7
MacDonell, Squadron Leader Aeneas Ranald Donald 'Don', 145–7, 150, 178, 188, 219–20, 223, 234–6, 256, 261
MacDougall, Pilot Officer Ian, 95
MacKenzie, Pilot Officer John, 180
Madle, Pilot Officer, 113
Malan, Group Captain Adolf Gysbert, 27, 46, 96–8, 170, 172, 193–4, 254–7, 262
Manlove, Pilot Officer Richard, 153, 155–6
Mann, Sergeant Jack, 220, 223, 236, 251, 260–1, 268
Manton, Squadron Leader Graham 'Minnie', 55, 106–107, 151
Marchfelder, *Leutnant* Richard, 32
Margate, 46, 136, 152, 165, 187, 261, 263, 287, 289, 291
Marsh, Sergeant Henry 'Taxi', 158, 271
Mather, Pilot Officer John, 2–3, 128
Matthews, Pilot Officer Henry, 136, 277
Matthews, Pilot Officers Peter, 100, 193
Mayers, Pilot Officer Howard, 238
Mayne, Warrant Officer Ernest, 257
McLure, Pilot Officer Andrew, 272
McDonough, Pilot Officer B.M., 37, 203–204
McGrath, Pilot Officer John, 237–8
McGregor, Pilot Officer Peter, 127–8

McGregor, Squadron Leader Hector, 269, 281
McKee, Alexander, 45, 164–5
McMullen, Flying Officer Desmond, 136
Measures, Flight Lieutenant William, 16
Merchant, Sergeant Henry, 193
Mermagen, Squadron Leader Herbert, 5–6
Miller, Pilot Officer Rogers, 53
Milne, Flying Officer Richard 'Dickie', 184
Milne, LAC John, 141
Ministry of Aircraft Production, 210, 217
Mitchell, Flying Officer Lancelot, 88
Mitchell, Pilot Officer Gordon, 24, 161
Mölders, *Major* Werner, 75, 170, 175–7, 209
Montgomery, Pilot Officer Cecil, 58–9
Morgan-Weld-Smith, Wing Commander Reginald, 204
Morris Motors, 211
Mortimer-Rose, Pilot Officer Edward, 249, 251
Morton, Pilot Officer James, 65, 72, 81
Moss, Sub-Lieutenant William, 76
Mottram, Pilot Officer Robert, 149
Mould, Sergeant Tony, 46, 170, 174, 194
Mounsden, Pilot Officer Maurice, 152
Mudie, Pilot Officer Michael, 58–9, 62
Mungo-Park, Flying Officer John, 16, 263

Navy, Army and Air Force Institutes, 48
Nelson-Edwards, Pilot Officer George, 250
Neville, Sergeant William, 258
Newhaven, 67, 231
Newling, Flying Officer Michael, 3, 46, 101

INDEX

Newton, Sergeant, 262
Norris, Pilot Officer, 148, 151, 246
North Foreland, 12, 278, 289
Norwell, Sergeant John, 54
Nutter, Sergeant Reg, 212–13, 236, 282

Observer Corps, 18, 88, 119, 234, 236
Oelofse, Pilot Officer Johannes, 247
Olive, Flight Lieutenant Gordon, 112
Orchard, Sergeant Harold, 112, 219
O'Meara, Pilot Officer James, 99, 256, 261
Oseau, *Oberleutnant* Walter, 15
Osmand, Pilot Officer Alexander, 75–6, 237, 246, 270, 281
Osterkamp, *Oberst* Theo, 54, 89, 205–207, 209
Ostowicz, Flying Officer Antoni, 101, 193, 268
Overton, Pilot Officer Charles 'Teeny', 53, 86, 282
Owles, Commander 'Mutt', 187–8, 233
Oxspring, Pilot Officer Bob 'Oxo', 182

Page, Pilot Officer Geoffrey, 55, 106–107, 152, 290–1
Pain, Pilot Officer D., 39
Pankratz, Flight Lieutenant Wilhelm, 280
Park, Air Chief Marshal Sir Keith, xi, 17, 49, 87, 89, 110–11, 113, 135, 162, 185, 206, 209, 249, 263, 284, 293
Parker, Pilot Officer Thomas, 250
Parker, Sergeant E.C., 114
Parkinson, Sergeant Cecil, 31, 52, 108, 109
Parrott, Pilot Officer Peter, 66–7, 84, 232, 242, 249–50, 279
Patterson, Midshipman Peter, 11
Pearce, Sergeant Leonard, 15
Pease, Pilot Officer Peter, 188–90
Peel, Squadron Leader John, 36, 46, 76, 88, 182, 232, 242, 263

Pemberton, Squadron Leader David, 100
Peterhead, 65, 72
Philippart, Pilot Officer Jacques, 237
Pickering, Pilot Officer John, 182
Pickering, Sergeant Tony, 157
Pidd, Sergeant Leslie, 271
Pinkham, Squadron Leader Phillip, 167, 195, 285
Pittman, Key, Chairman of the Senate Foreign Relations Committee, xv
Pittman, Pilot Officer Geoffrey, 40, 258
Phillips, Sergeant Norman, 234
Plymouth, xii, 169, 270
Pond, Flight Sergeant Arthur, 35, 156–7
Portland, xii, 23–7, 31, 36, 42, 44, 47, 52–3, 66, 68, 72, 81, 86, 101, 108, 143, 147, 158, 160, 230, 246–7, 263–6, 269–75, 295
  Harbour, 52, 273
  Naval base, 228, 230, 263
Portland Bill, 24, 30–1, 52, 152, 269–70, 272–3
Portsmouth, 34–6, 40, 44–5, 66, 228–9, 247–8, 278–80, 282–3, 285, 288, 295
Powell-Sheddon, Flight Lieutenant George, 8
Price, Pilot Officer Charles, 56–7
Proctor, Pilot Officer John, 109, 111, 288

Quill, Jefferey, 74, 286

Radar, 14, 21, 23, 30, 36, 39, 75, 81, 90, 130, 165, 178, 192, 218, 230, 232, 236, 257, 263, 275, 277–8, 283, 285, 288–9, 293, 295
  Airborne Interception radar, 130
  Chain Home, 230, 277–8, 283, 285, 295

Stations,
    Dover, 275, 277, 285
    Dunkirk, 275, 277, 285
    Pevensey, 277, 285
    Poling, 278
    Rye, 232, 277, 285
    Ventnor, 263, 275, 278, 279, 280, 283, 285
Raeder, Admiral Eric, 38–9, 71, 106, 115, 141, 191, 208–209, 228
Ramsgate, 67, 68, 81, 105, 165, 234, 278, 287
Rayner, Flying Officer Roddy, 101, 143
RDF, *see* Radar
Redhill, 88
Rhodes-Moorhouse, Flight Lieutenant Willie, 29, 35, 72–3, 263, 266–7
Riddle, Flying Officer Hugh, 33
Ridley, Sergeant Marmaduke, 200, 226
Ritchie, Flying Officer Ian, 72, 251
Roden, Sergeant Adrian, 178
Rolls-Royce, 8, 81, 139
    Glasgow factory, 81
    Merlin engine, 139, 210
Roberts, Aircraftman 1st Class Fred, 168
Robertson, Sergeant Fred, 2
Robinson, Sergeant Denis, 243, 246
Robinson, Sergeant James, 177
Robinson, Squadron Leader Marcus, 200, 226
Rogers, Captain J.C. Kelly, 217
Roosevelt, Franklin D., 222
Rowley, Flying Officer Michael, 280
Royal Air Force,
    Auxiliary Air Force, 24, 28, 59, 89, 148
    Bomber Command, 18, 37, 38, 49, 56, 63, 67, 73, 77, 87, 101, 104, 114, 122–3, 129, 131, 141, 152, 159, 169, 178, 185, 205, 207–208, 218, 250, 253, 275, 284, 296, 297

Groups,
    2 Group, 18–19, 49, 131, 141, 152, 159, 169, 178, 185, 191, 196, 205, 215, 218, 224, 226, 229, 234, 250–1
    3 Group, 226
    4 Group, 218
    5 Group, 67
Coastal Command, 19, 37, 39, 49, 57, 62–3, 67, 73, 77, 101, 113, 129–30, 141, 152, 159, 169, 178, 185–6, 191, 195, 203–205, 215, 217–18, 226, 229, 249, 251–2, 274, 284, 296–7
Fighter Command, xii, 2, 6, 8, 14, 17, 27, 34, 41, 52, 57, 63, 66–7, 72, 75, 82, 88, 99, 112, 116, 120, 130, 140, 152, 166–7, 170, 185, 188, 196, 199, 201, 206–209, 214, 217, 223, 227, 232, 234, 248–9, 251, 253, 263, 273–5, 281, 284–5, 293, 295–7
Fighter Command Pool, 8
Groups,
    10 Group, 45, 119, 143, 162, 209, 240, 249, 272, 279
    11 Group, 17, 81, 88, 119–20, 138, 147, 162, 167, 178, 185, 209, 225, 227–8, 234, 248–9, 263, 285, 288, 293
    12 Group, 5, 8, 11, 40–2, 77, 127, 141–2, 146, 166, 177, 185, 195, 209, 227, 249, 284
    13 Group, 64, 249
Headquarters, 8, 96
Fighter Interception Unit, 130
Photographic Reconnaissance Unit, 113, 203, 253
RAF Volunteer Reserve, 4, 8, 24, 89, 189, 193, 203, 223, 267

INDEX

squadrons,
- No.1 Squadron, 100, 147, 154, 263
- 3 Squadron, 130, 142
- 15 Squadron, 83
- 17 Squadron, 40, 183, 258
- 18 Squadron, 216, 234
- 19 Squadron, 5, 141, 157–9, 185, 195, 202, 214, 216, 285
- 22 Squadron, 19
- 32 Squadron, 14, 15, 98–9, 109, 111–12, 254–5, 288
- 41 Squadron, 150, 170, 174–5, 178–9, 223–4, 234, 274
- 43 Squadron, 44, 51, 99–100, 110, 120–1, 247, 277, 281
- 44 Squadron, 56
- 46 Squadron, 127
- 49 Squadron, 217, 226
- 53 Squadron, 57, 63, 84, 122, 130, 152, 274
- 54 Squadron, xiv, 53–4, 106–107, 119, 133, 135–6, 138, 145, 149–50, 163, 276, 286–7, 289
- 56 Squadron, 55–6, 65–6, 106–107, 151, 180–1, 257, 288–9
- 59 Squadron, 49, 57, 63, 77, 113, 130, 152, 203, 215, 217, 250–1, 275
- 64 Squadron, 16–17, 53–4, 75, 99, 133, 145–7, 150, 178–9, 188, 220, 223, 234–6, 251, 254–6, 260, 288–9
- 65 Squadron, 110, 112, 138, 144, 158, 219, 234, 277–8, 286–7
- 66 Squadron, 2–4, 6, 21, 128, 182–3
- 74 Squadron, 12–13, 16, 46, 96–7, 140–1, 170–4, 176, 193–5, 254–7, 259, 260, 262–3, 297
- 75 Squadron, 217
- 79 Squadron, 250
- 82 Squadron, 56, 178, 186, 253
- 85 Squadron, 22, 40–1, 182, 190, 225, 258–9
- 87 Squadron, 30–2, 34, 101, 133, 143, 159, 264, 272
- 92 Squadron, 13, 17, 66, 77, 132, 149, 158–9
- 97 Squadron, 57
- 101 Squadron, 87, 152
- 107 Squadron, 130
- 110 Squadron, 114, 131, 216, 253
- 111 Squadron, 15–16, 87, 90, 94–5, 192, 276
- 114 Squadron, 195, 203
- 115 Squadron, 216
- 139 Squadron, 217
- 141 Squadron, 88–92, 95–6, 98
- 144 Squadron, 253
- 145 Squadron, 3–4, 36, 46, 66–7, 76–7, 84, 88, 100–101, 128–9, 162, 182, 192, 200, 232–3, 241–2, 248, 250, 263, 267, 279
- 151 Squadron, 41–2, 57, 64, 139–40, 224, 278
- 152 Squadron, 37, 46–7, 52, 81–2, 143, 243, 264, 268, 270, 279–80
- 204 Squadron, 122
- 206 Squadron, 217, 224
- 213 Squadron, xii, 30, 66, 75–6, 237, 246, 250, 264, 269, 273, 281
- 217 Squadron, 37, 274
- 220 Squadron, 253
- 222 Squadron, 5, 142
- 224 Squadron, 130
- 234 Squadron, 45, 162, 169, 251
- 235 Squadron, 84, 217, 250

236 Squadron, 37, 84, 113, 203, 204, 218
238 Squadron, 30–1, 52, 53, 107–109, 119–22, 157–8, 160–1, 238–40, 248, 264, 270, 273
242 Squadron, 5–11, 21, 41, 130, 166, 202–203
253 Squadron, 4
257 Squadron, 88, 99, 170, 174, 212, 236, 279, 282
264 Squadron, 41, 88, 91, 95–6
266 Squadron, 279–80, 284
269 Squadron, 130, 141
302 (Polish) Squadron, 214
303 (Polish) Squadron, 211–13
310 (Czech) Squadron, 214
320 Squadron, 159
500 (County of Kent) Squadron, 39, 83, 195, 251
501 (County of Gloucester) Squadron, 23, 30, 44, 51, 109–10, 157, 178–9, 252, 277–8, 287, 291
541 Squadron, 253
600 (City of London) Squadron, 29
601 (County of London) Squadron, 28–30, 33, 35–6, 72, 107, 113, 156–7, 237, 263, 266–7
603 (City of Edinburgh) Squadron, 43, 64–5, 72, 81, 101, 107, 130, 133, 188
604 (County of Middlesex) Squadron, 274
605 (County of Warwick) Squadron, 251
607 (County of Durham) Squadron, 228
609 (West Riding) Squadron, 23–6, 28, 30, 42, 47, 52–3, 84–7, 203, 233–4, 238, 263–4, 273, 279, 281–2
610 (County of Chester) Squadron, 13, 57, 59, 81, 83, 110, 112, 134–5, 148, 151, 182, 257–8, 276
612 (County of Aberdeen) Squadron, 129
615 (County of Surrey) Squadron, 57–9, 62, 75, 87, 110, 112–13, 144–5, 165, 285
616 (South Yorkshire) Squadron, 29, 200, 226
University Air Squadrons, 189
Royal Fleet Auxiliary,
Vessels,
War Sepoy, 98–9
Royal National Lifeboat Institution,
Lifeboats,
Margate, 291
Selsey, 36
Weymouth, 34
Royal Navy, 129, 195, 241, 248, 295
Fleet Air Arm, 11, 66, 76, 112, 150–1, 201, 209, 217, 224, 242
812 Naval Air Squadron, 217
Warships,
Acheron, HMS, 109
Astral, HMS, 188, 217, 229, 233
Basset, HMS, 239
Borde, HMS, 218
Boreas, HMS, 149–52
Brilliant, HMS, 149–52
Bulldog, HMS, 232
Cedar, HMS, 280
Codrington, HMS, 162, 181
Delight, HMS, 230
Edwardian, 257
Elan II, HMS, 237
Europa, HMS, 188
Gladiolus, HMS, 129

INDEX

Glorious, HMS, 127
Green Fly, HMS, 237
Griffin, HMS, 99
Osprey, HMS, 273
Renee, HMS, 237, 247–8
Sandhurst, HMS, 162, 181
Scimitar, HMS, 66
Valorous, HMS, 66
Walpole, HMS, 162
Withrington, HMS, 37, 275
Wolverine, HMS, 37
Rubensdörffer, *Hauptmann* Walter, 51, 66, 83, 90, 190–1, 257, 275, 277
Rushmer, Flight Lieutenant Frederick 'Rusty', 130, 188–9
Rye, 191, 277

Salmon, Flying Officer H.N.E., 147
Sanders, Pilot Officer M.D., 63
Sandwich, 165, 178
Saunders, Pilot Officer Cecil, 77
Sawyer, Squadron Leader, 138, 286
Scarborough, 228
Schmid, *Feldwebel* Karl, 152, 177
Schmid, *Oberfeldwebel* Karl, 220
Schmid, *Oberst* Josef 'Beppo', 117–18, 208
Scott, Flying Officer William, 180
Scott-Malden, Pilot Officer David, xii, xv
Scunthorpe, 4
Sealion, Operation, xiv, 38, 50, 67–72, 106, 115–16, 118, 127, 141, 191–2, 198–9, 208, 225, 294–5
Sears, Pilot Officer Lionel, 201, 233
Selsey, 36, 67
  Beach, 36
Selsey Bill, 36, 63, 67, 84, 99, 107, 113, 128, 200, 232, 279
Shambles lightship, 34
Sheerness, 164–5
Shepley, Pilot Officer Douglas, 243, 268, 270, 281

Ships,
  Bestwood, 242
  City of Brisbane, 215
  Dlader, 62
  Fife Coast, 232
  Heworth, 66
  Holme Force, 232
  Hornchurch, 42
  Josewyn, 42
  Kirkwood, 257
  Lancastria, 201
  Mons, 62
  Oiltrader, 257
  Ouse, 232
  Polly M, 233
  Rye, 231–2
  Terlings, 122
  Warrior, 30
Sholto Douglas, Marshal of the Royal Air Force William, 1st Baron Douglas of Kirtleside, 195
Shoreham-by-Sea, 57, 101
Shuttleworth, Flying Officer Dickie, 242
Simpson, Flight Lieutenant John, 95, 100
Simpson, Pilot Officer Peter, 95
Sing, Flight Lieutenant John 'Jackie', 246
Sizer, Pilot Officer Wilfred, 250
Skinner, Sergeant Bill, 193
Slatter, Pilot Officer Dudley Malins, 96
Smart, Flying Officer Tommy, 287
Smithers, Pilot Officer Julian, 267
Smith, Flight Lieutenant Brian, 257–8, 276
Smith, Flight Lieutenant E.B.B., 81, 134
Smith, Flight Lieutenant Edward, 13
Smith, Flight Lieutenant Rod, 58
Smith, Pilot Officer Denis, 260
Smith, Pilot Officer H.T., 37
Smith, Sergeant Kenneth, 203–204, 236

Smith, Squadron Leader Andrew, 59, 148
Smith, Sub-Lieutenant Francis, 242
Smythe, Pilot Officer Rupert, 98, 288
Smythe, Sergeant George, 54, 56, 290
Snowden, Sergeant Ernest, 270
Southampton, 3, 23, 47, 72, 105, 122, 152, 211, 218, 224, 229, 247, 285
Spitfire Fund, 19, 22
Squires, Sergeant John, 234
Staines, 88
Staples, Pilot Officer Michael, 282
Stapleton, Pilot Officer Basil 'Stapme', 107
Stebrowski, Flying Officer Michal, 238, 271
Stephen, Pilot Officer H.M., 172, 263, 297
Stephenson, Squadron Leader Geoffrey, 5, 195
Stevens, Flying Officer Leonard, 258–9
Stevenson, Pilot Officer P.C.F., 12–13, 16, 46, 97–8, 170–1, 174, 177, 255
Stewart, Ada, 43
Stewart-Clark, Pilot Officer Dudley, 64–5, 72
St John, Flying Officer Peter, 13, 16, 83, 170, 173–4
Stocker, *Feldwebel* Wolfgang, 13
Stoney, Flight Lieutenant George, 287
Storrar, Pilot Officer Jas, 36, 66–7, 182, 280
Strickland, Flying Officer Claud, 269–70
Stuckey, Sergeant Sydney, 250, 281
St Margaret's Bay, xii, 59, 179
Stumpff, Generaloberst Hans-Jürgen, 118
Summers, Sergeant, 205
Sunderland, 66, 250–1
Supermarine, 74, 211, 286
Sutton, Pilot Officer Barry, 151–2, 290
Sylvester, Pilot Officers Edmund, 23, 110
Szlagowski, Sergeant Joseph, 251

Tamblyn, Pilot Officer Hugh, 93
Tanner, Flight Sergeant John, 258
Taylor, Flying Officer Donald, 17, 75
Tew, Flight Sergeant Phillip, 136
Thompson, Squadron Leader John, 15, 90, 147, 192, 262
Thorogood, Sergeant Laurence 'Rubber', 101
Tomkinson, Lieutenant Commander Michael, 149
Townsend, Group Captain Peter, 22, 258–9
Trautloft, *Hauptmann* Johannes, 89–94, 234
Trenchard, Marshal of the Royal Air Force, Hugh Montague, 41
Tucker, Flying Officer Aidan, 278
Tuck, Wing Commander Robert Roland Stanford, 149
Turley-George, Pilot Officer Douglas, 136, 145, 277
Turner, Flight Lieutenant Donald, 107–109, 120
Turner, Flight Lieutenant Eric, 239–40
Turner, Flight Sergeant Guy, 99
Turner, Flying Officer Stan, 5

Urbanowicz, Flying Officer Witold, 212, 279
Urwin-Mann, Pilot Officer Jack, 31, 109, 270, 271

Vickers-Armstrong, 211
Victoria Cross, 29, 267, 297
Vigors, Pilot Officer Tim, 142
von Brauchitsch, *General* Walther, 50, 105–106, 115, 191

Wainwright, Pilot Officer Michael, 145, 150–1
Walch, Flight Lieutenant Stuart, 31, 108, 121–2, 158, 238, 270–1

INDEX

Walker, Sergeant Wilfred, 220
Wallens, Pilot Officer R.W. 'Wally', 175, 234, 274
Wakeham, Pilot Officer Ernest, 182, 200–201, 242
Ward, Squadron Leader The Honourable Edward, 266
Warner, Flying Officer William, 13
Warren, Pilot Officer Charles, 82–3
Waterston, Flying Officer Robin 'Bubbles', 107
Way, Flight Lieutenant Basil 'Wonky', 54, 136, 145, 150
Weaver, Flying Officer Steve 'Squeak', 106–107, 180–1, 261, 289
Webster, Flight Lieutenant Terry, 163, 170, 174, 177, 179–80, 223–4, 235
Weir, Pilot Officer Nigel, 128, 268
Welford, Pilot Officer Harry, 228
Westland Aircraft Company, 66, 250
West, Warrant Officer Bernard 'Knocker', 8
Weymouth, 23, 31, 34, 47, 49, 52, 84, 87, 105, 109, 160–1, 233, 238, 263–5, 267–8, 270, 273
Wheeler, AC1 Raymond, 247
Whitehead, Sergeant Clifford, 15
Whitfield, Sergeant Joseph, 56
Whitstable, 165, 180, 288
Whittingham, Flying Officer Charles, 184
Wick, 2, 75, 107, 130, 142
Wick, *Oberleutnant* Helmut, 75
Wicks, Pilot Officer, 15
Wigglesworth, Pilot Officer John, 120
Wight, Flight Lieutenant Ronald, 270
Wildblood, Pilot Officer Timothy, 243, 268, 281
Wilkes, Sergeant Geoffrey, 281
Williams, Pilot Officer Dennis, 158, 159
Williams, Pilot Officer Dudley, 268
Williams, Pilot Officer Wycliff, 280
Winter-Taylor, Pilot Officer, 129
Winterton, 2
Withall, Flight Lieutenant Carr, 52, 281
Witorzenc, Flying Officer Stefan, 287
Wolton, Sergeant Ralph, 143
Woodhall, Wing Commander A.B. 'Woody', 5, 9
Woods-Scawen, Flying Officer Patrick, 182
Woods-Scawen, Pilot Officer Charles, 247
Woodward, Flying Officer Herbert, 54, 99, 220
Woolston, 211
Woolley, Sergeant Arthur, 35
Wootten, Pilot Officer Ernest 'Bertie', 153
Worrall, Air Vice-Marshal John, 98, 111
Worthing, 100, 182, 281
Wright, Sergeant John, 250

Yate, 17
Yeovil, 17
Young, Pilot Officer James, 174
Yule, Pilot Officer Robert, 3, 4, 46, 88, 201